GEOGRAPHICAL INDICATIONS IN INTERNATIONAL TRADE

Geographical Indications (GIs), widely used in the European context, are being promoted as vehicles for local development: but do they truly serve the interests of the Global South? Can they foster meaningful change in former colonial societies?

This open access book interrogates these questions through a critical legal lens grounded in Third World Approaches to International Law (TWAIL), to assess whether GIs – codified in international trade agreements like the EU-CARIFORUM Economic Partnership Agreement – can support 'development from within' for the small island developing states of the Caribbean.

Providing a fresh perspective on the colonial roots, current utility and future potential of GI laws, the book engages with Caribbean realities and includes global case studies from Demerara rum in Guyana, Ethiopian coffee, Indian Darjeeling tea, Colombian coffee, Mexican Tequila, and Barbados Rum.

In a world shaped by international trade rules, GIs and sustainable development offer a powerful lens into how the law of origin-linked products – like Champagne, Tequila, and Jamaican Rum – can shape futures for postcolonial states.

Geographical Indications in International Trade is essential reading for academics, policymakers, legal practitioners and development professionals seeking to understand the tensions between intellectual property law and sustainable development. It challenges readers to rethink international trade rules and consider how GI law can be reclaimed by third-world nations as a transformative tool for heritage-based, sustainable economic development.

Studies in International Trade and Investment Law: Volume 35

Studies in International Trade and Investment Law

Series Editors
Gabrielle Marceau
Krista Nadakavukaren Schefer
Federico Ortino
Gregory Shaffer

This series offers a forum for publication of original and scholarly analyses of emerging and significant issues in international trade and investment law - broadly understood to include the whole of the law of the WTO, the public international law of foreign investment, the law of the EU common commercial policy and other regional trade regimes, and any legal or regulatory topic that interacts with global trade and foreign investment. The aim of the series is to produce works which will be readily accessible to trade and investment law scholars and practitioners alike.

RECENT TITLES IN THIS SERIES:

Patent Games in the Global South: Pharmaceutical Patent Law Making in Brazil, India and Nigeria Amaka Vanni

The Nationality of Corporate Investors under International Investment Law Anil Yilmaz Vastardis

The Regulation of Product Standards in World Trade Law Ming Du

Investors' International Law Edited by Jean Ho and Mavluda Sattorova

Rethinking, Repackaging, and Rescuing World Trade Law in the Post-Pandemic Era Edited by Amrita Bahri, Weihan Zhou and Daria Boklan

Flexible Regional Economic Integration in Africa: Lessons and Implications for the Multilateral Trading System Timothy Masiko

International Investment Law: An Analysis of the Major Decisions Edited by Hélène Ruiz Fabri and Edoardo Stoppioni

State Capitalism and International Investment Law Edited by Panagiotis Delimatsis, Georgios Dimitropoulos and Anastasios Gourgourinis

The European Union and International Investment Law: The Two Dimensions of an Uneasy Relationship Francesco Montanaro

Financial Market Infrastructure and Economic Integration: A WTO, FTAs, and Competition Law Analysis George A Papaconstantinou

International Trade Law and Global Data Governance: Aligning Perspectives and Practices Neha Mishra

Hong Kong as an Actor in International Economic Law: Multilateralism, Bilateralism and Unilateralism Julien Chaisse

Economic Cooperation in the Shadow of Contested Sovereignty Chien-Huei Wu, Ching-Fu Lin and Han-Wei Liu

International Economic Dispute Settlement in Africa: Courts and Arbitral Tribunals as Socio-Legal Actors Harrison Otieno Mbori

Geographical Indications in International Trade: Towards Sustainable Development in the Caribbean Yentyl Williams

Geographical Indications in International Trade

Towards Sustainable Development in the Caribbean

Yentyl Williams

•HART•
OXFORD • LONDON • NEW YORK • NEW DELHI • SYDNEY

HART PUBLISHING
Bloomsbury Publishing Plc
Kemp House, Chawley Park, Cumnor Hill, Oxford, OX2 9PH, UK
1385 Broadway, New York, NY 10018, USA
Bloomsbury Publishing Ireland Limited, 29 Earlsfort Terrace, Dublin 2, D02 AY28, Ireland

First published in Great Britain 2026

1

A catalogue record for this book is available from the British Library.

A catalogue record for this book is available from the Library of Congress.

ISBN: HB: 978-1-50999-135-8
ePDF: 978-1-50999-137-2
ePub: 978-1-50999-136-5

Typeset by Amnet

Dedication and Acknowledgements

To my mummy Edith, daddy Leo, sister Asia, and niece Arielle.
My family are my rock, and with them, there is no hard place.

THIS WORK EVOLVED from my PhD thesis, supervised by Professor Clair Gammage, who believed in this project from our very first interaction and provided a steadfast constructive critique of my ideas and work throughout its development (2018–23). Professor Gammage's professional companionship throughout the entire process was exemplary, and I am blessed not only to have had her on that journey, but also for setting the standard that I now seek to emulate on my own academic–professional pathway. Professor Aurora Plomer exposed me to fundamental intellectual property texts and provided rigorous critique over the first few years of my PhD. I am indebted to her for these insights, and also for sharing her love of painting, which served as a healthy reminder to also invest in other passions besides my academic pursuits. Professor Greg Messenger has been a divine intervention, joining the supervisory committee and supporting me in the critical final stages of weaving the PhD together, and providing crucial insights. I also wish to acknowledge the team at the School of Law, both staff and fellow students. My PhD research would not have been possible without the generous funding from the UK's Economic and Social Research Council and the support of the School of Law.

I would also extend thanks to my dean, Professor Shazeeda Ali, who welcomed me to the MonaLaw family at the University of the West Indies (UWI, Mona – Jamaica). Professor Ali provided me with the opportunity to deepen and strengthen my research on and beyond GIs. I am grateful to Dr Natalie Corthésy, who invited me to be a tutor on her course, 'Intellectual Property Law'; to contribute to designing and directing the LLM/professional development course on 'GIs in the Global Market Place'; and to co-author my first edited collection on 'IP & Cannabis', alongside Professor Bonadio. I am indebted to Professor Bonadio for his stewardship, from examining my PhD to inviting me to collaborate on numerous publications, which has set a precedent for academic collaboration.

I am grateful for the editorial team led by Roberta Bassi, who made an impression on my inquisitive year 1 PhD mind from our first meeting. I feel entirely blessed and grateful to be part of productive ecosystems working towards sustainable development and beneficial international partnerships between our First and Third Worlds.

This work was supported by the Arts and Humanities Research Council, grant number ES/P000630/1.

Contents

Abbreviations

ACP	African, Caribbean and Pacific States
ADOPRON	Asociacion Dominicana de Prodoctores de Ron, Inc.
AO	appellation of origin
ARD	Asociación de Roneros Dominicanos
BIRPI	The United International Bureau for the Protection of Intellectual Property
CARICOM	Caribbean Community
CARIFORUM	Caribbean Forum
CARTFund	Caribbean Aid for Trade Regional Integration Trust Fund
CAAA	Central American Association Agreement
CDB	Caribbean Development Bank
CEDA	Caribbean Export Development Agency
CETA	Comprehensive Economic and Trade Agreement
CRNM	Caribbean Regional Negotiating Machinery
CSME	CARICOM Single Market and Economy
CSO	civil society organisation
CTEO	Chief Trade Enforcement Officer
DFID	Department for International Development
EAC	East African Community
EC	European Commission
ECDPM	European Centre for Development Policy Management
ECX	Ethiopian Commodity Exchange
EDF	European Development Fund
EPA	Economic Partnership Agreement
EU	European Union
EUIPO	European Union Intellectual Property Office
FCDO	Foreign, Commonwealth and Development Office
FITFIR	first in time, first in right
FTA	free trade agreement
GATT	General Agreement on Tariffs and Trade
GDP	gross domestic product
GI	Geographical Indication
GIZ	Germany Development Agency
IEL	international economic law
IICA	Inter-American Institute for Cooperation on Agriculture
IP	intellectual property
IPO	Intellectual Property Office
IPR	intellectual property rights

IS	indication of source
LDC	least developed country
MSME	micro-, small and medium-sized enterprises
NGO	non-governmental organisation
NYSE	New York Stock Exchange
OACPS	Organisation of African, Caribbean and Pacific States
OCTs	overseas countries and territories
ODI	Overseas Development Institute
OJ	Official Journal
OTN	Office of Trade Negotiations
PDO	Protected Designation of Origin
PGI	Protected Geographical Origin
RIP	Regional Indicative Programme
SADC	Southern African Development Community
SIDS	Small Island Developing States
SMEs	small and medium enterprises
SPS	Sanitary and Phyto-sanitary
SVEs	Small and Vulnerable Economies
TDC	Trade and Development Committee
TEU	Treaty on European Union
TFEU	Treaty on the Functioning of the European Union
TMO	Trade Marks Opposition
TRIPS	Trade-Related Aspects of Intellectual Property Rights
TSG	Traditional Speciality Guaranteed
TWAIL	Third World Approaches to International Law
UK	United Kingdom
US(A)	United States of America
USD	United States dollar
USMCA	United States–Mexico–Canada Agreement
USPTO	United States Patent and Trademark Office
WIPO	World Intellectual Property Organization
WIRD	West Indies Rum Distillery
WTO	World Trade Organization

Table of Cases

Table of Statutes and Legal Agreements

1

Introduction

> Humanity has the ability to make development sustainable to ensure that it meets the needs of the present without compromising the ability of future generations to meet their own needs. . . . technology and social organization can be both managed and improved to make way for a new era of economic growth. . . . sustainable development requires meeting the basic needs of all and extending to all the opportunity to fulfil their aspirations for a better life.[1]
>
> Brundtland Commission, Our Common Future (1987).

THE EARLY 2000S MARKED a shift in trading relations between the European Union (EU) and the African, Caribbean and Pacific (ACP) states, as a result of the banana dispute at the World Trade Organization (WTO).[2] This dispute brought into question the preferential post-colonial trading relationship between the EU and the ACP states, as distinct from the EU's trade with other banana-producing states,[3] and resulted in the move towards reciprocal trade relations in the form of Economic Partnership Agreements (EPAs).[4] The reciprocal trade relations are governed by WTO rules, namely Art XXIV of the General Agreement on Tariffs and Trade (GATT), which stipulates the liberation of 'substantially all trade' for a WTO-compatible agreement.[5] By October 2008, the Caribbean Forum (CARIFORUM) was the only regional

[1] The Brundtland Commission, 'Report of the World Commission on Environment and Development: Our Common Future' (UN) para 27, https://sustainabledevelopment.un.org/content/documents/5987our-common-future.pdf.

[2] The dispute was originally brought by Ecuador, Honduras, Guatemala, Mexico, and the United States on 8 May 1996. See WTO, *European Communities – Regime for the Importation, Sale and Distribution of Bananas* (25 September 1997) WTO/DS27/AB/R.

[3] While ACP states benefitted from duty-free and quota-free access for up to 775,000 metric tonnes of bananas, other countries, namely Latin American banana-producing nations, were subject to pay a duty of 176 euros per tonne. WTO, *European Communities – Regime for the Importation, Sale and Distribution of Bananas* (3 September 2007) WT/DS27.

[4] The 15 members of the CARIFORUM group are Antigua and Barbuda, Bahamas, Barbados, Belize, Dominica, the Dominican Republic, Grenada, Guyana, Haiti, Jamaica, Saint Lucia, Saint Vincent and the Grenadines, Saint Christopher and Nevis, Surinam, and Trinidad and Tobago. See Europa, 'Summary of Treaty' (*Europa*, 20 March 2017), https://ec.europa.eu/world/agreements/prepareCreateTreatiesWorkspace/treatiesGeneralData.do?step=0&redirect=true&treatyId=7407#:~:text=The%20CARIFORUM%20is%20a%20regional,Nevis%2C%20Surinam%2C%20and%20Trinidad%20and.

[5] For an overview, see Clair Gammage, 'Overcoming the Development Deficit of Article XXIV: Promoting Equality through North-South RTAs' (2016) 9 *Law and Development Review* 1.

grouping of the ACP states to have concluded a comprehensive EPA with the EU in advance of the original deadline for the conclusion of negotiations.[6] At the time, there were mixed reviews of this new agreement and its scope, consisting of commitments to liberalise not only trade in goods, but also services, investment, procurement, competition, and intellectual property (IP), under which Geographical Indications (GI) fall.[7]

The EPAs extend the EU's long-standing relationship with the ACP group and foreground that reciprocal trade between these historic partners can achieve sustainable development,[8] notwithstanding previously disadvantageous colonial and post-colonial trade relations.[9] Nonetheless, given that both sides had recognised that this preferential trading relationship had failed to benefit ACP states, concern remained over the capacity of ACP states to transition towards liberating 'substantially all trade' with their former colonial powers, albeit in a post-colonial setting.[10] For almost two decades, there have been few commentaries on the impacts of the provisions of the EPA, even as the timeline for the asymmetric liberalisation of trade nears completion.[11] In this context, this book presents an analysis on how the specific provisions on GIs as a subset of IP can contribute to fulfilling the aims of the EPA to promote sustainable development in the CARIFORUM region within the liberal economic free trade model. The theoretical enquiry focuses on the first and only comprehensive EPA to date concluded with the CARIFORUM, and its provisions on GIs.

GIs, as signs which protect the reputation, quality, and characteristics of goods originating in a specific territory, have gained prominence as a subject matter in international trade, especially via their inclusion in free trade agreements

[6] See 'Economic Partnership Agreement between the CARIFORUM States, of the one part, and the European Community and its Member States, of the other part' [2008] OJ L289/I/3 (hereinafter 'CARIFORUM–EU EPA').

[7] Caribbean Policy Research Institute (CAPRI), 'The Impact of the EPA on Caribbean Economies' (CAPRI Caribbean, 2009), https://www.capricaribbean.org/documents/impact-epa-caribbean-economies. For an overview, see Yentyl Williams, 'Shifting Between Hegemony and Dominance? A Neo-Gramscian Analysis of the EU as a Structural Foreign Policy Actor: The Singular Case of the Cariforum-EU Economic Partnership Agreement' (2015) 1 Bruges Regional Integration and Global Governance Papers 1–36.

[8] There are several references in the preamble of the CARIFORUM–EU EPA that specifically outline 'the need to promote economic and social progress . . . consistent with sustainable development'; 'their commitment to work together towards . . . poverty eradication, sustainable development'; and '[achieving] economic growth and social progress compatible with sustainable development'. This frames the objective of the EPA outlined in art 1(a), 'contributing to the reduction and eventual eradication of poverty through the establishment of a trade partnership consistent with the objective of sustainable development'. Moreover, art 3(1) explains that 'the objective of sustainable development is to be applied and integrated at every level of their economic partnership . . . especially the general commitment to reducing and eventually eradicating poverty in a way that is consistent with sustainable development'. It further foregrounds that 'sustainable development [is] centred on the human person who is the main beneficiary of development' (art 3(3)), CARIFORUM–EU EPA (n 6).

[9] See Williams, 'Shifting Between Hegemony and Dominance?' (n 7).

[10] See ch 4.

[11] ibid, for a discussion on the monitoring mechanisms.

(FTAs).[12] This prompts important questions about GIs in the contemporary context of globalisation and the pursuit of sustainable development to eradicate global inequalities within a context of economic liberalisation. This book aims to explain how GIs may further sustainable development by promoting 'development from within' for Third World producer communities of former colonial cash crops, even if the EPA falls short of achieving its ambitious aims more generally.[13]

The concept of 'development from within' foregrounds a holistic type of community-based development.[14] It draws on Sarah Bowen's use of this concept to assess the extent to which GIs can foster sustainable development in producer communities. It considers how GIs contribute to poverty eradication in the specific context of the Caribbean region, defined as one that has been subject to plantation economy exploitation over centuries of colonisation.[15] In light of the objectives of this book, 'development from within' provides a litmus test of the sustainable development potential of GIs in the Caribbean context.

FTAs can bring about structural changes, which can present both challenges and opportunities for their signatory parties. While further commitments are being made through other EU and multilateral trade agreements,[16] there are two prominent aspects of GI laws which remain under-researched: the history of GIs as a colonial construct of IP law; and legal analyses of the sustainable development potential of GIs for post-colonial societies. The impact of FTAs on formerly colonised countries requires an approach which recognises not only the historical and present endowments of post-colonial nations but also their post-colonial aspirations. An international economic law (IEL) approach that assesses not only the legal but also the normative foundations of GIs, rooted in an ontological understanding of post-colonial realities, is key to furthering knowledge in this area. Third World Approaches to International Law (TWAIL), with its focus on providing historically aware analyses of the law and how it can serve to emancipate post-colonial nations, provides this critical lens. TWAIL's linguistic preferences for terms that root and remind readership of historical realities is poignant and foregrounds the structural differences between developed and underdeveloped nations. For this reason, post-colonial underdeveloped nations are referred to as 'Third World'. The signifier 'Third World' is purposeful, since it distinctly locates formerly colonised territories and their underdeveloped realities in opposition to their First World counterparts – beneficiaries of hundreds of years of colonial exploitation.[17] It is from this optic that this book addresses the topic of GI laws across three themes:

[12] Billy Melo Araujo, *The EU Deep Trade Agenda: Law and Policy* (OUP, 2016).

[13] CAPRI report says EPA will not bring economic gains. See ch 4 on the reviews of the EPA (n 7).

[14] Sarah Bowen, 'Development from Within? The Potential for Geographical Indications in the Global South' (2010) 13(2) *Journal of World Intellectual Property* 231.

[15] George Beckford, *Persistent Poverty: Underdevelopment in Plantation Economies of the Third World* (first published OUP 1972, Zed Books 1983).

[16] See ch 3 for an overview of the GI provisions in the EU's FTAs with third countries.

[17] Makau Mutua, 'What is TWAIL?' (2000) *Proceedings of the ASIL Annual Meeting* 35.

1. GIs as colonial constructs.
2. GIs as tools for sustainable development, especially for Third World countries.
3. GIs as strategic tools to contribute to 'development from within' in the Caribbean.

These themes are concerned with examining the historical, legal, and socio-economic contexts within which GI law has developed. These themes are paramount, given the expansion of GI laws through IP multilateralism, EU bilateral trade agreements, and the emergence of GIs for the first time historically in Third World legal regimes. This research contributes to critically examining the conceptualisation of GI laws and the normative assumptions linked to GIs' historical usage by First World countries in international trade, though shifting the focus to the Third World Small Island Developing States (SIDS) context of Caribbean nations.

Understanding the emancipatory potential of GIs for Third World nations, particularly in the SIDS context of the Caribbean, requires an understanding of how GI laws can contribute to a transformative form of development suitable for such societies. Since the *Brundtland Report*, it has been internationally accepted that the principles of sustainability and sustainable development are defined, at least, across three main pillars – social, economic, and environmental – with culture also considered in some analyses.[18] The definition – 'to ensure that [development] meets the needs of the present without compromising the ability of future generations to meet their own needs'[19] – provides a foundational framework within which constructive debate and further analyses of inclusive, development-specific outcomes and impacts can be considered. It also recognises that there can be contestation over the linkage between the concept of sustainable development and law, and thus that relationship is accurately described as contested and complex.[20] This book aligns with the scholarship that considers the inclusive[21] and integrationist[22] elements of sustainable development. From this optic, the conceptualisation of sustainability must foreground the 'commensurability of difference',[23] to go beyond narrow, reductionist, or fractious analyses and applications of the concept, which can perpetuate marginalisations in access to

[18] Brundtland Commission, 'Our Common Future' (n 1).

[19] ibid.

[20] Margherita Pieraccini and Tonia Novitz, 'Introduction' in Margherita Pieraccini and Tonia Novitz (eds), *Legal Perspectives on Sustainability* (BUP, 2020) 1.

[21] Tonia Novitz and Margherita Pieraccini, 'Agenda 2030 and the Sustainable Development Goals: "Responsive, Inclusive, Participatory and Representative Decision-Making?"' in Pieraccini and Novitz (n 20) 40.

[22] Federico Ortino, 'Investment Treaties, Sustainable Development and Reasonableness Review: A Case Against Strict Proportionality Balancing' (2017) 30(1) *Leiden Journal of International Law* 83.

[23] I use this term to shift the emphasis on the transformational potential of difference as a language of emancipation, although the original usage refers to the 'incommensurability of difference'. See Dianne Otto, 'Subalternity and International Law: The Problems of Global Community and the Incommensurability of Difference' (1996) 5 *Social and Legal Studies* 360.

and the application of the law, procedurally and substantively. Furthermore, these ideals, as set out in the literature, must be based on inter-generational and intra-generational equity, and integrative decision-making.[24] This book foregrounds the transformational ideals of sustainability,[25] linked to poverty eradication that can achieve the aspiration towards a better life, as set out in the *Brundtland Report*[26] and worked on expeditiously by legal practitioners and scholars globally.[27]

This book grounds the assessment of GIs in a legal analysis, and draws insights from historical and IEL perspectives, to offer an original interdisciplinary contribution to the literature on this unique subset of IP: GI law. The critical assessment of GIs in this book makes four assertions. ***Firstly***, GIs are colonial constructs originally conceived to promote industrial development primarily, but not exclusively, between countries of the First World. In other words, GIs can lead to exploitation, and there is a risk that they perpetuate pre-existing inequalities in the global economy. As they are not designed for or by Third World countries, this book interrogates, challenges, and unpacks the reasonable assumption that they may not service the needs of Third World countries. ***Secondly***, notwithstanding GIs' colonial origins, GIs *may* have the potential to promote the 'development from within'. This investigation is assessed with reference to examples of GIs registered in Third World countries and, more specifically, in the Caribbean. ***Thirdly***, Third World countries have not been involved in the conception of GIs or other IPRs, and there is a lack of knowledge, understanding, and infrastructure to support the use of these development tools. This book shows the risk of norm export in the context of the EU–CARIFORUM EPA. ***Fourthly***, GIs are predominantly used by economically powerful businesses, and transnational capitalist classes,[28] with the capacity to navigate the institutional cognitive challenges to establish GIs, and Micro-, Small and Medium-sized enterprises (MSMEs) are missing out on the potential benefits of GIs for Third World countries.

This book has three key findings. ***First***, GIs *do* have development potential for countries in the Third World, but at present the evidence from GIs in the Caribbean does not appear to show that they are promoting 'development from within'. The language of GIs, and their current construction in treaties/trade

[24] This is explored, in the context of the institutions of the EPA, in ch 4. For a discussion on this, see Ortino, 'Investment Treaties, Sustainable Development and Reasonableness Review' (n 22) 83. See also Clair Gammage and Tonia Novitz, 'The Concept of Sustainability and its Application in International Trade, Investment and Finance' in Clair Gammage and Tonia Novitz (eds), *Sustainable Trade, Investment and Finance* (Edward Elgar, 2019) 4.

[25] See Gammage and Novitz (n 24) 1.

[26] Brundtland Commission, 'Our Common Future' (n 1).

[27] For example, see the work of the International Law Association (ILA), 'Sustainable Development and the Green Economy in International Trade Law', www.ila-hq.org/en_GB/committees/sustainable-development-and-the-green-economy-in-international-trade-law.

[28] BS Chimni, 'Third World Approaches to International Law: A Manifesto' (2006) 8 *International Community Law Review* 29.

agreements, does not preclude them from having this beneficial impact; their application and use in practice, however, might. ***Second***, and notwithstanding their colonial origins, GIs *do* have the potential to promote 'development from within', but Third World countries are ill-equipped to use them, especially in their *sui generis* form. Greater dissemination and understanding of GIs is needed to enable Third World-country negotiators to advocate for territory-specific sustainable development, or 'development from within'. ***Third***, across the Caribbean, large(r) businesses linked to transnational capital are using GIs, but smaller producers/exporters are not utilising the untapped development potential of GIs. Arguably, this illustrates how GIs can reinforce power asymmetries, and continue a 'dynamic of difference',[29] between large and small companies, as wealth and capital accumulation continues to flow towards, and be concentrated in, large businesses owned by the same (colonial) transnational classes. In this way, GIs are not promoting 'development from within', nor can they be framed as global-local laws contributing to poverty eradication. This book addresses these issues and offers recommendations on how GIs can promote 'development from within' and, therefore, be mobilised as emancipatory legal tools for GI producer communities in the Third World.

This book asserts that, in post-colonial times, the law must function to liberate producer communities, and GIs can be challenged to be emancipatory tools to spur sustainable development in communities that have been historically deprived of the opportunity to develop on their own terms. The historically aware approach lends itself to the legal analysis adopted to interrogate the historical, normative, and legal foundations of GIs. This book draws on Ruth Okediji's delineation of the three waves of IP multilateralism as a heuristic tool for conceptualising the developments of the legal regimes from the fifteenth century up until today.[30] The first wave refers to unequal trading relations between Europeans and non-Europeans, characterised by domination, dispossession, and accumulation, as part of the imperial and colonial era (1500s–1945).[31] The second wave of IP multilateralism is characterised by the extension of the international law doctrines of sovereignty, statehood, and self-determination to former colonies (1945–1990s). The third wave of IP multilateralism began with the establishment of the WTO and the signing of the TRIPS Agreement (1990s

[29] That is the way in which cultural difference was mobilised as part of the civilising mission. Anghie coined the term, referring to 'the endless process of creating a gap between two cultures, demarcating one as "universal" and civilized and the other as "particular" and uncivilized, and seeking to bridge the gap by developing techniques to normalize the aberrant society'. See Anthony Anghie, *Imperialism, Sovereignty and the Making of International Law* (CUP, 2014) 4, 28–30. See also Antony Anghie and BS Chimni, 'Third World Approaches to International Law and Individual Responsibility in Internal Conflicts' (2003) 2(1) *Chinese Journal of International Law*.

[30] Ruth Okediji, 'The International Relations of Intellectual Property: Narratives of Developing Country Participation in the Global Intellectual Property System' (2003) 7 *Singapore Journal of International & Comparative Law* 315.

[31] See also Eric Williams, *Capitalism and Slavery* (UNCP, 1994) and *From Columbus to Castro: The History of the Caribbean* (Vintage, 1984).

onwards).[32] This framing contextualises how GIs are colonial constructs, while also shedding light on how they can be conceived as tools for 'development from within', from a historically aware standpoint. That said, through deconstructing the historical development of GI laws at the national and international levels, it is possible to critically assess the sustainable development potential of GIs, framed as 'development from within' for Third World countries.

Leading IP scholars recognise that the linkage between IP and colonialism is under-researched in legal scholarship,[33] and that the conceptual underpinnings of GIs are unclear.[34] While there is limited literature confirming the linkage between copyrights, patents, and trademarks and colonialism, there is even less literature on the subject of GIs and colonialism. This book offers a novel contribution to the field in its discussion of GIs, as a unique subset of IPRs, and their linkage to the colonial epoch. It also extends the debate on the conceptual underpinnings of GIs to include a Third World perspective, particularly one which privileges Third World knowledge and heritage. These are themes explored throughout the book and explained in the chapter outline that follows.

Chapter two provides a legal analysis of GIs by mapping the legal architecture of GIs, as a subset of IP, at the international and multilateral levels. This chapter is concerned with addressing the following questions: *what are GIs? What are their origins and rationale in international law? And who and what was protected within these agreements?* The chapter demonstrates that GIs have their origins in the colonial period and are best understood as colonial constructs. The rationale for their protection was, equally, embedded in the colonial context of commercial expansion and control of industrial production. As such, industrialised First World countries and their products were protected across the key IP treaties considered in this chapter: the Paris Convention for the Protection of Industrial Property (1883); the Madrid Agreement for the Repression of False and Deceptive Indications of Source (1891); the Lisbon Agreement for the Protection of Appellations of Origin and Their International Registration (1958), including the Geneva Act (2015); and the WTO Agreement on Trade-Related Aspects of Intellectual Property Rights, concluded in 1995 (hereinafter 'TRIPS').[35] The chapter frames the critical assessment around the three waves of

[32] Okediji, 'The International Relations of Intellectual Property' (n 30) 333.

[33] Lionel Bentley, 'The "Extraordinary Multiplicity" of Intellectual Property Laws in the British Colonies in the Nineteenth Century' (2011) 12 *Theoretical Inquiries In Law* 1, 162.

[34] Dev Gangjee, *Relocating the Law on Geographical Indications* (CUP, 2012) 9.

[35] The legal regimes are hereinafter referenced as the Paris Convention, the Madrid Agreement, the Lisbon Agreement, and TRIPS. WIPO, 'The Paris Convention for the Protection of Industrial Property (as amended on September 28, 1979)', https://wipo.int/treaties/en/text.jsp?file_id=288514. The Madrid Agreement for the Repression of False or Deceptive Indications of Source on Goods of 1891 has been revised four times – Washington 1911, The Hague 1925, London 1934, and Lisbon 1958 – as well as an additional Act of Stockholm, in 1967; WIPO, 'The Madrid Agreement for the Repression of False or Deceptive Indications of Source', https://wipolex.wipo.int/en/text/286776; 'Lisbon Agreement for the Protection of Appellations of Origin and their International Registration' (WIPO, 1979), https://wipo.int/lisbon/en/legal_texts/lisbon_agreement.html#P15_193; WTO, 'Trade-Related Aspects of Intellectual Property Rights Agreement', https://wto.org/english/docs_e/legal_e/27-trips_01_e.htm.

IP multilateralism advanced by Ruth Okediji,[36] as a heuristic tool for conceptualising the developments of the legal regimes from the fifteenth century up until today. Understanding how GIs have evolved in international law foreshadows how they are now implemented across Third World countries. It demonstrates that GIs are colonial constructs, and exposes the neutral façade of the law by demonstrating how it has developed according to a 'dynamic of difference'.[37] As such, through the process of deconstructing the law, how the law privileges First World knowledge and ways of thinking, doing, and being over Third World realities is unpacked. This demonstrates that the universalism upon which this (colonial) law is based risks reproducing bygone structures of the colonial epoch that, as vestiges of formal empire, serve to keep Third World peoples marginalised.

Chapter three discusses the normative role of the EU as an exporter of GI norms via its FTAs. It provides an overview of the substantive provisions on GIs in the CARIFORUM–EU EPA,[38] and the analysis sheds light on how the international, and universalist, norms relating to GIs are expanding through the EU's bilateral FTAs with countries that do not have existing *sui generis* GI regimes. It questions whether EU FTAs, with their stated aim to create that level playing field, level out inequalities upon implementation or further entrench them, and the 'dynamic of difference',[39] in the bilateral and regional context. The assessment pays particular attention to the terms of protection, generic terms, the relationship between GIs and trademarks, future agreements, and Internet protection. These issues are assessed in relation to the CARIFORUM–EU EPA, with reference to other EU FTAs with Vietnam,[40] Singapore,[41] Canada,[42] Japan,[43] and Columbia/Peru,[44] for comparative analysis. This chapter demonstrates the now infamous adage of Jagdish Bhagwati that, where the EU cannot take the multilateral highway, it takes the bilateral country road with regard to achieving its trade goals relating to GI protection and intellectual property rights (IPR) enforcement.[45] In taking these bilateral country roads, the EU is also in the

[36] Okediji, 'The International Relations of Intellectual Property' (n 30) 7.

[37] See Anghie, *Imperialism, Sovereignty and the Making of International Law* (n 29). See also Anghie and Chimni, 'Third World Approaches to International Law and Individual Responsibility in Internal Conflicts' (n 29).

[38] CARIFORUM–EU EPA (n 6).

[39] Anghie, *Imperialism, Sovereignty and the Making of International Law* (n 29).

[40] Free Trade Agreement between the European Union and the Socialist Republic of Viet Nam [2020] OJ L186, 3-1400.

[41] Free trade Agreement between the European Union and the Republic of Singapore [2019] OJ L294, 3–755.

[42] Comprehensive Economic and Trade Agreement (CETA) between Canada, of the one part, and the European Union and its Member States, of the other part [2017] OJ L11, 23–1079.

[43] Agreement between the European Union and Japan for an Economic Partnership [2019] OJ L330, 3–899.

[44] Trade Agreement between the European Union and its Member States, of the one part, and Colombia and Peru, of the other part [2012] OJ L354, 3–2607.

[45] Jagdish Bhagwati, *Free Trade Today* (PUP, 2002) and Commission, 'Trade, Growth and Intellectual Property – Strategy for the Protection and Enforcement of Intellectual Property Rights in Third Countries' (2014) COM 389.

process of developing regional legal regimes, as a 'norm exporter'.[46] This chapter details the findings that the EU is developing GI legal regimes via its FTAs while also exporting its GI norms. It assesses whether these norms are based on a common good, namely whether they are inclusive and development-oriented. In other words, it questions whether the legal framing of GIs lends itself to be interpreted as a language of emancipation.[47] Or does the universality of the norms and practice of GIs that has been accepted in international law[48] continue to disadvantage the Other/subaltern,[49] in these FTAs? This book demonstrates that, for the most part, the laws are nonetheless framed as EU laws sanctioned by international law. Nevertheless, it is also shown that there is scope for reconceptualising the law to be framed as inclusive, and to function in the local interests of Third World nations, as a global-local law.[50]

Chapter four examines the institutions of the CARIFORUM–EU EPA and assesses their potential to promote dialogical manoeuvres to frame GIs as emancipatory legal tools for the CARIFORUM countries. The chapter considers whether these institutions are vestiges of informal imperialism that contribute to the continued marginalisation of Third World nations or whether, through the dialogical engagement, they are able to foreground the 'commensurability of difference'.[51] In this chapter, a detailed analysis of the monitoring and evaluation, joint institutions, and financing and implementation of the Agreement demonstrates how the CARIFORUM countries are projected de jure as the main beneficiaries of the EPA. A theory-of-change approach to monitoring the EPA privileges assessing the developmental potential of the EPA. However, this book explains that, in the absence of a dedicated monitoring mechanism, the potential emancipatory elements of the EPA are not being realised, and that GI laws may not be challenged to function as emancipatory tools contributing to sustainable development.

Chapter five provides insights into four case studies on GIs in the Third World: Guyana Demerara Gold,[52] the Ethiopia–Starbucks dispute,[53] the Café

[46] See James Thuo Gathii, *African Regional Trade Agreements as Legal Regimes* (CUP, 2011); Clair Gammage, *North–South Regional Trade Agreements as Legal Regimes: A Critical Assessment of the EU-SADC Economic Partnership Agreement* (Edward Elgar, 2017); Araujo, *The EU Deep Trade Agenda* (n 12).

[47] Anghie and Chimni, 'Third World Approaches to International Law and Individual Responsibility in Internal Conflicts' (n 29) 79.

[48] Mutua, 'What is TWAIL?' (n 17).

[49] BS Chimni, 'Capitalism Imperialism and International Law in the Twenty-First Century' (2012) 14 *Oregon Review of International Law* 17.

[50] See Valerie Phillips, 'Indigenous Peoples and the Role of the Nation State' (2007) *Proceedings of the ASIL Annual Meeting* 101, 319. See also Luis Eslava, *Local Space, Global Life, The Everyday Operation of International Law and Development* (CUP, 2015).

[51] Own usage (n 23).

[52] *Guyana Sugar Corporation (Guysuco) v Bedessee Imports Ltd* [2011] TMOB 102, 11 (*CanLII*), https://canlii.ca/t/fm8w7.

[53] Response to Office Action, Serial Number 78589307, US Patent and Trademark Office (17 January 2007) Application No 78589307 (*USPTO*), http://tmportal.uspto.gov/extemal/portal/tow?SRCH=&isSubmitted=true&details=&SELECT=U S+Serial+No&TEXT=78589307#.

de Colombia GI,[54] and the Indian basmati rice GI.[55] It demonstrates the challenges posed to Third World GIs by shedding light on how international law may continue to privilege First World knowledge. Notwithstanding the reconceptualisation of GI laws as inclusive and emancipatory, this chapter explores the vestiges of informal imperialism that challenge the implementation of global-local GI laws. It shows that Third World countries are not always successful in clawing back their origin names, but that reclaiming origin-linked names (most common in European cases such as port or sherry, feta, and Parmigiano Reggiano)[56] is one means to attempt to keep GI laws grounded in local realities. Furthermore, this chapter underlines that laws, as vestiges of informal imperialism, on some occasions, continue to marginalise the Third World insofar as international law continues to privilege First World knowledge. Given the sustainable developmental focus of this work, this chapter highlights the practical impediments to protecting GI products via a *sui generis* GI system. Drawing on the case study of Demerara Gold provides an example of how Third World countries de facto struggle to claw back their own origin names from First World countries (in this case, Canada and the USA). The Ethiopia–Starbucks dispute brings to the fore the issues of a Third World country's challenge to protection for origin-coffee against a First World company (based in the USA). It also demonstrates the practical impediments to establishing a *sui generis* legal regime in a Third World territory and the factors impacting Ethiopia's choice to opt for trademark protection for its origin products instead. The Café de Colombia GI is discussed as an example of a Third World success story of GI marketing and protection. Similarly, the Indian basmati rice case is highlighted to demonstrate a successful defence by a Third World country against a First World country (USA). These latter cases show, to varying degrees, the reversal of a classic European GI scenario, where countries in the Third World have utilised the GI system to their advantage. This demonstrates that Third World countries can successfully invoke their GI rights and claw back their origin names from the First World. If this serves as a cautionary tale for other Third World countries seeking protection for their GI products, it follows that Third World countries might be able to use the EU's own system to claw back from the EU. As such, this chapter demonstrates that GIs can begin to be used as emancipatory tools to foster sustainable development globally and 'development from within' locally.

[54] Café de Colombia and Juan Valdez have been protected as trade marks in 1967 – Denmark; 1975 – UK; 1988 – Poland, Slovenia; 1989 – Italy, Slovakia, Czech Republic; 1990 – Germany; 1992 – Portugal; 1999 – Greece. It was the first non-EU GI registered in the EU in 2007. See European Commission, Publication of an Application Pursuant to Article 6(2) of Council Regulation (EC) No 510/2006 on the Protection of Geographical Indications and Designations of Origin for Agricultural Products and Foodstuffs [2006] OJ C 320, 17.

[55] See Trade Mark application no UK00001081589, https://trademarks.ipo.gov.uk/ipo-tmcase/page/Results/1/UK00001081589.

[56] See Commission, 'WTO Talks: EU Steps up Bid for Better Protection of Regional Quality Products' (*Europa*, 28 August 2003), https://ec.europa.eu/commission/presscorner/detail/en/IP_03_1178.

Chapter six examines the first CARIFORUM GI to be registered in the EU, for (Guyana) Demerara Rum.[57] It draws on the analysis of 'development from within' in the literature for the oldest Third World GI, for tequila (Mexico), to test the extent to which GIs are functioning as emancipatory developmental tools in the Third World context. As such, the tequila GI case study provides lessons on how GIs in the Third World context can contribute (or not) to a global-local law for sustainable development, in practice. With a focus on the Caribbean rum industry, it demonstrates the challenges of the dialogical manoeuvres to shape the GI and to define what grounding GIs in local realities means in practice. The chapter provides insights on two GI case studies. The first case study is the Demerara Rum GI,[58] which is the first Caribbean rum GI protected within the EU, by Demerara Distilleries Ltd, the only rum producer in the Demerara region in Guyana. The second case study is the Barbados Rum GI, where there has been a deadlock between the four distilleries on the island around agreement on a GI. That said, the interests of the four distilleries analysed in this book point to preferences for Protected Designation of Origin (PDO) and Protected Geographical Indication (PGI) models,[59] distinctions which are de jure absent from the Barbados GI Act and other Caribbean jurisdictions. Drawing on Natalie Corthésy's scholarship on country names in IP,[60] this chapter affirms that GIs based on country names in the Caribbean can engage in a co-branding strategy (as a form of public–private partnership) to foster 'development from within' for producers and producing territories alike. This approach overcomes dichotomous issues – relating to water inputs or cask requirements – preventing the agreements for GIs, by foregrounding how GIs can be emancipatory tools contributing to sustainable development for Third World GI producer communities. This chapter shows that GIs in the Third World context risk replicating colonial structures wherein transnational capitalist classes who own GIs continue to reap the benefits of these legal tools. As such, 'development from within' is not guaranteed, and it follows that there is no guarantee for Third World GIs to function as global-local laws. Rather, in the Third World context, GIs are sites of contestation between First and Third World knowledges and, therefore, their ability to function as global-local laws is brought into question.

Chapter seven concludes the book. It explains that, notwithstanding the theoretical framing of GIs as emancipatory legal tools, there are impediments to the transformative potential of GI laws as contributors to poverty eradication and sustainable development in the Third World context. These include, and

[57] 'DEMERARA RUM' (File number: PGI-GY-02423 – 28.6.2018). Publication of an Application Pursuant to Article 17(6) of Regulation (EC) No 110/2008 of the European Parliament and of the Council on the Definition, Description, Presentation, Labelling and the Protection of Geographical Indications of Spirit Drinks and Repealing Council Regulation (EEC) No 1576/89 [2021] OJ C120/7.

[58] ibid.

[59] See ch 6.

[60] Natalie Corthésy, 'Country Name Designation and International IP Protection of National Competitive Identities' (2021) 16(4–5) *Journal of International Property Law & Practice* 357.

are not limited to, the threat that GI laws today may not have evolved beyond their colonial origins and may contribute to widening the gap between First and Third World producer communities, even when the assumed neutrality of GI laws are interrogated;[61] the risk that GI laws continue to marginalise Third World producer communities, as vestiges of informal imperialism, despite an attempt to reconceptualise GIs in Third World contexts;[62] and the prevalence of institutional and knowledge gaps that hinder GIs from realising their emancipatory potential as legal tools that can contribute to poverty eradication.[63] In other words, this book demonstrates that the legal language of GIs as expressed in EU FTAs and international law provides the interpretive space for reconceptualising GIs as inclusive legal tools; however, the reality is that First World knowledge continues to be privileged in practice, and this sustains the development gap between the First and Third Worlds. The chapter concludes that foregrounding the 'commensurability of difference' underpinned by heritage offers a launch pad from which Third World nations can transition from a place of marginalisation to one of inclusion in the global economy upon which emancipation in our post-colonial context is based. In this way, Third World countries, through mobilising GIs as emancipatory tools in post-colonial trade, continue to challenge international law to serve *all* nations and realise its global-local potential, upon which GI laws have developed. In doing so, albeit in today's post-colonial context, GIs can contribute to attaining sustainable development in Third World countries and 'development from within' in the Caribbean.

[61] See ch 2.
[62] See chs 3 and 4.
[63] See chs 5 and 6. See also the author's co-authored piece on the institutional and knowledge gaps identified in the case study of GI implementation in Jamaica: Enrico Bonadio, Natalie Corthésy, Marc Mimler, Dianne Daley McClure, Yentyl Williams, and Shadae Deslandes, 'Maximizing the Benefits of Origin Products in An Emerging Economy – the Impact of Geographical Indication Protection in Jamaica' (2023) *European Intellectual Property Review* 5, available at SSRN, https://ssrn.com/abstract=.

2

GIs as Colonial Constructs in International Law

[IP] law was not merely an incidental part of the colonial legal apparatus, but a central technique in the commercial superiority sought by European powers in their interactions with each other in regions beyond Europe.[1]

Ruth Okediji (2003).

2.1 INTRODUCTION

THIS CHAPTER RETRACES THE origins of Geographical Indications (GIs) and the rationale for their creation in international law. As a form of intellectual property (IP) protection, GIs seek to protect goods that originate in a particular location and, therefore, the specific designation of origin-linked property is protected by IP laws at the national, regional, and international levels. This chapter analyses the different international legal regimes that recognise and protect origin-linked designations: (i) the Paris Convention for the Protection of Industrial Property of 1883; (ii) the Madrid Agreement for the Repression of False and Deceptive Indications of Source of 1891; (iii) the Lisbon Agreement for the Protection of Appellations of Origin and Their International Registration of 1958, including the Geneva Act of 2015; and (iv) the WTO Agreement on Trade-Related aspects of Intellectual Property Rights (TRIPS), concluded in 1995.[2]

This chapter addresses the questions of *what are GIs?* and *what are their origins and rationale in international law?* It also poses the question, *who and*

[1] Ruth Okediji, 'The International Relations of Intellectual Property: Narratives of Developing Country Participation in the Global Intellectual Property System' (2003) 7 *Singapore Journal of International & Comparative Law* 324.

[2] The legal regimes are hereinafter referenced as the Paris Convention, the Madrid Agreement, the Lisbon Agreement, and TRIPS: WIPO, 'The Paris Convention for the Protection of Industrial Property (as amended on September 28, 1979)', https://wipo.int/treaties/en/text.jsp?file_id=288514; The Madrid Agreement for the Repression of False or Deceptive Indications of Source on Goods of 1891 has been revised four times – Washington 1911, The Hague 1925, London 1934, and Lisbon 1958 – as well as an additional Act of Stockholm in 1967; WIPO, 'The Madrid Agreement for the Repression of False or Deceptive Indications of Source', https://wipolex.wipo.int/en/text/286776; 'Lisbon Agreement for the Protection of Appellations of Origin and their International Registration' (WIPO, 1979), https://wipo.int/lisbon/en/legal_texts/lisbon_agreement.html#P15_193; WTO, 'Trade-Related Aspects of Intellectual Property Rights Agreement', https://wto.org/english/docs_e/legal_e/27-trips_01_e.htm.

what was protected within these agreements? The chapter contributes to theorising GIs as colonial constructs and, notwithstanding their origins in colonialism, an understanding of what role they can play in contributing to sustainable development. The chapter demonstrates that GIs had their genesis in the colonial period and are best understood as colonial constructs. The rationale for their protection was, equally, embedded in the colonial context of commercial expansion and control of industrial production. As such, industrialised countries and their products were protected across the key IP treaties, and Third World countries were marginalised in their access to intellectual property rights (IPRs).

The chapter begins by introducing the three waves of IP multilateralism as a heuristic tool for conceptualising the developments of the legal regimes from the fifteenth century up until today. Section 2.2 sets out the characteristics of the first wave of IP multilateralism and GI protection within this framing, through analysis of the Paris Convention and the Madrid Agreement. Section 2.3 explains the characteristics of the second wave of IP multilateralism and the protection afforded to GIs in the Lisbon Agreement. Section 2.4 sets out the characteristics of the third wave of IP multilateralism and the evolution of GI protection with regard to the TRIPS Agreement and the Geneva Act to the Lisbon Agreement. The conclusion of this chapter is that GIs are origin-linked products and their rationale for protection in international law is rooted in colonial industrial development. The legal analysis in this chapter demonstrates that the legal provisions functioned as colonial strategies whose rationale was aimed at assimilating, incorporating, and controlling colonial (Third World) territories and subjects.[3] Through the process of deconstructing the law, its neutral façade is exposed. It demonstrates that the universalism upon which this (colonial) law is based risks reproducing bygone structures while maintaining the gap between the First and Third Worlds.

2.1.1 Three Waves of IP Multilateralism – Protecting GIs over Five Centuries

This section draws on Okedjii's analytical three-waves approach to set out the history and rationale of IP protection.[4] The waves of IP multilateralism include: (i) the extension of the IP regime during the colonial period, from the 1500s through to 1945; (ii) the transition from colonised to independent territories subject to the same IP system, from 1945 to 1990s; and (iii) the third multilateralism established by the WTO, from 1990s to today.[5] Okediji's framing emphasises that IP

[3] Okediji, 'The International Relations of Intellectual Property' (n 1) 325.

[4] ibid 315; see also Peter Drahos, 'Developing Countries and International Intellectual Property Standard-Setting' (2005) 5(5) *Journal of World Intellectual Property* 766; Alexander Peukert, 'The Colonial Legacy of the International Copyright System' in Mamadou Diawara and Ute Röschenthaler (eds), *Staging the Immaterial. Rights, Style and Performance in Sub-Saharan Africa* (Sean Kingston, forthcoming) 14.

[5] Okediji, 'The International Relations of Intellectual Property' (n 1) 333. This framing goes beyond the conceptual debate on 'epistemic messiness' of GIs identified by leading GI scholar Dev Gangjee, as both epistemes – the communicative and *terroir* logics – are European in nature. For a discussion on the epistemes of GIs, see Dev Gangjee, *Relocating the Law on Geographical Indications* (CUP, 2012) 7.

rights were developed as part of the extractive colonial era to benefit the colonial commercial powers and not the colonised nations or peoples.[6] The next sections assess the key international IP regimes within the context of the three waves of multilateralism to deconstruct the evolution of the law and, where necessary, to expose any remnants that may linger today of the domination, dispossession, and accumulation that characterised the first wave of multilateralism.

2.2 CHARACTERISTICS OF THE FIRST WAVE OF IP MULTILATERALISM

2.2.1 Colonialism and Imperialism: 1500s–1945

According to Okedjii, the first wave of IP multilateralism occurred as part of the trading relations between Europeans and non-Europeans, initially with gold and spices, and then to trading of enslaved peoples and agricultural produce.[7] This trade became synonymous with unequal trading relations characterised by domination, dispossession, and accumulation, as part of the imperial and colonial era.[8] It also fuelled the Industrial Revolution and reinforced the ideology of European supremacy as part of the Age of Enlightenment era.[9] This historical contextualisation sheds light on the fact that the Berne and Paris Conventions could not be drawn up *in vacuo*. Rather, as Okediji explains,

> what the Paris and Berne Conventions initially accomplished was the establishment of a network of relationships between the European member countries—a relationship that consolidated colonial power by expanding the geographic scope of rights acquired in the governing country to the colonies and, in some cases, the protectorates.[10]

These Conventions, therefore, served to reify the regulations that secured the very exploitation and extraction typical of the colonial period through multilateral treaties amongst imperial and colonial powers. IP laws were a central technique in the colonial strategy.[11] These laws facilitated and secured the tenets of colonialism, which de-centred local inhabitants from their territorial context and socioeconomic and ecopolitical realities,[12] by securing European

[6] Okediji, 'The International Relations of Intellectual Property' (n 1) 333, 324.
[7] ibid 320–21.
[8] Eric Williams, *Capitalism and Slavery* (The University of North Carolina Press, 1994) and *From Columbus to Castro: The History of the Caribbean* (Vintage, 1984).
[9] Okediji, 'The International Relations of Intellectual Property' (n 1) 321–23.
[10] ibid 323–24.
[11] ibid 324.
[12] Lesley Green's work emphasises the importance of an ecopolitical approach, which ought to be added alongside socioeconomic and political realities, for a broader understanding of the subject matter. See Lesley Green, *Rock/Water/Life: Ecology and Humanities for a Decolonial South Africa* (Duke, 2020).

national trading interests in colonial territorial spaces. Additionally, former colonies acceded to these treaties as part of the colonial strategy,[13] as passive recipients of IP laws designed to facilitate their exploitation for European gains.[14] It is, therefore, paramount to assess the legal provisions contextualised as colonial strategies whose rationale aims at assimilating, incorporating, and controlling colonial territories and subjects.[15] The next section provides an overview of the emergence of GI protection in the first wave of IP multilateralism, with a focus on the provisions of the Paris Convention and the Madrid Agreement.

2.2.1.1 The Paris Convention 1883

This section assesses the specific provisions relating to GIs and, more broadly, the norms established by the Paris Convention. These provisions are considered alongside their amendments to the original Convention text across the three waves of multilateralism. The Paris Convention of 1883 was the result of preparatory work that took place over a decade prior to the agreement.[16] It resulted in the Union for the Protection of Industrial Property amongst the *High* Contracting States.[17] Article 1 sets out that:

> (2) The protection of industrial property has as its object patents, utility models, industrial designs, *trademarks*, service marks, trade names, *indications of source or appellations of origin*, and the repression of unfair competition.
>
> (3) Industrial property shall be understood in the broadest sense and shall apply not only to *industry and commerce proper*, but likewise to *agricultural*

[13] Okediji cites the colonial British administrator Lord Lugard, which emphasises the coloniser–colonised dynamics of this period: 'We develop new Territories as Trustees for Civilisation, for the Commerce of the World . . . As Roman imperialism laid the foundations of modern civilisation and led the wild barbarians of these islands along the path of progress, so in Africa today we are repaying the debt, and bringing to the dark places of the earth, the abode of barbarism and cruelty, the torch of culture and progress, while ministering to the material needs of our own civilisation.' Okediji, 'The International Relations of Intellectual Property' (n 1) 359.

[14] Okediji also succinctly notes, 'In essence, the extension of intellectual property rights was not directed at the inhabitants of the governed territories at all, but instead to facilitate commercial relations among colonial powers as trade between European powers occurred on and among the various territories on behalf of foreign sovereigns.' ibid 234, 323–25.

[15] ibid 325.

[16] The text of the Paris Convention was drafted and revised in 1873 and 1878, ahead of the Diplomatic Conference in Paris in 1880. The Additional Protocol was added in 1883. George Bodenhausen, 'Guide to the Application of the Paris Convention for the Protection of Industrial Property' (WIPO, 1968) 25, https://wipo.int/edocs/pubdocs/en/intproperty/611/wipo_pub_611.pdf. The 11 founding members comprised the King of Belgium, Emperor of Brazil, King of Spain, President of Republic of France, President of the Republic of Guatemala, King of Italy, King of the Netherlands, King of Portugal and the Algarve, President of the Republic of Salvador, the King of Serbia, and the Federal Council of the Swiss Confederation.

[17] By the 1911 Washington Act this was changed to 'contracting *States*', and eventually became 'contracting *countries*' by the London Act of 1934 (emphasis added). The change of wording is reflective of the geo-political changes of the time.

and *extractive industries* and to *all manufactured or natural products*, for example, wines, grain, tobacco leaf, fruit, cattle, minerals, mineral waters, beer, flowers, and flour.[18]

The definition of industrial property above includes both the indication of source (IS) and the appellation of origin (AO) as its subject matter, as well as both manufactured and natural products. This underlines the co-existence of at least two types of GI within this foremost IP regime: the IS and AO are the early instances of GIs and, indeed, the GI can also be considered an umbrella term regrouping these categories of indications of origin. They seek to protect the designation of a product by reference to its origin, and while their legal functions are similar, they may operate in different regimes and therefore have nuances between them.[19] For example, the IS is the simplest and broadest type of GI that indicates where a good originates, such as 'Made in China' or 'Swiss-made'. There is no requirement that the IS also indicates the quality, reputation, or other characteristics of the good. It is, therefore, the most basic type of GI that informs consumers of the place, region, or country that the goods come from. In contrast, an AO – which comes from the French '*Appellation d'Origine*' – indicates a link between the 'quality' and 'other characteristics' of the good, having an exclusive or essential link to its geographic origins. In terms of the protection they each afford their users, Dev Gangjee notes that the IS refers to a negative protection, namely preventing the use of the indication by others, compared with the positive protections that grant the use of an indication by a specified group.[20] These three terms – the GI, IS, and AO – inter alia, make up the alphabet soup of GIs. [21]

[18] In the 1925 revision conference, upon the request of Cuba, tobacco leaves were added to the original list of wines, grains, fruits, and cattle for 'agricultural' industries. At the same conference, 'mineral' was added alongside mineral water under 'extractive' industries. Beer, flowers, and flour were added during the revision conference in 1934. These are not exhaustive lists, but as the original Final Protocol advised, they are demonstrative of the broad conception of industrial property. Additionally, as membership expands alongside trade interests, these commodities are also illustrative of the goods traded at the time.

[19] In the *Exportur* case, the legal question concerned the distinction of the indication of source and the geographical designations. The judgment stated, 'Comparative examination of the national laws shows that indications of provenance (indications de provenance; *indicaciones de procedencia*) are intended to inform the consumer that the product bearing that indication comes from a particular place, region or country. A more or less considerable reputation may attach to that geographical provenance. A designation of origin (*appellation d'origine; denominación de origen*), for its part, guarantees, not only the geographical provenance of the product, but also that the goods have been manufactured according to quality requirements or manufacturing standards prescribed by an act of public authority and thus that they have certain specific characteristics.' (para 11). Accordingly, 'Jijona' and 'Alicante' could not be used in *Turrón* candies made in France, since they had a reputational link to Spain. *C-3/91 Exportur SA v LOR SA* 1992 E.C.R I-5529, I-5535.

[20] Gangjee, *Relocating the Law on Geographical Indications* (n 5) 135, fn 30.

[21] ibid 3.

The original scope of Article 1 of the Paris Convention of 1883 was to create a Union for the Protection of Industrial Property.[22] It was not until the 1911 revision conference that the IS was brought explicitly into Article 1.[23] Equally, the AO was also included for the first time in this international legal union in the 1925 revision conference (Article 1, Paris). This effectively reflects the legal discourse of the time, which was preoccupied with adequately identifying the IS and AO as IP subject matter and protecting it at the international level. Gangjee has highlighted how members were keen to negotiate that agricultural products, and specifically wines, were included as industrial products, in order to benefit from the broad protection established with the Paris Convention.[24] The inclusion of these products – 'natural' products alongside manufactured products – benefitted European trading interests and guaranteed their protection as products of industrial property. Additionally, in the *Guide to the Application of the Paris Convention*'s amendments at Stockholm, Georg Bodenhausen (then director of the United International Bureau for the Protection of Intellectual Property, 'BIRPI') explains that 'The purpose of the provision is merely to avoid excluding from the protection of industrial property activities or products which would otherwise run the risk of not being assimilated to those of industry proper.'[25] However, it is important to note that these activities and products are, namely, commodities traded by European powers during the colonial period.

A historical doctrinal (re)view of the Paris Convention shows that the IS was first included under the original Article 10 provisions, which relate to the use of false indications in trade. It was, therefore, originally included as subject matter of what constitutes an infringement with regard to the protection set out therein (Paris Convention, 1883). The original Article 10 of the Paris Convention of 1883 refers to the IS in the following context:

> The provisions of the preceding article will be applicable to all products that falsely bear, as the indication of source, the name of a given locality, as far as this indication is joint to a commercially fictitious or borrowed name with fraudulent intent.
>
> Any manufacturer or trader engaged in the manufacture or trade of the product and established in the locality falsely indicated as the source shall be considered as the interested party.[26]

[22] The term industrial property is broadly defined. The final protocol explains, 'Industrial property shall be understood in the broadest sense and shall apply not only to industry and commerce proper, but likewise to agricultural and extractive industries and to all manufactured or natural products, for example, wines, grain, tobacco leaf, fruit, cattle, minerals, mineral waters, beer, flowers, and flour.' Paris Convention, Final Protocol, 1883.

[23] The '*indication de provenance*', as it is known in the original French text, refers to the commonly translated IS that readers in English are more accustomed to.

[24] Gangjee, *Relocating the Law on Geographical Indications* (n 5) 25.

[25] Georg Bodenhausen, *Guide to the Application of the Paris Convention for the Protection of Industrial Property* (WIPO, 1968) 25, https://wipo.int/edocs/pubdocs/en/intproperty/611/wipo_pub_611.pdf.

[26] Translation by author of art 10, Paris Convention 1883, according to the '*texte authentique*' in French.

By virtue of this provision, the IS was subject to the provisions of seizure as established under the preceding Article 9 of the Paris Convention, 1883. Article 9 states:

> All products bearing an illicit trade mark or commercial name, could be seized at import in the States of the Union in which this mark or commercial name has the right to be protected legally.
>
> The seizure will take place at the request of either the public ministry or the interested party in conformity with the internal legislation of each State (Article 9, Paris Convention, 1883).[27]

The original text therefore permits the seizure of false IS products, as they are prohibited under the Convention. The colonial powers therefore envisaged enforcing protection against IS products from the outset of the foundational Paris Convention, first with regard to infringement (Article 10), and later through recognition of the IS as IP subject matter (Article 1).

The revisions referred to herein took place across a series of seven revision conferences: Brussels in 1900, Washington DC in 1911, The Hague in 1925, London in 1934, Lisbon in 1958, and Stockholm in 1967, including an additional amendment in 1979.[28] With each conference, membership of the Union grew by virtue of new contracting parties acceding to and ratifying the agreement, including, where applicable, for their overseas territories.[29] For example, the Washington Act (1911) included that these contracting countries could accede to the Paris Convention on behalf of their 'colonies, possessions, dependencies, [and] protectorates' (Article 16*bis*, Paris Convention, Washington Act 1911), wording which was not changed to 'territories' until the Stockholm Conference of 1967, under the second multilateralism.[30] The expansion in membership, including colonial territories, reflects the realities of the colonial period within

[27] Translation by author.

[28] Each revision conference was concluded with an Act bearing the name of the place it was concluded.

[29] Arts 20, 21, and 24, Paris Convention, as amended 1979. The Paris Convention currently has 177 contracting parties. The 1883 Paris Convention had 11 contracting parties: the King of Belgium, the Emperor of Brazil, the King of Spain, the President of Republic of France, the President of the Republic of Guatemala, the King of Italy, the King of the Netherlands, the King of Portugal and the Algarve, the President of the Republic of Salvador, the King of Serbia, and the Federal Council of the Swiss Confederation. To the Brussels Act, there were 23 contracting parties; 36 contracting parties to the Washington Act 1911; 33 contracting parties to the Hague Act 1925; 44 contracting parties to the London Act 1934; 52 contracting parties to the Lisbon Act 1958; and 146 contracting parties to the Stockholm Act 1967. See Paris Convention 'Contracting Parties' (WIPO), https://wipo.int/treaties/en/ip/paris/.

[30] These modifications reflect the changing political and legal times, including, inter alia, the decolonisation process that began with Ghanaian independence in 1957. What may appear as subtle differences in the language used are fundamental for understanding the geopolitical realities of the time and how the law, and changes in law, reflect these realities. For example, understanding the change of wording from 'High Contracting Parties' to 'contracting countries', alongside the shift from 'colonies' to 'territories', is reflective of how the King of Belgium and First Councillor of France could represent Tunisia during the 1900 Brussels Conference. Tunisia was a protectorate of France from 1881 to 1956.

which the Paris Convention was agreed and the changing geopolitical realities under which it was revised.

The Paris Convention laid certain foundational principles within the international trade law regime that have withstood the test of time.[31] These include the principles of national treatment and unfair competition. These principles shall now be considered, since they established the minimum standards that are considered across the three waves of IP multilateralism.

2.2.1.1.1 National Treatment

The Paris Convention establishes the protection of national treatment, which features in all subsequent intellectual property (IP) agreements.[32] From the outset, this principle established that members shall benefit from protection in the territory of the members on the same grounds as nationals, and this also extends to legal remedies under the law of the country where the infringement takes place (Article 3, Paris 1883):

> Subjects or citizens of States who are not party to the Union who are domiciled or have industrial or commercial establishments on the territory of one of the States of the Union are assimilated as subjects or citizens of contracting States.[33]

Under the 1911 Washington revision, the IS and unfair competition were added to the list of subject matter that benefits from national treatment. Although the Hague revision in 1925 removed the list and instead replaced it with the general term 'industrial property', it is understood to be implicitly included under the broad understanding of IP.[34] By the subsequent Washington revision, a new provision was included, which stated that there shall be no domiciliation or establishment requirement for nationals of the Union in the country where they claim their rights. This reflects the increasing trans-border nature of trade, whereby a legal person or entity is not obliged to be established or

[31] Under the Paris Convention, any separate Union seeking to advance certain aspects of protection relating to industrial property, therefore, would not need to repeat the breadth and scope of these provisions (art 15, Paris 1883; currently art 19, Paris 1979). Art 19 Paris Convention provides for 'Special Agreements': 'It is understood that the countries of the Union reserve the right to make separately between themselves special agreements for the protection of industrial property, in so far as these agreements do not contravene the provisions of this Convention.' Indeed, the later Madrid Agreement specifically focused on the means of repressing false IS (1981), and the Lisbon Agreement, after that, focused on protection relating to AOs and their registration (1958).

[32] The Paris Convention established that Members shall benefit from protection in the territory of the Members on the same grounds as nationals, and this also extends to legal remedies under the law of the country where the infringement takes place: 'Subjects or citizens of States who are not party to the Union who are domiciled or have industrial or commercial establishments on the territory of one of the States of the Union are assimilated as subjects or citizens of contracting States.': art 3, Paris Convention, 1883 (translation by author). Bodenhausen, *Guide to the Application of the Paris Convention for the Protection of Industrial Property* (n 25) 27.

[33] Translation by author.

[34] Bodenhausen, *Guide to the Application of the Paris Convention for the Protection of Industrial Property* (n 25) 25.

domiciled in the place where the product is sold. Rather, the provision clarifies that third-party rights are nevertheless protected in accordance with the law of that country where their goods are traded.[35] Contextualising this provision within the period of the first multilateralism is a reminder that it is imperial and colonial third-party rights that are protected in overseas territories, colonies, and protectorates.

The additional line added by the Hague revision further clarifies that the domestic laws shall determine the judicial and administrative proceedings, in regard to claims to protect the owners' rights to their industrial products (Article 2, para 1, Paris 1925):

> The nationals of each of the contracting countries will benefit from the protection of industrial property, the advantages that the respective laws accord currently or will accord to their nationals, without prejudicing the rights foreseen by the present Convention in all the other countries of the Union. As a consequence, they will have the same protection and same legal recourse against all affronts to their rights, within the means of the fulfilment of conditions and formalities imposed also on nationals.[36]

In addition, Article 3 provides that non-nationals can also enjoy the right of protection of their industrial property equal to that of subjects or citizens of the contracting states as long as they are domiciled or have an industrial or commercial presence on the territory of a Paris Member (Article 3, Paris 1883). This is significant since it contributes to establishing the network of European colonial trading interests – amongst both non-nationals and subjects or citizens alike – in territories of members of the Paris Convention. The Brussels Act of 1900 notably changed the nature of the establishment by adding the adjectives 'effective and serious' (Article 3, Paris 1900),[37] which remain in today's version of the text.[38] This additional level of subjectivity relating to the nature of the establishment serves to reinforce the standard-setting agendas of this wave of

[35] However, interestingly, trans-border protection was not explicitly included *expressis verbis* until art 2(2) Geneva Act of the Lisbon Agreement, 2015. See definition under art 1(xii) Geneva Act of the Lisbon Agreement, 2015.

[36] Paras 2 and 3 state: 'Equally, no requirement of domiciliation or establishment can be demanded of nationals of the Union in the country where the protection is sought in order to benefit from the rights of intellectual property. The provisions of the legislation of each of the contracting countries relative to the judicial and administrative procedure and competence are expressly reserved, as well as with regard to the assignment of the domicile or of the representative, which will be required by the laws on industrial property.' Translation by author. This domestic competence became para 3 of art 2 when enumeration was introduced in the text with the London Act 1934, and this provision has since remained unchanged. Additionally, under the London Act of 1934, 'contracting countries' was changed to 'countries of the Union'.

[37] 'Subjects or citizens of States who are not party to the Union who are domiciled or have effective and serious industrial or commercial establishments on the territory of one of the States of the Union are assimilated as subjects or citizens of contracting States.' Translation by author.

[38] In addition, the Hague Act replaced 'subjects or citizens' with nationals ('*ressortissants*', in French) in 1925, while the London Act in 1934 replaced contracting countries with 'countries of the Union'.

multilateralism, namely to expand the geographic scope of rights and secure trading interests of colonial powers.[39]

In Bodenhausen's *Guide to the Application of the Paris Convention for the Protection of Industrial Property*, it is usefully summarised that the provisions of national treatment have been revised with regard to: (i) the object of national treatment; (ii) how non-nationals are subject to its provisions; and (iii) under which circumstances non-nationals can benefit from protection provided therein.[40] As outlined above, the provisions on national treatment have endured not solely within the Paris Convention but also in subsequent legal regimes on IP, notably but not exclusively with the Madrid Agreement and the Lisbon Agreement.[41] Similarly, under the Geneva Act (2015) of the Lisbon Agreement, national treatment expressly applies as it relates to the refusal of international registration.[42]

Okediji underlines the significance of the provisions on national treatment, inter alia, as laying the foundations for 'a customary international practice with its own force of law'.[43] The prevalence of national treatment provisions – which transcends across all three instances of multilateralism and is evidenced in the legal texts of the IP regimes therein – attests to the importance of this provision in establishing the application of rights to secure the colonial trading relations of these powers. Having outlined the inclusion of national treatment provisions under the Paris Convention, the next section assesses the inclusion of unfair competition provisions under the same Convention.

2.2.1.1.2 Unfair Competition (and False Indications)

This section explains the provision on unfair competition and extends Okediji's analysis to consider that the Paris Convention also establishes a 'customary international practice' in IP law, similarly to the provision of national treatment.[44] The provisions on 'unfair competition' are set out under Article 10*bis*

[39] Okediji, 'The International Relations of Intellectual Property' (n 1) 323–24.

[40] Bodenhausen, *Guide to the Application of the Paris Convention for the Protection of Industrial Property* (n 25) 27.

[41] For example, national treatment expressly applies to the provision of art 1(4) of the Madrid Agreement vis-à-vis seizure: 'If the laws of a country permit neither seizure upon importation nor prohibition of importation nor seizure within the country, then, until such time as the laws are modified accordingly, those measures shall be replaced by the actions and remedies available in such cases to nationals under the laws of such country.' (art 1(4), Madrid Agreement (n 2)). It is worth noting, vis-à-vis protection, that prior to the Article's current wording, it did still allow for national treatment, albeit not in such explicit terms.

[42] Art 15(5) of the Geneva Act provides that 'Each Contracting Party shall make available to interested parties affected by a refusal the same judicial and administrative remedies that are available to its own nationals in respect of the refusal of protection for an appellation of origin or a geographical indication.' (art 15, Geneva Act of the Lisbon Agreement, 2015 (n 35)).

[43] Okediji, 'The International Relations of Intellectual Property' (n 1) 338.

[44] Okediji makes this reference in relation to national treatment. I extend it here in relation to unfair competition as well (ibid).

of the Paris Convention, while the 'repression of unfair competition' has also been provided for under Article 1 since the Washington revision conference of 1911. Article 10 and 10*bis* provide for seizure relating to false IS and protection against unfair competition, respectively. In the *Guide to the Paris Convention*, Bodenhausen explains that protection against unfair competition is brought under Article 1 since it is, in most cases, the same as protecting against an act infringing industrial property rights.[45] Gangjee has noted how this particularly satisfied French wine interests, due to a national differentiation of protecting manufactured objects *('objet fabriqué')* under the penal law of 1824, while natural products such as wine were protected under unfair competition *('concurrence déloyale')*.[46] In essence, the broad understanding of industrial property allowed wine to be considered as an industrial product, which could thereafter benefit from the broad minimum standards of protection set out under this regime. In the literature, wine is considered the archetypal GI,[47] and this also points to the Europeanness of the products and production that were protected at the outset within this colonial context. The next section explains how Article 10 has evolved with regard to false IS and unfair competition.

Under the first version of Article 10, the interested party, according to this law, was either the manufacturer or the merchant, and insofar as they were also established in the area ('locality') falsely indicated as the area of origin (1883).[48] At the 1900 Brussels revision conference there was a dual expansion of the terms of protection, not only with regard to the persons that can benefit from protection and the area designated, but also to the specific addition related to an act constituting unfair competition to which the protection applies:

> Any *producer*, manufacturer or trader engaged in the *production*, manufacture or trade of the product, and established in the locality falsely indicated as the source, *either in the region or where the locality is situated*, shall be considered as the interested party. (Article 10, Paris 1900).[49]

Equally importantly, the Brussels revision conference introduced Article 10*bis* specifying the terms of unfair competition, whereby countries of the Union

[45] Bodenhausen, *Guide to the Application of the Paris Convention for the Protection of Industrial Property* (n 25) 23.

[46] Gangjee, *Relocating the Law on Geographical Indications* (n 5) 26.

[47] ibid 66.

[48] 'The provisions of the preceding article will be applicable to all products that falsely bear, as the indication of source, the name of a given locality, as far as this indication is joint to a commercially fictitious or "borrowed" name with fraudulent intent. Any manufacturer or trader engaged in the manufacture or trade of the product, and established in the locality falsely indicated as the source shall be considered as the interested party.' (art 10, Paris Convention, 1883, translated by author).

[49] Translated by author. Italics indicate amendment.

are bound to protect against such an act.[50] This revision is fundamental, given that Article 10*bis* of the Paris Convention remains an internationally accepted legal reference on unfair competition that is referenced in subsequent agreements today. For example, under the GI provisions of the TRIPS Agreement,

> Members shall provide the legal means for interested parties to prevent: . . . (b) any use which constitutes an act of unfair competition within the meaning of Article 10bis of the Paris Convention (1967).[51]

This is precisely how the unfair competition provision, birthed in a colonial context under the first wave of IP multilateralism, has become customary in international law, as it continues to regulate IP provisions that apply to all WTO members within the current third wave of IP multilateralism.

The subsequent Hague revision added 'moral and physical persons' to the triptych of interested parties – the 'producer, manufacturer, merchant' – while rewording the geographic area implicated (Article 10, Paris 1911).[52] Article 10*bis* was also revised to ensure that Members provide '*effective*' protection. Although this may, at first glance, appear to be a minor qualification to the word 'protection', adding the word 'effective' introduces a new level of subjectivity vis-à-vis what type of protection is deemed effective or not. This new level of subjectivity is significant since it reinforces the standard-setting agendas of colonial powers, while also consolidating their agendas of assimilation and control of foreign territories and products in international trade. Importantly, the Act introduced a definition of unfair competition for the first time in an international legal regime on industrial property: Article 10*bis* as amended at the Hague conference established that '[a]ll acts of competition that are contrary to *honest usage* in industrial and commercial matters constitute an act of unfair competition' (emphasis added). This provision ought to be read objectively and with a critical lens. Such a reading should be taken into consideration, given the colonial context and the well-documented realities of colonialism as theft, conquest, and forced ownership and dispossession.[53] This is significant since it is emblematic of the perception of a colonial 'honest usage' of the period, which has come to be reified in international law today. It further lists such acts as being those which create confusion, include false allegations, or intend to discredit the products of a competitor, which henceforth should be prohibited (Article 10*bis*, Paris 1925).

[50] 'The nationals of the Convention (under Articles 2 and 3) will benefit, in all the States of the Union, from the protection accorded to nationals against unfair competition.' Translated by author.

[51] Article 22.2.b TRIPS.

[52] 'Any *producer*, manufacturer or trader engaged in the *production*, manufacture or trade of the product, and established in the locality falsely indicated as the source, *either in the region or where the locality is situated*, shall be considered as the interested party.' (art 10, Paris 1911, translated by author). Italics indicate the amendments.

[53] Williams, *Capitalism and Slavery* (n 8).

This was a landmark inclusion in 1925, but also in its legacy, as it remains a globally recognised reference point on unfair competition in international law today.[54]

Thereafter, the London Act of 1934 extended this protection under Article 10 to also include the country where the infringement takes place, namely the country in which the false indication is being used (Article 10(2) Paris, 1934).[55] In a similar vein, Article 10*bis* was also amended to bring clarity to the prohibition applying to an act of unfair competition which applies not only with regard to the product, but also to the establishment and industrial or commercial activity of the competitor (Article 10*bis*(3) Paris, 1934).[56] Article 10*ter* was also amended to include producers and traders, alongside trade unions and associations that can benefit from applying the law under this provision (Article 10*ter*(2) Paris, 1925).[57] In essence, the revision conferences reinforced the purpose of these amendments, namely to provide the framework within which the Union members could fulfil their colonial strategies within colonial trading networks.

The last revisions under Article 10 took place at the Lisbon revision conference in 1958. Article 10(1) was amended substantially. It now provided that

> [t]he dispositions of the preceding article [Article 9 on seizure] are applicable in the case of direct or indirect usage of the false indication with regard to the origin of the product or the identity of the producer, manufacturer or trader.[58]

It no longer referred to the product carrying the false indication (Article 10(1) Paris, 1934), but shifted the emphasis to the usage of the product and introduced the now common phrase vis-à-vis usage – whether it is 'direct or indirect'

[54] For example, TRIPS refers to Article 10*bis* Paris: see art. 22.2.b. In addition, the Hague Conference also added Article 10*ter*, which underlines that '[para 1] The contracting countries shall assure to nationals of other countries of the Union appropriate legal recourse to effectively prevent all acts foreseen under Articles 9, 10 and 10bis. [para 2] They shall also foresee measures to allow interested trade unions and associations representing industry and trade, of which their existence is not contrary to the laws of their country, to act in justice or in regard to the administrative authorities, in order to repress the acts foreseen under Articles 9, 10 and 10bis, insofar as the law of the country in which the protection is sought allows for trade unions and associations in the given country.' (art 10*ter*, Paris Convention, 1925).

[55] 'Whether a physical or moral person, the manufacture or trade of the product and having been established either in the locality falsely indicated as the place of origin, or the region or where the locality is situated, or in the country falsely indicated, or the country where the false indication of source is used, shall be recognised as an interested party' (art 10(2), Paris Convention, 1934, translation by author).

[56] 'Notably the following shall be forbidden: 1. All facts in spite of their nature which are liable to create confusion by any means of the establishment, the products or the industrial or commercial activity of a competitor; 2. The false allegations, in the exercise of trade, of a nature to discredit the establishment, products or industrial or commercial activities of a competitor.' (art 10*bis*(3), Paris Convention, 1934, translation by author).

[57] 'They undertake, moreover, to provide for measures to enable unions and associations representing the industry or trade concerned and whose existence is not contrary to the laws of their country, to take legal action before administrative authorities, with a view to the repression of acts provided for in Articles 9, 10 and 10bis, to the extent that the law of the country in which protection is requested allows trade unions and associations in that country.' Translation by author.

[58] Translation by author.

(Article 10(1) Paris, 1958). This reflects the normative assumption that false products may be, de facto, in circulation, but their usage is what amounts to an infringement.[59] The amendment to Article 10*bis* added that indications and claims to which their use in trade is susceptible to mislead the public about the good – its nature, process of manufacture, characteristics, usage, or quantity – shall be prohibited (Article 10*bis*(3)(iii), Paris, 1958).[60] Again, this reflects a number of normative assumptions – about the 'public' and what is 'susceptible to mislead', amongst others – that are central to the establishment of customary practices in law.

Unlike the provisions on national treatment, neither the Madrid Agreement nor the Geneva Act to the Lisbon Agreement (or the Lisbon Agreement before that) expressly refer to unfair competition *verbis expressis*.[61] Considering Gangjee's explanation of unfair competition's linkage to the communicative logic and trademark law,[62] this could suggest a shift towards the *sui generis* protection that characterises separate GI laws today. In other words, *sui generis* laws based on the *terroir* logic (origin-quality) no longer expressly rely on the communicative (origin-reputation) logic of the unfair competition provision, which is relied upon in trademark law. Nevertheless, the TRIPS Agreement does rely on this provision, and this, importantly, applies to *all* WTO Members (Article 22.2.b TRIPS). This effectively makes the provisions of 'unfair competition' – as set out in Article *10bis* Paris Convention – customary practice for *all* Members of the WTO, providing continuity across the three waves of IP multilateralism.

To summarise, both the IS and AO are considered as the earliest instances of GIs under the Paris Convention. The original 'High Contracting States' sought international legal protection for their industrial products – broadly conceived – and the provisions on national treatment and unfair competition provide evidence for the rationale for seeking this protection. In this period, it is evident that imperial powers and *their* internationally traded products benefitted from the protection established under this legal regime. In this section, the focus has been on the Paris Convention, precisely because it was the first multilateral treaty to

[59] Additionally, it also introduced the reference to the triptych of interested parties – *producer, manufacturer, or trader* – wherein the provisions of the Article apply if it concerns the origin of the product or the identity of these interested parties: art 10(1) Paris Convention, 1958. In sum, therefore, the definition of who was implicated as an interested party to claim infringement with regard to the false indication under art 10 was clarified and extended in geographical scope from interested parties, not merely established in the locality falsely indicated (Paris 1883), but also regions (Brussels Act of 1900), countries (Hague Act of 1925), and eventually to any interested party implicated in the false indication, either in the country falsely indicated or in the country where it is falsely used (Lisbon Act of 1958).

[60] Art 10*bis*(3) reads, 'the indications or allegation of the usage, in the course of trade, which is susceptible to mislead the public about the nature, mode of manufacture, the characteristics, aptitude of use or the quality of the product'. Translation by author.

[61] Under the third wave of multilateralism, the TRIPS provisions on GIs established that Members shall bear the duty of providing legal recourse for GI rights-holders by protecting against unfair competition 'within the meaning of art 10*bis* Paris Convention (1967)' (art 22.2.b TRIPS).

[62] Gangjee, *Relocating the Law on Geographical Indications* (n 5) 77–126.

establish broad norms of protection for industrial property, within which origin-linked products are included. In the following section, the second such treaty, the Madrid Agreement, is assessed within the context of this first wave of multilateralism. This section explores how these treaties facilitate the networks of colonial assimilation, incorporation, and control in relation to GI products.

2.2.2 The Madrid Agreement: Developing the Indication of Source Provisions from the Foundations of the Paris Convention

The Madrid Agreement for the Repression of False Indications of Source was created in 1891,[63] within a decade of the Paris Convention. It was born out of the current Article 19 Paris Convention (former Article 15) provision that allows for the establishment of other special agreements that aim to protect industrial property.[64] It goes beyond the foundational principles set out in the Paris Convention and is important for several broad reasons. It was the first agreement to utilise the Paris Convention provision to establish a new legal regime building on the Paris Convention provisions. The literature recognises that the rationale for the Madrid Agreement arose due to dissatisfaction amongst the Paris Convention founding members about the protection afforded to GIs under Article 10 Paris Convention, in turn broadly reflecting the limitations of the communicative approach to protection.[65] The Madrid Agreement effectively contributes to this shift away from the communicative logic (origin-reputation link) and towards an approach based on *terroir* (origin-quality link). It expands this in a number of ways, as set out in this section. Article 1 of the Madrid Agreement establishes that

> [a]ll goods bearing a *false or deceptive indication* by which *one of the countries* to which this Agreement applies, *or a place situated therein*, is directly or indirectly indicated as being the *country or place of origin* shall be seized on importation into any of the said countries.[66]

[63] Note that the current title, referring to 'False and Deceptive Indications', was not amended to include the 'Deceptive' element until 1958, under the Lisbon Act.

[64] 'It is understood that the countries of the Union reserve the right to make separately between themselves special agreements for the protection of industrial property, in so far as these agreements do not contravene the provisions of this Convention.' (art 19, Paris Convention).

[65] Gangjee, *Relocating the Law on Geographical Indications* (n 5) 65.

[66] The 'deceptive' terminology was not added until the last revision conference in 1958. Gangjee suggests that it has not been effectively translated, and that 'misleading' better emphasises the intention of this addition. Additionally, at the 1925 revision conference, a new line was included introducing special sanctions, inter alia, based on domestic laws referring to marks or tradenames, with the goal to prohibit the 'false' indications (art 1, para 5). This adds considerable flexibility in legal instruments available to members to ensure this repression and, in turn, to protect the IS right-holders. It is also remarkable as it allows IS to be protected or enforced through laws relating to marks, and thus introduces a flexibility into the regime on protection of IS. Arguably, this flexibility was always there, but not expressly stated (ibid 229).

The scholarship recognises that, although neither the Paris Convention nor the Madrid Agreement define the IS, the essence of an IS as a GI can be established from the wording of Article 1 of the Madrid Agreement, namely referring to both 'country' and 'place of origin'.[67] This is deemed important in the literature for at least two reasons. First, in the absence of an effective system for repressing false indications, protection was provided via a number of different laws: penal laws, tort, unfair competition, trade and merchandise marks laws, revenue and customs regulations, and niche labelling laws.[68] It is also important to recall the above-mentioned discussion that the IS was not included as an object of 'industrial property' until the 1911 revisions. Rather, it was after the establishment of the Madrid Agreement that the IS was brought under Article 1, as such clarifying both that it is protected as industrial property and that false indications are prohibited (Article 10, Paris Convention).

Second, although there was protection for both trademarks and collective marks in the Paris Conventions, in Article 6 and 7*bis* respectively, there was an ontological difference between the IS and the trademark.[69] Gangjee's historical account reviews 'the evidence that, analogous to the logic of a trademark protection, a collectively generated reputation formed the basis of including the IS within the Paris Convention'.[70] Trademarks were, therefore, deemed an inadequate basis of protection for a product with a collectively generated reputation. Hence, this led to the initiative by the few founding members to create a new Union specifically for the protection against false IS.

The Madrid Agreement, like the Paris Convention, has undergone the same series of revision conferences, and has equally been amended by Acts in Washington DC 1911, The Hague 1925, London 1934, and Lisbon 1958, as well as an Additional Act at Stockholm in 1967.[71] Much like the changes discussed above in relation to the Paris Convention, the Washington Act of the Madrid Agreement (1911) also brought substantial changes with regard to repressing false IS. Notably, the change in wording, from false IS '*can*' be seized to false IS '*shall*' be seized, is important (Article 1 Madrid, 1911). The use of mandatory language demonstrates a change in tone and objective of the agreement, in effect harmonising the action of seizure

[67] ibid 27.

[68] Gangjee draws on historical documentation, including a report from 'His Majesty's Representatives Abroad', as well as documentation from BIRPI. There is significant variation. For example, Belgium, Italy, and the Netherlands had penal codes; Germany had both unfair competition and trademark legislation; Brazil had a trademark law; Spain had niche legislation on labelling; Britain had the Merchandise Marks regime; Austria had none whatsoever, along with Japan, Norway, the Dominican Republic, Serbia, and Tunisia. Alongside this plethora of regimes were also different rights conferred for initiating legal proceedings, which were subject to different proceedings and, equally, different remedies (ibid 28–29).

[69] Lionel Bently 3, 28, in Lionel Bently, Jennifer Davis, and Jane C Ginsburg (eds), *Trade Marks and Brands: An Interdisciplinary Critique* (CUP, 2008) in Gangjee, *Relocating the Law on Geographical Indications* (n 5) 28. Also note the court's ruling in *Hanover Star Milling v Metcalf* [1916] 240 US 403, 412: 'The primary and proper function of a trademark is to identify the origin of ownership of the article to which the product is affixed' (Gangjee, ibid 27).

[70] Gangjee, *Relocating the Law on Geographical Indications* (n 5) 31.

[71] Similarly, membership has slowly risen from eight founding Members – Brazil, France, the UK, Portugal, Switzerland, Spain, Guatemala, and Tunisia – to the current 28 members.

amongst contracting countries. Similarly, the wording was also changed with respect to countries whose laws did not permit for seizure, and the Washington Act 1911 provides that such a country shall therefore undertake the necessary actions and means permitted under their domestic law (Article 1 Madrid, 1911).

Article 1 of the Madrid Agreement sets out that countries of the Union shall provide for seizure of false indications, which are prohibited amongst contracting countries, whether they are directly or indirectly false (Article 1 Madrid, 1891).[72] Two notable changes took place under Article 1 at the Hague 1925 and London 1934 conferences. At the Hague conference, a new line was included introducing special sanctions, inter alia, based on domestic laws referring to marks or tradenames, with the goal to prohibit *false* indications.[73] This adds considerable flexibility in legal instruments available to members to ensure such repression and, in turn, to protect IS right-holders. It is also remarkable as it allows IS to be protected or enforced through laws relating to marks, and thus introduces a flexibility into the regime on protection of IS. Arguably, this flexibility was always there, but not expressly stated.

At the 1934 London revision conference, 'source' was removed as a qualifying term to the 'indication', resulting in a new text referring simply and broadly to false indications to which the countries apply the Agreement (Article 1(1) Madrid Agreement, 1934).[74] This change emphasises the type of protection and is in line with the extension of the means of protection via marks and tradenames. Furthermore, the indication is broader than an IS and, again, links back to the possibility of protecting against false indications whether they are specifically indications of 'source' or not. This can be considered as an important verbatim change for non-geographic origin-linked products such as feta or Reblochon cheeses, which do not expressly refer to a source in their names, although they have a strong evocative origin link to their places of production in Greece and France, respectively.

The provision on seizure was also reworded, adding that countries, while adapting their legislation to be aligned to the provisions on seizure, shall, as before, undertake the necessary actions indicated at the national level. Although providing the flexibility to implement procedures via laws relating to marks under the Hague Act, this London Act revision obliges Members to adapt their

[72] The original art 1, 1911: 'Any product bearing a false indication of source in which one of the contracting countries, or a place in one of them, is directly or indirectly indicated as a country or as a place of origin, will be seized upon importation of the product in each of said countries. The seizure will also be made in the country where the false indication of source has been affixed, or where the product bearing the false indication has been presented. If the legislation of a country does not allow seizure on importation, this seizure will be replaced by the import prohibition. If the law of a country does not allow seizure within the home, such seizure shall be replaced by the actions and means which the law of that country assures in such a case to nationals.' Translation by author.

[73] 'In the absence of special sanctions ensuring the repression of false indications of source, the sanctions provided for by the corresponding provisions of the laws on trademarks or trade names will be applicable.' (art 1, para 5, translation by author).

[74] 'Any product bearing a false indication by which one of the countries to which this Arrangement applies, or a place situated in one of them, is directly or indirectly indicated as the country or as the place of origin, will be seized at the importation into each of these countries.' Translation by author.

domestic law. In effect, it removes the possibility that contracting countries may not have laws that allow for seizure, and, in turn, equates membership with the obligation to adapt laws as necessary under Article 1(4) London revision conference (Madrid Agreement, 1934). This is exactly the implantation of the colonial regime in national laws that is important to consider in this analysis. The obligation to provide the means of seizure is precisely the geographic extension of rights of colonial powers that is emblematic of the first wave of multilateralism. It effectively ensures the processes of assimilation and control of colonised territories, and their peoples and products, as part of a colonial strategy.

The final extension vis-à-vis the subject matter of false indications occurred under the Lisbon Act of the Madrid Agreement 1958, whereby 'deceptive' was added as a qualification to the indication, alongside 'false':

> All products bearing a false or deceptive indication . . . will be seized upon importation in each of the foresaid countries (Article 1(1) Madrid Agreement, 1958).[75]

This is an important extension, as it has implications with regard to both right-holders and duty-bearers, vis-à-vis both false and deceptive indications, and necessarily the infringement possible under this new category. Interestingly, the 1958 amendment also took place while formerly colonised nations were receiving their independences, and hence the deceptive nature of products shields against any type of potential competition from these newly independent states based on similar products from the former 'motherland'.

Article 4 of the Madrid Agreement is a landmark provision with an overt *terroir* influence, which establishes higher protection for 'products of the vine':

> The courts of each country shall decide what *appellations*, on account of their generic character, do not fall within the provisions of this Agreement, *regional appellations concerning the source of products of the vine being*, however, *excluded* from the reservation specified by this Article.[76]

Effectively this provision provides that 'products of the vine' cannot be considered generic, while national courts can rule on other appellations that have lost their distinctiveness.[77] This juxtaposes viticulture producers, embedded in a *terroir* logic, against other AO producers based on a communicative

[75] Translation by author.

[76] While other Articles went under Treaty revisions, art 4 was unchanged in the history of the Madrid Agreement revision Acts. Emphasis added.

[77] In the *'Feta'* case, the claimants (Denmark, France, Germany, UK) argued that feta had become generic, although the Court ruled against this, in favour of Greece. See Case C-465/02 and C-466/02 *Federal Republic of Germany and Kingdom of Denmark v Commission of the European Communities* [2005] ECR I-09115. In the context of discussions, see Gangjee's historical account that draws on the contribution of the Portuguese and French delegates, who proposed that all agricultural products and, thereafter, specifically viticulture products, respectively, should be subject to this art 4 exception. The French delegate, Mr Pelletier, importantly, drew on the combination of both natural and human factors that set wine products apart from the broader category of agricultural products that are not subject to the same levels of human intervention, and specifically threat from fraud. Gangjee, *Relocating the Law on Geographical Indications* (n 5) 69–70.

logic subject, inter alia, to unfair competition laws. In the subsequent revision conferences, this provision was debated vigorously with some (mainly European) countries calling for the expansion of the scope of Article 4 to include mineral water, beer, cheese, and traditional crafts, amongst others.[78] Meanwhile, BIRPI had also proposed adding an Article 4(2) to include qualifying terms – *method*, *genre*, *type* – that contribute to generic uses of GIs.[79] Nevertheless, and importantly for this research, while these terms did not enter the Madrid Agreement, they do appear in the subsequent Lisbon Agreement Article 3, and within Article 23.1.TRIPS.

Under the Madrid Agreement, the false and deceptive IS, as well as 'products of the vine', are considered GIs. The rationale for their inclusion was, in part, a response to the dissatisfaction with the earlier Paris provisions, and also a desire for stronger protection, as demonstrated in the provisions. The beneficiaries are the contracting parties, of which there were 36 in 1891 and currently are 24 (and their respective territories), to date.[80] At this stage, the GI – whether an IS or an AO – can be conceptualised as both a colonial construct and a tool for industrial development for the Paris and Madrid members, namely colonial trading powers of this period. The next section introduces the second wave of IP multilateralism that refers to the transition from colonialism to independence. Within this context, an overview of the Lisbon Agreement is provided.

2.3 CHARACTERISTICS OF THE SECOND IP MULTILATERALISM

2.3.1 The Legacy of Formalism: 1945–1990s

The second wave of IP multilateralism was characterised by the extension of the international law doctrines of sovereignty, statehood, and self-determination to former colonies, now Third World countries. Okediji notes that

> [t]he principle of self-determination provided the doctrinal justification to recognize the sovereignty of former colonies, and to legalize their participation in the

[78] Czechoslovakia made such proposals across the Washington, Hague, and London revision conferences, with Portugal also expressing this at the Hague conference; meanwhile, Italy, the UK, and Japan expressed concern about the special status afforded to wine, at the Lisbon revision conference 1958.

[79] The United International Bureau for the Protection of Intellectual Property (commonly referred to by its French acronym 'BIRPI', or as 'the Bureau' or 'the International Bureau') was established in 1893 to support the implementation of the Paris Convention. Although BIRPI was transformed into the World Intellectual Property Organization (WIPO) with its Convention of 1930, the reference to 'the Bureau' remains steadfast. On this history see, WIPO, 'WIPO – A Brief History', https://wipo.int/about-wipo/en/history.html. The proposal was never agreed, and thus never entered the legal text of the Madrid Agreement. It would have forbidden such terms as 'Champagne-style' or 'Swiss champagne': Gangjee, *Relocating the Law on Geographical Indications* (n 5) 73.

[80] The Madrid Agreement had 36 contracting parties in 1891, 14 in 1911, 18 in 1925, 23 in 1934, 25 in 1958, and 24 by the last Stockholm Revision Act 1967. See WIPO, 'Contracting Parties, Madrid Agreement for the Repression of False or Deceptive Indications of Source on Good', https://wipo.int/treaties/en/ip/madrid/#:~:text=According%20to%20the%20Madrid%20Agreement, importation%20must%20be%20prohibited%2C%20or.

> international community of states with all its processes, institutions and values. Paradoxically, . . . no more than an opportunity for developing countries to become more European.[81]

The conferral of rights and obligations under this new multilateralism did not alter the Europeanness of the pre-existing international order. As such, former colonies, territories, and protectorates were subsumed within the Western structures as part of the process of formalism, which relied on the very same doctrines of international law that previously subjugated them.[82] This phenomenon is aptly captured beyond the legal literature in the satirical reference to '*les soleils des indépendances*' (the suns of independence).[83] This term captures how the process of independence, in which formalism is essential, did not bring about the perceived autonomy and meanings embedded in the very terms of sovereignty, statehood, and self-determination. It represents, rather, a mere re-ordering of the framework of engagement, [84] or a shift from domination to hegemony.[85] This is further evidenced in the fact that rejection of the pre-existing legal order was structurally near impossible, given the extent to which legal norms were entrenched during the colonial era: only Burkina Faso (formerly Upper Volta) and Mauritius refused to sign the Berne Convention, in 1969 and 1971, respectively.[86]

[81] Okediji, 'The International Relations of Intellectual Property' (n 1) 325–26.

[82] 'Formalism effectively glossed over the purpose and functions of [IP] laws in developing countries and legitimized a process by which developing countries' continued adherence to colonial legislation was secured under the guise of an "international" law divorced from the domestic needs, priorities or constraints of countries.' (ibid 333 and 338). See, amongst others, Krishna, who asserts that "One of the key moments in the consolidation of neoliberal hegemony arises from our inability to conceive ourselves outside a national cartography of the world.' Sankaran Krishna, *Globalization and Postcolonialism: Hegemony and Resistance in the Twenty-first Century* (Rowman & Littlefield, 2009) 161.

[83] *Les Soleils des indépendances* is a West African francophone novel by Ahmadou Kourouma, which satirically refers to the light at the end of the tunnel of colonialism that was never fully achieved with independence: Ahmadou Kourouma, *Les Soleils des indépendances* (Éditions du Seuil, 1968).

[84] Okediji, 'The International Relations of Intellectual Property' (n 1) 327.

[85] Williams draws on the Gramscian definitions of hegemony and dominance, namely that hegemony is explained in relation to a shift away from 'pure' imperial and colonial dominance: '[hegemony is] a special case of dominance: it defines the condition of a world society and a state system in which the dominant state and dominant social forces sustain their position through adherence to universalised principles which are accepted or acquiesced in by a sufficient proportion of subordinate states and social forces': Stephen Gill (ed), *Gramsci, Historical Materialism and International Relations* (CUP, 1993) 57–58 in Yentyl Williams, 'Shifting Between Hegemony and Dominance? A Neo-Gramscian Analysis of the EU as a Structural Foreign Policy Actor: The Singular Case of the Cariforum-EU Economic Partnership Agreement' (2015) 1 *Bruges Regional Integration and Global Governance Papers* 9–10.

[86] Sara Bannerman, *International Copyright and Access to Knowledge* (CUP, 2016) 208. See also WIPO/BIRPI, 'Copyright, Monthly Review of the United International Bureaux for the Protection of Intellectual Property' (*WIPO*, 1 January 1970), https://wipo.int/edocs/pubdocs/en/copyright/120/wipo_pub_120_1970_01.pdf.

The mechanisms of formalism – international institutions, treaties, and laws[87] – define the tenets of the second multilateralism, namely re-ordering relations from the colonial period to the post-colonial period. BIRPI played a crucial role in facilitating the re-ordering of engagement through technical assistance to Third World countries,[88] including the drafting of a standardised declaration,[89] training for IP elites,[90] and drafting over 200 laws for these new sovereign post-colonial states.[91] This second multilateralism is, therefore, emblematic of a strategic shift from European powers to formally integrate Third World countries into the international legal system, effectively providing them with the tools to continue 'to build the master's house with the master's tools', to borrow from Audre Lorde.[92] The following section assesses the Lisbon Agreement as part of this process under the second multilateralism.

2.3.2 The Lisbon Agreement 1958: Defining the False Indication of Source and the Appellation of Origin

Under the Lisbon Agreement, Article 1 expressly reiterated the dual aims of the Agreement to (i) establish a Special Union within the framework of the Union for the Protection of Industrial Property; and (ii) to provide protection of appellations of origin via their registration at the Bureau (Article 1, Lisbon Agreement, 1958). Article 1(2) sets out the provision that countries shall undertake, within their territory, to protect appellations of origin recognised and protected in their country of origin and, thereafter, registered at the International Bureau. This Article remained unchanged until its 1979 amendments.[93] The Lisbon Agreement included AO in an international legal regime for the first time and defines an AO as:

> the geographical denomination of a country, region, or locality, which serves to designate a product originating therein, the quality or characteristics of which are due

[87] Okediji, 'The International Relations of Intellectual Property' (n 1) 329–30.

[88] BIRPI was the predecessor to WIPO and, similarly, was set up to administer the Paris and Berne Conventions.

[89] Okediji, 'The International Relations of Intellectual Property' (n 1) 330.

[90] The first meeting of the 'African Study meeting on Copyright' was held in August 1963 in Brazzaville. See Peukert, 'The Colonial Legacy of the International Copyright System' (n 4) 5–6 and 19–20.

[91] BIRPI provided technical assistance to 119 countries and regional organisations, for whom they drafted 214 IP laws: Drahos, 'Developing Countries and International Intellectual Property Standard-Setting' (n 4) 776.

[92] Audre Lorde, *Sister Outsider: Essays and Speeches* (Crossing Press, 2007).

[93] 'They [countries of the Lisbon Union] shall protect, within their territories, according to the terms of the present arrangement, the appellations of origin of products from other countries of the Union, recognised and protected in their country of origin and registered at the international Bureau of the Union for the protection of industrial property.' Translation by author.

> exclusively or essentially to the geographical environment, including natural and human factors. (Article 2(1) Lisbon Agreement, as amended 1979).

Article 2(2) of the Lisbon Agreement (1979) explained that an AO designation identifies that there is a link between the '*quality or characteristics*' of a product due to the '*exclusive or essential*' linkage to the territory from which it originates. Furthermore, it recognises that '*human and natural factors*' are also contributing factors to this origin link.[94] The definition of the AO in the Lisbon Agreement indicates a willingness to have an internationally agreed upon definition for an AO at a critical time in history.[95] Although neither the IS or the AO, nor any other subject matter of industrial property, were defined under the Paris Convention, the Paris Convention sought to establish the contours of the law pertaining to how these forms of industrial property should be protected internationally; that is, permitting members of the Union to use the definitions appropriate and in usage within their national jurisdictions. The Lisbon Agreement broke with this flexibility, since it formally defined the AO for the first time in an international legal regime, in 1958. It can be interpreted as a legal development typical of the changes under the second wave of IP multilateralism, namely an attempt by countries who have created IP unions to reify legal provisions with regard to origin-linked products. The next section explores the developments relating to GI protection under the Lisbon Agreement.

It is worth recalling the dual objectives of the Lisbon Agreement; that is, creating a Union for the protection of AOs and executing this via their registration in the international register (Article 1 Lisbon, 1979, now Article 2 Geneva Act of the Lisbon Agreement, 2015). On the 'content of protection', the former Article 3 (1979), which had previously remained unrevised, defines that

> [p]rotection shall be ensured against any usurpation or imitation, even if the true origin of the product is indicated or if the appellation is used in translated form or accompanied by terms such as 'kind,' 'type,' 'make,' 'imitation', or the like. (Article 3 Lisbon Agreement 1979).

Hence, there are at least three types of protection: (i) usurpation or imitation, even wherein there is a sign indicating the true geographic origin of the product; (ii) translations; and (iii) accompanying affixes, such as type, kind, like, and so on.

The literature points to a broader context that influences the provisions in the Lisbon Agreement,[96] aside from the subsequent revision conferences. For example, at the international level, the Stresa Agreement was established with the aim of protecting AOs for cheeses. At the bilateral level, three bilateral treaties were negotiated at the same time between the European trading powers of France, Germany, and

[94] 'The country of origin is the country whose name, or the country in which is situated the region or locality whose name, constitutes the appellation of origin which has given the product its reputation.' (art 2(2), Lisbon Agreement).

[95] Existing scholarship does not explain whether there is a link to the decolonisation process during this period.

[96] Gangjee, *Relocating the Law on Geographical Indications* (n 5) 132–33, 157.

Italy.[97] These bilateral agreements are especially considered to have had an impact on the Lisbon Agreement by serving as a model upon which to base the registration system.[98] In this regard, scholars have noted that the Lisbon Agreement is more akin to contract law, based on the trade logic of protecting products of 'mutual interest' via lists.[99] This is important for conceptualising the shift to protect AOs, away from an unfair-competition-based protection to one based on the law of contract and overtly linked to international trade interests. Equally important to note is that, according to the literature, the drafters of this Article intended that national courts can draw on the AO definition therein when deciding on AO matters.[100] However, in practice, and as the prominent series of *Budweiser* case law demonstrates,[101] the different interpretations of AO protections by national courts reflect the difficulty of scaling up national types of protections to the international level.

Under the Lisbon Agreement, the AO is captured under this analysis of GIs. The rationale builds from the desire of the original signatories to seek further *sui generis* protection for AOs, specifically via their registration. The members to this Agreement and their products are notable beneficiaries.[102] This demonstrates that GIs have been construed as tools for industrial development for industrialised countries, and they can be understood as relics of a colonial past. Therefore, the challenge is to understand how GIs can contribute to post-colonial sustainable development in the subsequent wave of multilateralism.

[97] Alongside Portugal, Spain, and Switzerland, these are the main European countries influencing the contours of the register (ibid 132). It is also important to reference that French laws had also transitioned from the AO to the AOC, and these types of developments are reflected at the international level. ibid 21–76.

[98] Again, it is overtly evident that European powers influenced the development of the legal provisions protecting AOs in the Lisbon Agreement (ibid 176).

[99] ibid. The bilateral EU FTAs are emblematic of this approach, since they list GIs to be protected by each party in the Annexes to the FTAs.

[100] ibid 137.

[101] The Czech town Budweis/Ceske Budejovice has been brewing beer since at least the thirteenth century, including labelling using the name 'Budweiser' since 1795; however, 'Budweiser' and 'Bud' have been registered trademarks in the US since 1895, by Anheuser-Busch ('AB'). While the (then) Czechoslovakian company (BB) had certain 'Budweiser' AOs registered under the Lisbon Agreement, the US did not have any registrations, since it was not party to the Agreement. Christopher Heath has summarised that, while BB has successfully relied on the absolute protection afforded to its AOs under the Lisbon Agreement in Israel, Bulgaria, and to some mixed extent in Hungary, the Italian and Portuguese Supreme Courts have been less favourable. As a result of the Italian Supreme Court decision of 2002, the Rome District Court (2005) and the Appeal Court in Rome (2007 and 2010) decided that BB could not rely on its Lisbon registrations for a 'Budweiser' denomination of origin, since 'a "*Budweiser*" beer could be produced anywhere'. In 2011, the Appeal Court Milan (2011) found that BB's trademark registration was 'unlawful because of the inherent risk of misleading consumers'. The Italian Supreme Court, in 2013, overturned these decisions, thereby annulling the revocation of BB's marks. The Appeal Court thereafter sought to assess BB's claim for its registration based on the Accession Treaty of Athens (2003) concerning the Czech Republic's accession to the EU. Similarly, where BB has sought to rely on GI protections in its bilateral treaties, there has been mixed success. These cases are drawn upon to demonstrate the difference between the theory of what the drafters of the Lisbon Agreement set out to achieve and the practice of how protection differs de jure. See 'Budweiser' [2003] 34 IIC 676 (Italian Supreme Court) and [2015] 46 IIC 888 (Italian Supreme Court).

[102] There were 29 contracting parties in 1967, and there are currently six contracting parties, including the EU, representing their 27 Member States. See WIPO, 'Contracting Parties, Lisbon Agreement', https://wipo.int/treaties/en/registration/lisbon/.

2.4 CHARACTERISTICS OF THE THIRD IP MULTILATERALISM

2.4.1 The Period of Consolidation: 1994–current

The third wave of IP multilateralism has been characterised by the intervention of the World Trade Organization (WTO) in IP law.[103] The TRIPS Agreement was signed in 1995 and entered into force as Annex 1(C) of the Marrakesh Agreement establishing the WTO. All WTO members are bound by the obligations and commitments set out under the TRIPS Agreement, and its provisions are enforceable by the WTO Dispute Settlement Body (DSB). The TRIPS Agreement is the first internationally binding legal regime that defines GIs, and is therefore a significant referent within this book.[104] Okediji summarises the objective of this wave of multilateralism:

> The TRIPS enterprise, then, was simultaneously to upgrade, update and reshape the laws of these countries to secure for intellectual property owners the benefits of ownership on a global scale for purposes of rent transfers from developing to developed countries.[105]

Nevertheless, Okediji also argues that this multilateralism is in its infancy,[106] due to the proliferation of bilateral and regional agreements with TRIPS-*plus* provisions – or, in other words, those obligations that go beyond the minimum standards established in TRIPS.[107] This is emblematic of the fact that TRIPS, and specifically its provisions on GIs, represented a compromise between the EU and the US.[108] Indeed, it is commonplace to refer to GI debates as divided along North–North lines, since the EU has developed a stand-alone *sui generis* system for protecting GIs, while the US has sought to protect GIs as trademarks.[109] Both TRIPS and the post-TRIPS agreements, therefore, represent attempts at maintaining a 500-year continuum of trade relations between European-colonial and

[103] Okediji, 'The International Relations of Intellectual Property' (n 1) 333.

[104] On the transition from GATT to TRIPS, see Catherine Field, 'Negotiating for the United States' in Jayashree Watal and Anthony Taubman (eds), *The Making of the TRIPS Agreement, Personal insights from the Uruguay Round negotiations* (WTO, 2015) 130–31.

[105] Okediji, 'The International Relations of Intellectual Property' (n 1) 336.

[106] ibid 338.

[107] For more on this and the implications for developing countries, see Andreas Rahmatian, 'Neo-Colonial Aspects of Intellectual Property Protection' (2009) 12(1) *Journal of World Intellectual Property* 44.

[108] For a discussion on GI negotiations, see Mogens Peter Carl, 'Evaluating the TRIPS negotiations: a plea for substantial review of the Agreement' in Watal and Taubman, *The Making of the TRIPS Agreement* (n 104) 116–17. On the compromises, see also Field, in Watal and Taubman, *The Making of the TRIPS Agreement* (n 104) 129, 146–48.

[109] For example, consider the numerous Budweiser litigations between the US and Czech companies. For an overview, see Christopher Heath, 'The Budweiser cases: Geographical Indications v Trade Marks' in Dev Gangjee, *Research Handbook on Intellectual Property and Geographical Indications* (Edward Elgar, 2018).

non-European-colonised countries.[110] These agreements reinforce the normative assumptions linked to protecting European trading interests in foreign markets, as such providing evidence of the path dependency linked to IP multilateralism.[111] The next section assesses the provisions relating to GIs in the TRIPS Agreement (1995) and the Geneva Act of the Lisbon Agreement (2015).

2.4.2 Trade-Related aspects of Intellectual Property (TRIPS)

TRIPS is the first multilateral treaty to define a GI. When reading the provisions relating to GIs set out in Articles 22–24 TRIPS, it is important to bear in mind the legally binding relationship between TRIPS and the Paris provisions set out under Article 2 TRIPS, namely that Members shall not derogate from prior obligations under the Paris Convention.[112] Under Article 22.1 TRIPS, the GI is defined as:

> indications which identify a good as originating in the territory of a Member, or a region or locality in that territory, where a given quality, reputation or other characteristic of the good is essentially attributable to its geographical origin (Article 22.1 TRIPS, 1995).

This provision also establishes that Members must ensure legal means to prevent the use of indications which may mislead the public as to the origin of the good (Article 22.2.a TRIPS), or those considered to constitute an act of 'unfair competition' according to Article 10*bis* Paris Convention (Article 22.2.b TRIPS). Article 22.3 TRIPS regulates the relationship between trademarks and GIs, namely that a trademark may be refused or invalidated if it is made up of a GI which is not also where the goods originate, or it misleads the public as to the true origin of the good:

> A Member shall, ex officio if its legislation so permits or at the request of an interested party, refuse or invalidate the registration of a trademark which contains or consists of a geographical indication with respect to goods not originating in the territory indicated, if use of the indication in the trademark for such goods in that Member is of such a nature as to mislead the public as to the true place of origin (Article 22.3 TRIPS).[113]

[110] For a critical overview, see Keith Aoki, 'Neocolonialism, Anticommons Property and Biopiracy in the (not-so-brave) New World Order of International Intellectual Property Protection' (1998) 6 *Indiana Journal of Global Legal Studies* 1.

[111] Okediji, 'The International Relations of Intellectual Property' (n 1) 338.

[112] '1. In respect of Parts II, III and IV of this Agreement, Members shall comply with Articles 1 through 12, and Article 19, of the Paris Convention (1967). 2. Nothing in Parts I to IV of this Agreement shall derogate from existing obligations that Members may have to each other under the Paris Convention.' (art 2 TRIPS).

[113] Moreover, interested parties may request the Member to refuse or invalidate a trademark registration if it includes a GI that does not correspond to the geographic origin indicated, as it may mislead the public, as set out in art 22.3 TRIPS. A Member, *ex officio* according to national laws, may also refuse or invalidate trademark registrations independent of a request by an interested party.

Article 22.4 TRIPS establishes that a GI cannot be used to protect a product of a true territory if that product does not originate from the true territory (Article 22.4 TRIPS). For example, a chocolate labelled 'Swiss chocolate' can only be considered to originate in a true territory if it is produced in Switzerland, and not France, Belgium, or elsewhere. Recalling the emphasis on the prohibition of false and deceptive indications in the Madrid Agreement, Article 22.2 TRIPS and Article 22.4 TRIPS, in particular, reinforce the spirit of that earlier Agreement. However, a more critical assessment of this provision illustrates that the law has been written so as to provide protection for the country of production, as opposed to (rural) producing communities, as aptly captured in the provisions. In other words, the law continues to privilege the transnational class while also continuing to marginalise producer communities. This is evidence of the vestiges of informal empire, which mark the continuum of colonial power imbalances that prevent structural transformation and emancipation, in a post-colonial context.

Article 23 TRIPS provides for protection against use of identical indications for GIs for wines and spirits, regardless of whether the public is misled on the origin of the product.[114] Article 23.1 TRIPS provides:

> Each Member shall provide the legal means for interested parties to prevent use of a geographical indication identifying wines for wines not originating in the place indicated by the geographical indication in question or identifying spirits for spirits not originating in the place indicated by the geographical indication in question, *even where the true origin of the goods is indicated or the geographical indication is used in translation or accompanied by expressions such as 'kind', 'type', 'style', 'imitation' or the like.*[115]

As such, the high level of protection afforded to AOs under the Lisbon Agreement is brought into TRIPS by way of Article 23. Indeed, the Article 3 Lisbon Agreement provisions wherein *-kind, -type,* and *-style* affixes are prohibited for wine and spirit GIs is repeated under Article 23 in TRIPS. The correlation of these provisions is important, since it underlines the continuities provided through the legal provisions on GIs across the three waves of IP multilateralism. Okediji has identified that the threefold purpose of TRIPS was to 'update, upgrade and reshape' the laws of newly independent countries.[116] This provision effectively extends the Lisbon provisions amongst all members

[114] art 23.1 TRIPS – Additional Protection for Geographical Indications for Wines and Spirits: 'Each Member shall provide the legal means for interested parties to *prevent use of a geographical indication identifying wines* for wines not originating in the place indicated by the geographical indication in question *or identifying spirits for spirits* not originating in the place indicated by the geographical indication in question, *even where the true origin of the goods is indicated or the geographical indication is used in translation or accompanied by expressions such as "kind", "type", "style", "imitation" or the like.* (emphasis added)'

[115] art 23(1) TRIPS.

[116] Okediji, 'The International Relations of Intellectual Property' (n 1) 336.

of the WTO, thereby ensuring their adhesion to these provisions. The italicised text shows the almost verbatim replication of the provisions under the former Article 3 of the Lisbon Agreement in Article 23.1 TRIPS.[117] One notable change is the example of the '*make*' affix under the Lisbon Agreement, which is replaced by the '*style*' affix under the TRIPS Agreement.[118] Compared to the low uptake of the Lisbon Agreement (30 members), it becomes evident that the translation of the same provisions and the spirit of the Agreement into the TRIPS Agreement at the WTO (160 members) is an important negotiating win for proponents of higher protection for GIs, particularly the EU.[119]

The higher protection set out for wines and spirits, as well as the commitment to a multilateral register, is recognised in the literature as evidence of the 'fixed-outcome logic' of negotiations.[120] According to this logic, proponents of higher GI protection, namely the EU or 'Old World' countries, specifically seek protection for national 'GI' champions that are thereafter included as a subject for protection in international negotiations. While the same logic was applied with low uptake for Lisbon, it is pervasive within the context of TRIPS, based on a trade-off between the EU representing the 'Old World' and the US representing the 'New World'.[121] Additionally, while the US had not been a contracting

[117] Art 3 of the Lisbon Agreement (1979) established that 'Protection shall be ensured against any usurpation or imitation, even if the true origin of the product is indicated or if the appellation is used in translated form or accompanied by terms such as "kind," "type," "make," "imitation," or the like.'

[118] Additionally, the higher protection for wine and spirits includes provisions on conflicting TMs (art 23.2 TRIPS), homonymous GIs (art 23.3 TRIPS), and (again) the establishment of a multilateral system of registration via the TRIPS Council (art 23.4 TRIPS). It is also important to understand the cultural variations in perspective on such wording. From the US point of view, such wording – '*kind*', '*type*', '*style*' – can inform the consumer, as opposed to deceiving or misleading them. Indeed, this recalls the famous EU Trademark case, *L'Oréal v Bellure* [2010] EWCA Civ 535, wherein LJ Jacobs was critical of the ECJ ruling against smell-alike perfumes on the grounds that poor consumers lose out. For a concise overview by the leading IP blog, see IP Kitten, 'Trade mark ruling muzzles free and honest speech says Court of Appeal' (*IPKitten*, 2010), http://ipkitten.blogspot.com/2010/05/trade-mark-ruling-muzzles-free-and.html.

[119] Yet there is no internal EU opinion on extending this higher protection to other GIs. See Annette Kur's dismissal of this in Justin Hughes, Lynne Beresford, Annette Kur, Kenneth Plevan, and Susan Scafidi, 'That's a Fine Chablis You're Not Drinking: The Proper Place for Geographical Indications in Trademark Law' (2007) 17(4) *Fordham Intellectual Property, Media and Entertainment Law Journal* 933.

[120] Taubman also, interestingly, compares this to other areas of IP and notes that this is certainly not the case for patents or copyrights: Anthony Taubman, 'Thinking Locally, Acting Globally: How Trade Negotiations Over Geographical Indications Improvise "fair trade" Rules' in Gangjee, *Research Handbook on Intellectual Property and Geographical Indications* (n 109) 221 and 251. See also Hughes' comments that '[t]he patent provisions and the copyright provisions of TRIPs, as well as its other trademark provisions, are all self-contained' and, rather, this presents a situation of agreeing to disagree (Hughes et al, 'That's a Fine Chablis You're Not Drinking' 935).

[121] Indeed, US commentators recognise the art 23 requirement as impacting on domestic law: 'the WTO treaty did not result in any general change in U.S. legal treatment of geographic marks. Rather, the only further change in U.S. law concerning geographic marks was a provision implementing the heightened protection for wines and spirits under Article 23': Robert Brauneis and Roger Schechter, 'Geographic Trademarks and the Protection of Competitor Communication' (2006) 96 *Trademark Reporter* 16.

state to either the Madrid or the Lisbon Agreement, and did not fully adhere to the Paris Convention, it was a driving force behind the inclusion of the TRIPS Agreement in the Uruguay Round negotiations. Literature suggests that the timing was right for a balanced trade-off to be achieved in the multilateral trading system between the US, favouring the inclusion of IP within the remit of the WTO, and the EU, who were reluctant to agree on the disciplines on agriculture in general.[122]

This trade-off between the so-called 'Old' and 'New' Worlds is evident, last but not least, within the provisions on 'international negotiations' and the 'exceptions' under Article 24 TRIPS. Known as the 'grandfather clause',[123] it provides that 'Members agree to enter into negotiations aimed at increasing the protection of individual geographical indications under Article 23'.[124] On the issue of further negotiations on GIs, the Agreement also commits Members to enter into negotiations to afford non-wine and non-spirit GIs a higher, 'AO-type', level of protection (as afforded to wines and spirits under Article 23 TRIPS and discussed below). This is a remarkable 'fixed-outcome' type of negotiation, emblematic of contract law based on the trade logic, as introduced via the Lisbon Agreement listing system. It is also evidence of the tensions around negotiation. Unlike its predecessors – Paris, Madrid, or Lisbon – which did not contain such binding commitments to further negotiations, this ambitious clause reveals substantial information about the conflicts, as opposed to the cohesion, around the incremental inclusion of GI as IP subject matter.

Importantly for the discussion in this book, it also protects against diminishing the protection of GIs (Article 24.3 TRIPS),[125] and equally permits the cohabitation of GIs and trademarks (Article 24.5 TRIPS). Under Article 24.5 TRIPS, it is established that:

> Where a trademark has been applied for or registered in good faith, or where rights to a trademark have been acquired through use in good faith either:

[122] Recall that the US had already made changes to domestic laws concerning GIs in NAFTA; therefore, art 23 was the commitment that required changes to domestic law. Handler discusses this as 'the product of hard bargaining in the form of concessions made to the EU in return for the EU agreeing in concurrent trade in agriculture negotiations to reduce its domestic subsidies': Michael Handler, 'Rethinking GI Extension' in Gangjee, *Research Handbook on Intellectual Property and Geographical Indications* (n 109) 149. See also WTO, 'Papers circulated in the negotiations' [WTO Docs IP/C/M 29 & IP/C/W289] (6 March 2001 and 29 June 2001), https://wto.org/english/tratop_e/trips_e/gi1_docs_e.htm.

[123] The following WTO module explains that 'the main *demandeurs* in the negotiations on GIs were not prepared to provide such exceptions, to "grandfather" pre-existing uses, without any possibility of obtaining full rights over their GIs at some stage in the future'. The grandfather clause, therefore, permits pre-existing uses (exceptions) as set out therein, albeit with the commitment to negotiate them in future negotiations. See WTO, 'Module IV Geographical Indications', https://wto.org/english/tratop_e/trips_e/ta_docs_e/modules4_e.pdf.

[124] art 24.1 TRIPS.

[125] 'In implementing this Section, a Member shall not diminish the protection of geographical indications that existed in that Member immediately prior to the date of entry into force of the WTO Agreement.' (art 24.3 TRIPS).

> (a) before the date of application of these provisions in that Member as defined in Part VI; or
> (b) before the geographical indication is protected in its country of origin;
>
> measures adopted to implement this Section shall not prejudice eligibility for or the validity of the registration of a trademark, or the right to use a trademark, on the basis that such a trademark is identical with, or similar to, a geographical indication.

Hence, trademarks and GIs can co-exist insofar as the trademark is registered and used in good faith, prior to the application and protection of GIs in its country of origin.[126] Read together, these provisions seem to imply that a GI cannot be diminished by a trademark but neither can an earlier trademark be diminished by a subsequent GI.[127] This neither clarifies nor privileges any higher protection of one over the other, even in spite of the higher protection afforded to wine and spirit GIs under Article 23 TRIPS.[128] Rather, it strikes the balance between First World powers' two protections for GI products.

[126] The *Consorzio Del Prosciutto di Parma v Parma Sausage Products Inc* case concerns the petition by the Italian *Consorzio* to cancel the registration of the 'Parma Brand' mark first registered in the US in 1969. The Court had to decide on whether the defendant's usage was geographically deceptively misdescriptive based on the good/place association and whether this was the case at the time of registration. The Court did not find that the *Consorzio* had proved a goods/place association, as US consumers did not link the Parma ham product to Parma, Italy. The Court also ruled that the existing Parma trademark had been originally registered in good faith at an earlier date. This case affirms the co-existence of the two marks, since the *Consorzio* now sell their ham under 'Prosciutto di Parma' [Registration: 2014629]. See *Consorzio Del Prosciutto Di Parma v Parma Sausage Products Inc* [1984] 23 U.S.P.Q.2d (BNA), [1992] WL 233379 (T.T.A.B.) ('*Consorzio*').

[127] See WTO Dispute Settlement 174 *European Communities — Protection of Trademarks and Geographical Indications for Agricultural Products and Foodstuffs* (WTO/DS/174/R) para 7.514. This dispute concerned the claims put forward by the US and Australia against the EU regarding the implementation of the EC Regulation 2081/92 on Protected Geographical Indications and Protected Dominations of Origin. The US put forward the dual claim that the Regulation did not allow for national treatment of GIs, nor did it provide for protection of pre-existing TMs. In the same year (17 April 2003), Australia also requested consultations concerning the same two issues. Pursuant to these requests, the DSB established one Panel with 12 countries utilising their third-party rights. The Panel confirmed that the Regulation did allow for de facto co-existence based on the evidence provided that the EC Regulation 2081/92 was construed as to allow for a 'limited exception' to trademark right-holders within the meaning of art 17 TRIPS. In this seminal case, regarding the co-existence of GIs and trademarks, the Panel specifically concluded that art 24.5 TRIPS neither implies a right to prevent confusing uses nor limits it. This, it further underlined, is expressly laid down in the object, purpose, and preamble of the TRIPS. Co-existence is defined as 'a legal regime under which a GI and a trademark can both be used concurrently to some extent even though the use of one or both of them would otherwise infringe the rights conferred by the other'. Anthony Taubman, *A Practical Guide to Working with TRIPS* (OUP, 2011) 99.

[128] While we have discussed the relations between the Agreements in a non-contentious manner, highlighting rather how the earlier Agreements have fed into the later ones, there are no doubt some tensions. For example, Heath, in his discussion of the *Budweiser* cases, notes that '[t]he Lisbon Agreement thus envisages no co-existence between the indication of origin and a registered or unregistered trademark. This is hardly in line with TRIPS, yet the Lisbon Agreement falls under the exemption provision in Art 5 of TRIPS as a special Agreement under art 19 of the Paris Convention." Heath in Gangjee, *Research Handbook on Intellectual Property and Geographical Indications* (n 109) 428–29.

According to their drafting history, Articles 22–24 TRIPS are largely based on the 'Dunkel draft', which was a merged text of both EU and US texts on the GI provisions.[129] For some, it represents 'a messy, politically expedient compromise between the EU and the US'.[130] Indeed, this can be deciphered from how the text reads in a rather disjointed manner, at first setting out the scope of protection and then presenting the exception to it.[131] Additionally, despite the fact that the agreement appears to establish so many rules, it is silent as to the means of protection, which underscores the flexibility of the system wherein obligations shall be fulfilled via domestic laws.[132] Indeed, since there is no obligation to harmonise the means of protecting GIs, multiple legal regimes continue to co-exist today, notably through *sui generis* systems or trademark protection, or via unfair competition laws, amongst others.

Under the TRIPS Agreement, GIs are expressly protected, as they are defined for the first time in an international treaty. Although first defined therein, this analysis has demonstrated that GIs had their origins in the Paris Convention and have also been the subject of later international regimes, namely the Madrid and Lisbon Agreements. The rationale for their inclusion here has been considered, namely as a trade-off between the major economic powers of the First World. In theory, all WTO members can benefit from the GI provisions, and yet, in reality, the GI debate is still largely considered to be one dominated and influenced by First World concerns. As such, and from this perspective, GIs remain colonial constructs and their sustainable developmental potential for countries of the Third World is unclear.

[129] This was named after the former GATT director Arthur Dunkel, who was chair of the Trade Negotiating Committee responsible for drafting the final TRIPS text.

[130] Handler, in Gangjee, *Research Handbook on Intellectual Property and Geographical Indications* (n 109) 146. Equally, on the compromise, see José Manuel Cortés Martin, 'International protection of Geographical Indications: the WTO multilateral register negotiations' in Gangjee (ibid) 185–94.

[131] For example, art 2.1 TRIPS reads '1. Members agree to entering into negotiations aimed at increasing the protection of individual geographical indications under art 23. The provisions of paragraphs 4 through 8 below shall not be used by a Member to refuse to conduct negotiations or to conclude bilateral or multilateral agreements.' Then, art 24.6 TRIPS provides the exception that '[n]othing in this Section shall require a Member to apply its provisions in respect of a geographical indication of any other Member with respect to goods or services for which the relevant indication is identical with the term customary in common language as the common name for such goods or services in the territory of that Member'. The full paragraph also notes that this extends to include products of the vine too! Another indication of the outright compromise is spelt out clearly in reference to para 4-8, art 24 TRIPS: 'The provisions of paragraphs 4 through 8 below shall not be used by a Member to refuse to conduct negotiations or to conclude bilateral or multilateral agreements.' (art 24.1 TRIPS).

[132] Recall that the TRIPS Agreement establishes minimum standards, as set out in art 1.1 TRIPS, that 'Members shall give effect to the provisions of this Agreement. Members may, but shall not be obliged to, implement in their law more extensive protection than is required by this Agreement.' See also Taubman, who charts how the provision of Paris created a reality whereby 'new world producers were in principle free to evoke or allude to the geographical penumbra surrounding their traditional competitor's goods' in contrast to the interests of the advocates of stronger GI norms (Taubman, 'Thinking Locally, Acting Globally' in Gangjee, *Research Handbook on Intellectual Property and Geographical Indications* (n 109) 232).

2.4.3 Geneva Act of the Lisbon Agreement 2015

Two decades after the TRIPS Agreement introduced the first internationally agreed upon definition of a GI, the GI was added to the Lisbon Agreement on 20 May 2015, through an amendment of the Geneva Act. This is a significant chronological development, since the Geneva Act is innovative in at least two key regards. First, it adds the definition of a GI alongside the definition of an AO, which was first defined in the original 1958 Agreement. By extension, it therefore legally recognises the AO and GI as different forms of IP protection for origin-linked products in international law. This is significant since it has the impact of distinguishing both categories for the first time in a multilateral treaty. Second, this Act allows for accession by international organisations, and with the accession of the EU in February 2020, the Agreement entered into force with new meaning, as its membership expanded more significantly than ever before.[133] This increased membership does reinforce the buy-in to the definition of the GI subject matter therein.

Under the former Article 2(1) of the Lisbon Agreement, an AO was defined as

> the geographical denomination of a country, region, or locality, which serves to designate a product originating therein, the quality or characteristics of which are due exclusively or essentially to the geographical environment, including natural and human factors (Article 2(1) Lisbon Agreement, as amended 1979).

Under the new Article 2(1)(i) of the Geneva Act of the Lisbon Agreement, an AO refers to

> any denomination protected in the Contracting Party of Origin consisting of or containing the name of a geographical area, or another denomination known as referring to such area, which serves to designate a good as originating in that geographical area, where the quality or characteristics of the good are due exclusively or essentially to the geographical environment, including natural and human factors, and which has given the good its reputation.

Under the new Article 2(1)(ii) of the Geneva Act of the Lisbon Agreement, a geographical indication is defined as:

> any indication protected in the Contracting Party of Origin consisting of or containing the name of a geographical area, or another indication known as referring to such area, which identifies a good as originating in that geographical area, where a given

[133] See Matthijs Geuze, 'Some Memories of the Unique TRIPS Negotiations' in Watal and Taubman, *The Making of the TRIPS Agreement* (n 104) 125–26. Wasescha notes, '[i]t is also the TRIPS GIs section which contains the highest incidence of constructive ambiguity, at least from my point of view . . . We get either a spaghetti bowl or, more optimistically, a lasagne plate': Thu-Lang Tran Wasescha, 'Negotiating for Switzerland' in Watal and Taubman, *The Making of the TRIPS Agreement* (n 104) 177–82. See also Jörg Reinbothe, 'Negotiation for the European Communities and their Member States' in Watal and Taubman, *The Making of the TRIPS Agreement* (n 104) 189, 194, 197.

> quality, reputation or other characteristic of the good is essentially attributable to its geographical origin.

Furthermore, the Geneva Act of the Lisbon Agreement also adds a paragraph on the definition of a geographic area under Article 2(2):

> A geographical area of origin as described in paragraph (1) may consist of the entire territory of the Contracting Party of Origin or a region, locality or place in the Contracting Party of Origin. This does not exclude the application of this Act in respect of a geographical area of origin, as described in paragraph (1), consisting of a trans-border geographical area, or a part thereof.

These definitions must be considered consecutively, while also recalling the foundational TRIPS definition of a GI.[134] In the first instance, the two primary definitions of an AO (Lisbon, 1958) and a GI (TRIPS, 1995) in international law reveal a narrow and broad conceptualisation of the subject matter, respectively. The AO, for example, is due '*exclusively and essentially*' to its geographic area of origin, whereas the GI is only '*essentially attributable*'. The product that links an AO exclusively or essentially to a geographic milieu is its '*character or quality*', while for a GI product, the triptych of attributes – '*quality, reputation or characteristic*' – links the product to its geography. The AO definition as set out in the original Lisbon Agreement also notes the contributing factor that natural and human inputs make to the AO product, whereas this is not explicitly mentioned in the GI definition. These definitional developments are remarkable, and are emblematic of second- and third-wave IP multilateralism that departs from the broad definition of industrial property set out under the foundational Paris Convention.[135] This represents the reshaping, upgrading, and updating of IP laws that Okediji recognises as central to the third wave of IP multilateralism.[136]

With regard to the Geneva Act of the Lisbon Agreement, it is easily discernible how both new definitions have been inspired by their earlier texts. The new AO definition maintains the crucial elements defined in 1958: '*character or quality*'; '*exclusively and essentially*'; '*human and natural factors*'. It does also, however, innovate beyond this definition in two key aspects. Firstly, it no longer refers to a 'geographic denomination'; instead, it refers to '*any denomination*'. Second, it adds a final phrase, complementing the aforementioned elements, 'and which has given the good its *reputation*' (Article 2(1)(i) Geneva Act of the Lisbon Agreement 2015). In doing so, this broadens the conceptualisation of a denomination, recognising that it need not be restricted to a geographic

[134] 'indications which identify a good as originating in the territory of a Member, or a region or locality in that territory, where a given quality, reputation or other characteristic of the good is essentially attributable to its geographical origin': art 22.1 TRIPS.

[135] Recall that the definition was not established in the Paris Convention per se; rather, industrial property was to be conceived in its 'broadest sense' (art 1, Paris Convention).

[136] Okediji, 'The International Relations of Intellectual Property' (n 1) 336.

area.[137] This has practical significance for products that do not bear geographic names but can still be protected as an AO, such as feta or Reblochon. This also better aligns it with the TRIPS definition, which refers more broadly to '*indications*', not only geographical names, that are known to be related to a specific area. Furthermore, the explanation of a geographical area under Article 2(2) of the Geneva Act of the Lisbon Agreement introduces that this can also be a '*trans-border area*', a recognition which was previously absent at the international level.

The addition of the reputation linkage brings the AO definition here closer to the TRIPS definition of a GI, which also recognises the attribute of the reputation linkage to origin products.[138] As the Agreement only entered into force in 2020, it is too early to assess the practical implications of what can be interpreted as a narrowing of the gap between the AO and the GI definitions, where in practice the main difference now lies in the fact of whether a product is also '*exclusively*' attributable to its geographic area of origin. The Geneva Act definition of a GI maintains the key elements defining a GI under TRIPS, namely as '*essentially attributable*' and referring to '*quality, reputation or characteristics*'.

Based on the former Article 3 protection, Article 11(2) Geneva Act has abandoned the reference to usurpation and now simply refers to imitation. It reads:

> Paragraph (1)(a) shall also apply to use of the appellation of origin or geographical indication amounting to its imitation, even if the true origin of the goods is indicated, or if the appellation of origin or the geographical indication is used in translated form or is accompanied by terms such as 'style', 'kind', 'type', 'make', 'imitation', 'method', 'as produced in', 'like', 'similar' or the like.

Some commentators argued that usurpation was not a commonly used or understood term in international law.[139] Rather, Article 11(2) of the Geneva Act sets out, as before, to prohibit imitations even if true origin is indicated, translated, or affixed, and goes further, by naming several new affixes: 'style',[140] 'method', 'as produced in', '"similar" or the like'. Again, like the previous Article 3 of the Lisbon Agreement (1979), this list should not be considered exhaustive but merely explanatory. However, the new Article 11(2) on imitation, and with regard to the new affixes, only applies in relation to similar or dissimilar goods (in the trade logic of the Lisbon Agreement), and not to misleading the public (in the context of unfair competition). The Geneva Act provisions are evidently

[137] Recall that a similar amendment to art 1 of the Madrid Agreement took place during the 1934 London revision conference, wherein indication of source was amended to simply refer to 'indication'.

[138] This could, arguably, blur the lines of distinction: Anna G Micara, 'The Geneva Act of the Lisbon Agreement for the Protection of Appellations of Origin and Their International Registration: An Assessment of a Controversial Agreement' (2016) 47(6) *International Review of Intellectual Property and Competition Law* 673–96.

[139] ibid.

[140] As under TRIPS but not the former art 3 Lisbon, 1979.

broader, as they apply to all AO and IS, and not just to wine and spirits, as with the TRIPS Agreement provisions.

Under the Geneva Act, both the AO and GI are defined. This Act extends who can benefit from the provisions, since it is provided that international organisations can accede, and therefore regionally protected products can benefit from the provision therein. In this regard, GIs can expand their scope as tools for sustainable development for entire regional groups insofar as they understand the colonial construction of these laws and their contemporary potential to contribute to 'development from within'.[141]

2.5 CONCLUSION

This chapter has explored the origins and history of GIs through a detailed legal analysis of their treaty bases. As part of this analysis, the chapter has also posed the question, *who and what was protected within these agreements?* In doing so, this chapter has drawn on the three waves of IP multilateralism as a heuristic tool to demonstrate how the IP regimes have evolved through the colonial and post-colonial periods. It charted the evolution and expansion of GI subject matter – the IS, AO, and GI – across the four IP regimes: (i) the Paris Convention; (ii) the Madrid Agreement; (iii) the Lisbon Agreement, including the Geneva Act; and (iv) the TRIPS Agreement of the WTO.

The chapter has demonstrated that GIs have their genesis in the colonial period, and therefore they can be considered as colonial constructs within international law. The rationale for their protection was, equally, embedded in the colonial context of commercial expansion and control of industrial production. As such, industrialised countries and their products were protected across the key IP treaties. In contrast, post-colonial nations acceded to these agreements after the majority of Acts had been passed, with the exception of the TRIPS Agreement, of which there is abundant literature on its controversies.[142] Therefore, newer members may be 'included' formally – as an act of formalism[143] – however, the comparatively low rate of GI registrations from Third World countries attests to the ineffective inclusion of these countries in these regimes.[144] In regard to the broader research discussions in this book, this chapter has demonstrated that GIs can be conceptualised as both colonial constructs *and* tools for sustainable development. Third World countries, albeit latecomers to the GI debate, can choose to strategically engage with these tools for their own

[141] See Sarah Bowen, 'Development from Within? The Potential for Geographical Indications in the Global South' (2010) 13(2) *Journal of World Intellectual Property* 231; ch 6.

[142] See, eg Peter Yu, 'TRIPS and its Discontents' (2006) 10 *Marquette Intellectual Property Law Review* 369.

[143] Okediji, 'The International Relations of Intellectual Property' (n 1) 333, 338.

[144] See the interactive map of registrations of AOs, WIPO, 'Appellations of Origin', https://wipo.int/ipdl/en/lisbon/lisbon-map.jsp.

sustainable development, while learning from the rich history of IP development and enforcement in this domain. This chapter, therefore, concludes that if Third World countries are seeking to use these forms of protection, they may need to seek new ways to engage with and interpret the law in order to derive benefits from a system that was not initially conceived for their inclusion.[145] The following chapter will examine the role of the EU as an exporter of GI norms via its FTAs, particularly drawing on the EU–CARIFORUM EPA as a case study.

[145] Equally important is understanding the broader agenda of the 'global IP ratchet' to carve out the best combination of IP protection in a context of increasing use of IPRs outside of the WTO framework. See Susan Sell, 'The Global IP Upward Ratchet, Anti-Counterfeiting and Piracy Enforcement Efforts: The State of Play,' (2010) PIJIP Research Paper no 15, American University Washington College of Law, Washington DC. See also Christopher May and Susan Sell, *Intellectual Property Rights: A Critical History* (Lynne Rienner Publishers, 2006).

3

The EU as a GI Exporter in the Caribbean

Each generation must (. . .) discover its mission, fulfil it or betray it.[1]

Frantz Fanon (1961).

3.1 INTRODUCTION

THIS CHAPTER ASSESSES HOW the EU exports Geographical Indication (GI) norms in its free trade agreements (FTAs), and the significance of this practice for its Third World partners. An overview of the substantive provisions on GIs in the Caribbean Forum–European Union Economic Partnership Agreement (CARIFORUM–EU EPA) will be presented, with particular attention given to the terms of protection, generic terms, the relationship between GIs and trademarks, future agreements, and Internet protection.[2] The analysis sheds light on how the international, and universalist, norms relating to GIs are expanding through the EU's bilateral FTAs with countries that do not have existing *sui generis* GI regimes. The rationale for focusing on the EU is due to the fact that GIs are de facto EU IP tools, and through EU FTAs there are increasing commitments to implement GI laws.

This chapter questions whether EU FTAs privilege First World EU knowledge in their provisions on GIs and, by extension, whether they embed a 'dynamic of difference' in the bilateral and regional context.[3] The chapter assesses whether these GI norms are based on a concept of common good between the EU and its partners, namely whether they are inclusive and development-oriented. In other words, the chapter assesses whether the legal framing of GIs in the EU's FTAs is according to a language of emancipation.[4] As the EU's universality of the norms

[1] Frantz Fanon, *The Wretched of the Earth* (first published SARL, 1961; Grove Press, 2004).

[2] Economic Partnership Agreement between the CARIFORUM States, of the one part, and the European Community and its Member States, of the other part [2008] OJ L289 (hereinafter 'CARIFORUM–EU EPA').

[3] Anthony Anghie, *Imperialism, Sovereignty and the Making of International Law* (CUP, 2014) 4. See also Antony Anghie and BS Chimni, 'Third World Approaches to International Law and Individual Responsibility in Internal Conflicts' (2003) 2(1) *Chinese Journal of International Law*.

[4] Anghie and Chimni, 'Third World Approaches to International Law and Individual Responsibility in Internal Conflicts' (n 3) 79.

and practice of GIs has been given sanction though international law,[5] there is merit in conducting this assessment to understand how GIs can be reconceptualised to benefit Third World nations.[6] The role of the EU as a GI norm exporter is analysed in the assessment of the CARIFORUM–EU EPA, and with reference to other EU FTAs with Vietnam,[7] Singapore,[8] Canada,[9] Japan,[10] and Columbia/Peru,[11] for comparative analysis. This chapter also demonstrates the now infamous adage of Jagdish Bhagwati that, where the EU cannot take the multilateral highway, it takes the bilateral country road with regard to achieving its trade goals relating to GI protection and intellectual property rights (IPR) enforcement.[12] In taking these bilateral country roads, the EU is also in the process of developing regional legal regimes as a 'norm exporter'.[13] This contributes to the claim that, through the processes and institutions of formalism,[14] the EU continues to play a role shaping international trade and its corresponding norms. Notwithstanding, drawing on Frantz Fanon's statement that '[e]ach generation must discover its mission, fulfil it or betray it', this chapter demonstrates how EPA implementation can be harnessed to contribute to this generation's mission to transition from plantation economy to sustainable development for GI producer groups in today's post-colonial context.

This chapter begins by introducing the CARIFORUM–EU EPA. Section 3.2 sets out the GI provisions in the EPA with particular attention to the objectives and the nature and scope of obligations in the EPA. Section 3.3 assesses the substantive provisions on GIs – in particular, terms of protection, as well as generic terms, plant varieties, and animal breeds. Section 3.3.3 assesses the

[5] Makau Mutua, 'What is TWAIL?' (2000) *Proceedings of the ASIL Annual Meeting* 17.

[6] BS Chimni, 'Capitalism Imperialism and International Law in the Twenty-First Century' (2012) 14 *Oregon Review of International Law* 17.

[7] Free Trade Agreement between the European Union and the Socialist Republic of Viet Nam [2020] OJ L186 (hereinafter 'EU–Viet Nam FTA').

[8] Free Trade Agreement between the European Union and the Republic of Singapore [2009] OJ L294 (hereinafter 'EU Singapore FTA').

[9] Comprehensive Economic and Trade Agreement (CETA) between Canada, of the one part, and the European Union and its Member States, of the other part [2017] OJ L11 (hereinafter 'EU–CETA Agreement').

[10] Agreement between the European Union and Japan for an Economic Partnership [2018] OJ L330, 3–899 (hereinafter 'EU–Japan EPA').

[11] Trade Agreement between the European Union and its Member States, of the one part, and Colombia and Peru, of the other part [2021] OJ L354 (hereinafter 'EU–Colombia and Peru Agreement').

[12] Jagdish Bhagwati, *Free Trade Today* (PUP, 2002). On the EU's IPR enforcement, see Commission, 'Trade, Growth and Intellectual Property – Strategy for the Protection and Enforcement of Intellectual Property Rights in Third Countries' (2014) COM 389.

[13] See James Thuo Gathii, *African Regional Trade Agreements as Legal Regimes* (CUP, 2011); Clair Gammage, *North–South Regional Trade Agreements as Legal Regimes: A Critical Assessment of the EU–SADC Economic Partnership Agreement* (Edward Elgar, 2017); Billy A Melo Araujo, *The EU Deep Trade Agenda* (OUP, 2016). On the EU as a normative power, see Ian Manners, 'Normative Power Europe: A Contradiction in Terms?' (2002) 40(2) *Journal of Common Market Studies* 235.

[14] Ruth Okediji, 'The International Relations of Intellectual Property: Narratives of Developing Country Participation in the Global Intellectual Property System' (2003) 7 *Singapore Journal of International & Comparative Law* 315.

relationship between GIs and trademarks, as well as future agreements and Internet usage. The conclusion summarises that the EU is a GI norm exporter in the case of the CARIFORUM–EU EPA, and that this may have the impact of hindering the region's trade relations with its major trading partner, the United States (US). However, through a comparative analysis of GI provisions in other FTAs, it is also demonstrated that there are lessons for CARIFORUM countries to heed, from the cumulative use of GI and trademark protection, to expressly considering the beneficiaries of GIs to foster sustainable development.

3.1.1 Context and Background: The CARIFORUM–EU EPA

The CARIFORUM–EU EPA was signed on 15 October 2008 between the EU and 15 Caribbean states, known as the 'CARIFORUM' group.[15] The EPA marked a substantive shift in the trading relations between both parties since it ushered in a new era of trade relations based on trade reciprocity.[16] The CARIFORUM–EU EPA emerged in the context of a long history of trade relations between the EU and the Organisation of African, Caribbean and Pacific States (OACPS).[17] The need to have WTO-compatible trade relations, and the Cotonou Partnership Agreement,[18] were driving forces behind the shift in trading relations to establish an FTA in line with Article XXIV of the General Agreement on Tariffs and Trade (GATT).[19] Under the EPA, the preferential and non-reciprocal trading

[15] The CARIFORUM grouping includes the Dominican Republic and the Caribbean Community (CARICOM) states, Antigua and Barbuda, The Bahamas, Barbados, Belize, Dominica, Grenada, Guyana, Haiti, Jamaica, St Kitts and Nevis, Saint Lucia, St Vincent and the Grenadines, Suriname, and Trinidad and Tobago. Montserrat, although a member of CARICOM, is a British Overseas Territory.

[16] See Yentyl Williams, 'Shifting Between Hegemony and Dominance? A Neo-Gramscian Analysis of the EU as a Structural Foreign Policy Actor: The Singular Case of the Cariforum-EU Economic Partnership Agreement' (2015) 1 *Bruges Regional Integration and Global Governance Papers* 1–36; Yentyl Williams, 'The EU as a Foreign Policy Actor: Shifting Between Hegemony and Dominance' (2015) 3(1) *Caribbean Journal of International Relations and Diplomacy* 7. Lorand Bartels, 'The Trade and Development Policy of the EU' (2007) 18(4) *European Journal of International Law* 715; Gammage, *North–South Regional Trade Agreements as Legal Regimes* (n 13); and Peg Murray-Evans, *Power in North–South Trade Negotiations Making the European Union's Economic Partnership Agreements* (Routledge, 2019).

[17] 'The Organisation of African, Caribbean and Pacific States (OACPS) evolved from the ACP Group, founded via the Georgetown Agreement in 1975. It comprises 79 African, Caribbean, and Pacific States. The main goals of the OACPS centre around the sustainable development of its Members and their gradual integration into the global economy, with the ultimate objective of reducing and eventually eradicating poverty; coordination of OACPS activities in the framework of the implementation of the existing Partnership Agreement with the European Union', amongst others. See OACPS, 'About Us', https://www.oacps.org/.

[18] Partnership agreement 2000/483/EC between the members of the African, Caribbean and Pacific Group of States of the one part, and the European Community and its Member States, of the other part, signed in Cotonou on 23 June 2000 – Protocols – Final Act – Declarations [2020] OJ L317, 3–353.

[19] Piet Eeckhout, *External Relations of the European Union: Legal and Constitutional Foundations* (OUP, 2004).

relationship was transformed into a reciprocal free-trade relation based on the progressive and asymmetrical liberalisation of 'substantially all trade' over a 25-year period, in line with GATT and World Trade Organization (WTO) law.[20]

The CARIFORUM–EU EPA is considered a landmark agreement, as it was the first, and remains the only, 'full EPA' between the EU and the states belonging to the OACPS, covering not only trade in goods but also some aspects of trade in services, intellectual property, and public procurement.[21] Since its inception, however, CARIFORUM exports to the EU have shrunk by 2 per cent, while the EU's exports to CARIFORUM states have grown by 4 per cent.[22] The total export value of EU exports was 5.1bn euros, while CARIFORUM exports totalled 3.9bn euros.[23] Although there are legal and policy analyses that deal with IPRs in the CARIFORUM EPA,[24] statistical information in this area is lacking. Rather, there are only general statistics on the 1.3bn euro 'food and live animal' trade within the scope of the Agreement, representing 600m euros and 700m euros exported and imported from the EU, respectively.[25] The lack of statistical information can serve to exemplify power imbalances which facilitate the functioning of a 'dynamic of difference', and continues to privilege First World knowledge. After all, disaggregated data is available for First World trade, and this allows for evidence-informed policy-making. As such, Third World countries are disadvantaged and remain marginalised, whereby they are not able to access credible and disaggregated data to inform decisions that contribute to their sustainable development.

The EU had intended to negotiate full EPAs with all OACPS regions, but the Caribbean region remains, to date, the only one to have a full EPA.[26] However,

[20] While the EU allowed for duty-free and quote-free access of CARIFORUM goods immediately, CARIFORUM states will liberalise 86.9% of their imports, equivalent to 'substantially all trade' with the EU, over a period of 25 years. 82.7% is due to be liberalised in the first 15 years, with exceptions for agricultural products such as sugar and rice. Errol Humphrey, 'CARIFORUM EPA Negotiations: Initial Reflections on the Outcome' (*Europa*, 13 February 2008) 3, https://trade.ec.europa.eu/doclib/docs/2008/april/tradoc_138606.pdf. CRNM, 'The Cariforum-EC Economic Partnership Agreement (EPA) Special and Differential Treatment Provisions in the EPA' (CARICOM), https://caricom.org/documents/9679-special_and_differential_treatment_provisions.pdf.

[21] The substantive provisions of the CARIFORUM–EU EPA have not been amended since the UK left the EU. Rather, the UK and CARIFORUM states have opted for their own UK–CARIFORUM EPA, including the very same provisions discussed herein. See EPA between the CARIFORUM States, of the one part, and the United Kingdom of Great Britain and Northern Ireland, of the other part [MS No.18/2019].

[22] Commission, 'Ex-Post Evaluation of the Economic Partnership Agreement (EPA) between the European Union and CARIFORUM' (Publications Office of the European Union, 2021) 13.

[23] ibid 66.

[24] Center for International Environmental Law (CIEL), 'Intellectual Property in European Union Economic Partnership Agreements with the African, Caribbean and Pacific Countries: What way Forward after the Cariforum EPA and the interim EPAs?' (2008), https://ciel.org/Publications/Oxfam_TechnicalBrief_5May08.pdf.

[25] Statista, 'Main Traded Goods between the European Union and the Caribbean Forum in 2018 *(in billion euros)*', https://statista.com/statistics/1101582/eu-cariforum-trade-by-product/.

[26] Commission, 'The EU-CARIFORUM Economic Partnership Agreement' (*Europa*), https://trade.ec.europa.eu/access-to-markets/en/content/eu-CARIFORUM-economic-partnership-agreement.

both the EU–Southern African Development Community (SADC) EPA and the EU–East African Community (EAC) EPA contain commitments relating to GIs.[27] Thereafter, the EU has negotiated several FTAs within the context of its 'Global Europe 2020' strategy,[28] which emphasises the importance of open markets, reduced barriers to trade, and the necessity of strengthening IPRs in a globalised world. The FTAs concluded within this framework also include commitments on GIs: EU–Vietnam, EU–Singapore, EU–Canada, EU–Japan, and EU–Columbia/Peru. References to the relevant provisions within these Agreements are provided within the analysis of this chapter, for comparative purposes.

The following section provides an analysis of the substantive provisions on GIs in the CARIFORUM–EU EPA.

3.2 GI PROVISIONS IN THE CARIFORUM–EU EPA

The provisions on GIs are set out in Chapter 2, on innovation and IP, in the CARIFORUM–EU EPA: in Article 145 on 'GIs', Article 144F on trademarks, and Article 164C on co-operation between the signatory parties. GIs are first mentioned in relation to the principles of the Agreement, referring to the nature and scope of the obligations, namely that GIs fall within the remit of IPRs (Article 139C).

In the first instance, the context of the Agreement, set out in Article 131, explains that the CARIFORUM and EU hold a shared view that enhanced competitiveness is linked to promotion of innovation and creativity, which are key ingredients of trade and sustainable development between the partners. It also emphasises what appears as an added value solely for the CARIFORUM party, namely that the Agreement fosters the CARIFORUM countries' integration in the world economy (Article 131.1).[29] This is part of a broader context of long-standing co-operation between the parties, which, from the EU's side, has always sought to integrate CARIFORUM (and OACPS) into the global economy as part of a post-colonial objective of the Lomé Agreements,

[27] The GI provisions can be found in art 16 and Protocol 3 of the SADC EPA and Article 74 of the EAC EPA: Economic Partnership Agreement between the European Union and its Member States, of the one part, and the SADC EPA States, of the other part [2016] OJ L250, 3–2120. Interim Agreement with a view to an Economic Partnership Agreement between the European Community and its Member States, of the one part, and the Central Africa Party, of the other part [2009] OJ L57, 1–360.

[28] Commission, 'Global Europe: Competing in the World, A Contribution to the EU's Growth and Jobs Strategy' COM (2006) 567 final.

[29] 'The Parties agree that fostering innovation and creativity improves competitiveness and is a crucial element in their economic partnership, in achieving sustainable development, promoting trade between them and ensuring the gradual integration of CARIFORUM States into the world economy.' (art 131.1, CARIFORUM–EU EPA (n 2)).

the precursor framework to the Cotonou Agreement.[30] Yet, integration into the world economy must serve the development interests of Third World nations and not merely privilege First World knowledge on how this integration may take place. In this way, integration in the global economy can stay grounded in local realities and serve the developmental needs of states, previously marginalised under the vestiges of formal empire. On the CARIFORUM side, there are critical appraisals as to what this integration means in practice, and, importantly, questions raised around whether this integration facilitates a long-standing dialectic of development and underdevelopment between the regions, as pertinently outlined by Walter Rodney. Rodney's seminal work, *How Europe Underdeveloped Africa*, published in 1972, demonstrates how the process of colonialism was exemplified by exploitation and underdevelopment of the colonised world, with Africa as a synonym, as such, for the developing or colonised countries, while the coloniser countries of Europe enriched themselves and developed.[31] This critical perspective serves as a reminder that, if the EPA is meant to benefit both parties, it must overcome this historic imbalance and truly set in place a level playing field, as EU IP communications proclaim that the EU seeks to do.[32] Such an approach privileges a 'commensurability of difference'[33] and seeks to overcome the historic marginalisation of the Third World.

In the second instance, the context of the Agreement also reinforces and upholds the claims put forth in EU communications on IPR enforcement, namely that protecting IP brings both economic returns and sustainable development to both sets of signatories (Article 131.2).[34] While EU communications emphasise the added economic benefits of IPRs, CARIFORUM countries (and CARICOM) are still coming to grips with how IPR enforcement might serve the region, while simultaneously understanding how much they have lost through the lack of IPR protection nationally and internationally.[35] A case in point is the Trinidad and Tobago steel pan, the iconic

[30] This was considered one of the reasons why the former non-reciprocal trade relations were unsuccessful. Karel de Gucht, then EU trade commissioner, stated, 'as regards the economic fundamentals, the truth is that the current system has failed; that ACP countries have become increasingly marginalized in world trade, even with the generous tariff preferences since the Cotonou and Lomé agreements'. See Karel De Gucht, 'A Partnership of Equals' (*EuroParl*, 4 December 2010) 4, https://europarl.europa.eu/intcoop/acp/60_20/pdf/speech_de_gucht_en.pdf.

[31] Walter Rodney, *How Europe Underdeveloped Africa* (Pambazuka Press, 2012).

[32] Commission, 'Trade, Growth' (n 12).

[33] Own usage, ch 1 (n 23).

[34] 'They also recognise that the protection and enforcement of intellectual property plays a key role in fostering creativity, innovation and competitiveness, and are determined to ensure increasing levels of protection appropriate to their levels of development.' (art 131.2 CARIFORUM–EU EPA (n 2)).

[35] At the request of CARICOM Ministers for IP, a series of meetings were facilitated by WIPO from at least 1999: 'WIPO-CARICOM Seminar on Intellectual Property' (WIPO), https://wipo.int/meetings/en/details.jsp?meeting_id=3717; CARICOM Today, 'Intellectual Property in Focus' (*CARICOM Today*, 2020), https://today.caricom.org/2020/01/31/intellectual-property-in-focus/.

symbol of cultural heritage of the twin-island nation, a creative by-product of the country's oil industry and the only new musical instrument made in the twenty-first century.[36] Despite its undisputable origins in Trinidad and Tobago, its patent is held in the UK and Japan.[37] In 2024, Pan Trinbago Inc. received the GI for steel pan, to protect the authenticity of the instrument, preserve its cultural heritage, and support the industry's economic growth and global reputation.[38]

Additionally, there have been instances of media-driven backlash for claims of cultural appropriation of Caribbean practices and words, for example against the British chef Jamie Oliver, who produced a 'jerk rice' when 'Jamaican Jerk' is a registered GI and 'jerk' is famously linked to Jamaican culinary traditions.[39] While anyone can freely use the term 'jerk', since it is 'Jamaican Jerk' that is subject to GI protection, this does demonstrate how local traditions and cultural knowledge interplay with the concepts on GI standard-setting and the economic returns linked to GI terms. In this case, even in the absence of the geographic reference to Jamaica, the diasporic reaction evidences that Jamaica was evoked, even if not directly referred to. The extent of the backlash did, indeed, lead to a name change, to 'Jerky rice'.

Another example is the public outcry in response to actor Michael B. Jordan's attempted launch of a rum product called 'J'ouvert'.[40] The brand name chosen, 'J'ouvert' – coming from French/patois '*jour ouvert*' – is an important cultural term which refers to the festivities that open the day of Trinidad and Tobago's carnival, a festive activity that is now a staple across most Caribbean island carnival celebrations. The consequent name change is responsive to the public backlash as a result of what the Caribbean public perceived as an attempt to appropriate cultural heritage for personal gains. It also signals a broader public interest to 'claw back' names associated with its cultural heritage, to reap the associated economic rewards locally while contributing to sustainable development. In this way, if the EPA can fulfil its aim, there is significant scope for the virtuous circle of IP protection to create economic benefits for the CARIFORUM

[36] See UN, 'United Nations Gifts', https://www.un.org/ungifts/steel-pans.

[37] Kris Rampersad, 'Intellectual Property Issues Strike at the Heart of the Steelpan' *Trinidad and Tobago Guardian* (Port of Spain, 29 July 2011), https://guardian.co.tt/article-6.2.447523.a608c18300.

[38] TTIPO, 'The Steelpan GI: A Milestone for Pan Trinbago and Trinidad and Tobago' (IPO 2024), https://ipo.gov.tt/the-steelpan-gi-a-milestone-for-pan-trinbago-and-trinidad-and-tobago/.

[39] The issues summarised: 'The decision to label the microwavable rice "jerk" has been criticised, because the product doesn't contain many of the ingredients traditionally used in a Jamaican jerk marinade.' ('Jamie Oliver's "jerk rice" accused of cultural appropriation' (*BBC Newsbeat*, 21 August 2018)), https://bbc.co.uk/news/newsbeat-45246009. See also Zoe Williams, 'Here's the Main Issue Behind the Jamie Oliver Jerk Rice Row – and it's not Cultural Appropriation' *The Guardian* (London, 22 August 2018), https://theguardian.com/commentisfree/2018/aug/22/heres-the-main-issue-behind-the-jamie-oliver-jerk-rice-row-and-its-not-cultural-appropriation.

[40] 'Actor Michael B Jordan to Rename J'Ouvert rum after Nicki Minaj Criticism' (*BBC*, 23 June 2021), https://bbc.co.uk/news/entertainment-arts-57581240.

region,[41] notwithstanding the need for legal, political, and social safeguards to be in place to protect against cases of imitation, misuse, or evocation.[42]

The next section provides an overview of the objectives of the EPA, which can shed light on how GIs may be (re)conceptualised as tools for sustainable development in Third World contexts.

3.2.1 Objectives

Chapter 2 of the CARIFORUM–EU EPA was drafted with eight objectives in mind (Article 132). The first objective refers to fostering innovation, and importantly lists eco-innovation in businesses. This is important for the CARIFORUM countries, which, although classified as middle-income countries by the World Bank, are also classed as Small Island Developing States (SIDS).[43] They are also recognised as Small and Vulnerable Economies (SVEs), based on their size and vulnerability to external shocks, including financial and environmental vulnerabilities.[44] There is clearly a potential for this in relation to GI industry by-products, such as sugar.[45] The second objective aims to encourage competitive businesses, especially those considered micro-, small and medium-sized enterprises (MSMEs). This may prove to be significant for CARIFORUM states, since there are a high number of MSMEs operating in the region. Additionally, as small and medium enterprises (SMEs) have traditionally been the focus of much attention on business competitiveness,[46] this shift to specifically recognise MSMEs could be interpreted as specifically having taken into consideration the development needs of CARIFORUM countries and the region as a whole. The third objective links with this, since it aims to promote the production and trade of such products deemed 'innovative and creative'.

[41] The virtuous circle of IPR enforcement refers to its ability to contribute to driving innovation, growth, and employment. See Commission, 'Trade, Growth' (n 12).

[42] Evocation has been the subject of much EU case law. Accordingly, 'the concept of "evocation" covers a situation in which the sign used to designate a product incorporates part of a [GI], so that when the consumer is confronted with the name of the product in question, the image triggered in his or her mind is that of the product whose indication or designation is protected'. See CJEU Press Release No 154/21, Judgment in Case C-783/19 *Comité Interprofessionnel du Vin de Champagne*, ECLI:EU:C:2021:713.

[43] SIDS are recognised for their unique social, economic, and environmental vulnerabilities. See UN, 'About Small Island Developing States', https://www.un.org/ohrlls/content/about-small-island-developing-states#:~:text=Small%20Island%20Developing%20States%20(SIDS,social%2C%20economic%20and%20environmental%20vulnerabilities.

[44] SVEs are recognised for their unique vulnerability to economic and environmental uncertainties: WTO, 'Briefing note: Small, Vulnerable Economies', https://www.wto.org/english/thewto_e/minist_e/min11_e/brief_svc_e.htm#:~:text=Small%2C%20vulnerable%20economies%20(SVEs),uncertainties%20and%20environmental%20shocks%201.

[45] See Marsha Cadogan, 'A TWAIL Constructivist Critique of the IP and Development Divide in the Age of Innovation – Has the Protection of Place-based Goods Changed the Narrative for the Caribbean?' in Susy Frankel (ed), *The Object and Purpose of IP* (Edward Elgar, 2019).

[46] Commission, 'Internal Market, Industry, Entrepreneurship and SMEs' *(Europa)*, https://ec.europa.eu/growth/smes_en.

The fourth objective of the chapter refers to establishing 'adequate and effective' protection and enforcement of IPRs. Although CARIFORUM and Caribbean Community (CARICOM) public documents are sparse on the issue, some policy debates in the region indicate that there is institutional engagement on the issue.[47] The fifth objective concerns facilitating technical innovation, including the transfer of technology and know-how. This is particularly interesting, since if there is no level playing field to start with, it can be assumed that this provision is applied unilaterally, from the EU to CARIFORUM countries. Objectives six and seven set out to foster research and development between both parties, in the areas of science and technology and creative industries, respectively. The last objective pertaining to innovation and IP encourages regional co-operation between the EU's outermost regions (or overseas countries and territories (OCTs)) and CARIFORUM countries. It is couched in language which refers to 'regional proximity' and 'neighbours', while encouraging a regional innovative and competitive area.

While these objectives do appear progressive, there are many political, economic, and linguistic hurdles that can be listed as impediments to them. In a post-colonial context, a historically aware approach highlights that the knowledge, know-how, and expertise of colonised peoples were used, extracted, and exploited for colonial trade ends. Notwithstanding the inequality that stemmed from colonial plantation economies,[48] it is hoped that these objectives can bring forth the development goals that the CARIFORUM region aspires to and that the EU seeks to support, in order to foster sustainable development.

Having outlined the context and objectives of the EPA's chapter on innovation and IP, the next section addresses the scope and obligations of this chapter in the EPA.

3.2.2 Nature and Scope of Obligations

The provisions on GIs in the CARIFORUM–EU EPA are generally seen to be novel because the Caribbean region had never before signed an agreement that included these IP issues.

GIs are first mentioned in the EPA under Article 139, in relation to the nature and scope of obligations. This article recognises the parties' commitments to IPR protection at the multilateral level via the TRIPS Agreement:

> The [European Community] EC Party and the Signatory CARIFORUM States shall ensure an adequate and effective implementation of the international treaties dealing

[47] The last public conference was held in 2015, underlining this: CARICOM, 'Building Geographical Indications for the Caribbean's Origin Linked Products' (22 July 2015), https://caricom.org/building-geographical-indications-for-the-caribbeans-origin-linked-products/.

[48] George Beckford, *Persistent Poverty: Underdevelopment in Plantation Economies of the Third World* (first published OUP, 1972; Zed Books, 1983).

> with intellectual property to which they are parties and of the Agreement on Trade-related Aspects of Intellectual Property, contained in Annex IC to the Agreement establishing the World Trade Organization (Article 139.1 EU–CARIFORUM EPA).

The provision imposes a future obligation: henceforth, the parties come under an obligation not to derogate from the norms established within the cited international IP treaties. Therein, 'adequate and effective' implementation refers to implementing these GI provisions and ensuring enforcement of the contingent rights as *jus cogens* rules. Implementation is framed not merely as a region-to-region issue but one that concerns international trade, through the reference to the TRIPS Agreement and the WTO. Given that CARIFORUM countries are newcomers to *sui generis* GI laws, such a provision can be considered as a region-to-region stepping stone for achieving international norms relating to GIs and IPR. This may, additionally, have specific legal weight for the Bahamas, the only CARIFORUM nation and only nation in the Western Hemisphere that is not a member of the WTO and, therefore, also not a signatory of the TRIPS Agreement. This provision could be analysed as EU standard-setting with regard to enforcing multilateral rules at the bi-regional level, although not de jure producing any new obligation. This is also consistent with the historical overview that the EU and, prominently, its Member States, have been key drivers of such provisions in international agreements, from the Paris Convention (1883) to TRIPS (1995).[49] However, the type of implementation is open to interpretation by both parties, since there is no obligation to implement, besides the correlative practices set out therein.[50]

The subsequent paragraph, Article 139.2 of this chapter,[51] specifies that both parties adhere to Article 8 of TRIPS:

> The Parties also agree that an adequate and effective enforcement of intellectual property rights should take account of the development needs of the CARIFORUM States, provide a balance of rights and obligations between right holders and users and allow the EC Party and the Signatory CARIFORUM States to protect public health and nutrition (Article 139.2).

This is important because it provides a legal foothold for exceptions and legitimate adjustments. The key point to note here is that the obligation, whilst categorical, is qualified through the specific reference to Article 8 TRIPS. There are two important dimensions in relation to Article 8 TRIPS. Firstly, laws and regulations should protect public health and nutrition, and areas of public

[49] See ch 2.

[50] Reference to art 10*bis* Paris at art 145.B.3.a, for example: WIPO, 'The Paris Convention for the Protection of Industrial Property (as amended on September 28, 1979)', https://wipo.int/treaties/en/text.jsp?file_id=288514 (hereinafter, 'Paris Convention').

[51] It is preceded by the sentence, 'The EC Party and the Signatory CARIFORUM States agree that the principles set out in Article 8 of the TRIPS Agreement apply to this Section. . . . Nothing in this Agreement shall be construed as to impair the capacity of the Parties and the Signatory CARIFORUM States to promote access to medicines.' (art 139.2 CARIFORUM–EU EPA (n 2)).

interest, which are key to socioeconomic and technological needs of the Member and consistent with TRIPS (Article 8.1 TRIPS). Secondly, Members can adopt measures to prevent abuse of IPRs by right-holders, or practices that may impede trade or affect technological transfers, again insofar as they are consistent with the provisions of TRIPS (Article 8.2 TRIPS).[52] The EPA provisions also repeat that 'adequate and effective' enforcement must specifically take into account the development needs of the CARIFORUM users, balancing rights and obligations of IPR holders and users, while protecting public health and nutrition for both parties. The focus on CARIFORUM's developmental needs reinforces a claim of this book that there is a 'development–underdevelopment dialectic' between the regions, which the parties aim to address, in part at least, through the promotion of trade.[53]

Lastly, Article 139.3 states that the Agreement should not be interpreted as impairing the capacity of either party to facilitate access to medicines. This is significant, especially given the context within which this book has been written – from the inception of, and throughout, the global COVID-19 pandemic. From policy institutes and the Caribbean Public Health Agency (CARPHA) to local WhatsApp groups, peoples in the Caribbean region are acutely aware of the dynamics around access to medicines.[54] This ranges from organisations, such as CARPHA, promoting a regional approach to access medicines relating to the coronavirus (COVID-19), to local approaches, which favour herbal and local traditional medicinal approaches to tackling the COVID-19 virus. There is literature which outlines the historic and ongoing threats around traditional knowledge and medicine, the role of Western pharmaceuticals,[55] and patenting scandals of natural products, such as turmeric, neem, and jamun.[56] While there is literature on GIs and traditional knowledge,[57] more research is needed

[52] Art 8 TRIPS sets out: '1. Members may, in formulating or amending their laws and regulations, adopt measures necessary to protect public health and nutrition, and to promote the public interest in sectors of vital importance to their socio-economic and technological development, provided that such measures are consistent with the provisions of this Agreement. 2. Appropriate measures, provided that they are consistent with the provisions of this Agreement, may be needed to prevent the abuse of intellectual property rights by right holders or the resort to practices which unreasonably restrain trade or adversely affect the international transfer of technology.'

[53] Rodney, *How Europe Underdeveloped Africa* (n 31).

[54] CARPHA, 'COVID19 Response,' (14 October 2020), https://carpha.org/More/Media/Articles/ArticleID/366/CARPHA-COVID-19-Response#prettyPhoto.

[55] See, eg Vandana Shiva, Biopiracy: The Plunder of Nature and Knowledge (North Atlantic Books, 2016). Earlier, in 2009, the United Nations Economic and Social Council convened a discussion on considering traditional medicine on the same standing as Western medicine. See UN, 'Potential of Traditional Medicine Should be Fostered, Economic and Social Council President Tells Panel on Attaining Millennium Development Goals in Public Health (2009), https://un.org/press/en/2009/ecosoc6385.doc.htm.

[56] WIPO, 'Intellectual Property and Traditional Medical Knowledge', https://wipo.int/export/sites/ibid/tk/en/documents/pdf/background_briefs-e-n6-web.pdf.

[57] For example, Patrick Martens, 'Can Traditional Knowledge Owners and Producers in Developing Countries Use GIs for Protection and Economic Development Gain' (2012) SIEL 3rd Biennial Global Conference, available at SSRN, https://ssrn.com/abstract=2083680.

specifically on the subject of natural remedies, even if GIs may not be the first or most appropriate law to protect medicinal, health-related agrofood produce.

Paragraph 3 of Article 139 lists GIs amongst the IPRs protected under the Agreement and includes the oft-cited reference to the Paris Convention's Article 10*bis* – protection against unfair competition.[58] Again, this is important for reinforcing the linkage of GI protection and the iterative process of protecting GIs through legal regimes, set in place since 1883. While unfair competition is defined under the Paris Convention as referring to 'an act of competition contrary to honest practices in industrial or commercial matters',[59] within the historically aware approach adopted herein, asking who sets the terms for 'unfair competition' in global trade from 1883 to today is fundamental. Furthermore, as the WTO Panel in *Australia-Tobacco Plain Packaging* confirmed that dishonest practices do extend to matters relating to GIs,[60] it is even more important to closely analyse provisions which claim to support sustainable development, inter alia, through protecting against a given interpretation of unfair competition. Labelling products such as 'Belgian chocolate', 'Swiss chocolate', and 'Italian coffee' are examples that could be considered to be dishonest and a practice of miseducation which misleads consumers from the standpoint of chocolate- and coffee-producing countries of the Third World.[61]

Article 139.4 proceeds to speak specifically to the scope of the Agreement and the obligations contained therein:

> In addition and without prejudice to their existing and future international obligations, the EC Party and the Signatory CARIFORUM States shall *give effect to the provisions* of this Section and ensure their *adequate and effective implementation no later than 1 January 2014 unless the CARIFORUM-EC Trade and Development Committee determines otherwise taking into account the development priorities and levels of development of the Signatory CARIFORUM States*. The EC Party and the Signatory CARIFORUM States shall be *free to determine the appropriate method of implementing the provisions* of this Section within their own legal system and practice (emphasis added, Article 139.4).

This paragraph contains several elements. First, it recognises existing and future international obligations. Existing obligations pertaining to GIs are interpreted as referring to international obligations under the Paris Convention, the Madrid

[58] 'For the purpose of this Agreement, intellectual property rights include . . . geographical indications; trade marks for goods or services; . . . protection against unfair competition as referred to in Article 10bis of the Paris Convention for the Protection of Industrial Property.' (art 139.3 Paris Convention (n 50)).

[59] ibid.

[60] WTO, *Australia—Certain Measures Concerning Trademarks, Geographical Indications and Other Plain Packaging Requirements Applicable to Tobacco Products and Packaging: Reports of the Panels* WT/DS435/R, WT/DS441/R, WT/DS458/R, WT/DS467/R, 816.

[61] A similar point has been made in relation to rum. See Ian Burrell, 'Rum Colonisation has to Stop' (*Harpers*, 22 March 2022), https://harpers.co.uk/news/fullstory.php/aid/30060/Soapbox:_Rum_colonisation_has_to_stop.html.

Agreement, and the Lisbon Agreement, including its Geneva Act, as well as any other FTAs to which the WTO's most-favoured nation (MFN) clause would apply. In terms of future agreements, this may be intended to apply to future negotiations on GIs as set out under Article 23 TRIPS, on negotiating an international register for GI products, beyond the wines and spirits category (Article 23.4 and Article 14.1 TRIPS). This is known in the literature as the Article 23 extension debate, since Article 23 TRIPS provides a higher level of protection to wine and spirit products than that applied to other agricultural GIs.[62] As such, when higher protection beyond the minimum requirements set out in TRIPS is provided for beyond wine and spirit GIs (or other provisions in general) within bilateral agreements, the issue is referred to as TRIPS-*plus*. The CARIFORUM provision may also include any future agreement which both parties enter into which also includes GI protection. This could benefit CARIFORUM countries in terms of implementing existing commitments that support their development priorities and bolster their legal systems and practices. However, there is also an element of harm that could come from such a provision, which speaks to a 'future' obligation without details of what this could be. In this regard, the open-ended nature of the future obligation could serve to bind CARIFORUM countries into commitments that they are unable to fulfil, precisely because of the level of development of their existing legal systems and practices.

Second, it sets out that parties shall give effect to the GI provisions and their adequate and effective implementation, unless the Trade and Development Committee (TDC) determines that it is not possible to give effect to or implement the provisions, based on CARIFORUM's level of development and its development priorities. The TDC is composed of senior officials from *both* parties, and they are entrusted with assisting the Joint Council, to whom it also reports (Article 230.1).[63] This is interesting, given that it distinguishes between levels of development, on the one hand, and development priorities, on the other. Yet, at the same time, this is considered not only by the CARIFORUM side as an autonomous recognition of its own endogenous reality and priorities. Rather, given the joint composition of the TDC, it is assumed that both sides determine this. On the EU side, a director within Directorate-General (DG) Trade at the European Commission may co-chair. On the CARIFORUM side, the Director of the CARIFORUM Directorate is mandated to represent the CARIFORUM states (Article 230.1). This can be interpreted as an imbalanced provision, since the EU exerts a unilateral (neocolonial) power in considering the level of development and the development priorities of the CARIFORUM parties in the course of implementation of the Agreement. This is neither reciprocal nor mutually applied, thereby implicitly recognising the unlevel playing field upon which this

[62] See, eg Irene Calboli, 'Expanding the Protection of Geographical Indications of Origin Under TRIPS: "Old" Debate or "New" Opportunity?' (2006) 10 *Marquette Intellectual Property Review* 181.

[63] See ch 4.

trade relationship plays out, and whose knowledge is privileged. However, given the substantive basis of the TDC,[64] it is expected that it should effectively take into consideration issues brought forward by the CARIFORUM side, even if the process of determining the terms of development (level and priority) is a joint one.

Third, the final line of this Article 139.4 recognises that parties 'shall be free' as to the means of implementing IPRs, in general, in their legal systems. In relation to GIs as a subset of IPRs, this ought to be interpreted as nationally for the CARIFORUM states, since a regional framework equivalent to the EU's Regulation 1151/2012 on GIs does not exist at the time of writing, nor is it foreseen. In this regard, the EPA could, therefore, be interpreted as encouraging a regional approach to GI implementation indirectly. Billy Melo Araujo had already noted how, through the influence of the EU on GI developments in the region, GI implementation in the Caribbean region was likely to have a European flavour.[65] In other words, GIs may be implemented *in* the Caribbean region, but that process is likely to be shaped by the EU. This may already be evidenced in the GI registration for Jamaica Rum, which the EU has refused to register in its territory due to, inter alia, disputes over the existing Jamaica Rum specification nationally.[66] In this regard, given the existing literature, which takes note of the EU's influence on the Caribbean's legal regime and GI protection regime in particular, it is questionable as to how 'free' CARIFORUM states may be with regard to IPR implementation. In practice, CARIFORUM countries are likely to be supported through the mechanisms of the EPA and tools of inter-regional co-operation with the EU to implement the provisions therein.[67]

The subsequent Article 139.5 states that parties 'shall not be obliged' to implement more extensive protection than that set out in the section.[68] However, a comparative analysis of the GI provision in this CARIFORUM FTA and other EU FTAs shows that such a provision on GIs and Internet use (Article 145.E CARIFORUM EPA is a 'more extensive' provision than that which is implemented elsewhere.[69] This is significant in the CARIFORUM context, and more generally in relation to the EU's norm-setting role, since it has introduced an innovative standard in relation to GIs and Internet usage.[70]

[64] In relation to development, the TDC is specifically tasked with: assisting the Joint Council in relation to development cooperation (art 230.3.b.i); monitoring implementation and actions with third-party donors (art 230.3.b.ii); provision of recommendations in the area of trade-related cooperation (art 230.3.b.iii); periodic reviews of the EPA, including the addition of new priorities as deemed appropriate (art 230.3.b.iv); and revision of cooperation in the area of regional integration and its implementation (art 230.3.b.v).

[65] Araujo, *The EU Deep Trade Agenda* (n 13) 142, 154.

[66] Huntley Medley, 'Rum Fight gets New Referee' *The Gleaner* (Kingston, 20 September 2019), https://jamaica-gleaner.com/article/business/20190920/rum-fight-gets-new-referee.

[67] Commission, 'Ex-Post' (n 22).

[68] 'The EC Party and the Signatory CARIFORUM States may, but shall not be obliged to, implement in their law more extensive protection than is required by this Section, provided that such protection does not contravene the provisions of this Section.' (art 139.5).

[69] The UK–CARIFORUM EPA repeats this provision (n 20).

[70] Discussed below.

Crucially, while this is framed in non-mandatory language, it is nevertheless restricting when considering the aims of the CARIFORUM region, amongst many others in the Third World, to also protect non-agrifood products through GI laws.[71] After all, even if CARIFORUM countries protect their traditional knowledge products through national GI schemes, the EU has only recently introduced GI protection for handicraft products at the EU level.[72] This has been a long-standing complaint waged by Third World countries against the EU.[73] While the EU has produced Communications to the effect that they are now considering means to protect non-agrifood GI products,[74] there is no guarantee on how long this will take and how accessible it will be to Third World countries' non-agrifood GIs currently protected or being considered for protection in their national legal systems. Additionally, there is the risk that, although a latecomer to the debate on protecting non-agrifood GI products, the EU may set a new standard, which would prove to be a challenge for protecting Third World country non-agrifood products in the EU's legal system. This feeds into the neocolonial nature of how the EU continues to structurally influence legal and policy developments, and by extension, sustainable development in the Caribbean. For example, although registered nationally, the EU has requested that Caribbean GI owners of Jamaica Jerk and Jamaica Rum GIs amend the Code of Practice in line with the (more stringent) requirements for GI protection in the EU.[75] These are potential challenges for the adequate and effective protection of IPRs both within and beyond the scope of this Agreement.

Article 140, which concerns least developed countries (LDC), is not assessed here, since Haiti is the only LDC in the CARIFORUM grouping, and it is not

[71] Non-agrifood is noted as an area that several countries seek to protect, not just nationally but also internationally. See Miranda Risang Ayu Palar, Ahmad M Ramli, Dadang Epi Sukarsa, Ika Citra Dewi, and Saky Septiono, 'Geographical Indication Protection for Non-agricultural Products in Indonesia' (2021) 16(4-5) *Journal of Intellectual Property Law and Practice* 405–14; Michelle Okyere and Janice Denoncourt, 'Protecting Ghana's Intellectual Property Rights in Kente Textiles: the Case for Geographical Indications' (2021) 16(4-5) *Journal of Intellectual Property Law and Practice* 415–26; Hasan Kadir Yilmaztekin and Banu Eylül Yalçın, 'Turkish Law on Infringement of Geographical Indications and its Degree of Alignment with the EU Law' (2021) 16(4-5) *Journal of Intellectual Property Law and Practice* 376–83; Patricia Covarrubia, 'The EU and Colombia/Peru Free Trade Agreement on GIs: Adjusting Colombian and Peruvian National Laws?' (2021) 6(5) *Journal of Intellectual Property Law and Practice* 330–38.

[72] Commission, 'Intellectual property: Commission Boosts Protection of European Craft and Industrial Products in the EU and Beyond' (*Europa*, 13 April 2022), https://ec.europa.eu/commission/presscorner/detail/en/IP_22_2406.

[73] Alexander Peukert, 'The Colonial Legacy of the International Copyright System' in Mamadou Diawara and Ute Röschenthaler (eds), *Staging the Immaterial. Rights, Style and Performance in Sub-Saharan Africa* (Sean Kingston, forthcoming).

[74] Commission, 'Study on Control and Enforcement Rules for Geographical Indication (GI) Protection for Non-agricultural Products in the EU' (EU Publications Office, 2021), https://data.europa.eu/doi/10.2873/82711.

[75] JIPO, 'GIs and the Cannabis' (Zoom conference, 30 March 2022). Additionally, the EU has recognised the need for a shorter and simpler GI registration process. See Commission, 'Commission Strengthens Geographical Indications to Preserve High Quality and Reinforce Protection' (*Europa*, 31 March 2022), https://ec.europa.eu/commission/presscorner/detail/en/IP_22_2185.

currently implementing the EPA. For the purpose of this analysis, therefore, Haiti sits outside the legal regime established by the EPA. Having provided an overview of the scope and obligations of the provisions (Article 139) of Chapter 2 on innovation and IP, the next section looks specifically at the EPA's provisions on Gis, set out under Article 145.

3.3 GEOGRAPHICAL INDICATIONS – SUBSTANTIVE PROVISIONS AND LESSONS

Article 145 CARIFORUM–EU EPA, entitled 'Geographical Indications', provides the core provisions relating to GIs. Paragraph 1 states that

> Nothing in this Agreement shall require the EC Party and the Signatory CARIFORUM States to protect in their territories [GIs] that are not protected in their country of origin.

While there is no obligation to protect GIs that are not nationally protected, this Article can be interpreted to mean that GIs should be protected in their country of origin in order to benefit from GI protection under the EPA. Indeed, this is commonplace for GI protection under TRIPS (Article 24.9),[76] the Lisbon Agreement (Article 9, Geneva Act of the Lisbon Agreement),[77] and other EU FTA GI provisions and case law. It can also be read as illustrating an imbalance and inequality in the EU's export of its own norms, since EU GIs are protected in their country of origin, unlike CARIFORUM (or other third-country) GIs that are not even listed in the annexes of the Agreements and protected even if unregistered.[78] In other words, Caribbean states will only benefit from the EU (external) protection if they introduce GI protection in their own states first, and thereafter they can be protected within the EU. Another interpretive variation on this may regard the EU as a neocolonial norm exporter, given its role in inducing legislative development in third countries.[79] Such provisions have standard-setting impacts, and, as such, impose an EU modus operandi of implementing and benefiting from GI laws.

Paragraph 2 establishes the commitment by CARIFORUM states to 'establish a system of protection of GIs in their respective territories' by 1 January 2014. It establishes that the TDC shall be the forum of co-operation between both

[76] 'There shall be no obligation under this Agreement to protect geographical indications which are not or cease to be protected in their country of origin, or which have fallen into disuse in that country.' (art 24.9 TRIPS).

[77] Art 9 Geneva Act of the Lisbon Agreement states, 'Each Contracting Party shall protect registered appellations of origin and geographical indications on its territory, within its own legal system and practice'. It is also noteworthy that GIs shall no longer be protected internationally if they are no longer protected in their territory of origin (art 8 Geneva Act).

[78] The Protection of Geographical Indications Act 5 of 2004 (Jamaica).

[79] Sophie Meunier and Kalypso Nicolaïdis, 'The European Union as a Conflicted Trade Power' (2006) 13(6) *Journal of European Public Policy* 906–92.

parties, particularly pertaining to the development of GIs within CARIFORUM countries in line with Article 164.2.C, and that, six months after the entry of force of the Agreement, the TDC should receive a list of CARIFORUM GIs to be discussed. This responsibility appears to naturally fall within the ambit of the TDC, namely to ensure the 'effective implementation' of Article 145 and to be a forum of mutual exchange between both parties on legislative and policy information related to GIs (Article 145.A.3). Currently, the minutes of the meetings of the TDC are not public, and there is no public list of the CARIFORUM GIs to be protected under the EPA. Rather, the products to be protected can be identified from public (news) sources and private-sector commentary on national GI implementation (for the aforementioned rum, sugar, and cocoa products, for example).

The next section provides a closer analysis of these provisions and assesses them in relation to the role of the EU as a GI exporter, vis-à-vis CARIFORUM countries, with comparative references to the EU's FTAs with Vietnam, Singapore, Canada, Japan, and Columbia/Peru.

3.3.1 Terms of Protection

Under the Agreement, protection is granted under the legal systems of the parties and is renewable indefinitely:

> Protection afforded in respect of geographical indications in the EC Party and the Signatory CARIFORUM States shall be granted *in accordance with the legal system and practice of the EC Party or the relevant Signatory CARIFORUM State* as the case may be, and shall be *indefinite* (emphasis added, Article 145.B.1).

Indefinite protection, in the first instance, appears to mean that protection lasts forever. However, a footnote to this provision clarifies that it is, in fact, renewable for a period of 10 years, or rather, 'not less than' a period of 10 years. This provision, therefore, creates a legal standard between the regimes, that GI products are protected indefinitely, which in practice means for a consecutive period of 10 years or more. Moreover, the same provision also qualifies this protection as indefinite insofar that the good continues to be produced according to its product specification:

> Such protection shall ensure that the use of [GIs] of goods protected pursuant to paragraph 1 *be exclusively reserved in the EC Party and the Signatory CARIFORUM States to goods originating in the geographical area concerned* and that are *produced in accordance with the relevant product specifications* (emphasis added, Article 145B.2).

Therefore, any change in production from the registered product specification can jeopardise the protection afforded to GI products under this Agreement. This is significant, as it implies that GI products must not deviate from their specification, and where they do, it implies that the product specification would need to be updated. Otherwise, it is assumed that GI protection would, therefore, become finite and cease at a certain date. It is questionable as to what extent there is flexibility on GI registers to change specifications based on environmental concerns or climate change aspects that may impact GI production.[80] While it may seem questionable, from a First World perspective, as to how production could be impacted for a period of 10 years, in the SIDS of the Caribbean a hurricane can wipe out entire crops, which can take decades to grow anew.[81] Implementing this in practice, in post-natural-disaster situations, can serve as an impediment to GI development in the region. Moreover, these provisions also appear to assume that legal systems in place in both parties' territories provide for such indefinite protection. This can be interpreted as a practice of the EU transplanting its own legal norms and privileging its own knowledge on GI implementation and indefinite protection, so long as GI terms do not become generic, and are not in disuse, opposed, or cancelled.

Reading Articles 145B.1 and 145B.2 together sheds light on the type of protection expected for GI products under the Agreement. For example, the Demerara Rum GI will be accorded indefinite protection in the EU insofar as it maintains its protection in its country of origin. While this might seem like a reciprocal protection between the parties, the list of GI products to be protected reinforces the unequal playing field between the EU and CARIFORUM countries, most of which are only now implementing GI legal protections for the first time in their territories. The EU signatories have listed more than 100 products to be protected; protection that is now 'indefinite' in CARIFORUM countries. Taking into consideration the context of the Agreement – to foster development, business competitivity, and so forth – there is a genuine risk that EU GI registrations pose a threat to the development of Caribbean GIs. If the EU benefits from the GI provisions in the EPA, and CARIFORUM states do not, it could demonstrate that the law not only privileges EU knowledge but also undermines the developmental commitments of the EPA. Rather, it seems plausible that, once EU GIs are able to make use of CARIFORUM's national GI registration process, support to business competitiveness for EU businesses would follow. The risk here is that the GI laws, with their colonial origin, having been sanctioned by international law and transposed in CARIFORUM states, would provide a framework that could

[80] Quinones-Ruiz and others point out that, since 2001, cheese has been the product class with the highest number of amendments, followed by fruits, vegetables and cereals, meat, and oils. Reasons for modification include market factors (market and consumer demand, and new technologies); descriptions of the products (perhaps due to higher impurities, size changes, or new varieties) and method of production (restricting synthetic chemicals or changes in farming practices for example) are areas most subject to modification. Few specifically refer to environmental factors, let alone historical or traditional knowledge factors (which must be taken into consideration in CARIFORUM cases). See Flavia Guerrieri, 'The Farm to Fork Strategy as an External Driver for Change: Possible Impacts on Nested GI Rule Systems' (2021) 16(4-5) *Journal of Intellectual Property Law and Practice* 331–40. While the EU has a clear procedure for amendments – art 53 of Regulation (EU) 1151/2012 and art 10 of Implementing Regulation (EU) 668/2014 – there is no clear procedural route on the CARIFORUM side.

[81] There is ample evidence of this in the Caribbean: Grenada's ongoing recovery from Hurricane Ivan in 2004; Dominica's ongoing recovery from Hurricane Maria in 2017; or St. Vincent's loss of 100% of its agricultural land when La Soufrière volcano erupted on 9 April 2021.

foster the implantation of EU businesses with the potential to spur takeovers in the region.[82] This is just one example amongst many of how European producers continue to have a stronghold in the Caribbean business sector, precisely due to the colonial history whereby the regions' economies are still structured colonially to benefit transnational capital. This clearly raises broader political economy issues, linked to origin and geographical location of not only products but business owners and their businesses in post-colonial trade.[83]

The CARIFORUM–EU EPA GI provisions provide for both direct protection of GIs, as listed in the annex of the Agreement, and those due to be added from the CARIFORUM side (Article 145.A.2 and 145.E), as well as a cancellation procedure, which is discussed below. The terms of direct protection stipulate that the EU and CARIFORUM parties, *ex officio*, shall prohibit or prevent, including at the request of a given 'interested party', the following:

> *regardless of the class of product* on which it is used, the use in their territory of any means in the *designation or presentation of a good that indicates or suggests* that the *good in question originates in a geographical area other than the true place or origin* in a manner which *misleads the public* as to the true geographical origin of the good; or any other use which *constitutes an act of unfair competition* within the meaning of *Article 10bis of the Paris Convention* (emphasis added).

The wording here is important since it applies to *any* 'class of product' and, therefore, not only agricultural products but other goods. It also outlines that either the 'designation or presentation' may be considered in testing whether the product 'indicates or suggests' a link to an origin which is not the true origin of the product. The wording, therefore, allows for more direct false usage via designations *and* indications, as well as more indirect usage via presentation *and* suggestions, which opens the door for 'evocation'-type infringements. Given the rise of evocation litigation, both within the EU and in EU–US cases,[84] this provision is significant, especially as it applies broadly, 'regardless of the class of product'. The provision, like its precedents in the Paris Agreement and other

[82] For an example, see the Italian company Campari's takeover of Jamaica's most famous national rum, J. Wray and Nephews rum company 'J Wray and Nephew Limited' (Campari Group), https://camparigroup.com/en/news/2019-12-31/j-wray-nephew-limited.

[83] Cadogan notes that elites are due to benefit unless there are normative adjustments: 'A TWAIL Constructivist Critique of the IP and Development Divide' (n 45) 58.

[84] Although there have been several judgments on evocation, such as *Morbier*, *Queso Manchego*, *Gorgonzola*, *Glen*, and *Parmigiano Reggiano*, it has been noted that 'the Court [CJEU] has not undertaken any effort to systematize an "evocation test" that ensures consistency among decisions and provides legal certainty': Vicente Zafrilla Diaz-Marta and Anastasia Kyrylenko, 'The Ever-Growing Scope of Geographical Indications' Evocation: from Gorgonzola to Morbier' (2021) 16 (4-5) *Journal of Intellectual Property Law and Practice* 442–49. See also Gunzel, who makes a similar suggestion regarding *Morbier*, in which they suggest that the CJEU has opened up Pandora's box by interpreting 'any other practice' (art 13(1)(d) EU Regulation 1151/2012) as being 'open-ended', therefore possibly including shape and appearance characteristics: Ortrun Gunzel, 'Ashes to Ashes for Cheese Featuring the 'Morbier' Visual Appearance?' (2021) 16 (4-5) *Journal of Intellectual Property Law and Practice* 294.

IP treaties, makes use of the 'misleading the public' test and prevents uses which would fall under the Paris Convention category of unfair competition within the meaning of Article 10*bis*.

By contrast, the terms of protection for products of the *same* class include the prohibition and prevention of products not originating in the geographical region indicated, even if:

(i) the *true origin* of the good is indicated;
(ii) the geographical indication in question is used in *translation*;
(iii) the name is accompanied by terms such as *'kind'*, *'type'*, *'style'*, *'imitation'*, *'method' or other expressions* of the sort (emphasis added).

These higher 'Article 23 TRIPS' protections are commonplace in GI provisions. As such, Article 23 TRIPS-level of protection is applied to GI products within the same class in this Agreement.[85]

The EPA also sets out that

> It shall be possible to cancel the registration of a [GI]. The procedure to this effect shall allow for the participation of any natural or legal person having a legitimate interest (Article 145.B.4).

Cancellation is also possible with regard to GIs and Internet usage, whereby infringement can lead to either the transfer or cancellation of a domain name (Article 145.F). In this latter instance, it seems reasonable, within the scope of the agreement, that if an infringement were to take place, 'regardless of the class of product' or for the 'same class', this would also lead to the cancellation or transfer of the GI name.

While the CARIFORUM–EU EPA provides for this direct protection – regardless of the class and for the same classes – and a cancellation procedure, this is not commonplace in all FTAs including GIs. Rather, there is variation across EU FTAs. Before delving into these, it is also important to note that the language of 'classes' of products is not commonplace either. In this case, classes of products refer to the Harmonised System (HS) code, which is a standardised system of codes used to classify goods for export.[86] Elsewhere, as in the Geneva Act (Article 11.1.a.i and Article 11.1.a.ii) and other agreements, some agreements refer to 'goods *[that are not]* of the same kind' (emphasis added).

In general, the EU's FTAs including GI provisions can be divided into those that include direct protection – listing GIs to be mutually protected, for example in the Annex of the Agreement – and those referred to as indirect protection. From the outset, literature on the topic has already outlined that the EU prefers direct protection as an automatic guarantee of GIs protected in the territory of

[85] See ch 3.
[86] Harmonised System (HS) Code (*Trade.gov*), https://trade.gov/harmonized-system-hs-codes#:~:text=The%20Harmonized%20System%20is%20a,taxes%20and%20for%20gathering%20statistics.

the third-party signatory to an FTA.[87] For example, such agreements include Comprehensive Economic and Trade Agreements (CETAs) with Canada,[88] Columbia/Peru (Article 208),[89] CARIFORUM,[90] the SADC,[91] and Japan. [92] These examples show that it prefers this approach irrespective of the development status of the partner, whereas the approach to cancellation differs. However, even within agreements providing for direct protection, there is still some divergence on the type of protection and the possibility of cancellation. In the case of the CETA, direct protection is afforded to both parties' GIs; however, there is no opposition or cancellation procedure stipulated within the Agreement. This is quite remarkable, given the public interest in, and media coverage of, the CETA, as well as the particular issue of GIs. Rather, the only way a GI can be cancelled under the CETA is where it is not used or no longer protected in its national territory.[93] Yet, this is not uncommon, since in both the Columbia/Peru (now known as the 'Andean Agreement' since Ecuador joined on 1 January 2017)[94] and the SADC Agreements, there are no procedures for opposition or cancellation. Rather, it has been suggested that, within the course of negotiations, wherein GIs were considered for protection and examined by both parties, there was an opposition procedure embedded in this prior process.[95] Hence, the Agreement allows for direct protection based on the provisions therein. More akin to the CARIFORUM Agreement, the EU–Japan EPA both provides for a direct protection for GIs and includes provisions for objection and cancellation (Article 14.23(2)(c)(d)). There are also specific provisions relating to translations, which are assessed on a case-by-case basis,[96] and transliteration. It is explained

[87] Masayoshi Omachi, 'A Tale of Two Approaches: Analysis of Responses to EU's FTA Initiatives on Geographical Indications (GIs)' (2019) 18 *Chicago-Kent Journal of Intellectual Property* 153.

[88] art 20.19.1, EU–CETA Agreement (n 9).

[89] art 208, EU–Colombia and Peru Agreement (n 11).

[90] CARIFORUM–EU EPA (n 2).

[91] Protocol 3, art 3, Economic Partnership Agreement between the European Union and its Member States, of the one part, and the SADC EPA States, of the other part [2016] OJ L250, 3–2120.

[92] art 14.22.3, EU–Japan EPA (n 10).

[93] 'There shall be no obligation under this Sub-section to protect geographical indications which are not or cease to be protected in their place of origin, or which have fallen into disuse in that place. If a geographical indication of a Party listed in Annex 20-A ceases to be protected in its place of origin or falls into disuse in that place, that Party shall notify the other Party and request cancellation.' (art 20.19(7) EU–CETA Agreement (n 9)).

[94] Bolivia is also a member of the Andean Community and can accede to the Agreement, although it has not acceded to date. Commission, Andean Community (*Europa*), https://ec.europa.eu/trade/policy/countries-and-regions/regions/andean-community/index_en.htm.

[95] 'Having completed an objection procedure and having examined the geographical indications of a signatory . . . [Party] listed in the Appendix 1 of Annex XIII (Lists of Geographical Indications) which are registered by such signatory . . . [Party], the [Andean/EU] Party will protect the same according to the level of protection laid down in this Section.' (arts 208.1 and 208.2). See also Canada, 'Technical Summary Of Final Negotiated Outcomes: Canada-European Union Comprehensive Economic And Trade Agreement' (2013), http://international.gc.ca/trade-agreements-accords-commerciaux/assets/pdfs/ceta-aecg/ceta- technicalsummary.pdf; Omachi, 'A Tale of Two Approaches' (n 87).

[96] EU–Japan EPA (n 10) n 1, 375.

that 'transliteration covers the conversion of characters following the phonetics of the original language or languages of the relevant geographical indication'.[97]

Literature on GI provisions in EU FTAs suggests that the EU prefers directly protecting GIs in its FTAs,[98] as evidenced in the CARIFORUM, CETA, Columbia/Peru, Japan, and SADC Agreements. However, neither the Singapore nor the Korea Agreements have allowed for this. In the case of Singapore, this was mainly because there was no pre-existing domestic legislation there.[99] In Omachi's view, '[t]his testifies to the EU's desire for direct protection of GIs, and implies that its negotiations with Singapore were tough for the EU'.[100] Rather, the Singapore Agreement provides detailed information on the system for protection of GIs via a domestic register, administrative verification, and objection and cancellation proceedings, with the express aim to ensure that legitimate third-party interests are considered (Article 10.17.2). It may be suggested that, if Singapore had already had domestic legislation in place, the Agreement may have contained a list of GIs for direct protection. The lack of pre-existing domestic protection for GIs, therefore, gave Singapore leverage to negotiate the GI clauses to their advantage, based on their legal reality. At a broader level, it also demonstrates the cleavage between countries that directly protect GIs and those that do so indirectly; the case of Singapore demonstrates that, for countries that do not yet have national legislation in place, this can be used as a lever in negotiations with the EU. It may be one of the few areas in which countries without GI legislation may be able to delay adopting full commitments to protect EU GIs through direct protection, as they develop their own GI systems according to their own national needs and priorities. This can be an important leverage for countries of the Third World and the OACPS countries that do not yet have the requisite domestic legislation in place, in the grand scheme of power relations in the global economy.

Once this has been established, and similar to CARIFORUM, it is set out that the parties within the remit of the Trade Committee (akin to the TDC in the CARIFORUM case) shall meet to adopt a decision as to which GIs shall be protected under Annex 10-B (Article 10.17.3). Already, Annex 10 A contains a list of 196 products to be protected from the EU side, while none have been listed for the Singapore side. Similarly, in the CARIFORUM case, while the EU did list their GIs to be protected, the CARIFORUM side did not include a list. However, a list has since been drawn up and shared in subsequent TDC meetings. These lists are not exhaustive, and GIs can be added according to the parties' intention to protect their GIs.

A review of the Singapore GI provisions and existing literature confirms that the approach adopted by Singapore is, in fact, largely based on the existing EU

[97] ibid n 2.

[98] Omachi, 'A Tale of Two Approaches' (n 87).

[99] Letter from Lim Hng Kiang, Minister for Trade and Industry, Singapore, to Karel De Gucht, European Commissioner for Trade (*Europa*, 21 January 2013), http://trade.ec.europa.eu/doclib/docs/2013/september/tradoc_151779.pdf, in ibid.

[100] Omachi, 'A Tale of Two Approaches' (n 87) 175.

Regulation.[101] However, this is less surprising when assessed alongside all EU FTAs with GI provisions,[102] or for countries interested in setting up GI schemes in general, as the EU's own GI system often appears as a model.[103]

Within the EU–Korea Agreement, both parties recognised the equivalent systems of protection – the Council Regulation (EC) No 510/2006 and the Agricultural Products Quality Control Act, respectively – and undertook to protect the GIs listed in Annex 10-A (Article 10.18.3-10.18.4). Similar to the Singapore Agreement, reference is made to a domestic register, an administrative verification and amendment procedure, and an objection procedure which takes into consideration the legitimate interests of third parties (Article 10.18.6(a)(b)(c)(f). In addition, there is also scope for 'control provisions applying to production' and 'legal provisions laying down that a registered name may be used by any operator marketing the agricultural product or foodstuff conforming to the corresponding specification' (Article 10.18.6(d)(e)). These two additional requirements are more extensive, and suggest that a bigger burden is placed on both parties to ensure that these provisions are complied with. This is further bolstered by specific provisions on the enforcement of protection, in which both parties commit to protect GIs, based on their own initiative by means of intervention by their authorities, as well as upon the request of interested parties (Article 10.22). Such burdensome provisions would be difficult for CARIFORUM countries to implement, especially given the nascent stage of GI development in the CARIFORUM region. The SADC Agreement does also contain enforcement provisions; however, the SADC region – and South Africa in particular – has experience in protecting wine products from the region (Article 8). The colonial flavour of the South African wine industry, and by extension its experience of trading and protecting wine – steeped in (neo)colonial relations – has given it pre-existing experience in protecting GIs.

The Korea Agreement sets out that each party shall meet to discuss GIs to be added to the Annex (Article 10.24), within the framework of the GI Working Group, which is the equivalent of the Trade [and Development] Committee in other agreements (Article 10.25). The GI Working Group also has the mandate to modify the Annexes.

In addition to the issue of direct protection, there is also the issue of the level of protection afforded, specifically in relation to the higher (Article 23 TRIPS level of) protection afforded to agricultural products broadly. Third World

[101] Regulation (EU) No 1151/2012 of the European Parliament and of the Council of 21 November 2012 on Quality Schemes for Agricultural Products and Foodstuffs [2012] OJ L343.

[102] ibid. See also Liam Sunner, 'How the European Union is Expanding the Protection Levels Afforded to Geographical Indications as Part of its Global Trade Policy' (2021) 16(4-5) *Journal of Intellectual Property Law and Practice* 341–46.

[103] For example, see Andrea Zappalaglio and Evgeniia Mikheeva, 'The New Russian Law of Geographical Indications: A Critical Assessment' (2011) 16(4-5) *Journal of Intellectual Property Law and Practice* 368–75; Sunner, 'How the European Union is Expanding the Protection Levels' (n 102); Yilmaztekin and Banu, Turkish Law on Infringement of Geographical Indications' (n 71).

countries, such as India, have argued that the limited coverage within the WTO is unfair since they are obliged to protect wine and spirits through a higher level of protection while the same products are considered generic in other important markets, such as the US and Canada.[104] Ritika Banerjee and Mohar Majumdar explain how India's interest in extending Article 23 TRIPS protection to all products is linked to their aim to reduce the Third World–First World divide, protect their biodiversity, and prevent the exploitation of their indigenous communities and traditional knowledge.[105] India's position is emblematic of many developing countries who recognise that European wine and spirit GIs have been granted the highest protection while (non-wine and spirit) GI products from Third World countries cannot benefit from the same protection. As such, the extension of the Article 23 TRIPS-level of higher protection can be interpreted as levelling the playing field amongst WTO members in relation to the (higher) protection of *all* GI products. While the authors do recognise that there may be associated added costs – for the consumer, producer, and government – they note that there is already an unfair burden on producers to prove consumer confusion, which may lead to producers outside the region taking advantage of an existing reputation so long as the public is not misled. Citing the examples of the neem and basmati patent controversies,[106] the authors note that the benefits of higher protection should outweigh the cost.

Patricia Covarrubia, writing on the EU–Columbia/Peru Agreement, also recognises the developing-country coalition that sought to extend this protection to boost local earnings, while also protecting from usurpation.[107] Covarrubia notes that the opposing countries of the New World not only defended the current level of protection, but equally denied theft accusations stemming from migrations of methods and knowledge linked to GI products from the Old World to the New World.[108] In reminding us that GIs are not only culturally valuable products but also business assets, she highlights how *EU* Traditional Speciality Guaranteed (TSG) products benefit from higher protection under Peru/Columbia GI law because such a level of protection for TSG products does not exist in their domestic law. Rather, TSG as a category is a European invention within the EU's GI legal regime. As such, the EU benefits from a higher protection in countries without an equivalent scheme. Additionally, there is further discrepancy pointed out here, since handicrafts are not protected within the Agreement, precisely because EU laws did not provide for protection of handicraft products as GIs at the time of signing of the Agreement. These are two key areas that CARIFORUM states implementing GI laws must be critically engaged with if GI implementation is

[104] Ritika Banerjee and Mohar Majumdar, 'In the Mood to Compromise? Extended Protection of Geographical Indications under TRIPS Article 23' (2011) 6(9) *Journal of Intellectual Property Law and Practice* 659.

[105] ibid 660.

[106] ibid.

[107] Covarrubia, 'The EU and Colombia/Peru Free Trade Agreement' (n 71) 330.

[108] ibid 331–32.

to promote 'development from within'.[109] First, it is important to know which TSG products have made their way into the CARIFORUM–EU EPA and, as a result, benefit from the higher level of protection afforded to GIs. Second, an understanding of how the EU is engaging with countries wishing to protect their handicraft products as GIs, especially as the EU develops its own system, is key if Third World countries are to protect their own GI space. These are two areas where research should be conducted to build capacity in Third World countries.

The next section considers one of the biggest costs in failing to adequately protect origin products: the possibility that an indication may be considered generic and, therefore, unable to be protected in law.

3.3.2 Generic Terms, Plant Varieties, and Animal Breeds

Within the CARIFORUM–EU EPA, the now oft-cited provision protecting against the process of 'genericide' – the phenomenon of regional names becoming generic and losing their profitable communicative link to their original place of production – is included. Protection is not required for GI goods whose indication is identical to a term deemed 'customary in common language' for such goods in the parties' territories (Article 145.C.1). A case in point is Cheddar cheese, which does not refer to cheese from the Cheddar region in the UK, but rather a general type of hard cheese. This issue is a key interest of EU GI exporters, and has been the subject of case law. Most prominently, in the *Feta* litigation, Advocate General Colomer stated, '[t]he process of genericide is fatal because the sign no longer functions to indicate geographical origin'.[110] In that case within the EU, producers of the famous Greek cheese won the right to protect the use of feta as evocative of Greek cheese, albeit not the direct name of a region.[111] A similar case was fought in the US, where the Communité de Roquefort won their case to protect the Roquefort term in the US, based on their traditions of producing the blue-veined cheese in caves in Roquefort since the fifteenth century.[112] However, in the more recent *Gruyère* case in the US, unfortunately for the producers from Interprofession du Gruyère and Syndicat Interprofessionnel du Gruyère, the 'relevant' American public did not link this type of hard cheese with Switzerland or France.[113] The pendulum has surely

[109] Sarah Bowen, 'Development from Within? The Potential for Geographical Indications in the Global South' (2010) 13(2) *Journal of World Intellectual Property* 232. See chs 1 and 6.

[110] 'Parmesan' Case C-132/05 *Commission of the European Communities v Federal Republic of Germany* [2008] ECR I-00957; 'Feta' Joint cases C-465/02 and C-466/02 *Federal Republic of Germany and Kingdom of Denmark v Commission of the European Communities* [2005] ECR I-09115.

[111] Joint *Feta* cases (n 110).

[112] *Cmty Of Roquefort v William Faehndrich Inc*, 303 F.2d 494, 133 USPQ 633 (2d Cir. 1962).

[113] The 'Marvin' two-part test consists of asking: (i) what is the origin of goods and services? (ii) does the relevant public link the designation primarily to the origin of the given goods or services? In these cases, the opposing party bears the burden of proof: David Schiavetti, 'Genericness in US Certification Marks: the 'GRUYERE' Case' (2021) 16(4-5) *Journal of World Intellectual Property* 298–300.

swung from GI recognition in the *Roquefort* case to genericide in the *Gruyère* case. The key elements of the two-part test considered: (i) what is the origin of goods and services? (ii) does the relevant public link the designation primarily to the origin of the given goods or services? A central part of this assessment is the provision of evidence linking the product to the origin, by the opposing party that bears the burden of proof, and these can include: dictionary explanations; third-party use; media-driven coverage; non-capitalised terms, including on the Internet; and administrative regulations, amongst others.[114] Given these precedents, CARIFORUM countries should be vigilant in the establishment of their product specifications in the first place, as well as marketing in third-party territories.[115] In this regard, the role of the national IP offices in providing support and guidance in the process of writing up the GI specification and understanding the GI process is crucial.[116]

The issue of generics did not pose a 'direct' issue in the CARIFORUM negotiations, given that CARIFORUM countries – unlike 'New World' countries like the US, Canada, and Australia – are not producers of GI goods that the EU attempts to 'claw back'. Nonetheless, elsewhere, it has been well documented how the EU attempts to 'claw back' certain terms,[117] precisely to avoid them being used as 'customary terms in common language' of another territory. Interestingly, the EU has significant experience negotiating the protection for these terms within its own case law, which is now used as a benchmark for international negotiations for the protection of GIs outside the EU. The issue was prominently raised in the *Spanish Champagne* case, wherein producers of Champagne lobbied the French courts and government to not protect Scotch whisky, given that the UK courts, at first instance, did not deem that Spanish champagne would confuse consumers. After all, the UK courts reasoned that consumers would be aware that this sparkling wine originated in Spain, as the composite country name – Spain – accompanied the drink, champagne. As a result of the French backlash, the UK courts reversed their decision and protected Champagne produced by French *vignerons*, which in turn led to the creation of 'cava', the now globally recognised word denoting Spanish sparkling wine.[118] As a result of the above-mentioned *Feta*

[114] ibid 300.

[115] See Demerara Rum case study, ch 6.

[116] Currently, the EU-funded CarIPI project supports CARIFORUM intellectual property offices. It has four objectives: create stronger IP offices offering high-quality, state-of-the-art services to users; ensure availability of effective IPR enforcement mechanisms; contribute to the development of a sustainable and innovative private sector; make doing business between the EU and CARIFORUM, and particularly within the CARIFORUM region, easier: 'CARIFORUM Intellectual Property Rights and Innovation' (*International Cooperation*), https://internationalipcooperation.eu/en/caripi.

[117] The shortlist of 41 products is featured here: Commission, 'WTO Talks: EU Steps up Bid for Better Protection of Regional Quality Products' (*Europa*, 28 August 2003), https://ec.europa.eu/commission/presscorner/detail/en/IP_03_1178.

[118] Dev Gangjee, 'Spanish Champagne: An Unfair Competition Approach to GI protection' in Rochelle Cooper Dreyfuss and Jane C Ginsburg (eds), *Intellectual Property at the Edge: The Contested Contours of IP* (CUP, 2014).

and *Champagne* litigations within the EU, a precedent has been set for protection against genericide occurring outside the EU.

While internal EU case law has refined how GIs are protected, the 2021 decision by the Russian government not to protect Champagne in their territory[119] reflects the legal loopholes that exist with regard to GI enforcement because there is no multilateral GI register. Furthermore, it demonstrates the economic bargaining power that Russia has in comparison with France and the EU, to insist on new labeling requirements. Under this new law, Champagne exporters must add 'sparkling wine' to the label of exports to Russia. Only sparkling wine produced in the Russian territory can be called 'Russian champagne' *(Russian Shampanskoye)*, akin to the 'Soviet champagne' popularised from the 1930s in that territory.[120] This is a 'hard' power that the SIDS of the CARIFORUM states could hardly attempt to emulate.[121] It is hardly conceivable that CARIFORUM countries would amend their legislation, at this current time, with regard to expanding the category of sparkling wine, or to locally label 'champagnes'. With the exception of the Dominican Republic, the English-speaking territories aptly refer to *any* sparkling wine as a 'champagne'. Yet it does not appear that they possess the requisite market power to create, for example, a 'Jamaican champagne'. After all, Russia has USD 1.48 trillion gross domestic product (GDP),[122] compared with the CARICOM's USD 82 billion[123] and the Dominican Republic's USD 78 billion.[124] While the French champagne producers and the EU yielded to Russia's demands, it is unlikely that a similar scenario would yield the same outcome in the Caribbean region. The outcome would most likely lead to costly litigation and intense press coverage of Caribbean producers attempting to free-ride on a long-standing French/European tradition. This rather demonstrates the global imbalances in negotiating the protection of GIs, as well as the historic relations between European countries and the Caribbean. It implies that the EU's own legal system will continue to have an impactful role on the development of the region's GI laws,[125] coupled with its development aid support programmes.

[119] Anastasiia Kyrylenko, 'Russia Adopts Law that Shakes Cognac and Champagne Importers' (*IP Kitten*, 3 July 2021), https://ipkitten.blogspot.com/2021/07/russia-adopts-law-that-shakes-cognac.html. Kim Willsher and Andrew Roth, 'Shampanskoye, French Champagne Industry in a Fizz over Russian Law' *The Guardian* (London, 5 July 2021), https://theguardian.com/world/2021/jul/05/shampanskoye-french-champagne-industry-in-a-fizz-over-russian-law.

[120] Kyrylenko, 'Russia Adopts Law that Shakes Cognac and Champagne Importers' (n 119).

[121] Willsher and Roth, 'Shampanskoye' (n 119).

[122] World Bank, 'GDP (current US$) – Russian Federation' (*World Bank*), https://data.worldbank.org/indicator/NY.GDP.MKTP.CD?locations=RU.

[123] 2021 statistics drawn from compiling World Bank data. Elizabeth Morgan, 'CARICOM: GDP as an indicator of the status of national economies – a false impression' (*CARICOM*, 21 December 2021), https://today.caricom.org/2021/12/15/caricom-gdp-as-an-indicator-of-the-status-of-national-economies-a-false-impression/#:~:text=On%20a%20regional%20level%2C%20the,income%20is%20US%244%2C%20348.

[124] 'GDP (current US$) – Dominican Republic' (*World Bank*, 2020), https://data.worldbank.org/indicator/NY.GDP.MKTP.CD?locations=DO.

[125] See Araujo, *The EU Deep Trade Agenda* (n 13) 142, 154.

The CARIFORUM EPA goes beyond the standard protection against genericide for goods, since it extends to grape, plant, and animal varieties (Article 145.C.2, as does Korea Article 10.24.3). This is significant, as not all FTA texts extend the protection for GI terms to plant and animal varieties. While it is not included in the Andean Agreement, plant and animal varieties are mentioned *verbis expressis* in Japan Article 14.25.4.a and CETA Article 20.22.3.b. Additionally, the possibility to protect plant and animal varieties as GIs would only be permitted if domestic legislation allows in the Korea Agreement, Article 10.22.8. As such, within the CARIFORUM Agreement, GI protection is not afforded to terms deemed 'customary in common language' (Article 145.C.1.), or for identical GIs for grape and plant varieties and animal breeds already protected prior to the entry into force of the EPA (Article 145.C.2.).

Terms considered as homonymous GIs are protected, insofar as there is sufficient distinction between earlier GIs and later homonymous terms, wherein the consumer must not be misled and producers ought to be treated equitably. The phrasing of this provision recalls the longstanding proactivism of the EU to obtain the limited exception to trademark holders' rights, for later GIs that are allowed to co-exist with earlier trademarks as a matter of a limited exception (as affirmed in *WTO DS 174*).[126] Here, it seems that the EU has sought to protect earlier GIs while not spelling out the protection for later GIs vis-à-vis earlier homonymous terms. Furthermore, what if those terms are not protected in law but are customary in common language? It seems likely that these issues may arise before CARIFORUM courts, given the linguistic, historical, and to some extent cultural, entanglements of the regions. After all, there is no legal precedent as to what amounts to 'sufficient distinction in practice' between GIs and homonymous terms in case law, or what exactly 'equitable treatment' refers to, given the recognition of the imbalanced IPR playing field. Given that Article 23.3 TRIPS applies mutatis mutandis,[127] this implies that, according to the TRIPS language, each party shall determine practically how terms are to be differentiated. What is somewhat confusing, however, is that while the CARIFORUM provision notes that Article 23.3 TRIPS should apply, the TRIPS text does not refer to a GI *and* a homonymous term, but rather to the homonymous terms in general. This difference in the CARIFORUM text, therefore, can be read as establishing a hierarchy between the legally protected GI term and the unprotected

[126] WTO, *European Communities — Protection of Trademarks and Geographical Indications for Agricultural Products and Foodstuffs* (15 March 2005) WT/DS/174/R, incorporates the complaint by Australia, 'WT/D290/R' of 15 March 2005. The second request for consultation, issued on 4 April 2003, concerned the enforcement procedures, in which the US claimed that third-party nationals were discriminated against, and therefore these provisions were also inconsistent with TRIPS. 13 countries (Sri Lanka, Australia, Hungary, India, Argentina, Bulgaria, Cyprus, the Czech Republic, Malta, Slovenia, Romania, the Slovak Republic, and Turkey) requested to join the WTO/DS/174 consultations. 15 countries requested to join WT/D290/R consultations (Bulgaria, Cyprus, the Czech Republic, Malta, the US, Hungary, Slovenia, New Zealand, Romania, the Slovak Republic, Chinese Taipei, Turkey, Argentina, Colombia, and Mexico).

[127] See ch 2 (n 118).

homonymous term. In this case, the future case law would no doubt raise not only pertinent legal questions but important political economy ones that should draw on how entwined the regions' colonial and historical developments have been, and on issues of production, labelling, and IPR trade today.

The issue of homonymous terms, alongside 'component' terms deemed generic, may be of particular interest to the development of GI products in CARIFORUM countries. The components issue deals with terms that constitute GIs. For example, the terms 'aceto', 'balsamico' and 'aceto balsamico' are not protected as a GI without the reference to 'Modena', and hence the recognised GI, 'aceto balsamico di Modena'. [128] There is ample EU case law on the issue.[129] Like cheddar, and unlike 'West Country Farmhouse Cheddar', there are many component cheese terms in particular that are now considered as lacking a distinctive link: 'Gouda' and 'Edam', but not 'Gouda Holland' or 'Edam Holland'; 'Camembert' or 'Emmental', but not 'Camembert du Normandie' or 'Emmental de Savoie'; or 'ricotta' but not 'Ricotta Romana'.[130]

Given that US producers and exporters make use of these generic terms that the EU tries to 'claw back', the Caribbean region can strategically engage with the issue of component terms and homonymous terms when implementing their GI regime for the benefit of Caribbean consumers. An area which may be relevant is in the development of the local and regional CARIFORUM wine industry, which local experts say are less wines and more liquors. For example, sorrel, sea grape or even cannabis wines are local produce that may also bear affiliations to European counterparts. While there is no outstanding case law or litigation pending, this is an issue that may arise in future with the development of a GI legal regime in the CARIFORUM and the increased trade in GI products inter-regionally with the EU. This relates to the concept of 'development from within', since it challenges First World knowledge on GI subject matter – wines – and proposes a reconceptualisation of a GI which is grounded in local Caribbean realities.[131]

CARIFORUM's provisions on generic products can be interpreted as lying in a middle ground compared with other EU FTAs. For example, only within the EU–Korea and EU–EAC Agreements are provisions on generic terms absent. This suggests that GIs cannot become generic in these territories, whether they are legally protected or not. This may indicate that neither party is on an

[128] Magali Contardi, 'No Proprietary Protection for Individual Non-geographical Components of Protected Geographical Denominations, says AG Hogan' (2019) 14(11) *Journal of Intellectual Property Law and Practice* 838–40, 838. Opinion of Advocate General Hogan in C-432/18, *Consorzio Tutela Aceto Balsamico di Modena v BALEMA GmbH*, ECLI:EU:C:2019:650.

[129] For example, see Judgment of 26 February 2008, 'Parmesan' (n 110), paras 43–44; Judgment of 2 July 2009, '*Bayerisches Beer*', C-343/07 *Bavaria NV and Bavaria Italia Srl v Bayerischer Brauerbund eV*, EU:C:2009:415, para 108.

[130] Contardi, 'No Proprietary Protection for Individual Non-geographical Components' (n 128) 839. On the Andean Agreement, see Covarrubia, 'The EU and Colombia/Peru Free Trade Agreement' (n 71) 337.

[131] See ch 6.

offensive to protect their GIs in the other's territory.[132] The EU–SADC EPA states plainly:

> Protected GIs shall not be deemed to become generic in the territories of the Parties (Article 5.2 EU–SADC EPA).

However, the reality is that, without a multilateral register, CARIFORUM GIs may be deemed generic in certain territories. This is certainly the issue at hand currently with the government of Guyana's attempts to protect Guyana Demerara sugar in the US and Canada.[133] What this demonstrates is that, in fact, the GI commitments can have an effect of locking in GI trade and deepening (post-colonial/neocolonial) path dependencies between the CARIFORUM and the EU. From this optic, the decision to opt for GI protection must be carefully weighed against the costs and benefits of not only adopting and using a GI but considering the export market of the product. After all, CARIFORUM products can be protected as certification marks in the US, as successfully demonstrated in the *Café de Colombia* case, and less successfully in the *Tequila* case.[134]

The EU–Columbia/Peru Agreement, more precisely, only refers to 'common language':

> geographical indications protected in accordance with this Title shall not, for as long as they remain protected in their country of origin, be considered the common or generic designation of the product that they identify (Article 207(h), emphasis added).

Meanwhile, Canada, Singapore, Japan, and CARIFORUM all refer to terms that have become 'customary in common language as the common name'. In the Singapore Agreement, this provision is extended since it applies to both goods and services (Article 10.22.5). According to Singapore's national GI law, wherein this applies to terms used within a GI, the third party may request qualification of rights conferred (Article 46(1)(2)(5)(7)). Therefore, there are exceptions for GIs which are identical to common names in Singapore. Omachi explains that this accommodates the CJEU *Feta* decision.[135] GI names that are deemed common can, therefore, be cancelled in Singapore. This is remarkable, since it directly contrasts with the EU's position on this issue – that, once protected, GIs shall not become generic.

An overview of the CETA Agreement presents several ways that Canada strategically negotiated for exceptions to GI protection (Article 20.21). For example, the CETA provision on exceptions to protection applies to translations, given that Canada is a bilingual francophone–anglophone territory (Article 20.21(7)). The provision sets out that:

[132] Indeed, the EAC agreement did not contain EAC GIs to be protected in the EU. Rather, it is the EU that seeks to protect its GIs, offensively, via its FTAs.

[133] See ch 5.

[134] See chs 5 and 6.

[135] Joint 'Feta' cases (n 110).

> If a *translation of a geographical indication* is identical with or contains within it a term *customary in common language as the common name* for a product in the territory of a Party, or if *a geographical indication is not identical with but contains within it such a term*, the provisions of this Sub-section [exception] shall not prejudice the right of any person to use that term in association with that product in the territory of that Party (emphasis added, Article 20.21(7) CETA).

This provision shows how Canada was able to use its bilingual reality to influence GI provisions, in effect to allow for translations of direct GIs, and their component terms, even if they are not identical. For example, translations are also permitted for certain terms listed, such as Parmesan and St George cheese, and thus prior trademark-holder rights to these products in Canada are maintained unless the public may be misled as to geographic origin (Article 20.21.11, part A, Annex 20B). Additionally, Canada has grandfather clauses for four of the 19 products listed for 'clawback', namely feta, Asiago, Fontina, and Gorgonzola, as well as Munster, which was added during negotiations (Article 20.21.2.) Canada also managed to maintain the rights for the terms used in commerce for this product class prior to the date of the Agreement, namely 18 October 2013 (Article 20.21.2.). Interestingly, expressions including 'kind,' 'type', 'style', 'imitation' or the like are not prevented outright (Article 20.21.1). Indeed, joint correspondence from US Congress, Secretary of State, and Trade Representative points out that Canada should not include certain generic terms in the grandfather clauses,[136] since future protection of these terms, such as feta, could impair future trade and market access for US products to Canada, such as feta indications produced in the US, where the term is not protected.[137] In this regard, the clauses on generic names, such as in CARIFORUM, can function to exclude US producers of terms deemed 'common' under US law, such as feta, which are protected in the EU, and now under the CARIFORUM–EU EPA.

There are some lessons to be heeded on the potential of language and linguistics that can be gleaned from the EU–China Cooperation Agreement signed on 14 September 2020. Michele Ferrante advises that 'rights owners should also create and register Chinese language translations and transliterations of their GIs to facilitate recognition by Chinese consumers'.[138] On this backdrop, and with hindsight on these provisions, which were agreed to in later EPAs/FTAs, translations and transliterations are issues that CARIFORUM negotiators could have considered. That said, in the Caribbean, traditional knowledge is held by the elders, many of whom speak European dialects or patois, and all CARIFORUM

[136] The grandfather clause permits pre-existing uses (exceptions), albeit with the commitment to negotiate them in future negotiations. See WTO, 'Module IV Geographical Indications', https://wto.org/english/tratop_e/trips_e/ta_docs_e/modules4_e.pdf.

[137] Omachi references the letter from 55 senators of the US Congress to Tom Vilsack, Secretary of the US Department of Agriculture, and Michael Forman, US Trade Representative ('A Tale of Two Approaches' (n 86)).

[138] Michele Ferrante, 'Food for Thought: the EU–China Agreement on GIs' (2021) 16(4-5) *Journal of Intellectual Property Law and Practice* 295.

countries have European languages as their mother tongue (English, Dutch, and Spanish).

Some FTAs demonstrate how GI development can be considered a quid quo pro: therefore, in spite of the literal disadvantage that the CARIFORUM has with fewer GIs in the first place, co-operating with the EU can be beneficial for the development of its own regime. In the case of the EU–Central American Association Agreement (CAAA), Adrian Esquivel has recognised that, in spite of the EU's trade diplomacy and its soft power – which is exercised through capacity-building programmes and training schemes – with GIs, its trade agreements nevertheless have the potential to galvanise dormant GI infrastructure in third parties.[139] As such, the trade-off with GIs may be considered a quid pro quo: giving up some GIs, such as 'Gorgonzola' or 'provolone', even if they have acquired local goodwill in usage in third-party territories, can be balanced against support to the local GI infrastructure and higher-value exports of local origin products. This is certainly the suggestion put forth in the CAAA case, in two instances. In Guatemala, the US Dairy Export Council opposed several cheese GIs, and in Costa Rica, the administrative courts dodged the issue, since the trademarks, although in use for many years, had not been registered.

This offers two precautionary lessons for CARIFORUM countries. On the one hand, it is important to understand who the local interested parties are that can seek to oppose, not only third-party GI registrations, but equally those being registered by CARIFORUM nationals. And, on the other hand, it would be important to check which marks are registered, since, following on from the Costa Rican courts, registration rights through usage may be overridden by the registration requirement. This speaks to the interests of diverse trade stakeholders, who, contrary to the EU's position, may have a preference for trademarks registrations for GI products. This is the topic of the next section below.

3.3.3 Relationship between GIs and Trademarks

GIs are first mentioned under the provisions on trademarks – Article 144F, which sets out a limited exception to trademark-holder rights in relation to GI terms:

> The EC Party and the Signatory CARIFORUM States shall provide for the fair use of descriptive terms, including geographical indications, as *a limited exception* to the rights conferred by a trade mark. Such limited exception shall take account of the legitimate interests of the owner of the trade mark and of third parties.[140]

[139] Adrian Esquivel, 'Will Coffee be the New Wine? The EU–Central American Association Agreement and the European Shaping of GIs in Costa Rica' (2021) 16 (4-5) *Journal of Intellectual Property Law and Practice* 310–15.

[140] Emphasis added.

This provision implements the exception set out to TM right-holders in Article 17 TRIPS, albeit emphasising the contractual nature of the exception in the EPA, insofar as parties '*shall provide*' it, as opposed to the option for such an exception exemplified by the use of '*may provide*' in the TRIPS text.[141] This is significant, as the EPA uses mandatory language to oblige the EU and CARIFORUM states to provide the exception. While Article 144F CARIFORUM–EU EPA provides for a limited exception to trademark holders' rights for fair use of descriptive terms including GIs, Graeme Dinwoodie has suggested that '[t]he same clamor for mandatory exceptions has not been seen in trademark law'.[142] This can be added to the list of evidence of how the EU pushes for co-existence of GIs alongside trademarks.

In the CARIFORUM–EU EPA, the relationship between GIs and trademarks is set out in the provisions of Article 145.D.1. Under this Article, it is established that later GIs cannot be registered if they are capable of misleading consumers about the origin of the product specifically in relation to the trademark's reputation, renown, and duration of use. In a similar vein, Article 145.D.2 clarifies that later trademarks cannot be registered where they are identical or similar to existing GIs, and as a consequence, any such registered trademarks must be invalidated (Article 154.D.3). Article 145.D.4 provides for the co-existence of earlier trademarks and GIs, in line with obligations set out under WTO or the EPA, insofar as there are no grounds for their revocation or invalidity. As such, the CARIFORUM–EU EPA establishes a co-existence regime between GIs and (earlier) trademarks. A comparative analysis on this issue across EU FTAs and other GI regimes can provide lessons for CARIFORUM countries, as they can strategically engage with both laws to protect their GI products.[143]

While there is literature pointing to the EU's preference for co-existence regimes,[144] the EU's FTAs with Singapore, Canada, and Korea do not have provisions establishing a co-existence regime, ie a provision pertaining to protecting later GIs conflicting with earlier trademarks. In the literature, it has been noted that this is unsurprising, given that both Singapore and Korea also have FTAs with the US agreeing to the first in time, first in right (FITFIR) principle, which recognises the right-holder as the first to register the mark, and this is used to resolve disputes, and Canada and Singapore are signatories to the Trans-Pacific Partnership that also uses the FITFIR principle.[145] Omachi has highlighted how

[141] 'Members may provide limited exceptions to the rights conferred by a trademark, such as fair use of descriptive terms, provided that such exceptions take account of the legitimate interests of the owner of the trademark and of third parties.' (art 17 TRIPS).

[142] Graeme B Dinwoodie, 'Developing Defenses in Trademark Law' (2009) 13 *Lewis & Clark Law Review* 99, 103.

[143] See chs 4 and 5.

[144] ibid.

[145] Korea–US arts 18.2.4, 18.2.15 and US–Singapore Free Trade Agreement, art 16.2.2, Singapore–US, May 6, 2003, Office of the US Trade Rep, and TPP arts 18.20, 18.32.1, in Omachi, 'A Tale of Two Approaches' (n 87) 170. On FITFIR, see Dev Gangjee, *Relocating the Law on Geographical Indications* (CUP, 2012) 225.

Singapore's 2014 GI Act sets out how conflicts may be resolved (in the future),[146] underscoring a prominent point of his article – domestic laws matter for GI implementation. With regards to CETA, Omachi underscores that

> CETA shows the result of negotiations addressing the relationship of prior conflicting trademarks and subsequent GIs, instead of rules governing the relationship . . . It is inferred from the above that the CETA negotiations included some dispute settlement elements concerning individual GIs.[147]

Interestingly here, Omachi identifies a cognitive dissonance between both parties' narrative on this aspect of the Agreement: for the EU, the clawing back of certain terms at the negotiation stage represents an EU win, wherein Canada has deviated from the FITFIR principle in order allow for the co-existence of EU GIs, such as 'Prosciutto di Parma'. In contrast, for Canada this protection does not prejudice pre-existing trademarks.[148] Of particular interest in CETA, Omachi notes that similar GIs may be added to CETA's Annex, as only identical GIs may not be added (Article 20.22.3(a)), which accordingly demonstrates a lack of compliance with Article 16.1 TRIPS (which sets out protections for trademarks).

Michele Ferrante notes that both China's trademark law and *sui generis* GI law 'shall be used cumulatively to reach the highest possible level of protection on the Chinese territory'.[149] This is remarkable, since it suggests that China aims to allow for origin protection through the dual usage of both types of laws. Indeed, champagne was the first GI to be protected in China, being afforded protection via an administrative decree of 1989 and thereafter through the revision of its trademark law in 1993. According to Ferrante, the discussion around the evolution of GIs in China is based on the important economic trade amounting to 15billion euros in agricultural trade, including high-end food and wine, being cited as one of the factors behind the 2021 agreement.[150] CARIFORUM states implementing the GI provisions can learn from this precedent set by China. Currently, there are no development co-operation programmes on GIs that are led by Third World donors for the Third World beneficiaries. Existing programmes represent First World–Third World co-operation, as they are led by the EU, EU agencies, and European institutions. However, it is not unlikely that, in the future, there could be fruitful Third World–Third World exchanges. The lesson to be heeded here is that CARIFORUM countries should use the legal tools they deem fit to protect their GIs, and where necessary this may be a combination of both trademark and GI legal regimes.[151]

[146] Omachi, 'A Tale of Two Approaches' (n 87) 170.
[147] ibid 171.
[148] EU-CETA Agreement (n 9).
[149] Ferrante, 'Food for thought' (n 138) 295.
[150] See Commission, 'Agri-Food Trade Statistical Factsheet' (*Europa*, 13 March 2020) 296, https://ec.europa.eu/info/sites/info/files/food-farming-fisheries/farming/documents/agrifood-china_en.pdf.
[151] See ch 4.

3.3.4 Future Protection Agreement

Article 145.E commits both parties to further negotiations of an agreement for the protection of GIs, notwithstanding ongoing requests for protection. This provision is an innovation in the EPA, since it commits both parties to a separate agreement on GIs that sits apart from the EPA, albeit intrinsically linked to the legal regime that the EPA establishes. The parties have stated that 'negotiations between CARIFORUM States and the EU to implement Article 145.E are ongoing'. [152] This is interesting, given the divergences in GI protections amongst the ACP group: while there is a region-to-region African Union (AU)–EU GI Strategy, one does not exist for the CARIFORUM. Although the forthcoming agreement may be similar in content to the AU–EU GI Strategy, under this provision, the expected forthcoming EU–CARIFORUM GI Agreement should have a legally binding effect, since it is a result of the EPA.[153] In this regard, the EU is achieving the same normative standards in contributing to international trade. On the CARIFORUM side, while the group is still establishing a list of GIs to be protected in the EU, Guyana's Demerara Rum has become the first CARIFORUM GI to be registered in the EU, as of 4 August 2021.[154] The slow pace of implementing GI protection, both regionally and in the EU, may be an indication that any GIs listed under the future protection agreement may suffer a similar fate of slow or – worse – no implementation.

3.3.5 Internet Use

Article 145.F sets out that the parties agree that a legal framework is needed to protect GI right-holders on the Internet, and in e-commerce. It establishes that such a framework should address protection against usurpation and evocation, acquisitions done in bad faith, infringements, and unfair competition, as well as remedies, inter alia, relating to the transferral or cancellation of domain names. To this end, the Article states the parties' intention to apply the WIPO

[152] 'Economic Partnership Agreement Between The Cariforum States And The European Union (Goods And Services) Questions And Replies' (*WTO*, 04 October 2018), https://docs.wto.org/dol2fe/Pages/FE_Search/FE_S_S009-Html.aspx?Id=248529&BoxNumber=3&DocumentPartNumber=1&Language=E&HasEnglishRecord=True&HasFrenchRecord=True&HasSpanishRecord=True&Window=L&PreviewContext=DP&FullTextHash=371857150. See also Commission, 'The EU-CARIFORUM Economic Partnership Agreement', https://trade.ec.europa.eu/access-to-markets/en/content/eu-CARIFORUM-economic-partnership-agreement.

[153] See ch 4.

[154] The application for registration was submitted, received no opposition, and was thereafter registered. 'DEMERARA RUM' (File number: PGI-GY-02423 – 28.6.2018). Publication of an Application Pursuant to Article 17(6) of Regulation (EC) No 110/2008 of the European Parliament and of the Council on the Definition, Description, Presentation, Labelling and the Protection of Geographical Indications of Spirit Drinks and Repealing Council Regulation (EEC) No 1576/89 [2021] OJ C120/7, 7–12.

recommendations with regard to protecting marks and other IPRs on the Internet (Article 145.F).[155] The provisions of the Joint Recommendation aim to establish a clear legal framework for trademark right-holders usage on the Internet and in e-commerce, specifically facilitating the application of existing laws in determining infringement and settling remedies.[156] For example, the use of a sign on the Internet is understood to have effect only if it is considered a 'commercial use' (Article 2), in accordance with the non-exhaustive factors, such as level of business activity, customer base, and sales (Article 3). Additionally, it also sets out some criteria regarding usage on the Internet that would constitute bad faith, namely prior knowledge of an identical or existing sign when the sign was first used or acquired, or whether the sign takes 'unfair advantage' or 'unjustifiably impairs' the specific character or reputation of a protected sign (Article 4). Importantly, it sets out that the applicable law for the implementation of the provisions shall be determined by the private international law of its members (in regard to infringements and remedies, Articles 6–8 and 13–15, respectively). Given the practical importance of applicable laws of members, it will be important to keep an eye on legal developments in this domain of EU and CARIFORUM countries. Additionally, given that the CARICOM group has made commitments generally towards a digital transformation in the region[157] – and despite no equivalent parliamentary legislation or policy documents, such as the EU's 'Future of Food'[158] – the partnership in this area could be viewed as mutually reinforcing the region's transformative agendas. Considered alongside the nascent stage of GI development across CARIFORUM countries, it would be hoped that leapfrogging into this domain of GIs and Internet usage helps rather than hinders the CARIFORUM's sustainable development. This is clearly an interesting innovation and one that needs further research.

Given the difference in (GI) development between the regions, the drive to protect the GI online ought not to override the importance of including all stakeholders offline, in the creation of an inclusive GI system. This shall be considered in the final chapters of this book.

[155] This is framed to be in accordance with the 'WIPO at the Thirty-Sixth Series of Meetings of the Assemblies of the Member States of WIPO, 24 September to 3 October 2001'.

[156] WIPO, 'Joint Recommendation Concerning Provisions on the Protection of Marks, and Other Industrial Property Rights in Signs, on the Internet', https://wipo.int/edocs/pubdocs/en/wipo_pub_845.pdf.

[157] CARICOM, 'ICT Ministers Approve CARICOM Secretariat Led Action Plans to Fast Track Digital Transformation' (*CARICOM*, 11 February 2022), https://caricom.org/ict-ministers-approve-caricom-secretariat-led-action-plans-to-fast-track-digital-transformation/.

[158] See Pilar Montero, 'Towards a Core Unitary Legal Regime for Geographical Indications in the European Union Digital Market' (2021) 16(4-5) *Journal of Intellectual Property Law and Practice* 427–34. The Final Proposal is available here, although the original text dealt with the draft version. The 'Future of Food and Farming' outlined the importance of future-proofing the EU's Common Agricultural Policy, in which making GIs more attractive to both farmers and consumers, as well as a simpler GI system, including easier registration and specification approvals, were highlighted. It provided a key background from which the proposal was based.

3.4 CONCLUSION

This chapter has mapped the legal provisions within the EPA and evaluated how those provisions could sustain power asymmetries between the two regions. The legal analysis has shown that the EU is a GI norm exporter in the case of the CARIFORUM–EU EPA, and plays a decisive role in international GI standard-setting through its FTAs. An overview of CARIFORUM's commitments on GIs shows that the legal regime may help the parties' inter-regional trade; however, it may also hinder the CARIFORUM's trading relations with its major partner – the US. The CARIFORUM's commitment to protect EU GI terms deemed generic in the US, or the commitments to provide higher protection for GIs over trademarks, are two such areas. By discussing the commitments in other EU FTAs, this chapter sought to demonstrate lessons that could be learnt for the region. Cumulatively using both GI and trademark regimes for protecting the region's origin products is one such lesson to impact the strategic implementation of (GI) laws so as to contribute to levelling the international trade playing field and contributing to sustainable development.

A comparative analysis of GI provision in the EU's FTAs has elucidated several areas in which the CARIFORUM–EU EPA GI provisions have far-reaching IPR provisions; however, there is one area in which, perhaps, it has not gone far enough – identifying the intended beneficiaries under the agreement. The EU–Andean Agreement expressly states the GI beneficiaries within its legal text, as it underlines that the use of a GI is

> reserved exclusively for *producers, manufacturers or craftsmen with production or manufacturing establishments in the locality or region* within the Party identified or evoked by that indication [as well as] public or private bodies that represent beneficiaries of geographical indications or bodies designated for that purpose shall have at their disposal mechanisms allowing for the effective control over the use of protected geographical indications (Art 20(e)(g)).

No other Agreement expressly states the beneficiaries of GI IPRs, in what can be interpreted as an exhaustive list here. Yet, the EU–Japan Agreement refers to the 'end user' in the context of the obligation to consider public policy objectives while pursuing innovation, creativity, and competition via IPRs, inter alia, via the sharing of knowledge and culture, technology, and art (Article 14(2)). The provision concludes by underlining the imperative of taking 'into account the interests of relevant stakeholders including rightsholders and users' (Article 14(2)). Liam Sunner, writing on this Agreement, notes that, although the end is still commercial, the means of achieving it nevertheless places primary importance on the user.[159] By contrast, the CARIFORUM–EU EPA only references beneficiaries within the general provisions (Article 61), and within the meaning of

[159] Sunner, 'How the European Union is Expanding the Protection Levels' (n 102) 346.

Article 3 on 'sustainable development' at the beginning of the EPA that sets out the Agreement as a 'Trade Partnership for Sustainable Development'.[160] Given the reference to end users and listing of beneficiaries, the lack of such references in the EU–CARIFORUM EPA can, therefore, be perceived as a missed opportunity for the GI producer communities and peoples of the CARIFORUM region.

In the next chapter, the institutions of the EPA within which GIs are subject to dialogical engagements amongst EU and CARIFORUM stakeholders are examined. The purpose of this analysis is to demonstrate that institutions exist within the treaty framework that could provide dialogic spaces for contesting, reinterpreting, and reconceptualising the GI provisions in a way that promotes sustainable development in Third World countries.

[160] Foregrounding a human-centred approach to food systems is raised as a priority in the UN Special Rapporteur on the Right to Food Report. See UN Policy Brief, 'Last Chance to Make the Food Systems Summit Truly a "People's Summit"' (*OHCHR*, 19 August 2021), https://ohchr.org/sites/default/files/Documents/Issues/Food/Policy_brief_20210819.pdf.

4

The CARIFORUM–EU EPA: Monitoring and Evaluating GI Implementation

> [W]hat can make evaluation of trade agreements an effective process is to capture the hearts and minds of those responsible for evaluation by focusing on the intended social impact of the trade deal. . . . It needs to act as a tool for continuous improvement of implementation plans for the benefit of a country and its citizens . . . how the agreement will make a difference to people's lives.[1]
>
> Dr Nicholas Charalambides, Imani Developments

4.1 INTRODUCTION

THIS CHAPTER DISCUSSES THE institutions of the Economic Partnership Agreement (EPA), within which GIs are subject to dialogical engagements, or manoeuvres,[2] amongst European Union (EU) and Caribbean Forum (CARIFORUM) stakeholders. It explains how dialogical engagements within the institutions of the EPA can contribute to implementing the post-colonial guarantees that the EU and CARIFORUM countries seek through law. Dialogical engagement, in theory, allows for the reconceptualisation of a law, to take into consideration the inclusive and integrative aspects of sustainable development;[3] that is, how the law and its processes can be transformed, thus embodying a language of emancipation for its beneficiaries, notably Third World GI producers. It suggests that, if the EU is the only benefactor, this is contrary to the spirit of agreement. Therefore, given that the EU is the more powerful actor in regard to sustainable development, the focus of this chapter is how Caribbean peoples benefit from this EPA.

[1] Imani Development, 'Interview with Dr Nicholas Charalambides on M&E in Trade Agreements', https://imanidevelopment.com/interview-with-dr-nicholas-charalambides-on-me-in-trade-agreements/.

[2] Makau Mutua, 'What is TWAIL?' (2000) *Proceedings of the ASIL Annual Meeting* 36.

[3] See ch 1.

This chapter relies, inter alia, on the five- and ten-year reviews,[4] as valuable resources for understanding the state of implementation of the EPA, and its institutions. Within monitoring methodologies, the changes sought through law are often discussed within the framework of implementing a theory of change.[5] Within this theory-of-change approach, the EPA implementation is the intervention that is expected to bring about the objectives of the EPA, which is the change sought by both parties. Within this methodology, the importance of stakeholder buy-in is key and, therefore, to this end, education, sensitisation, and motivating stakeholders is a key part of achieving the objectives of the Agreement, namely allowing the change to manifest. The analysis herein highlights the opportunities where dialogical engagements can foster implementation of the EPA within the framing of the theory of change, which is aimed at benefiting the peoples of both regions and achieving the post-colonial guarantees sought *through* the EPA.

This chapter is concerned with addressing how *the institutions and laws within the EPA contribute to a theory of change to bring about the post-colonial guarantees of sustainable development sought with the EPA*. The chapter demonstrates that the ambitions of the EPA may be muted by the lack of a formalised monitoring mechanism. The rationale for this premise is based on the unfulfilled commitments to design a monitoring mechanism to carefully track the sustainable development impacts of the agreement, especially as it is 18 years since the agreement was signed. This threatens the sustainable development objectives of this agreement, namely that Caribbean peoples would be beneficiaries of the post-colonial guarantees of the Agreement as intended, inter alia, under Article 1 of the EPA. From a theoretical standpoint, it also threatens the shift from a 'dynamic of difference' to the 'commensurability of difference' that arises out of framing alternative GI norms based on dialogical manoeuvres within these institutions;[6] that is, the ability to monitor a process that allows for cultural engagement in the process of establishing universal norms, based on the recognition of multiple identities and heterogeneity.[7] This is aligned with the

[4] See the five-year review: European Commission, Directorate-General for Trade, Sacha Peter Silva, Ranjit Singh, Keisha-Ann Thompson, and Paul Hare, *Monitoring the Implementation and Results of the Cariforum–EU EPA: Final Report* (Publications Office, 2015). See the EU's ten-year review: European Commission, Directorate-General for Trade, Nora Plaisier, Tahmina Shafique, Michael Fuenfzig, David Luff, and Simone Snoeijenbos, *Ex-Post Evaluation of the EPA between the EU and its Member States and the CARIFORUM Member States: Final Report* (Publications Office, 2021). See the CARIFORUM's ten-year review: Audel Cunningham, 'Consultancy to Prepare Technical Position Paper on CARIFORUM's priorities for the Second Five Year Review of the CARIFORUM–EU EPA' (Final Report, 13 December 2020).

[5] Theory of change is the management principle used to monitor and evaluate the SADC–EU EPA. See 'Interview with Dr Nicholas Charalambides' (n 1).

[6] On 'dynamic of difference' see ch 1 (n 29); Anthony Anghie, *Imperialism, Sovereignty and the Making of International Law* (CUP, 2014) 4. On 'commensurability of difference' (own usage), see ch 1 (n 23).

[7] James T Gathii, 'Rejoinder: Twailing International Law' (2019) 98(6) *Michigan Law Review* 2071.

framing of sustainable development as inclusive and based on the principles of integration.[8]

The chapter begins by introducing the 'tailor-made' aspects of the CARIFORUM region. Section 4.2 provides a general overview of monitoring and evaluating the EPA and its institutions with reference to the theory of change. The joint institutions assessed (in section 4.3) include: the Joint CARIFORUM–EU Council, the CARIFORUM–EU Trade and Development Committee (TDC), the CARIFORUM–EU Parliamentary Committee, and the CARIFORUM–EU Consultative Committee. Section 4.4 sets out the financing and EPA implementation, with regard to national EPA implementation units, the regional implementation unit – the CARIFORUM Directorate – and support to the private sector. Section 4.5 sets out the shortcomings of EPA reviews in relation to monitoring, evaluation, and implementation. The Conclusion (section 4.6) summarises that implementing a monitoring mechanism according to a theory of change, which speaks specifically to the social impact of the Agreement, can be a tool for tracking and evaluating the sustainable development impact of the EPA, specifically in relation to GIs. However, this chapter shows that, due to current (socioeconomic) power imbalances, EU funding may impact on implementation of GI provisions. In this sense, advances in GI implementation may be as much a tool for sustainable development in the Caribbean, while also reinforcing EU interests, as such blurring the lines between a 'dynamic of difference' and a 'commensurability of difference'.

4.1.1 The CARIFORUM Region: Tailor-made for the EPA?

This section explores the origins of the CARIFORUM group with reference to socioeconomic and political economy contextualisations of its emergence. It also discusses how the EU is a hegemonic structural foreign policy actor,[9] based on its ability to incentivise the formation of the CARIFORUM group, which deepens and extends the region's own process of integration despite pre-existing regional tensions.

The CARIFORUM is a grouping comprising the 15 Caribbean Community (CARICOM) states[10] and the Dominican Republic. The CARIFORUM group did not pre-exist the EPA; it emerged due to the EU's preference to negotiate a free trade agreement (FTA) with both the CARICOM and the Dominican Republic combined, for at least two reasons. First, the Dominican Republic's gross domestic product (GDP) of USD 124 billion is almost the same as all

[8] See ch 1 (n 23).

[9] Yentyl Williams, 'Shifting Between Hegemony and Dominance? A Neo-Gramscian Analysis of the EU as a Structural Foreign Policy Actor: The Singular Case of the Cariforum-EU Economic Partnership Agreement' (2015) 1 *Bruges Regional Integration and Global Governance Papers* 1–36.

[10] Anthony Payne, *The Political History of CARICOM* (Ian Randle, 2007).

CARICOM countries combined.[11] While CARICOM GDP wavered around the same GDP as the Dominican Republic, it is projected to reach USD 150 million by 2025.[12] Second, the Dominican Republic's population of 10 million provides substantially more market access in the same geographic area as CARICOM countries, whose total population is 16 million.[13] Thus, an FTA with the CARIFORUM offers the EU a strategically more attractive trade agreement with 16 countries, as opposed to 15, within the same region of the Caribbean Sea and Atlantic Ocean. Importantly, also, it pushes intra-Caribbean regional integration further than before, since the Dominican Republic requested to accede to CARICOM on two occasions.[14] CARICOM members, however, fearful of the Dominican Republic's economic and demographic size in the region, rejected the accession request.[15] Instead, CARICOM–Dominican Republic relations had been regulated though their own FTA,[16] although the CARIFORUM EPA's provisions deepen regional integration via its trade liberalisation commitments.

Much of the literature discusses the Caribbean Forum (CARIFORUM) group as 'tailor-made'.[17] This author's earlier work considered the EPA as a structural foreign policy tool, which has long-term influences on the Caribbean region's political, legal, economic, social, and security structures.[18] By extension, the EU is described as a structural foreign policy actor, which refers to the EU's ability to influence other countries' political, legal, economic, social, and security structures.[19] This is exemplified in the EU's role in forging the CARICOM–Dominican Republic union for the purpose of the EPA, beyond the CARICOM's very own

[11] World Bank, 'GDP (current US$) – Dominican Republic' (2024), https://data.worldbank.org/indicator/NY.GDP.MKTP.CD?locations=DO.

[12] IMF, Caribbean, (IMF DataMapper, 2025), https://www.imf.org/external/datamapper/profile/CBQ#:~:text=World%20Economic%20Outlook%20(October%202025,Caribbean, accessed 14 December 2025.

[13] ibid.

[14] 'Dominican Republic – CARICOM: Unfinished Business' (4 December 2013), https://ecdpm.org/work/political-economy-of-regional-integration-volume-2-issue-7-october-2013/dominican-republic-caricom-unfinished-business.

[15] See Yentyl Williams, 'The Caribbean-EU EPA – Lessons for African-EU EPAs' (10th Ghent–Africa Platform Symposium, Centre of EU Studies (CEUS) Ghent University, 9th December 2016). Available via Yentyl Williams, 'The Caribbean-EU EPA – Lessons for African-EU EPAs' (*YouTube*, 10 January 2017), https://youtube.com/watch?v=VN9Xl2InTcQ.

[16] Caribbean Community (CARICOM) Dominican Republic Free Trade Act 2001.

[17] Bruce Byiers and Quentin de Roquefeuil, 'Monitoring Regional Integration in Practice: Reflections from the EU-CARIFORUM Economic Partnership Agreement' in Philippe De Lombaerde and Edgar J Saucedo Acosta (eds), *Indicator-Based Monitoring of Regional Economic Integration: Fourth World Report on Regional Integration* (Springer, 2017) 185.

[18] Williams, 'Shifting Between Hegemony and Dominance?' (n 9).

[19] 'Structural foreign policy can be defined as a policy which, conducted over the long term, seeks to influence and shape sustainable political, legal, economic, social, and security structures on various relevant levels (from the individual to the global level), with the degree of internalisation influencing this sustainability.' Stephan Keukeleire, *Structural Foreign Policy* (forthcoming), cited in Williams, 'Shifting Between Hegemony and Dominance?' (n 9) 7. See, more generally, Stephan Keukeleire and Tom Delreux, *The Foreign Policy of the European Union* (Routledge, 2014).

impetus to deepen regional integration.[20] According to a former CARIFORUM negotiator, the new CARIFORUM grouping 'has effectively overhauled the CARICOM–Dominican Republic FTA and replaced it with a more dynamic and ambitious arrangement'.[21] It supports the suggestion that the CARIFORUM group is tailor-made, since the EU conveyed its strategic interest to negotiate with the CARIFORUM grouping, as opposed to the pre-existing CARICOM grouping, based on a number of (economic) factors.[22] Some of these facts may go unnoticed since there is sparse literature on CARIFORUM's history and how the EU has incentivised the formation of the CARIFORUM group. The EPA also offers an opportunity to deepen intra-regional integration. This has been expressed both within the preamble of the EPA and as one of the objectives of the Agreement:

> Promoting regional integration, economic cooperation and good governance thus establishing and implementing an effective, predictable and transparent regulatory framework for trade and investment between the Parties *and* in the CARIFORUM region (Article 1.b, emphasis added).

Importantly, it is not just the inter-regional element which is the focus of integration, but Article 1.b foregrounds CARIFORUM's own intra-regional integration alongside the trade commitments between the EU and CARIFORUM. The de facto existence of the CARIFORUM group overcomes some pre-existing tensions between the Dominican Republic and CARICOM, arising from the linguistic, cultural, and historic 'mutual incomprehension' of the former as a Spanish-speaking country and the latter as its anglophone counterpart.[23] It also seeks to spur integration beyond the historic weight of its trade structures, wherein flows are significantly skewed towards each parties' former colonial centres – Spain and the UK, respectively. For example, within the period of 10 years of the EU–CARIFORUM EPA, Dominican Republic exports to Spain, as its entry point into the EU market, totalled USD 138 million, while trade statistics between the Dominican Republic and CARICOM are not compiled, and are piecemeal.[24] CARICOM exports to the UK were at a value of USD 507 million,[25] and following the UK's exit from the EU in 2020, Spain became the number one

[20] Williams, 'The Caribbean-EU EPA' (n 15).

[21] Junior Lodge, 'A Trade Partnership for Sustainable Development' in Americo Zampetti and Junior Lodge (eds), *The CARIFORUM-EU Economic Partnership Agreement: A Practitioners' Analysis* (Kluwer Law International BV, 2011) 32–34, in Williams, 'Shifting Between Hegemony and Dominance?' (n 9) 26.

[22] Williams, 'The Caribbean-EU EPA' (n 15).

[23] ibid.

[24] These are 2019 statistics after 10 years of EPA implementation. In 2024, this was USD 130m. Trading Economics, 'Dominican Republic Exports to Spain was US$129.92 Million during 2024' (*UN COMTRADE*, 2024), https://tradingeconomics.com/dominican-republic/exports/spain.

[25] Similarly, these are 2019 statistics, but in general, there is no aggregated CARICOM data on exports to the UK. See 'The Caribbean Trade with Europe Moving into a New Era' (*CARICOM Today*, 25 June 2020), https://today.caricom.org/2020/06/25/the-caribbeans-trade-with-europe-moving-into-a-new-era/.

export destination, accounting for 17 per cent of CARICOM exports into the EU. Tensions concerning the Dominican Republic's migration policies towards its Haitian neighbour and Haitian descendants who work there have been used as a stick against the Dominican Republic's accession bid to CARICOM.[26] This gives an overview of a fragmented region, where historical structural relations bear down heavily on regional integration impetuses. Nonetheless, through the EU's consistent, and now post-colonial, relations with the region, it has been able to influence and forge a deeper level of integration in the region, via the EPA, than that previously achieved.

This overview has shown that the CARIFORUM grouping ought to be considered as a complex yet united 'tailor-made' entity, for the purpose of achieving the sustainable development objectives of the EPA. It has also been shown that the external influence from the EU was needed in order to speed up a process of intra-regional integration with the CARICOM–Dominican Republic FTA that had arguably stalled.[27] The following sections assess the monitoring and evaluation of the EPA more than a decade on.

4.2 MONITORING AND EVALUATING THE EPA AND ITS INSTITUTIONS

Much has been written about the monitoring and evaluation of the EPA, both at the time of negotiation (2008) and the review phases (2015 and 2020).[11] A large part of the literature focuses generally on the monitoring of the agreement, and a few works offer a detailed account of the IP commitments.[28] This section will discuss the issues relating to the monitoring and evaluation of the EPA, de jure and de facto, and then focus on the specific nature of the IP commitments of the EPA.

4.2.1 Monitoring the EPA De Jure: Article 5

The Joint Declaration on the Signing of the EPA reinforces the nature of monitoring, which is not just continuous within the meaning of Article 5, but also comprehensive, as stated therein.[29] A closer look at the methodological approaches

[26] CARICOM, 'Crisis Related to Dominicans of Haitian Descent and Haitian Migrants in the Dominican Republic' (13 October 2015), https://caricom.org/crisis-related-to-dominicans-of-haitian-descent-and-haitian-migrants-in-the-dominican-republic/.

[27] CARICOM Dominican Republic FTA (n 16).

[28] 'EPA Negotiations: State of Play and Strategic Considerations for the Way Forward' (South Centre, February 2008) 10, http://southcentre.org/publications/AnalyticalNotes/Other/2008Feb_State_of_Play_and_Way_Forward.pdf. See also Lodge, 'A Trade Partnership for Sustainable Development' (n 21).

[29] Joint Declaration on the Signing of the Economic Partnership Agreement [2008] OJ L289/1953, 1955.

and sectors covered in the review sheds light on what a comprehensive review may look like. It is also expected that such a review would necessarily take into consideration the costs and consequences of implementing the Agreement, as well as including recommendations vis-à-vis any adjustments that may be necessary. A key prerequisite of understanding the impact of the Agreement, as stated therein, lies with understanding the link between monitoring and the objectives of the EPA.

This section sets out the importance of Article 5 on monitoring, in conjunction with its reference to achieving the objectives of the Agreement, namely its linkage to Article 1 of the EPA. It underscores that 'proper implementation' of the EPA will ensure that the benefits for the people of both regions can not only be reaped, but 'maximised'.

Article 1 sets the intention of both parties to conduct a trading relationship aimed globally at poverty reduction and eradication (Article 1.a), *inter*-regional integration (Article 1.b), and to develop a new inter-regional trade and investment dynamic between the EU and CARIFORUM (Article 1.f). Specifically, at the CARIFORUM level, fostering integration into the world economy (Article 1.c), improved trade capacity (Article 1.d), and enhancing supply-side capacity (Article 1.e) are the aims set out. This comprehensively ties together the ambitious intentions of the drafters of the EPA, wherein monitoring EPA implementation is set out as a means to achieve the ends (objectives). Yet, without obligations with regard to monitoring, it can be inferred that the current wording of Article 5 merely relies on the parties' goodwill. Monitoring the EPA was not conceived as an ad hoc activity; rather, it was written into Article 5 of the EPA:

> The Parties undertake to *monitor continuously* the operation of the Agreement through their *respective participative processes and institutions, as well as those set up under this Agreement*, in order to ensure that the *objectives* of the Agreement are realised, the Agreement is *properly implemented* and the *benefits* for men, women, young people and children deriving from their Partnership are *maximised*. The Parties also undertake to consult each other promptly over any problem that may arise.[30]

Within the meaning of Article 5, monitoring must be a continuous process, via 'participative processes and institutions'. These include participative processes via the Consultative Committee, and institutions such as the Joint Council created under Part V of the EPA (amongst others discussed below). The final line of this Article 5 encourages consultation amongst the parties, and hence it underscores that this participative approach is expected to overcome any problems in implementation through consultative deliberation. This creates

[30] Emphasis added. Economic Partnership Agreement between the CARIFORUM States, of the one part, and the European Community and its Member States, of the other part [2008] OJ L289 (hereinafter 'EU–CARIFORUM EPA'), art 5.

a virtuous circle of consultation and participative processes with the aim of maximising the benefits of the EPA. Additionally, the Joint Declaration on the Signing of the EPA provides for

> *comprehensive review* of the Agreement [to] be undertaken *not later than five (5) years* after the date of signature and at subsequent *five-yearly intervals*, in order to determine the *impact* of the Agreement, including the *costs and consequences* of implementation and we undertake to *amend its provisions and adjust their application as necessary*[31] (emphasis added).

Yet, the wording of Article 5 – relying on the goodwill of the parties to ensure that it is continuous, participative, and beneficial for the peoples of the regions – may have contributed to the current state of play of the monitoring of EPA implementation and the lack of an enforceable monitoring mechanism today.

Existing literature on participative processes within the EU–ACP partnership, particularly in relation to deliberations at the EU–ACP Joint Parliamentary Assembly,[32] is valuable for assessing deliberation amongst EPA institutions more generally. Although the aim is not necessarily to assess deliberation here, it offers an insight into how the intentions of Article 5 may be achieved by way of aiming for an ideal type of deliberation whereby consultative and participative processes are mandated within the Agreement. For example, procedurally, deliberation can set the scene for an equal debate even where the relationship is asymmetrical.[33] Substantially, it offers an opportunity for divergent views and interests to engage in constructive debate.[34] This would prove beneficial in EU–ACP relations whereby there are power asymmetries, and tensions around some aspects of implementing both the pre-existing partnership agreements and the current EPA (as will be explored further below). In addition, deliberation can be assessed in relation to at least five criteria: (i) inclusiveness with regard to participation; (ii) openness with regard to views represented; (iii) consideration of the societal common good; (iv) contribution to constructive politics; and (v) the ability of the rules of procedures to neutralise power imbalances.[35] More generally, understanding how effectively deliberation takes place allows for broader assessments of the EU as a trade and development partner to Third

[31] Joint Declaration (n 29).

[32] Sarah Delputte and Yentyl Williams, 'Equal Partnership Between Unequal Regions? Assessing Deliberative Parliamentary Debate in ACP-EU Relations' (2016) 1(4) *Third World Thematics* 490–507. See also Sarah Delputte and Yentyl Williams, 'Equal Partnership between Unequal Regions? Assessing Deliberative Parliamentary Debate in ACP-EU Relations' in Mark Langan and Sophia Price (eds), *Sustainable Development in Africa-EU Relations* (Routledge 2018) and Sarah Delputte and Yentyl Williams, 'Parliamentary Deliberation in Inter-regional Relations: Insights from the ACP-EU JPA' in Kolja Raube, Meltem Müftüler-Baç, and Jan Wouters (eds), *Parliamentary Cooperation and Diplomacy in EU External Relations* (Edward Elgar, 2019) 373–86.

[33] Delputte and Williams, 'Equal Partnership' (n 32) 493.

[34] ibid.

[35] ibid 493–94.

World countries.[36] Critically, it allows for an interrogation into how the institutional mechanism of formalism – international organisations, treaties, and laws[37] – continues to shape the EU's relationship with its former colonies, in this current post-colonial trade relationship. It can also expose opportunities to forge inclusive sustainable development based on the tripartite principle of integration.[38]

The next section discusses the monitoring of the EPA in practice, with reference to the five- and ten-year review processes. The overview of the legal text here is intended to provide a contextualisation of the sustainable development intentions of the drafters of the EPA,[39] from which the practice of monitoring the Agreement's implementation can be further understood.

4.2.2 Monitoring the EPA in Practice: The Five- and Ten-year Reviews

Since the conclusion of the EPA in 2008, two sets of reviews have taken place marking the Agreement's fifth and tenth years of implementation. This section provides an overview of the reviews, and explains how the sectors for analysis are chosen, as well as the evaluative tools used and the methodology of the report. This overview sheds light on the data included in the report, the relationship between the five- and ten-year reviews, and, eventually, any omissions within the reports.

4.2.2.1 Methodology, Evaluative Tools and Sector Analysis

The first five-year review was a joint exercise conducted by a four-person team of EU and Caribbean experts and funded by the EU.[40] Entitled *Monitoring the Implementation & Results of the Cariforum–EU EPA* (hereinafter the 'joint five-year review'), it was published in September 2014, and its analysis covered the

[36] The above-mentioned work on deliberation has been cited in several assessments of the EU's development approach, including Jan Orbie, 'The Graduation of EU Development Studies: Towards a Post-colonial Turn?' (2021) 7(4) *Global Affairs* 597–613; Johanne Døhlie Saltnes and Sebastian Steingass, 'Fit for Creating Partnerships of Equals with the Global South? Tensions in the EU's Development Policy Post-2020' (2021) 7(4) *Global Affairs* 523–40'; Mark Langan and Sophia Price, 'The EU and "Pro-Poor" Contributions to Sustainable Development in the post-2015 Consensus' (2016) 1(4) *Third World Thematics* 431–36.

[37] Ruth Okediji, 'The International Relations of Intellectual Property: Narratives of Developing Country Participation in the Global Intellectual Property System' (2003) 7 *Singapore Journal of International & Comparative Law* 315. See ch 2 (nn 82 and 87).

[38] Inter and intra-generational, and equitable dialogue, as set out by Ortino in ch 1. See Federico Ortino, 'Investment Treaties, Sustainable Development and Reasonableness Review: A Case Against Strict Proportionality Balancing' (2017) 30(1) *Leiden Journal of International Law* 83.

[39] See ch 1, n 8.

[40] The project team included Ranjit Singh, Keisha-Ann Thompson, Sacha Peter Silva, and Paul Hare on the EU side. Funding was provided by the EU, and the project was implemented by the consultancy B&S Europe. European Commission, *Monitoring the Implementation* (n 4).

period 2008–13. The joint five-year review's approach and sectoral analysis is set out around three questions that the review's authors posed:

1. Are the provisions of the EPA being complied with?
2. What is the quantitative and qualitative impact of the EPA in relation to the objectives and principles set out therein?
3. What are the key issues of the five-year review and their potential to improve implementation?[41]

The methodological approach adopted draws from the EU's Sustainable Impact Assessment's priority-setting approach, which focuses on the economic, environmental, and social impacts on sectors of the Agreement, with a focus on areas that have a marked difference in status from pre-EPA implementation.[42] In addition, priority sectors were also drawn from those raised in negotiations and stakeholder consultations.[43] While the study does evaluate all areas of the EPA, the analysis differs in depth and detail.

From the fore, the authors underline that the Agreement 'represents a major and complex milestone'.[44] They also underline that any part of the agreement could be its own stand-alone study, given the breadth of the EPA, and the fact that it is 'one part of a much larger trade and development toolbox available to EU and CARIFORUM policymakers'.[45] Unsurprisingly, there are a number of limitations, given the extensive scope of the EPA. The authors highlight in particular, that it is

> nearly impossible to separate clearly [the 'wide spectrum of sectors, stakeholders and variables — economic, social and political'], particularly in a context of two highly diverse economic integration initiatives (the EU and CARIFORUM), and a time period which saw significant upheaval at the global, regional and national level.[46]

Hence, they note from the outset that the study presents a limited perspective on the EPA and its potential impact.[47] The methodological approach included extensive desk research and primary data collection (in-person field research,[48] phone and email interviews, questionnaires) with EU and Caribbean stakeholders

[41] European Commission, *Monitoring the Implementation* (n 4).

[42] Additionally, the authors have pragmatically, where relevant, referred to the following groupings of countries within the review: 'the big four', which comprises Barbados, the Dominican Republic, Jamaica, and Trinidad and Tobago; the 'small economies' of the Organisation of Eastern Caribbean States of Antigua and Barbuda, Saint Kitts and Nevis, as well as the Windward Islands of Dominica, Grenada, Saint Lucia, and Saint Vincent and the Grenadines); the 'mainland countries' of Belize, Guyana, Suriname; and lastly, Haiti. This approach draws on the earlier 2004 Sustainability Impact Assessment, which also uses the same references.

[43] European Commission, *Monitoring the Implementation* (n 4) 4.

[44] ibid 2.

[45] ibid 4.

[46] ibid.

[47] ibid.

[48] Antigua and Barbuda, Barbados, Belize, Brussels, Dominica, the Dominican Republic, Guyana, Jamaica, Saint Lucia, Suriname, and Trinidad and Tobago.

(public officials from national and regional organisations, private and civil society representatives, and trade experts) between 2013 and 2014.[49]

The second period of review has, notably, taken a different approach, as separate reviews have been conducted by each party. The EU conducted its own ten-year review, drawn up by a five-person team of EU consultants and funded by the EU.[50] This study, referred to as the *Ex-post Evaluation of the Economic Partnership Agreement (EPA) between the European Union and CARIFORUM* (hereinafter the *EU* ten-year review), was published in March 2021 and reviews the period 2008–18. The EU's ten-year review is based on a combination of reviews of primary data, including trade literature and data, economic modelling, sector-specific case studies, and data from 200 stakeholder consultations.[51] It focuses on the following sectoral analyses: overview of EPA implementation, results of development co-operation, economic impact, sustainability impact, and four case studies – CARIFORUM's cultural and creative industries, beverage export from CARIFORUM countries, EU foreign direct investment (FDI) in the Caribbean tourism sector, and EU dairy exports under the EPA.

On the CARIFORUM side, the report, the *Consultancy to Prepare Technical Position Paper on CARIFORUM's priorities for the Second Five Year Review of the CARIFORUM–EU EPA* (hereinafter the 'interim CARIFORUM ten-year review'), was published on 13 December 2020 and financed by the EU.[52] The interim CARIFORUM review responds to the Terms of Reference for the consultancy to provide a technical paper, and to conduct two sets of stakeholder consultations. It was drawn up by one of the region's top international law and trade consultants, Audel Cunningham, and it sets out the CARIFORUM group's priorities in light of the second review exercise. The resulting methodological approach is one that draws both on a review of literature and on stakeholder consultations. The interim CARIFORUM review focuses on five issues: trade in goods, trade in services, development co-operation, Cotonou and post-Cotonou implications, and subject-specific review issues. These have been drawn up taking into consideration the priorities of the CARIFORUM Council of Ministers, and the EU's proposal of priorities for the joint review,[53] between which there is considerable overlap.[54]

[49] The full list of stakeholders is included in Annex II: European Commission, *Monitoring the Implementation* (n 4) 128.

[50] Nora Plaisier, Tahmina Shafique, Michael Fuenfzig, David Luff, and Simone Snoeijenbos are the authors of the EU's 10-year report, prepared by Ecorys and Appleton Luff consulting agencies: European Commission, *Ex-Post Evaluation* (n 4).

[51] ibid 12.

[52] Cunningham, 'Consultancy to Prepare Technical Position Paper' (n 4).

[53] These include: The EPA and CARIFORUM's Development Imperatives; CARIFORUM–EU Trade Performance; Outstanding Issues from the 2015 Review of the CARIFORUM–EU EPA; Challenges converting Market Access into Market Presence – Good and Services; Status of Implementation of Commitments; Matters to be Negotiated/Re-Negotiated; and Unresolved Issues at the Level of the Joint Institutions. This joint review focuses on: Trade in Goods; Trade in Services; Trade Related Issues; Development Cooperation; and Institutional and Horizontal Matters. Cunningham, 'Consultancy to Prepare Technical Position Paper' (n 4) 10.

[54] ibid.

Already, the difference of approach between the five- and ten-year reviews is discernible: whereas the five-year review was a joint exercise, the ten-year reviews were conducted separately; the EU's ten-year review is an 'ex-post evaluation', whereas the interim CARIFORUM review is a report intended to prepare the CARIFORUM side for the ten-year review; all review exercises have, nonetheless, been financed by the EU, which would be in line with its development co-operation commitments via the European Development Fund (EDF). While it is notable that there is overlap between the sectors covered and the methodological approaches (technical reporting with economic modelling, as well as stakeholder consultations), there has not been a clear and consistent methodological approach adopted from the first era of review and the second, or an explanation as to the different methodological approaches adopted.

The reviews generally have the objective of evaluating the implementation of the EPA and to what extent the EPA contributes to the objectives set out therein. In so doing, the reports typically outline the effectiveness and efficiency of EPA implementation, where bottlenecks may lie, and the coherence of the EPA to other policy agendas.

The EU's ten-year review of the CARIFORUM EPA has opted for, and demonstrates, a preference for a 'theory of change' model, similar to SADC EPA monitoring system. Nick Charalambides, director of Imani Development, who designed the SADC EPA monitoring and evaluation system, has explained how a theory-of-change approach is capable of assessing the usage of the EPA, namely by tracing the results of its implementation, use, outcome, and impacts. A brief overview of the approach taken by the SADC region is informative here. Charalambides notes that:

> A monitoring system must alert implementers as to whether users are actually taking advantage of the agreement provisions and if not, why not. If this is not picked up and addressed early enough in the implementation process (through the provision of advisory services and support) the agreement is likely to fail.[55]

Charalambides outlines an issue which is not stated as overtly in CARIFORM cases, but may be as equally true:

> the SADC region has inherited an approach to trade negotiation and agreement, which suits other contexts, such as America, China or Europe, where trade law, technical specification and standards have a long history . . . more emphasis and resources need to be invested in the design and operationalisation of trade agreements.[56]

Within this theory-of-change methodology, the EPA implementation is, therefore, the intervention that is expected to bring about the objectives of the EPA, which is the change sought by both parties. Within this methodology, as

[55] 'Interview with Dr Nicholas Charalambides' (n 1).
[56] ibid.

is generally expected in monitoring processes, the importance of stakeholder buy-in is key, and therefore, to this end, education, sensitisation, and motivating stakeholders is a key part of achieving the objectives of the Agreement, namely allowing the change to manifest. If implementation is to benefit the peoples of both regions – that is, the post-colonial guarantees sought *through* law – as set out in Article 5, it seems that adopting a theory of change which speaks specifically to the social impact of the Agreement in a context-specific manner is vital. In this regard, the earlier concluded CARIFORUM–EU EPA can borrow from the intentions of the SADC–EU EPA monitoring process.

The principle of the theory of change will be considered in the subsequent analysis of the reviews. The next section draws on the five-year review's five issues of ratification; support to EPA implementation units (national and regional); private sector support; and establishing the TDC sub-committee and Consultative committee and the joint mechanism. These provide a springboard from which the broad topics of trade in goods or services can be discussed, and importantly they deal with the foundational issues of the EPA's obligations, institutions, and processes. The issue of ratification will be discussed in this section, whereas EPA implementation and private sector support will be discussed under financing EPA implementation, and the joint institutions will be discussed under institutional arrangements of the Agreement. The monitoring mechanism is discussed throughout, alongside the sectoral issues identified in the two ten-year reviews.

4.2.3 Implementation and the Issue of Ratification

Although the Agreement was signed in 2008, by the first five-year review only seven of the 15 CARIFORUM countries and 16 of the 28 EU countries had ratified the Agreement. By the ten-year review, the number of states that had ratified rose to 10 of the 15 CARIFORUM states and 25 of the 28 EU Member States.[57] Ratification is an essential part of taking the necessary steps towards implementing any trade agreement. The speed at which ratification is done, therefore, must also be assessed as reflecting the engagement of parties to implement the Agreement. At the stage of the five-year review, it was underlined that Article 243(3) EPA sets a deadline for provisional application of the EPA, although several CARIFORUM states' legal systems (Antigua and Barbuda, Dominican Republic, and Suriname) do not allow for such application. The EU's ten-year report noted that ratification

[57] Notifications are pending for the following countries: Luxembourg, Hungary, Poland, and Slovenia on the EU side, and the Bahamas, Haiti, Jamaica, Suriname, and Trinidad and Tobago on the CARIFORUM side. Commission, *Ex-Post Evaluation* (n 4) 27. All CARIFORUM states, with the exception of Haiti, have provisionally applied the EPA since 2008. See Commission, *EU Aid for Trade Progress Report 2020: Review of Progress on the Implementation of the Updated EU Aid for Trade Strategy of 2017* (Publications Office, 2020) 174–76.

was at 79 per cent of all parties to the EPA.[58] More recent data shows that the Agreement has entered into force for all states.[59]

4.3 JOINT INSTITUTIONS

While monitoring must be undertaken, it must be done by both parties' respective institutions as well as the joint institutions. The duality between respective institutions and joint ones is an issue that is central to this chapter. Four joint institutions have been set up in line with the provisions of the EPA: the Joint CARIFORUM–EU Council (Article 227); the CARIFORUM–EU Trade and Development Committee (TDC, Article 30); the CARIFORUM–EU Parliamentary Committee (Article 231) and the CARIFORUM–EU Consultative Committee (Article 232). Besides the formal joint institutions, sub-committees and special committees may be established to support EPA implementation. For example, there is a special committee on customs co-operation and trade facilitation, and there is a sub-committee to assist the TDC.

The five-year review notes that the EPA emphasises the establishment of a regular dialogue to support both regions' mutual knowledge and understanding (as indicated in the preamble of the EPA).[60] It also considers the input from consultation that, in light of ongoing exchanges, the scope and quality of dialogue can be enhanced. Equally, the EU ten-year review also highlights the need to boost capacity for enhanced political and technical dialogue, for more solution-oriented outcomes (recommendation number 5 of 12). While the interim CARIFORUM report has highlighted unresolved issues relating to the joint institutions as a priority area for CARIFORUM ministers, the report does not delve into detail on this. On this backdrop, the following section considers the processes of implementation and dialogue within the joint institutions, both de jure and de facto. It specifically provides an overview of the four joint institutions (Articles 227–32).

4.3.1 The Joint CARIFORUM–EU Council (Articles 227–29)

The Joint CARIFORUM–EU Council is a ministerial body that meets at regular intervals to monitor the implementation of the EPA (Article 227.1) It is composed of members of both the Council of the EU and the European Commission (EC),

[58] Commission, *Ex-Post Evaluation* (n 4).

[59] 'When no dates are specified, the dates shown in "Entry into Force" (above left) and "Signature" (above right) apply, except in the case of acceding Parties.' In 'Economic Partnership Agreement between the CARIFORUM States, of the one part, and the European Community and its Member States, of the other part', https://consilium.europa.eu/en/documents-publications/treaties-agreements/agreement/?id=2008034.

[60] It contextualises this in contrast to the Cotonou era of relations. Commission, *Monitoring the Implementation* (n 4) 12.

as well as representatives of CARIFORUM states (Article 228.1) and a designated representative to act on behalf of all of CARIFORUM (Article 228.2). This body provides reports to the Council of Ministers in line with Article 15 Cotonou Agreement (Article 228.4).[61] Cotonou Article 15 set out that the Council's function is to conduct political dialogue (Article 15(2)(a); to adopt policy guidelines for the implementation of the provisions of the Agreement (Article 15(2)(b); and to examine any issues that might hamper the implementation of the Agreement and its objectives (Article 15(2)(c)).

Under this provision, and without prejudice to the pre-existing arrangements under Cotonou Article 15, the Joint Council is responsible particularly for the operation and implementation of the Agreement, including issues that may arise in the process of implementation, whether at the bilateral, multilateral, or international levels, in order to fulfil the objectives of the Agreement (Article 227.2). The Joint Council can take legally binding decisions on any matter of the EPA in the aim of fulfilling the objectives of the Agreement (Article 229.1), and these decisions are legally binding for both parties (Article 229.2). Additionally, the Joint Council can make recommendations (Article 229.3). The Joint Council can also assess proposals and recommendations coming from the signatory parties (Article 227.3). It is noted that, where CARIFORUM states act collectively, the Joint Council can adopt a decision or recommendation by a mutual agreement (Article 229.4). Where a decision is not taken collectively by the CARIFORUM states, adoption of the agreement is required (Article 229.4). This non-binding wording and provision, which addresses CARIFORUM's (dis)unity, underscores the institutional differences and robustness in EU and CARIFORUM functioning. Whereas the EU has a very robust institutional structure, this latter provision specifically speaks to the needs of CARIFORUM states, whether they act collectively or separately. There is, of course, no equivalent provision for the EU, since the European Commission is responsible for the EU's Common Commercial Policy (Article 207 Treaty on European Union (TEU)). This clause, in effect, is pragmatic vis-à-vis the institutional differences between the CARIFORUM and the EU.

As a ministerial body, the Joint Council may suffer from a political weakness, given that governments can change every five years, on average, at election time. This can impact on the implementation of the Agreement. In the case of the UK, it seems that Brexit offered an opportunity for further strengthening UK–CARIFORUM relations.[62] Furthermore, given that the UK has been a key partner for CARIFORUM countries and EPA implementation previously, there

[61] See ch 3 (n 30). The Cotonou Agreement (Partnership agreement 2000/483/EC between the members of the African, Caribbean and Pacific Group of States of the one part, and the European Community and its Member States, of the other part, signed in Cotonou on 23 June 2000 – Protocols – Final Act – Declarations [2020] OJ L317, 3–353) preceded the EPA.

[62] See Economic Partnership Agreement between the CARIFORUM States, of the one part, and the United Kingdom of Great Britain and Northern Ireland, of the other part [MS No.18/2019], Foreign and Commonwealth Office, 22 May 2019.

is a substantial expectation that the UK–CARIFORUM EPA will benefit both parties.[63] In the case of EU27, while Germany has proved its support to the EPA bilaterally via the Germany Development Agency (GIZ), other EU countries must now also step in to fill the gap created by the UK.

Although meetings should be held at regular intervals, there was a hiatus of two to three years between the each of the second (Brussels, 26 October 2012), third (Georgetown, 16 July 2015),[64] and fourth (Brussels, 17 November 2017) Joint Council meetings.[65] Notwithstanding the time lapse between the meetings, the minutes of the Joint Council are important sources, at the highest level of the contentious issues that arise in the implementation of the Agreement.

Two issues of relevance to this analysis on monitoring and its linkage to the objectives of the Agreement, amongst others, have been raised at the Council meetings. At the second Joint Council meeting, the issue of 'differentiation' – that is, the process the EU uses to differentiate the development assistance provided[66] – was raised within the context of EU Development Assistance.[67] CARIFORUM states argued that GDP per capita is not an appropriate sole indicator to be considered for differentiation. Rather, other factors should be taken into consideration, such as levels of poverty, risk of vulnerability, climate change, and shocks from natural disasters. Although there was mention from the EU side that internal consultations are under way on the issue, it was equally stated that the EU has no intention to change the level of co-operation with CARIFORUM countries. This is a strong signal, at ministerial level, that what was negotiated within the EPA, and beyond Cotonou, sets the stage for the parties' new relationship. While it may seem that this is an issue that should have been raised at negotiation stage and not ex post at implementation stage, the Joint Declaration does refer to amendment of provisions where necessary. Yet, de facto, even if the Joint Council has the powers to make legally binding

[63] UK FCDO, UK–CARIFORUM EPA (Zoom conference, 13 June 2023).

[64] 'Joint Communiqué: Third Meeting of the Joint CARIFORUM-EU Council' (*MICM*, 16 July 2015), https://micm.gob.do/images/pdf/direcciones/comercio-exterior/Joint-Communique-Tercera-Reunion-del-Consejo-Conjunto-EPA---CARIFORUM.pdf.

[65] 'Minutes of the Fourth Meeting of the Joint CARIFORUM-EU Council' (*Parlament*, 17 November 2017), https://.parlament.gv.at/PAKT/EU/XXVI/EU/04/11/EU_41137/imfname_10852841.pdf.

[66] For more on differentiation policy, see Brecht Lein, Florian Krätke, Jeske van Seters, Niels Keijzer, and Annita Montoute, 'Differentiation in ACP-EU Cooperation: Implications of the EU's Agenda for Change for the 11th EDF and Beyond' (*ECDPM*, 2 October 2012), https://ecdpm.org/wp-content/uploads/2013/10/DP-134-ACP-EU-Cooperation-Implications-EU-Agenda-Change-11-EDF-2012.pdf; European Parliament, Directorate-General for External Policies of the Union, Josep Coll, *Criteria for Differentiation and Methods for Phasing out EU's Development Cooperation in light of the Commission's Proposal for a Development Cooperation Instrument (DCI) for 2014–2020* (Publications Office, 2012); and Svea Koch, 'From Poverty Reduction to Mutual Interests? The Debate in Differentiation in EU Development Policy' (DIE–GDI, 2013), https://die-gdi.de/en/briefing-paper/article/from-poverty-reduction-to-mutual-interests-the-debate-on-differentiation-in-eu-development-policy/.

[67] 'Joint Communiqué' (n 64).

decisions, these must nevertheless be jointly agreed. In this example, the EU does not support the claims of CARIFORUM countries for differentiation, despite the opportunities of deliberation.[68] Nonetheless, the CARIFORUM side has repeated its call for differentiation in subsequent Joint Council meetings,[69] as part of the deliberative exchange within the institution.

A second case in point is that the CARIFORUM side has expressed that revenue losses and the trade deficit resulting from EPA implementation were not offset by financial and technical support provided by the EU.[70] The CARIFORUM side specifically highlighted that, in order to overcome capacity constraints, additional support should be granted via the Regional Indicative Programme (RIP) of the European Development Fund (EDF), as one possible avenue for support. The EU, in turn, highlighted that almost 2 billion euros was provided from the 10th and 11th EDF over two five-year programming cycles, of which 160 million euros was via the RIP. Yet, broken down, these financial envelopes are actually quite small. For example, the programme of support to the implementation of the EPA Sanitary and Phyto-sanitary (SPS) measures, which aims to increase compliance with international standards, is to be implemented by the Inter-American Institute for Cooperation on Agriculture (IICA) over three years and receives 1.25 million euros.[71] For an issue that has long been signalled as an obstacle to enhanced EU–Caribbean trade, this budget, over three years, does not seem proportional. In addition, standby facilities that support both EPA and Caribbean Single Market and Economy (CSME) implementation at the national levels receive 8.75 million euros over four and a half years, and are managed by the Caribbean Development Bank (CDB). Over a four-year period, across CARIFORUM countries, this budget is broken down significantly.[72]

Despite commitments to promote mutual understanding and to boost CARIFORUM's trade policy, as set out in the Joint Declaration and EPA objectives, respectively, it is clear that there is a discrepancy between de jure commitments and de facto actions. In this regard, the minutes of this joint institution, amongst others, provide ample evidence of the issues subject to dialogical engagement that plague effective implementation of the Agreement. They also supply ample evidence of the divergent views which may have led to separate ten-year reviews of EPA monitoring and evaluation.

[68] Recall the five criteria for deliberation: Delputte and Williams, 'Equal Partnership' (n 32) 493–94.

[69] 'Joint Communiqué' (n 64) 11. Within the context of Brexit, it seems that, if this is an issue that the UK can be lenient on, it may further deepen the cleavage between UK and EU trading relations with CARIFORUM, wherein the UK would effectively be regarded as a partner who truly takes into consideration the developmental needs of the CARIFORUM bloc.

[70] ibid 8.

[71] Commission, *EU Aid for Trade* (n 57) 54–55.

[72] ibid.

4.3.2 The CARIFORUM–EU Trade and Development Committee (TDC, Article 230)

The TDC is composed of senior officials from both parties, and it is entrusted with assisting the Joint Council, to whom it also reports (Article 230.1). On the EU side, a director of the Directorate-General for Trade at the European Commission may co-chair. On the CARIFORUM side, the director of the Cariforum Directorate is mandated to represent the CARIFORUM states (Article 230.1) Any party may raise any issue concerning the implementation of the Agreement and the fulfilment of its objectives (Article 230.1). The TDC is tasked with a number of roles specifically related to trade: monitoring implementation and making recommendations in this regard (Article 230.3.a.i); evaluating results of implementation (Article 230.3.a.ii); dispute resolution (Article 230.3.a.iii); assisting the Joint Council (Article 230.3.a.iv); overseeing regional integration, economic, and trade relations (Article 230.3.a.v); assessing the implementation in relation to sustainable development (Article 230.3.a.vi); acting upon areas that facilitate opportunities relating to trade, investment, and business (Article 230.3.a.vii); and raising issues that impact on attaining the objectives of the EPA (Article 230.3.a.viii). In relation to development, the TDC is specifically tasked with: assisting the Joint Council in relation to development co-operation (Article 230.3.b.i); monitoring implementation and actions with third-party donors (Article 230.3.b.ii); provision of recommendations in the area of trade-related co-operation (Article 230.3.b.iii); periodic reviews of the EPA, including the addition of new priorities as deemed appropriate (Article 230.3.b.iv); and revision of co-operation in the area of regional integration and its implementation (Article 230.3.b.v).

The establishment and oversight of the special sub-committees falls within the competence of the TDC (Article 230.4.a). Besides establishing the sub-committee, the TDC is, importantly, competent with regard to its composition, duties, and rules of procedure (Article 230.4.a). This gives specific powers to the TDC not only to appoint members to the sub-committee, but to dictate the times they must meet (Article 230.4.b), and the issues to be discussed and actions to be taken (Article 230.4.c), in such a manner as to give effect to the objectives of the Agreement. Where the power to take a decision or to furnish a recommendation is delegated by the Joint Council, the TDC follows the conditions of the above-mentioned Article 229.4, according to whether CARIFORUM states act collectively or separately. In general, the TDC meets annually on a rotating basis between the regions and discusses the issues of trade and development (Article 230.3a and b) within this setting (Article 230.5). It is an interesting fact that the TDC established the rules of procedure of the special sub-committees, which must be viewed, therefore, as bodies that execute the intentions of the TDC. In comparison, both the Joint Council and TDC establish their own rules of procedures (Article 228.3 and Article 230.2). Although the data is not publicly available, it is questionable as to whether the experts appointed perceive this as helpful or a hindrance to their functioning as a sub-committee.

The TDC, importantly, reports to the Joint Council. At the fourth meeting of the Joint Council in Brussels, on 17 November 2017, the TDC reported several vital points in relation to the implementation of the Agreement and GIs.[73] During the first meeting of the Special Committee on Agriculture and Fisheries, held on 24 October 2017 in Santo Domingo, there was a dedicated meeting on the subject of Gis, to finalise technical discussions on the establishment of a CARIFORUM–EU GI Agreement.[74] The minutes explain that there was progress in the text of the Agreement and the GI specifications therein, and that the final draft of the Agreement would be ready by March 2018.[75] Yet, there is no further public information on this stand-alone agreement today, signalling, in fact, a failure of the deliberative process despite the production of minutes. This impacts on the ability of the EPA to bring about the purported benefits of adopting GI regimes across CARIFORUM countries. The minutes contextualised the significance of the Agreement for the CARIFORUM group:

> The Agreement on GIs will allow CARIFORUM States to take full advantage of the culture and tradition rooted in their products. Their products, with a culturally distinctive background will be able to create value for local communities and support local production and development since Geographical Indications are becoming a beneficial intellectual property right, particularly for developing countries.[76]

In the absence of the CARIFORUM–EU GI Agreement, and notwithstanding several dialogical engagements in this area – such as the CARIFORUM–EU Workshop on Intellectual Property (IP) Tools, Networks and Cooperation held in September 2016[77] – these tangible absences, of both the GI Agreement and a monitoring mechanism, undermine the ability of the EPA to fulfil its promise with regard to the development that GIs can foster. This further undermines the deliberative process which is at the heart of the functioning of these institutions. Nevertheless, there have been some benefits. For example, this regional forum, importantly, allowed for co-production of ideas and discussions between the CARIFORUM and European Union Intellectual Property Office (EUIPO) that led to the identification of collaboration opportunities. In addition, at the 2017 TDC meeting, the EU also reiterated its intention to support the CARIFORUM Directorate's technical operation with a number of the EU's technical institutions,

[73] 'Minutes of the Fourth Meeting' (n 65).
[74] ibid 24.
[75] ibid 23.
[76] ibid.
[77] This regional forum, importantly, allowed for co-production of ideas and discussions between the CARIFORUM and EUIPO that led to the identification of collaboration opportunities. In addition, at the 2017 TDC meeting, the EU also reiterated its intention to support the CARIFORUM Directorate's technical operation with a number of the EU's technical institutions, including the EUIPO.

including the EUIPO.[78] Arguably, this is being followed through via the establishment and support from CarIPI project;[79] that is, in the absence of a stand-alone GI Agreement as set out within the EPA, the participation and open exchange in this forum has led to some advances around advancing the implementation of some of the provisions concerning GIs.

The interim CARIFORUM report draws on the minutes of the eighth and ninth TDC meetings, where CARIFORUM officials presented the progress of the region's tariff commitments.[80] It notes that what was presented at the TDC is at variance with the claims made in the EU report. It also references the TDC to demonstrate where concerns on EPA commitments have been presented by the CARIFORUM party and not heeded by the EU party.[81] It can be gleaned that there is also an important inter-institutional functioning of the institutions, in practice. For example, whereas it may be recommended that the Joint Council suggest that a special sub-committee monitor a relevant aspect of the Agreement, it may also be suggested that the TDC is not an effective stakeholder engagement entity, and thus such responsibilities may be better placed elsewhere.[82] In all three review documents, there is no questioning of the role of the TDC; rather, this institution is referenced in relation to the dialogue therein. This suggests that the TDC is functioning according to its role set out, and that the minutes of meetings provide valuable insight into the functioning of this joint institution, in terms of its compliance with the ambitions of the EPA, its impact, and its use.

4.3.3 The CARIFORUM–EU Parliamentary Committee (Article 231)

The CARIFORUM–EU Parliamentary Committee consists of members of both parties' parliaments, to encourage an exchange of views between CARIFORUM national delegates, on the one hand, and members of the European Parliament, on the other (Article 231.1 and 2). There are 15 members from each side, and on the EU side there is the further requirement that nine of these Members of the European Parliament (MEPs) sit in the Trade Committee and six also sit in the Development Committee.[83] This suggests that the EU side of the Committee has

[78] 'Minutes of the Fourth Meeting' (n 65) 24–26.

[79] Currently, the EU-funded CarIPI project supports CARIFORUM IP offices. It has four objectives: create stronger IP offices offering high-quality, state-of-the-art services to users; ensure availability of effective IPR enforcement mechanisms; contribute to the development of a sustainable and innovative private sector; make doing business between the EU and CARIFORUM, and particularly within the CARIFORUM region, easier. CarIPI, 'CARIFORUM Intellectual Property Rights and Innovation', https://internationalipcooperation.eu/en/caripi.

[80] Cunningham, 'Consultancy to Prepare Technical Position Paper' (n 4) 22.

[81] ibid 40.

[82] ibid 78.

[83] European Parliament, 'DCAR: The Delegation to the CARIFORUM-EU Parliamentary Committee', https://.europarl.europa.eu/delegations/en/dcar/about/introduction.

put this measure in place to strike a balance between MEPs' knowledge, understanding, and engagement on the issues of trade and development broadly, as well as in the specific case of this EPA. The Parliamentary Committee determines when meetings shall be held, and it is expected to co-operate with the Joint Parliamentary Assembly as established under Article 17 of the Cotonou Agreement (Article 231.1). Under Article 17, the role of the EU–ACP Joint Parliamentary Assembly includes the promotion of dialogue and consultation as part of a democratic process; facilitating inter-regional understanding between the peoples of both regions, with specific reference to development issues; and adopting resolutions and providing recommendations to the Council of Ministers aimed at fulfilling the objectives of the Agreement (Article 17(2)). As such, Article 231.1 fosters coherence between the Joint Parliamentary Committee under the EPA and the Joint Parliamentary Assembly under Cotonou,[84] from which the Committee's own legal basis was drawn.

The Parliamentary Committee establishes its own rules of procedure, which are communicated to the Joint Council (Article 231.3), although it is pre-established and commonplace that chairing the committee shall alternate between both parties (Article 231.4). According to the rules of procedure established, the Committee should meet once per year; however, the Committee's website notes that, regrettably, due to challenges, the Committee has only met three times since its establishment.[85] The Committee can also request relevant information relating to EPA implementation, and the Joint Council is expected to supply it (Article 231.5). A review of the minutes does not indicate that such a specific request has been made; rather, it speaks to specific sectoral issues of EPA implementation, including showing support or concern vis-à-vis the process of implementation.[86] Additionally, the Parliamentary Committee is informed of the decisions or recommendations of the Joint Council (Article 231.6), and it may equally make recommendations to the Joint Council or TDC (Article 231.7).

The Joint Parliamentary Committee has not received substantive coverage across all three review publications. While the minutes may be a valuable resource, they also have the practical limitation that minutes are drawn up consensually. This means that some issues of tension or dispute may be glossed over in technical language, and therefore omitted from the public domain and scrutiny. Or, according to the literature, the Committee may have, in actual fact, engaged in participative and open dialogue, and thus the minutes reflect the common good achieved though adherence to the power-neutralising mechanisms of such deliberative fora.[87]

[84] The author has written on the EU–ACP JPA. See Delputte and Williams texts (n 32).
[85] European Parliament, 'DCAR' (n 83).
[86] 'Third Meeting of the CARIFORUM-EU Parliamentary Committee' (*Europa*, 1 November 2017),https://europarl.europa.eu/cmsdata/162842/1153920EN.pdf.
[87] Delputte and Williams, 'Equal Partnership' (n 32).

4.3.4 The CARIFORUM–EU Consultative Committee (Article 232)

The Consultative Committee is the civil society body established to support the Joint Council in the promotion of dialogue and co-operation between its members, consisting of academic, social, and economic actors (Article 232.1). The text of the Agreement states that dialogue and co-operation concerns '*all* economic, social and environmental' areas (Article 232.1, emphasis added), and the minutes of the Consultative Committee meetings confirm this.[88] The language is used to be inclusive; to ensure that the Consultative Committee can hear issues relating to any area of economic, social, and environmental concerns. For example, GIs can cover all three aspects from the social context of worker's rights, the economic gains to be reaped from this protection, or the environmental aspects of protection embedded in the specification. Although the issue of GIs has not arisen within the context of the Consultative Committee, this is an example that demonstrates that the drafters of the EPAs perceived dialogue in this regard as both non-exhaustive and also pertaining to the three pillars (social, economic, and environmental) of sustainable development.[89]

The Joint Council decides on the membership of the Consultative Committee and aims to ensure a broad representation (Article 232.2). On the EU side, members apply and the application is reviewed within the Joint Council. This author has been a member of the Consultative Committee since 2017, and an observer since its establishment and first meeting in 2014, including at the establishment of its rules of procedure (Article 232.4, notably in accord with the Joint Council). The Committee generally meets prior to the TDC meeting, in order to provide recommendations when the TDC convenes (Article 232.3). To date, and perhaps due to institutional and capacity constraints, few meetings take place outside of this framework, although the Committee can meet upon its own initiative. The Consultative Committee has met eight times since its foundation, and makes joint statements that include recommendations to the TDC and Joint Council.[90] The issue of GIs has not been raised, since there is no member of the Committee that works directly on this niche area. A number of related issues – agriculture, and trade in services, amongst others – have been raised. A procedural issue was also raised at the fourth meeting, in St Lucia, where the Consultative

[88] See point 1, 'Joint Statement from the Fifth Meeting of the CARIFORUM-EU Consultative Committee' (*EESC*, 09 December 2019), https://eesc.europa.eu/en/documents/joint-declaration/joint-statement-fifth-meeting-cariforum-eu-consultative-committee.

[89] On this, it also links to the pragmatism of conducting the five-year review: 'The analysis in this study — mirroring the "priority-setting" approach used by the 2004 Sustainability Impact Assessment (SIA) on the CF-EU EPA prepared for the European Commission (1) — focuses on significant sectors from an economic, environmental and/or social perspective where changes can be expected from the implementation of the CF-EU EPA, particularly those areas of the Agreement that marked clear departures from the pre-2008 status quo.' Commission, *Monitoring the Implementation* (n 4) 5. For more on sustainable development, see ch 1.

[90] For example, see EESC, 'Joint statement from the 8th meeting of the CARIFORUM-EU Consultative Committee' (*EESC Europa*), https://www.eesc.europa.eu/sites/default/files/2025-03/Cariforum-EU-Joint-Statement_20032025_Bahamas.pdf.

Committee expressed that it wanted to adjust its position from sounding board to an advocate of civil society issues arising within the EPA.[91] This is important, since it signals a shift from a reactive consultative body that, in essence, reports issues already on the TDC agenda, to one which represents issues of civil society actors coming from the region. Yet, with the disruption of COVID-19 and the changing membership of the Committee, this adjustment is unlikely to take place. The functioning of the body is an important participatory mechanism and its functioning, so far, evidenced by its declarations, shows the constructive engagement that representatives have sought through deliberations in this body.

A reference to the Consultative Committee is notably absent from the interim CARIFORUM report; however, there is mention of the progress of the participatory mechanism in the five-year report, and the EU's ten-year review does have a reference to it. A case in point is the reference to co-operation in the field of education, notably via the CARIFORUM–EU Centre, a joint partnership between the University of the West Indies and the European University Institute.[92] The report also notes that the Committee's work plan includes youth exchanges; however, at the level of the EPA, concrete outcomes are absent.[93] In a footnote in relation to the role of the Committee and deepening co-operation, it is pertinently noted that 'the plans for more monitoring by the Consultative Committee lack concrete implementation plans and budgets'.[94] This succinctly highlights the limits of the Consultative Committee: it can fulfil its mandate de jure, promoting dialogue and consultation; however, more concrete actions relating to issues of members' interests, plans, and budgets are likely to be executed outside the remit of the Committee. Therefore, the deliberative process therein can also stimulate further deliberation and implementation beyond the body itself.

Since the EU–CARIFORUM EPA established the Consultative Committee, there has been an emergence of literature that looks specifically at civil society meetings in EU trade agreements.[95] This literature, in general,

[91] Yentyl Williams, 'ACP YPN at the 4th CARIFORUM EU Consultative Committee, St Lucia' (ACP YPN, 12 April 2018), http://acpypn.com/2018/12/04/acp-ypn-at-4th-cariforum-eu-consultative-committee-st-lucia/.

[92] Cunningham, 'Consultancy to Prepare Technical Position Paper' (n 4) 199.

[93] ibid 132. The author made this recommendation, which was included in the Committee's work plan, on behalf of the civil society body the 'ACP Young Professionals Network', which the author represents at the Consultative Committee.

[94] Cunningham, 'Consultancy to Prepare Technical Position Paper' (n 4) 339.

[95] Jan Orbie, Deborah Martens, and Lore Van Den Putte, 'Civil Society Meetings in European Union Trade Agreements: Features, Purposes, and Evaluation' (2016) 3 *Centre for the Law of EU External Relations* 1–48. Deborah Martens, Jan Orbie, Lore Van den Putte, and Yentyl Williams, 'Civil Society Meetings in EU Trade Agreements. Recommendations and Lessons for EPAs' (2016) 93 *ECDPM: The Centre for Africa–Europe Relations* 1–10; Jan Orbie, Deborah Martens, Myriam Oehri, and Lore Van den Putte, 'Promoting Sustainable Development or Legitimising Free Trade? Civil Society Mechanisms in EU Trade Agreements' (2016) 1(4) *Third World Thematics* 526–46. This builds on an earlier body of literature which critically interrogates how CSOs engage in international trade institutions, namely the WTO. For example, see Kristen Hopewell, 'Multilateral Trade Governance as Social Field: Global Civil Society and the WTO' (2015) 22(6) *Review of International Political Economy* 1128–58.

seeks to understand the features and purposes of the meetings, and evaluate the functioning of these Committees. This body of literature draws on primary data collected with committee members and outlines four perceptions around the purpose of the committees: (i) instrumental, referring to their ability to canvas support for the agreement; (ii) functional, in relation to the task of monitoring the agreement; (iii) deliberative, through their convening powers with the aim of engaging civil society organisations (CSOs) in a process of structured dialogue; and (iv) policy, referring to their ability to advise and provide recommendations on the implementation of the agreement, especially in relation to sustainable development issues.[96] It exposes the issue that there is uncertainty surrounding the purpose, amongst members, and ambiguity documented around their functioning. Yet, the literature also recognises that CSO actors within such committees, set up within EU FTAs more generally, have adopted a constructive approach to the participative process, albeit recognising the virtues and the vices of such institutions, ie the ability to deliberate important trade issues while also being challenged by organisational, representative, and accountability issues.[97] It discusses that, '[i]n addition to criticisms concerning the institutional dimension of the meetings (e.g., financial support and representativeness), they also point to frustrations with limited impact and lack of substantive dialogue'.[98] The most important contribution of this literature is in highlighting the dichotomy between business and non-profit CSO members in such committees. It is explained that 'there is a risk that the civil society mechanisms further reinforce the existing asymmetric power relationship between business and non-profit organisations when it comes to trade policy influence, rather than balancing them in favour of sustainable development'.[99] This is counter to the aims of a deliberative process, which should provide power-neutralising mechanisms to allow participative and open deliberation with the aim of achieving a common good. It is critical in terms of achieving the objectives of the Agreement that there is broad representation in such committees, since this influences the type of deliberation in such a participative process.

This section has provided an overview of the functioning of the joint institutions. It has also demonstrated the joint institutions' compliance with the spirit of the legal text of the EPA, and how its impact and use play out in practice. The next section focuses specifically on the national and regional institutions of the CARIFORUM party.

[96] Martens, Orbie, Van den Putte, and Williams, 'Civil Society Meetings' (n 95) 2–3.

[97] Orbie, Martens, Oehri, and Van den Putte, 'Promoting Sustainable Development' (n 95) 528–29.

[98] ibid 540.

[99] ibid. This builds on literature which criticises EU trade policy's ability to contribute to sustainable development. See Lucy Ford, 'EU Trade Governance and Policy: A Critical Perspective' (2013) 9(4) *Journal of Contemporary European Research* 578–96.

4.4 FINANCING AND EPA IMPLEMENTATION

4.4.1 The National EPA Implementation Units

The five-year report summary recognises the fact that the negotiation phase was difficult, and cautions that the implementation is the 'far more difficult task'.[100] Implementation in this sense, as the summary points out, is in relation to the specific and general obligations of the official EPA text, but also, importantly, 'using the CF-EU EPA as a platform for trade and development, as intended under the Agreement's stated principles and objectives'.[101] Implementation roadmaps had been drawn up and assistance was provided, for example bilateral assistance from EU Member States.[102] However, the report notes that, while implementation is sought, the capacity to do so varies considerably. This will be the focus of this next section.

National EPA implementation units have been established. Although they are not mentioned *verbis expressis* in the EPA, Article 234 speaks of the role of EPA co-ordinators to 'facilitate communication and ensure the effective implementation of the Agreement'. Despite different rates of ratification of the Agreement, all countries have designated EPA co-ordinators, who are government-appointed officials. The contrast of ratification versus the allotment of specified EPA co-ordinators sheds light on the disparity between legal ratification and administrative implementation. It also demonstrates that there is impetus to co-ordinate the EPA nationally, despite what the status of ratification may be. The following two examples demonstrate this.

A case study of Antigua and Barbuda reveals that, within the same month of ratifying the EPA (December 2009), the twin-island nation swiftly moved to establish their EPA unit, which became operational by November 2010.[103] It was established within the office of the National Authorising Officer (NAO) for the EDF, within the government's Ministry of Finance, Economy and Public Administration. The establishment of this office relied on external funding from the EU via financial support from the Caribbean Aid for Trade Regional Integration Trust Fund (CARTFund), managed by the Caribbean Development Bank (CDB). This case study is an example of a case where EU funding contributes to the fulfilment of EU objectives in the framework of the EU–CARIFORUM EPA. The work of the unit is guided by the CARICOM-devised 'Road Map for EPA Implementation'. The unit's mission is defined as 'seeking to meet obligations of the . . . Economic Partnership Agreement, while accessing opportunities

[100] Commission, *Monitoring the Implementation* (n 4) 2.

[101] ibid.

[102] ibid 3.

[103] Clarence Henry, Barbara Williams, and Alana Benjamin, 'Moving Forward with EPA Implementation in the Caribbean: The Example of Antigua and Barbuda' (2011) 10(1) *Trade Negotiations Insights* 8.

to increase economic growth and enhance development'.[104] This is implemented via four objectives. The first of these is assisting the private sector to benefit from the opportunities of the Agreement. Within this objective, the unit has undertaken consultations with the private sector on a range of issues, including IP, and aims to support small and medium enterprises (SMEs) in their export goals. The second is assisting the public sector to benefit from the opportunities of the EPA. This includes seeking development co-operation support from external founders, providing advisory services, and monitoring and evaluating EPA implementation. The third is monitoring national implementation. It is particularly interesting to note here the intention to have quarterly consultations with both private and public sector stakeholders, with the aim of contributing to a review and monitoring system. It was intended that briefs from these consultations would thereafter be presented to cabinet ministers; however, there is no record that this intention has been followed through as intended, quarterly. The fourth objective is raising awareness about the EPA. Public awareness, sensitisation, and education are deemed critical, especially as the country (and region) moves from preferential to reciprocal trading relations. In this regard, an effective communications strategy was deemed necessary to support the work of the unit. The authors of the aforementioned report are actively contributing to this process, as Ambassador Dr Clarence Henry is the head of unit, Barbara Williams is the national EPA implementation coordinator, and Alana Benjamin is the trade and customs officer, and together they comprise the core staff of the unit.

At the end of February 2020, Belizean media reported that a meeting had been held with the Belizean Directorate General for Foreign Trade on the results-based management system being put in place to monitor EPA implementation.[105] Margaret Ventura, EPA co-ordinator at the Belizean Directorate General for Foreign Trade stated, 'we are now looking at developing a monitoring and evaluation system to be able to *monitor the progress* being made with EPA implementation and also *to assess whether we are truly benefiting* from this agreement'.[106] Ventura's statement underlines the crux of the monitoring system, which, through the means of monitoring, aims to achieve the end goals of assessing how the region is benefiting or not from the agreement. Errol Humphrey, international trade consultant, was also quoted, adding that, 'we want to ensure that the agreement is delivering *long term development benefits* for the region'.[107] This latter statement expresses the intention that the benefit ought not to be of a short-term nature but be addressed to the region long-term. Equally, a case study on Belize also suggests concern for non-tariff barriers: 'if

[104] ibid.

[105] 'A Management System to Monitor & Evaluate Impact of EPA' (*Channel 5 Belize*, 27 February 2020), https://edition.channel5belize.com/archives/199108.

[106] ibid (emphasis added).

[107] ibid (emphasis added).

current market access conditions persist, Belize would likely face constraints in accessing the EU market for its (Belize's) most important export sectors, namely agricultural and agri-food exports'.[108] Non-tariff barriers related to agricultural and agrifood products refer to issues such as SPS issues. These are, notably, areas in which the EU has high internal standards which could act as a (non-tariff) barrier that restricts exports, notably an issue that has challenged the EU's trade policy with its Third World partners since post-colonial relations were governed by the Lomé and Cotonou EU–ACP treaties.[109] Addressing such issues would amount to delivering on the long-term development objectives of the region and the partnership.

The joint five-year review discusses the mandate of the Barbados implementation unit. The work of this national EPA unit concerns, inter alia, liaising with the public and private sector bodies on the issue of development assistance; raising the profile of the EPA and opportunities therein through sensitisation; and working with governmental bodies to strengthen the national regulatory environment. The report equally notes the varying institutional capacities of the national EPA units. Antigua and Barbuda has been highlighted as demonstrating leadership on EPA issues despite being a small office. This underscores the interesting reality that EPA units such as Antigua and Barbuda's may be driving forth EPA implementation, yet they have not ratified the Agreement, and their laws do not provide for provisional implementation. Yet, de facto, the EPA unit is funded, resourced, and playing a role in EPA implementation. There is also variation in staffing, from Grenada, which has two officials, to the Dominican Republic, which has a unit of 40 people dedicated to overseeing EPA implementation.[110] Additionally, the five-year report recognises that success rates are due to strong political support, particularly with reference to the case of Barbados.[111]

[108] David M Gomez, *Implications of EU-CARIFORUM Economic Partnership Agreement for Belize – A Forward Assessment* (Belize Chamber of Commerce & Industry, Belize City, 2007) 89.

[109] Trade Commissioner Karel de Gucht summarised the challenges faced by the ACP countries in the following words: 'as regards the economic fundamentals, the truth is that the current system has failed; that ACP countries have become increasingly marginalised in world trade, even with the generous tariff preferences since the Cotonou and Lomé agreements' (Karel De Gucht, 'EU-China Investment: A Partnership of Equals' (*Europa*, 2008), http://europa.eu/rapid/pressReleasesAction.do?reference=IP/08/1510&type=HTML, in Williams, 'Shifting Between Hegemony and Dominance?' (n 9) 5. Williams considers this a cognitive failure between EU–OACP officials: 'ACP contributors to this debate whole-heartedly disagree that the preferential tariff regime was the reason for marginalisation in the world economy, but evoke other issues related to EU rules and standards.' Williams also draws on Van Genderen-Naar, who notes, 'According to the European Commission in its Green paper 1996, COM(96)570 final,. .. it was clear that ACP States had not benefited from the EU trade preferences as the market share of ACP states fell back from 6.7% in 1976 to only 2.8% in 1997. The ACP countries did not agree and said that the complex rules of origin, EU procedures and standards were the major reason they could not benefit from the non-reciprocal trade preferences.' See 'The Cariforum-EU EPA Five Years After' (*Norman Girvan*, November 2012), http://.normangirvan.info/wp-content/uploads/2012/12/NAR-Development-Content-of-CF-EPA-Nov-12.pdf, in Williams, 'Shifting Between Hegemony and Dominance?' (n 9) 4–5.

[110] Commission, *Monitoring the Implementation* (n 4) 10.

[111] ibid.

Although currently relying on national budgets, the EPA units have received start-up funding from both the UK's Foreign, Commonwealth and Development Office (FCDO, formerly the Department for International Development (DFID)) and the German Development Agency (GIZ). The CARTFund and EPA Implementation Support Programmes, funded respectively by the UK and Germany, have provided operational funds, and co-ordinated activities around the establishment of the units. Despite this initial funding, the perception of the provision of these resources was deemed inadequate by stakeholders consulted as part of the five-year review process. Two GIZ surveys (2010 and 2014) have demonstrated that two-thirds of the EPA units are dependent on government financial support.[112] Moreover, the fact that these units were funded via DFID and GIZ programmes from the outset puts into question their long-term sustainability, as funding ends and budget constraints are felt. For example, data shows that only 11 per cent of EPA units established perceived the funding allocation to be adequate.[113] There was also an expectation that more funds would be disbursed within the framework of the 10th EDF (considered for the period of review) via the Caribbean Development Bank's EPA and the CSME Standby Facility. Outlining the role of these units is important, since it has been noted that they played a key role in co-ordinating the four joint institutions. Yet, these units remain vulnerable to resource supplies in practice, despite being key institutional areas linked to the implementation of the EPA.

While a regional roadmap has been drawn up, the five-year report is inconclusive as to how much this map provides for guiding EPA implementation. The 'Reworked Roadmap for Implementation of the CARIFORUM–EC Economic Partnership Agreement In Chronological Order', as its title suggests, set out a timeline for implementing commitments under the EPA. The five-year report outlines that this has been used by national implementation units in drawing up their own plans and matrices; however, in reality it serves more as a background document, since national efforts are dictated by EPA units locally. Again, resource constraints appear to impact on the level at which this regional roadmap can be used as a yardstick, or a mere background document, for national units. While the roadmaps are not mentioned in the EU's ten-year report, there is discussion of the budget-constrained national EPA units. The report references interviews with EPA co-ordinators, who have reported that offices are understaffed; that, where funding has been provided, disbursement may be slow; and that some even have to work in absence of budget lines.[114] The role of EPA co-ordinators, units, or roadmaps is not mentioned in the interim CARIFORUM review.

[112] ibid.
[113] ibid.
[114] ibid.

4.4.2 The Regional Implementation Unit – The CARIFORUM Directorate

At the regional level, an EPA unit was also established within the CARICOM Secretariat in 2009. By 2011, the regional EPA unit had been subsumed within the CARIFORUM Directorate. The experts therein provide technical assistance to CARIFORUM states, from legislative drafting to the organisation of consultations on specific sectors of the EPA. The unit also plays a role in organising the meetings of the joint institutions. It faces similar resource supply-side constraints as its national counterparts, and it has been stated that it must seek out donor funding for its activities.[115]

It is useful to reiterate here that the five-year report succinctly underlines that 'CARIFORUM is not an institution per se but a coordinating forum'.[116] It does not have a separate legal personality based on a treaty arrangement, but it functions according to agreed Rules of Procedure. CARIFORUM does not have a secretariat of its own, a formally agreed mandate, or a formally agreed delineation of its activities. CARIFORUM is dependent on EU regional funding (for the majority of its resources) and the CARICOM Secretariat in Georgetown (for office space and resources).

In 2011, the role of the CARIFORUM Director-General was created, and the DG also serves as the EPA's regional co-ordinator. 4.2million euros was earmarked in the 10th EDF, for the CARIFORUM Directorate (2008–13). This funding aimed to provide institutional support to the CARIFORUM Directorate and ensure its effective participation in the joint institutions of the EPA.[117] This appears as an oxymoron, as the co-ordinating forum of the CARIFORUM side of the EPA is largely funded by the EU, in order to ensure its effective operations. This reinforces the old adage that 'who pays the piper picks the tune'. In this case, evidently, the EU is playing the tune that the CARIFORUM Directorate responds to. What is made explicit in the report is that the ecosystem of EPA-implementing institutions and stakeholders – EPA Coordinators and Ministries, in particular – rely on an effective Directorate to play its co-ordinating role for implementing the EPA.[118]

One of the biggest challenges that the CARIFORUM Directorate faces, unlike the EC, is the lack of a formal co-ordination mandate. Whereas the EC negotiates trade rules on behalf of its Member States, where it has exclusive competence to do so (Treaty on the Functioning of the European Union (TFEU), art 3),[119] the CARIFORUM Directorate does not benefit from such

[115] ibid 10-11.
[116] ibid 14.
[117] Commission, *Ex-Post Evaluation* (n 4) 49.
[118] ibid.
[119] The Union has exclusive competence in common commercial policy, under art 3(1)(e). Furthermore, under art 3(2) it is emphasised that 'The Union shall also have exclusive competence for the conclusion of an international agreement when its conclusion is provided for in a legislative act of the Union or is necessary to enable the Union to exercise its internal competence, or in so far as its conclusion may affect common rules or alter their scope.'

autonomy. Rather, decisions are made at ministerial level, and this can impact on implementation processes.[120] A case in point is the controversial history of negotiating the EPA, with regard to the role of the former Caribbean Regional Negotiating Machinery (CRNM). During the negotiation phase, the CRNM was mandated to negotiate the EPA on behalf of CARIFORUM Member States and was financed by the EU. However, there was a perception that the CRNM acted autonomously,[121] and, pursuant to the conclusion of the EPA, not only did CARICOM change its rules on third-party funding for negotiations, but it dissolved the CRNM, rebranded it as the Office of Trade Negotiations (OTN), and moved it within the CARICOM Secretariat.[122] Earlier primary research demonstrates the controversy surrounding the CRNM in negotiations:

> [S]ome seem to feel that the CRNM exceeded its mandate and thereby killed itself, others seem to be of the view that the negotiators did a good thing but in a bad way and as such, they were a force for forced integration as opposed to a motor for integration.[123]

A CRNM negotiator also stated, 'the decision of negotiation was a European decision [as] imposition rather than negotiation'.[124] As documented, this reflects the 'big-stick' tactics of the EU to achieve its trade ambitions,[125] and is emblematic of the EU's structural foreign policy actorness to influence all the structures of its third-country partners through its trade agreements.

Additionally, and in spite of this example, perhaps as a result of this limited capacity, there is also a false perception of the capacity of the Directorate in the region. For example, it is noted in the ten-year report that several of the region's business associations perceived that there was a lack of engagement and visibility vis-à-vis the Directorate and the private sector.[126] While this may be factual, contextualising the capacity constraints of the Directorate as a co-ordinating body also sheds light on its limitations. In this regard, it also emphasises the importance of continued and enhanced funding to support EPA implementation in the region; and to better connect the private sector with the relevant institutions to support their ability to contribute to trade and, in turn, the objectives of the EPA.

Notwithstanding the important co-ordinating role the CARIFORUM Directorate plays, the sustainability of it as an organisation has been brought into

[120] Commission, *Ex-Post Evaluation* (n 4) 50.

[121] CRNM negotiator, Interview, Port-of-Spain, 8 August 2011 in Williams, 'Shifting Between Hegemony and Dominance? (n 9). See also Tony Heron, 'Asymmetric Bargaining and Development Trade-offs in the CARIFORUM-European Union Economic Partnership Agreement' (2010) *Review of International Political Economy* 328–57.

[122] Williams, 'Shifting Between Hegemony and Dominance?' (n 9) 13.

[123] Caribbean Ambassador, Interview, ibid.

[124] Anonymous, Interview, ibid.

[125] 'OP-ED: Tenth Anniversary of EPA Negotiations: Not a Time for Celebration' Huntington News (Ohio, 2012), http://huntingtonnews.net/45124.

[126] Commission, *Ex-Post Evaluation* (n 4) 50.

question. The ten-year report highlights that 'it was not clear if the CARIFORUM Directorate has developed any strategy to sustain its operation beyond the current funding arrangements, both for implementing its programmes and for its administrative operations'.[127] Additionally, the report draws on an earlier evaluation which underlines that the Directorate is dependent on both EU and donor funds, and should these funds cease, the institutions may also cease to exist.[128] This threatens not only EPA implementation but regional coherence and co-operation with regard to the EPA. It also, remarkably, shows the lack of regional support to implementing the EPA, if the Directorate faces the very real spectre of ceasing to exist if the external funds supporting its operations stop. This overview points out that holistic and concerted efforts need to be made to ensure coherence at the national and regional levels. Otherwise, as the practice shows, there will be variation in implementation, co-ordination and, ultimately, effectiveness and efficiency of EPA implementation at all levels.

The interim CARIFORUM review makes ample reference to the information put forth by the CARIFORUM Directorate and, importantly for this book, it puts forth the substantive recommendation that 'the CARIFORUM Directorate should provide assistance to the CARIFORUM States in carrying out an inventory of the state of compliance with the intellectual property obligations of the EPA and conducting a gap analysis'.[129] Yet, having outlined the institutional vulnerability of budget constraints, it has been made explicit how EPA implementation is subject to follow where the funding flows. In that regard, the report has also noted that the Directorate is in dialogue with GIZ, for capacity-building support, and the Caribbean Export Development Agency (CEDA), on mutual recognition agreements.[130]

4.4.3 Support to Private Sector

From the outset, it should be stated that some Member States have been lauded for their support to EPA implementation, most notably the UK and Germany, through their development assistance and capacity-building programmes.[131] Although the review notes that there is a perception of an 'information deficit' – a lack of information vis-à-vis rights and responsibilities – especially for the private sector, it is the modest ambition of this book to provide further insight into that area in regard to GIs in particular. After all, there is ample evidence that not only is the language and structure of the EPA considered complex,

[127] ibid 51.

[128] Commission, 'Evaluation of the 10th EDF Institutional Support to CARIFORUM/EU Development Cooperation and EPA Implementation' (2017) FWC BENEF 2013 Lot 10 Trade, Standards and Private Sector, Final Report, 38 in ibid.

[129] Cunningham, 'Consultancy to Prepare Technical Position Paper' (n 4) 4, 111.

[130] ibid 76–77. CEDA is also referred to as Caribbean Export.

[131] Commission, *Monitoring the Implementation* (n 4) 10.

but firms are challenged to benefit from the EPA as a result.[132] Germany, via its development agency, GIZ, has also provided critical support to the EPA implementation process. The regional CEDA has also been recognised for its pertinent support to the EPA implementation process. In this regard, all meetings on GIs and private sector trade in the region have been convened by or with CEDA.

It is remarkable how the 10th EDF fund, towards this end, spells out how integration into the global economy should take place. It is outlined that this should be done via private sector competitiveness and innovation; intra-CARIFORUM trade and export development; CARIFORUM and Overseas Countries and Territories (OCTs) trade and investment; stronger CARIFORUM–Dominican Republic trade and investment; and enhanced institutional capacity of Caribbean Export (CEDA) to run effective trade and investment programmes regionally.[133]

There are a number of issues that may prove problematic in the linkage of the objectives of this agreement, linked to regional integration via private sector enhancement. First, private sector competitiveness is largely impacted by historical (colonial) structural issues,[134] as well as financing issues.[135] In today's context, through EU support, and specifically via the EPA, this is meant to be rectified. This critique of exogenous support, especially coming from EU countries previously involved in highly extractive, unequal, and detrimental trading relations, extends to the ambitions to support further intra-Caribbean trade in a region historically divided specifically because of the EU's influence therein. For example, while enhanced trade between CARICOM and OCTs – particularly the French overseas islands – and the Dominican Republic make logical sense due to their geographical proximity, these countries have more established trade routes with the metropole than with their neighbours, with whom they shared their joint colonial history.

Second, building the CEDA's capacity was not only an objective, amongst the others mentioned above, but CEDA received 28 million euros between March 2011 and June 2016 to implement this programme. Support has been provided

[132] Commission, *Ex-Post Evaluation* (n 4) 35.

[133] ibid 51.

[134] See ch 2, which demonstrates how IP rights were colonial tools, and therefore were rights accorded to colonial businesses at the expense of development and innovation. The legacy of this underdevelopment is documented in the (post-colonial) literature also. See Walter Rodney, *How Europe Underdeveloped Africa* (first published Bogle-L'Ouverture Publications 1962; Pambazuka Press, 2012); and Kwame Nkrumah, *Neo-Colonialism, The Last Stage of Imperialism* (International Publishers Co, 1965).

[135] The five-year review points to limited productive capacity and supply side constraints affecting the private sector, as well as the need for trade and investment promotion: Commission, *Monitoring the Implementation* (n 4). The ECDPM report discusses an information deficit which impacts on accessing the opportunities of the EPA. See ECDPM, 'EPA Challenges CARIFORUM Region', https://ecdpm.org/application/files/8616/5547/2490/DP-117-Economic-Partnership-Agreement-Challenges-CARIFORUM-Region-2011.pdf. See also Sheldon McLean, Errol Humphrey, and Jeetendra Khadan, 'Trade and Development Nexus: Reflections on the Performance of Trade in Goods under the CARIFORUM-European Union Partnership Agreement. A CARIFORUM perspective' (*EU-LAC Foundation*, 2014), https://intranet.eulacfoundation.org/en/system/files/trade_and_develop.pdf.

via grants, trade missions and training, and support to investment agencies and business networks, as well as directly to CEDA and its Market Intelligence System.[136] Nevertheless, the report is transparent in noting that there was unequal follow-up on grant awardees, and that further review is needed of this system, including technical assistance support and third-party monitoring. Furthermore, the fact that only 30 per cent of businesses that received support saw growth in export sales undermines the ability to see this support as a success. Rather, it reinforces why there might be the suggestion that third-party oversight may be necessary, as such, implying that due diligence has been undermined in grant disbursals. This is a critical area to address, since a third of the firms receiving grants work in the agricultural, aquaculture, and agro-processing sectors – an area identified as the backbone of inter-regional cooperation. Indeed, the 2020 EU Trade Policy Review mentions that 'CARIFORUM's agri-food exports to the EU increased by 11% in 2019, driven by strong exports of rice, beer, cigars, tropical fruit and rum'.[137] This is recorded on the backdrop of the reality that there is very low take-up of FTA preferences by (M)SMEs, even though these account for a significant proportion of economic actors.[138]

The ten-year report underlines another issue that is a key challenge: 'The programme design had ambitious targets, but these were too much spread out compared to the budget available. For example, the focus was on too many countries, sectors and a range of expected results.'[139] This is highly unfortunate, as it shows the capacity constraints of implementing the EPA, if it cannot serve all countries and the demands stemming from the region. In addition, the ten-year report states that 'it is not clear if CEDA is working towards a sustainable business model that can cater to the private sector to effectively sustain without long-term donor funding'.[140] This effectively puts CEDA in a very similar predicament to the CARIFORUM Directorate. It demonstrates that, without exogenous third-party support, the institutions that are meant to implement the EPA may fail at that very task.

The interim CARIFORUM review commends the work of CEDA, underscores the value of EU financial assistance, and recommends that the CARIFORUM side should secure a commitment for funding from the EU.[141] The report also extensively cites the findings of a CEDA-funded study on firm-level review of the region, conducted by former CARIFORUM trade negotiator Ramesh Chaitoo.[142]

[136] Commission, *Ex-Post Evaluation* (n 4) 52.

[137] Low take-up is attributed to resource dependence, in this Report. See Commission, 'Report from the Commission to the European Parliament, the Council, the European Economic and Social Committee and the Committee of the Regions on the Implementation of EU Trade Agreements 1 January 2019 – 31 December 2019' COM (2020) 705, 27.

[138] On the EU side, 'SMEs and family businesses represent around 99% of all companies in the EU, and account for half of Europe's GDP' (ibid).

[139] Commission, *Ex-Post Evaluation* (n 4) 52.

[140] ibid 53.

[141] Cunningham, 'Consultancy to Prepare Technical Position Paper' (n 4) 3.

[142] ibid 18–20.

The overview has shed light on an insidious truth: that the EPA is not a panacea for '*contributing to* the reduction and eventual eradication of poverty' or '*promoting* regional integration',[143] even when considered alongside the EU's package of initiatives aiming to enable further integration of its Third World trade partners into the world economy. Unfortunately, however, the Agreement does portray itself as a panacea, whereas both the five- and ten-year reports, as well as perceptions from the region, demonstrate otherwise. And tensions remain in implementation, whereby it has been pointed out that, 'in several cases programmes focused more in addressing regional needs, rather than national needs'.[144] And, '[i]n other cases, programmes show a lack of understanding on the context of CARIFORUM countries, and capacity of agencies'.[145] These realities point to a cognitive dissonance between the drafters of the EPAs and those destined to implement them.[146] This is further reflected in the fact that the ten-year report underlines that the sustainability of support and EPA institutions is questionable.[147] Given the issues raised in this section which demonstrate a questionable institutional sustainability, the next section delves further into an analysis of the shortcomings of the EPA review processes.

4.5 SHORTCOMINGS OF EPA REVIEWS: MONITORING, EVALUATION, AND IMPLEMENTATION

The ECDPM report *Monitoring the EU-CARFIORUM EPA, Where are We and What are the Next Steps?* cautioned that the Agreement's impact, the Agreement's use, and compliance with the provisions of the Agreement are three very different issues.[148] This is a useful reminder to assess each of these issues separately. This section considers the shortcomings of monitoring, evaluating, and implementing the EPA in light of the review process. It first considers the lack of a monitoring mechanism, then the divergent perspectives around the evaluation and implementation process.

4.5.1 Monitoring: Lack of a Mechanism 18 Years On

Just two years shy of two decades of EPA implementation, a dedicated monitoring mechanism has still not been established. Although there was provision for this under Article 5 EPA, the only monitoring exercise that takes place is

[143] art 1 CARIFORUM–EU EPA. Emphasis added.
[144] Commission, *Ex-Post Evaluation* (n 4) 53.
[145] ibid.
[146] McLean, Humphrey, and Khadan, 'Trade and Development Nexus' (n 135).
[147] Commission, *Ex-Post Evaluation* (n 4) 53.
[148] Bruce Byiers and Quentin de Roquefeuil, *Monitoring the EU-CARFIORUM EPA, Where are We and What are the Next Steps?* (ECDPM, 2012) 2.

at the level of the national implementation units. The five-year review noted that only Barbados and the Dominican Republic EPA units conduct routine monitoring.[149] Although monitoring is part of the mandate of these units, the above-mentioned resource constraints are an indication, inter alia, of why this is not taking place.

In the EU ten-year review, the authors dedicate recommendation number 3 (of 12) to the need to adopt a functional monitoring mechanism. Accordingly, it suggests that the mechanism should contain instructions for indicators, format, frequency, and responsibility of relevant actors in the process. Yet, the five-year review highlights two key issues that should remain at the fore of discussions on this highly anticipated mechanism. On the one hand, it has cautioned that, 'arguably the most important metric of monitoring – the use of the Agreement by its target stakeholders and the specific impact of the Agreement on them – a purely numerical approach may be insufficient'.[150] On the other hand, it also highlights the suggestion that there should be more targeted, detailed and thus frequent reviews, or "snapshots" of different areas of the Agreement, which thereafter can be aggregated.[151] These issues may indeed underscore the complexity of establishing an effective and efficient monitoring mechanism, and may be an indication of why one has not been established. Broad indicators would undermine the ambitions of the Agreement, and although reviews have been undertaken, more strategic snapshots of different sections of the Agreement can contribute to having a more accurate indication of how aspects of the Agreement are being implemented.[152] The interim CARIFORUM review does not mention the establishment of a separate monitoring mechanism.

While several reports may underscore the importance of establishing a mechanism, and some even suggest what it may entail,[153] the reality is that, more than a decade and a half after signing the EPA, there is no agreed joint monitoring mechanism. For example, David Jessop's commentary highlights the lack of a monitoring mechanism: 'Most notably, in an almost throwaway line, the report observes "the lack of a joint mechanism for EPA monitoring". . . . Without a public measure any further decline in the Caribbean's relationship with Europe will go unnoticed.'[154] This echoes the general sentiments around EPA implementation – without the monitoring system, how can one know what is being implemented? And, perhaps more worryingly, the relationship of the two regions bound by the ambitious framework of the EPA may be at stake.

[149] Commission, *Monitoring the Implementation* (n 4) 16.
[150] ibid 120.
[151] ibid.
[152] ibid 120-121.
[153] ibid 118-121; Commission, *Ex-Post Evaluation* (n 4) 216.
[154] David Jessop, 'Has the EU-CARIFORUM EPA Worked?' *Dominican Today* (Roseau, 5 February 2021), https://dominicantoday.com/dr/opinion/2021/02/05/has-the-eu-cariforum-epa-worked/.

4.5.2 Evaluation: Divergent Views in the Public Domain

The EU's ten-year EPA review has received substantial scrutiny. CARIFORUM ministers have publicly expressed concerns about the EU's approach to EPA evaluation in the regional press.[155] This Council of Ministers of the CARIFORUM publicly stated:

> As a region, we are particularly troubled that in spite of the detailed concerns raised by our senior officials in writing, this document remains in the public sphere, including on the official site of our partner under this Agreement. It is being regarded by some as an accurate assessment of the operation of the Agreement.[156]

The detailed concerns have, in part, been outlined in the Audel Cunningham review referred to herein as the interim CARIFORUM review. What is concerning, and is expressed in this quote, is the reference to the document being in the public domain and, as a result, being considered an accurate assessment as opposed to one view of the EPA review process. This is a reminder of the importance of agreeing to a metric of assessment, and where there is no agreement, 'overstanding' that there are always different interpretations of any given situation.[157] In this case, the EU review and the CARIFORUM review may differ substantially.

The news article highlights a disregard from the EU side of concerns coming from the CARIFORUM group, such as remaining regulatory barriers to the EU market (including mode 4, for trade in services), as well as 'unfounded general statements' which imply that CARIFORUM states are non-compliant with their EPA obligations.[158] The examples cited include the statement that CARIFORUM states do not have independent judicial systems that are able to provide final rulings and injunctions in IPR cases. The statement is clear in its disapproval of the report:

> the number of inaccuracies in the Report, at the expense of CARIFORUM, is unacceptable. In the absence of any specific analysis or provision of evidence to support, CARIFORUM is branded non-compliant, even in circumstances where the observations are not applicable to all CARIFORUM States.[159]

[155] 'CARIFORUM Ministers Express Concerns at EPA Evaluation' *Loop News* (Kingston, 12 November 2021), https://caribbean.loopnews.com/index.php/content/cariforum-ministers-express-concerns-epa-evaluation.

[156] ibid.

[157] Overstanding is a Rastafari-Caribbean expression of the word understand, which denotes precisely that there may be multiple perspectives and expressions for any given reality. See Yentyl Williams, Aleema Gray, and Chevy Eugene, 'Groundings and Rastafari: Re-territorializing Caribbean Indigenous Knowledges' in Camille Nhakid, Margaret Nhakid-Chatoor, Anabel Fernandez Santana, and Shakeisha Wilson-Scott (eds), *Affirming Methodologies, Research and Education in the Caribbean* (Routledge, 2022) 163.

[158] *Loop News* (n 155).

[159] ibid.

The statement concludes that the CARIFORUM group is hopeful that the upcoming review will highlight the EU's very own need to raise awareness of EPA amongst its stakeholders – both operators and border and regulatory agencies – as a means to curtail the barriers that CARIFORUM stakeholders experience, especially for trade in services.[160]

Equally, in the region, Caribbean trade commentator Alicia Nicholls' commentary on the EU's ten-year review critiques EU positions that are taken to the detriment of a joint understanding of a topic, such as tax jurisdictions and the EU's blacklisting of certain CARIFORUM countries as tax havens.[161]

In addition to this, the EU has its own independent monitoring of its FTA implementation and enforcement. The EU has produced its first Annual Report on Implementation and Enforcement, which replaces the former annual Trade Policy Review Report.[162] This new report also responds to the institutional development of a new role at the EC, of the first Chief Trade Enforcement Officer (CTEO) in the Commission, on 24 July 2020. It also specifically responds to the current realities, namely a decade of concluding EU FTAs, and the new challenges in global trade policy, including 'structural imbalances, level playing field and market access issues, and the political use . . . of unjustified restrictive unilateral measures'.[163] The report discusses implementation and enforcement of EU FTAs, which refers to the elimination of barriers to trade and investment in third-country partners. The 2021 review states how the institutions set up within the framework of the FTA contribute to its implementation. While there is nothing specific on GIs in the context of the CARIFORUM–EU EPA, there is information on GI developments between the EU and other third parties. For example, progress on the specific issue of GIs is credited to ministerial trade meetings for Korea and Japan agreements.[164] It also discusses how dedicated committees have averted trade irritants and removed laws or regulations that would otherwise have restricted the trade in GI products (feta to Egypt and wine to Canada, respectively). In the former case, the EU–Egypt SPS Committee, responsible for animal and plant health, drew up a new feta standard which removed the reference to the higher yeast content, which was previously restricted. In the latter, through the deliberations of the Wines and Spirits Committee, Canada will remove its federal excise duty on wine,

[160] Repeated here: 'CARIFORUM Slams "Glaring Weaknesses" in European Commission Evaluation of EPA' *Our Today* (Kingston, 13 November 2021), https://our.today/cariforum-slams-glaring-weaknesses-in-european-commission-evaluation-of-epa/.

[161] Alicia Nicholls, 'EU-CARIFORUM EPA Monitoring Report finds Five-fold Increase in EU FDI to CARIFORUM' (*Caribbean Trade Law*, 29 January 2021), https://caribbeantradelaw.com/2021/01/29/eu-cariforum-epa-monitoring-report-finds-five-fold-increase-in-eu-fdi-to-cariforum/.

[162] Commission, 'Report from the Commission to the European Parliament, the Council, the European Economic and Social Committee and the Committee of the Regions on Implementation and Enforcement of EU Trade Agreements' (2021) COM 654 final.

[163] ibid 2.

[164] ibid 12.

and discriminatory measures will be removed in Ontario and Nova Scotia.[165] Also in relation to wine, the EU–Japan EPA Committee on Regulatory Cooperation facilitated further trade through recognising, in their domestic regulations, uses of enzymes and additives used by the other party.[166]

On monitoring the agreement, the Report notes specifically that there is a dual lack of administrative capacities on the part of EPA agencies and lack of awareness of the EPA on the side of business, including in relation to transparency obligations.[167] These inadequacies become obstacles to EPA. Poignantly, in relation to a key issue of this chapter, it also states that, 'given the development dimension of the EPA, its successful implementation by the 14 CARIFORUM States depends significantly on the relevant development cooperation funding'.[168] And, in the EU's view, SMEs can harness the partnership for development purposes, since 'Trade agreements with developing countries offer market access opportunities that local SMEs are eager to seize, and they provide incentives for reform that development cooperation can further build on.'[169] It should be borne in mind that these may be EU incentives that lead to the type of development *à l'EU*, which may in fact depart from reforms sought endogenously by local SMEs. The Report references how the EU's Aid for Trade policy aims to address internal constraints to trade, inter alia, through its development.[170] The evidence herein supports the objective of this chapter, namely to highlight how the EU's institutions continue a post-colonial legacy of formalism via the EPA institutions. This section has also shown how these institutions are also capable of influencing other mechanisms of formalism, such as laws, through the institutions' ability to foster dialogue on and fund trade-policy measures aimed at reducing barriers to trade and investment for the EU in third-party markets.

4.6 CONCLUSION

This chapter examined the institutions of the CARIFORUM–EU EPA and assessed their potential to promote dialogical manoeuvres to frame GIs as emancipatory legal tools for Third World countries in the CARIFORUM region. The chapter has argued that these institutions may function as vestiges of informal imperialism that contribute to the continued marginalisation of Third World nations, but they could equally foster dialogical engagement between the parties to foreground the 'commensurability of difference'. It has discussed the current state of play of monitoring and evaluation, particularly that, in the absence of a dedicated mechanism written into the Agreement, the five- and ten-year

[165] ibid 13.
[166] ibid 14.
[167] ibid 20.
[168] ibid 20.
[169] ibid 21.
[170] Commission, *EU Aid for Trade* (n 57).

reviews become valuable resources for understanding the state of implementation. That being said, it is widely recognised that the reviews provide only a snapshot of implementation,[171] and therefore cannot fully address all issues that may contribute to sustainable development. This is an area that requires further research. Yet, the divergence from joint reporting in the five-year review to separate reports at the ten-year stage, and significant delays in publishing the reviews in general,[172] has shown that the ambitions of the EPA may be muted by the lack of a formalised monitoring mechanism. In this regard, while the CARIFORUM regional grouping has been tailor-made, it seems a shortfall that its monitoring system has not also been tailor-made. As the EPA approaches its eighteenth anniversary, there is certainly scope for reimagining the monitoring mechanism to ensure that Third World interests are being promoted and protected in the context of trade liberalisation. A theory-of-change approach to monitoring the EPA privileges assessing the developmental potential of the EPA. However, this chapter concluded that, in the absence of a dedicated monitoring mechanism, GI laws may struggle to function as emancipatory tools that would contribute to an inclusive global-local law. This undermines the opportunity for an inclusive framing of sustainable development grounded in the integrationist principle that fosters inter- and intra-generational, and equitable, dialogue.[173] The remaining chapters of this book examine case studies of GIs in the developing world to illustrate the challenges and opportunities of GIs for promoting sustainable development and 'development from within'.

[171] Commission, *Monitoring the Implementation* and *Ex-Post* (n 4).

[172] The five-year review 2008–13 was published in 2015, and the ten-year review 2008–18 was published in 2021 for the EU, and the CARIFORUM's consultancy report was published in 2020.

[173] See ch 1 (nn 20–22). Tonia Novitz and Margherita Pieraccini, 'Agenda 2030 and the Sustainable Development Goals: "Responsive, Inclusive, Participatory and Representative Decision-Making"?' in Margherita Pieraccini and Tonia Novitz (eds), *Legal Perspectives on Sustainability* (Bristol University Press, 2020) 40; Federico Ortino, 'Investment Treaties, Sustainable Development and Reasonableness Review: A Case Against Strict Proportionality Balancing' (2017) 30(1) *Leiden Journal of International Law* 83

5

GIs in the Third World: Lessons for a Strategic Approach to GIs as IP Assets in the Caribbean

In considering how legal protection of GIs can be used to improve coffee and cocoa producers' incomes we should focus neither on certification mark versus sui generis GI protection nor on Article 22 versus Article 23 [TRIPS] protection. Instead, we should concentrate on practical obstacles, problems, and dangers.

. . . we must not lose sight of the desired 'GI effect': successful marketing that (a) produces higher economic rents and (b) is controlled by or at least directly benefits farmers.[1]

Justin Hughes (2009).

5.1 INTRODUCTION

THIS CHAPTER PROVIDES AN overview of Third World GIs, the rationale for their protection locally and internationally, and the contestation to reclaim these GIs in First World jurisdictions. As a form of appropriating GI names, the issue of 'clawback' – reclaiming origin-linked names – which is most common in European cases (from port and sherry to feta and Parmigiano Reggiano) is discussed.[2] Theoretically, this assesses how Third World GI owners, as the subaltern,[3] previously marginalised voices, can keep international law grounded in local realities. As such, Third World GI owners, through using GIs as intellectual property (IP) assets, are using the law inclusively to foster a

[1] The risks identified include policy-makers' assumptions that GI protection leads to higher incomes automatically (conflating legal protection and marketing), and that GIs also automatically protect traditional knowledge. Justin Hughes, 'Coffee and Chocolate – Can We Help Developing Country Farmers through Geographical Indications?' (2009) *Intellectual Property Institute* 1–152.

[2] Commission, 'WTO Talks: EU Steps up Bid for Better Protection of Regional Quality Products' (*Europa*, 28 August 2003, https://ec.europa.eu/commission/presscorner/detail/en/IP_03_1178.

[3] On the subaltern, see Dianne Otto, 'Subalternity and International Law: The Problems of Global Community and the Incommensurability of Difference' (1996) 5(3) *Socio-Legal Studies* 337–64, 360.

global-local law.[4] The chapter analyses the issue of subaltern uses of GIs as IP assets, and the issue of clawback, with reference to four Third World case studies: (i) Demerara Gold sugar in Guyana;[5] (ii) the Ethiopia–Starbucks dispute;[6] (iii) the Café de Colombia GI;[7] and (iv) the Indian basmati case.[8]

This chapter addresses how *Third World countries claw back origin-linked names from First World jurisdictions*. It also considers the effectiveness of *sui generis GI regimes in Third World country contexts and how GIs contribute to sustainable development and poverty eradication for Third World countries*. The chapter demonstrates that GIs can be valuable IP assets for Third World countries; however, a *sui generis* GI regime is not the only means of protecting GI signs. As such, contextually relevant legal protection such as trademarks could be sought. The rationale for the protection of GIs in today's post-colonial epoch, similarly to that in the colonial epoch, remains contextually linked to the economic benefit that can be derived from commercial expansion and industrial production to foster sustainable development *within* Third World territories. However, Third World GI owners must be attentive to how, through challenges to clawing back GIs, they are in fact challenging the international law – which continues to privilege the historical, intellectual, and cultural experiences of the First World[9] – particularly in relation to, but not limited to, GI laws. The challenge facing Third World GI owners is framed as a challenge against the vestiges of informal imperialism,[10] which continues to undermine Third World aims of mobilising law as an emancipatory tool to achieve 'development from within' for GI producers in today's post-colonial context.

The chapter introduces the issue of clawing back GI names. Section 5.2 sets out the case study of Demerara Gold sugar and the attempt by the government of Guyana to 'claw back' this origin-linked name in the First World jurisdictions

[4] See Valerie Phillips, 'Indigenous Peoples and the Role of the Nation State' (2007) 101 *American Society of International Law* 319. See also Luis Eslava, *Local Space, Global Life: The Everyday Operation of International Law and Development* (CUP, 2015).

[5] *Guyana Sugar Corporation (Guysuco) v Bedessee Imports Ltd* [2011] TMOB 102, 11 (*CanLII*), https://canlii.ca/t/fm8w7.

[6] USPTO, Response to Office Action, Serial Number 78589307, US Patent and Trademark Office, Application No 78589307 (*USPTO*, 17 January 2007), http://tmportal.uspto.gov/extemal/portal/tow?SRCH=&isSubmitted=true&details=&SELECT=U S+Serial+No&TEXT=78589307#.

[7] Café de Colombia and Juan Valdez have been protected as trademarks in 1967 – Denmark; 1975 – UK; 1988 – Poland, Slovenia; 1989 – Italy, Slovakia, Czech Republic; 1990 – Germany; 1992 – Portugal; 1999 – Greece. The Café de Colombia GI was the first non-EU GI registered in the EU, in 2007. See European Commission, Publication of an Application Pursuant to Article 6(2) of Council Regulation (EC) No 510/2006 on the Protection of Geographical Indications and Designations of Origin for Agricultural Products and Foodstuffs [2006] OJ C 320, 17.

[8] See Trademarks, Trade Mark Application no UK00001081589, https://trademarks.ipo.gov.uk/ipo-tmcase/page/Results/1/UK00001081589. See Commission, 'WTO Talks: EU Steps up Bid for Better Protection of Regional Quality Products' (*Europa*, 28 August 2003), https://ec.europa.eu/commission/presscorner/detail/en/IP_03_1178.

[9] Makau Mutua, 'What is TWAIL?' (2000) 94 *American Society of International Law* 31.

[10] Luis Eslava, 'TWAIL Coordinates' (Critical Legal Thinking, 2 April 2019), https://criticallegalthinking.com/2019/04/02/twail-coordinates/.

of Canada and the US. Section 5.3 highlights the practical impediments to protecting GI products via a *sui generis* system, with reference to the Ethiopia–Starbucks dispute case study. Section 5.4 discusses the best-practice case studies of the Café de Colombia GI and Indian basmati rice GI to demonstrate how Third World countries are successfully protecting – and, where necessary, clawing back – their valuable origin-linked names. In the Conclusion (section 5.5), it is summarised that GIs are valuable IP assets that can be used by Third World countries; however, they must be strategically used in a context-specific manner to reap the benefits of protecting origin-linked names in trade in today's post-colonial epoch.

5.2 DEMERARA SUGAR/GOLD: THE THIRD WORLD CLAWING BACK FROM THE FIRST WORLD?

This section sheds light on one of Guyana's most prized exports: its sugar from the Demerara region, known as Demerara sugar, or by its commercial name, Demerara Gold. It begins by providing an overview of the legal case around the Guyanese government's attempt to invalidate the trademark registration of Demerara Gold by a member of its diaspora in Canada. It also considers the libel case that ensued as a result of the failed opposition proceedings. The chapter also sheds light on how Demerara sugar has been produced and exported from other parts of the world, with reference to the EU/ACP-funded study that considers the viability of protecting Demerara sugar coming from beyond Guyana. It discusses the issues of clawing back geographical names, the genericide of Third World geographical names, and some of the lessons that can be learnt from Demerara Gold as a case study.

The Guyanese law on GIs was adopted in 2005 and enacted in 2008.[11] As early as 2002, the Guyanese Ministry of Foreign Trade and International Cooperation had written on the strategic priority of GIs for Guyana,[12] and this was also addressed in the very first WTO Trade Policy Review conducted for the country, in 2003.[13] It was, equally, the subject of a 2005 CARICOM report.[14] However, in a 2010 ACP study, research was conducted on the viability of a Demerara sugar GI for Mauritius (discussed separately below). Meanwhile, the Guyanese Sugar Corporation (Guysuco)[15] registered the Demerara Gold trademark in the EU in

[11] The Co-operative Republic of Guyana Geographical Indications Act of 2005 and GI Act Commencement Order of May 14, 2008.

[12] Ministry of Foreign Trade and International Cooperation (MOFTIC) Digest, 'Geographical Indications in the Context of Guyana' (*SICE*, 2003) 4, 8, http://ctrc.sice.oas.org/TRC/Articles/Guyana/Moftic4.pdf.

[13] WTO, 'Trade Policy Review – Guyana (WT/TPR/S/122)' (1 October 2003), https://docsonline.wto.org/dol2fe/Pages/SS/directdoc.aspx?filename=Q:/WT/TPR/S122-0.pdf&Open=True.

[14] CARICOM, 'A Review of Agricultural Policies – Case Study of Guyana' (2005) in Dev Gangjee, 'Demerara Sugar: A Bitter Pill to Swallow?' (2011) 24 *Intellectual Property Journal* 1.

[15] 'Guyana Sugar Corporation Inc', https://guysuco.gy/index.php?lang=en.

14 August 2008, and Demerara has been a registered trademark by Demerara Distillers Ltd since 28 January 2010.[16] Oppositions were filed against Bedessee's Demerara Gold applications by both Guysuco and Demerara Distillers Ltd; however, the literature has focused on the former, since the same reasonings were relied upon in both decisions.[17] The focus hereunder will be on Guysuco's opposition proceedings, although considering the argumentation of the parties is important, since 'Demerara' is now a GI-protected term in Guyana for sugar and molasses, while the Demerara Rum GI is protected in Guyana and the EU. The next section will outline the legal case that ensued between Bedessee Imports Ltd and Guysuco.

5.2.1 Opposition Proceedings

Bedessee Imports Ltd applied to register the trademark 'Demerara Gold' in relation to sugar, glucose, rice, and coconut oil products on 18 February 2004, based upon prior usage in Canada since January 1984. Bedessee also claimed the exclusive right to use 'Demerara' as part of the trademark in relation to sugar and glucose. This was opposed by Guysuco, who filed their opposition to the application on 25 February 2005. Guysuco's opposition was based on the grounds that, inter alia, the mark was deceptively misdescriptive with regard to the character, quality, and origin of the goods, and thus not registrable under section 12(1)(b) of Canada's Trademarks Act.[18] Guysuco further claimed that it was the only producer of authentic Demerara sugar from Demerara, Guyana, and thus the trademark 'Demerara Gold' would cause confusion with their product in Canada (s 16(1)(b), Trademarks Act).

Under the section 12(1)(b) grounds for opposition, Guysuco pleaded that Bedessee's 'Demerara Gold' was deceptively misleading in two regards.[19] First, and in relation to the character and quality of the sugar, it was argued that Demerara sugar was produced in the eponymous region in Guyana, and that its golden hue was a key characteristic of Demerara sugar. Hence, in the first instance, the combined usage of the words 'Demerara' and 'gold' was put forth as being deceptively misleading. Second, Guysuco claimed to be the only producer, manufacturer, and exporter of the authentic Demerara sugar of Guyana. Hence, in the opponent's view, Bedessee could not therefore claim exclusive rights to the use of the term 'Demerara Gold', as Bedessee's products did not originate

[16] 'Demerara Gold' (*EUIPO*), https://euipo.europa.eu/eSearch/#details/trademarks/006068779; 'Demerara' *(EUIPO)*, https://euipo.europa.eu/eSearch/#details/trademarks/007577661. One other trademark exists, for Danish Demerara sugar: 'Dan Sukker Råsocker Strö Rørsukker Demerarasukker Ruokokidesokeri' (*EUIPO*), https://euipo.europa.eu/eSearch/#details/trademarks/002557965.

[17] Gangjee, in 'Demerara Sugar' (n 14) 10, notes that the reasoning that led to the same decision in both cases are almost identical.

[18] Trademarks Act 1985 RSC (c T-13).

[19] *Guysuco v Bedessee* (n 5).

from Demerara in Guyana or from Guysuco. As such, it was argued that an application to use the trademark 'Demerara Gold' was deceptive and likely to be misleading to consumers.

The court relied on the test of whether the general public would be misled, as set out in *Atlantic Promotions Inc. v Registrar of Trade Marks*:[20]

> the proper test to be applied to the determination as to whether a trade mark in its entirety is deceptively misdescriptive must be *whether the general public in Canada* would be misled into the belief that the product with which the trade mark is associated had its origin in the place of a geographic name in the trade mark.[21]

The court considered the type of evidence that would be used to demonstrate the reputation of the geographic area amongst the relevant Canadian public.[22] Both the applicant and opposition presented affidavits, and all of the opposition's affiants were cross-examined. While Guysuco's evidence pointed to the production of Demerara sugar in the Ogle Estate of East Demerara dating from the 1800s,[23] it was unable to demonstrate the link that the Canadian public was aware of this reputation. Nisa Surujubally, Guysuco's managing director, while at first presenting international sales of Demerara sugar, later corrected the reference to state that the statistics related to sales within the Caribbean Community (CARICOM) and not Canada, or internationally. Additionally, there was no evidence of advertising of Demerara sugar within Canada.[24] Ironically, an affidavit presented by Jennifer Stecyk on behalf of Guysuco demonstrated that Demerara sugar was manufactured, produced, and exported from Mauritius, Malawi, and Jamaica,[25] a piece of evidence which was also presented by the applicant. Additionally, Bedessee's affidavit also indicated that 'DEMERARA *style* sugars . . . were refined in Canada and none indicate that they emanate from Guyana'.[26] This was the basis from which it was concluded that 'DEMERARA is a style of sugar which is not particularly associated with a single source location'.[27]

The court's decision was also supported by the precedent of the *Anderson v Britcher* (1913) case, which first concluded that Demerara sugar does not refer solely to sugar of the eponymous region in Guyana.[28] In that case, although the respondent had originally been charged with the unlawful sale of a sugar that had been produced in Mauritius and dyed in colour as 'Demerara sugar', the charge was later dismissed by the magistrate. It was dismissed on the grounds

[20] *Atlantic Promotions Inc. v Registrar of Trade Marks* [1984] 2 C.P.R. (3d) 183 at p 186 (F.C.T.D.).
[21] ibid [15], emphasis in original text.
[22] ibid [17]–[19].
[23] ibid [18].
[24] ibid.
[25] ibid [19].
[26] ibid. Emphasis added.
[27] ibid [20].
[28] ibid [21]; *Anderson v Britcher* [1913] EWHC (KB).

that Demerara sugar was deemed generic, and thus applicable to any sugar, independent of origin, colour, or other attributes. Therefore, the sale of Mauritian dyed sugar as 'Demerara sugar' did not prejudice the rights of other 'Demerara sugar' salespersons. Even upon appeal, the matter was dismissed.[29]

While it was not disputed that Demerara is the name of a region in Guyana and the description of a style of sugar, the court had to determine whether Demerara Gold in its entirety was deceptively misdescriptive. It considered that, while the map of Guyana was printed on Bedessee Ltd's packaging, the Canadian public would not recognise the outline of the country.[30] In particular, the court made reference to the ordinary public and stated that there was no evidence to suggest that such a consumer would either recognise the map or be deceived by its use.[31] And, crucially, although Demerara may be the region where Demerara-style sugar originated, it has been shown to be produced in other places globally.[32] Additionally, the reference to 'Gold', which could be linked to the hue of the sugar or its superior quality, was not considered as grounds to prevent the registration of Demerara Gold based on a deceptive misdescription of the character, quality, or origin of the product. The court referred to the dictionary explanation of the word 'gold' as referring to a colour, metal, or superior quality, but underlined that none of these factors that could be linked to the characteristics, reputation, or quality of the trademark name precluded its registration.[33] Additionally, the fact that Guysuco did not file any evidence supporting their use of the 'Demerara Gold' trademark in Canada weighed against their claims in this opposition proceeding. The decision of 30 June 2011, therefore, established that Demerara Gold was not deceptively misdescriptive of the character, quality, and origin of sugar sold in Canada by Bedessee Ltd.

5.2.2 Libel Claim and State Immunity

In addition to the opposition proceedings, Bedessee initiated a libel claim against Mr Robert Persaud, Guyana's minister of agriculture, and Guysuco. A libel claim refers to a published statement which is considered to be false and damaging to the reputation of the person or entity that it targets. In this case, Bedessee outlined how Mr Persaud, as part of the government's marketing campaign of its own 'Demerara Gold', made claims that Bedessee had dishonestly marketed its products in Canada.[34] Persaud was accused of making defamatory statements regarding Bedessee's business and products, while Guysuco

[29] 'Trademark Battle over Demerara Gold' (*Caribbean Review*, September 2010), https://caribbeanreview.org/2010/09/trademark-battle-over-%E2%80%98demerara-gold%E2%80%99/.
[30] *Atlantic Promotions Inc.* (n 20) [24]–[29].
[31] ibid [29].
[32] ibid.
[33] ibid [30].
[34] Libel and Slander Act 1990 RSO (c L12), ibid [30], [34], [58], [67].

was implicated for funding public advertisements and providing a brief for Mr Persaud to initiate a public affront on Bedessee. This libel claim was grounded in the harm that these false statements would impact on the existing registration and reputation of the 'Demerara Gold' brand that Bedessee had, with the Canadian (and American) public.

Mr Persaud as minister, acting on behalf of Guysuco – the state-owned sugar corporation – sought to rely on the State Immunity Act to prevent the libel investigation.[35] The Justice Strathy relied on common law antecedents to determine that immunity shall not be granted to court proceedings that concern a commercial activity of the state,[36] nor shall it be granted when it concerns loss or damage to property in the geographic territory of Canada.[37] In other words, the immunity would only apply had it concerned *acts jure imperii* (public acts), as opposed to this case of *acts jure gestionis* (private acts). This ought to provide a lesson to be learnt for other countries of the Third World in the marketing of any terms that may already be protected in First World jurisdictions.

5.2.3 Lessons on Clawing Back for Third World Countries

Understanding and unpacking this case is of vital importance for countries of the Third World considering protection of their GI products. This section discusses the Demerara Gold opposition proceedings and the libel case with reference to the challenges relating to clawing back terms when relying on third-country courts' interpretation of the relevant public and the issue of economically valuable geographical terms being considered generic. It concludes by suggesting that assessing the issues faced as concerning the public policy orientation of GIs offers a prism of hope for countries of the Third World facing similar challenges.

Demerara sugar has been a product of the sugar cane industry of the Demerara region of Guyana since the 1800s. Currently, the government-owned Guysuco is the largest sugar producer, employer, and foreign exchange earner in Guyana.[38] This sugar accounts for approximately 10 per cent of the country's gross domestic product (GDP).[39] While sugar has been a commodity produced and exported en masse since the colonial period, Guysuco moved from marketing unlabelled 50kg bags of sugar with the launch of its own retail brand of sugar, 'Demerara Gold', in 2003.[40] By October of the same year, Guysuco had written to

[35] State Immunity Act 1985 RSC.

[36] ibid, s 5.

[37] ibid, s 6(b), as had been previously done by Lord Wilberforce in *Congreso Del Partido* at the House of Lords in *Owners of Cargo Lately Laden on Board the Marble Islands v Owners of The I Congreso del Partido* [1983] 1 AC 244, at 263.

[38] Gangjee, 'Demerara Sugar' (n 14) 2.

[39] Ministry of Agriculture, 'Guysuco', https://agriculture.gov.gy/guysuco/.

[40] 'Bedessee Can Use Demerara Gold Trademark in North America – GuySuCo' *Starbroek News* (Georgetown, 4 March 2015), https://stabroeknews.com/2015/03/04/news/guyana/bedessee-can-use-demerara-gold-trademark-in-north-america-guysuco/.

a member of the Guyanese diaspora and potential distribution partner, Lionel Bedessee, who had established Bedessee Imports Ltd in 1977, with distribution, manufacturing, and sales of Caribbean products in Canada and the US. While his products were, in the most part, of Caribbean origin, they were not exclusively Caribbean, since Bedessee's sugar, although using the label 'Demerara Gold', was in fact sourced (both produced and exported from) elsewhere. This reflects a reality of globalised trade and names in trade, since Demerara sugar has also been produced and exported from Mauritius, Barbados, India, and Malawi.[41]

In the legal proceedings discussed above, it was shown that the Opposition Board concluded that Demerara-style sugar does not have a single source and was, therefore, considered generic. Gangjee finds the reasoning of the Opposition Board to be problematic. In his opinion, this is an incomplete reasoning, since it heavily relies on an 'outsider's' use of the term as a determinant of the generic status of GI product,[42] which disadvantages those seeking to protect – or claw back – the GI. In this case, Demerara Gold was not deemed a GI term by the Canadian public; however, it would most likely be a significant term for the Guyanese diaspora consumers of the product in Canada. Gangjee notes that Guysuco's concerns were most likely with this narrower category of the Guyanese diaspora, as opposed to the Court's reasoning, which relied on the misleading-the-public test based on the Canadian public at large.[43] This observation most prominently brings to the fore the issues that can emerge when a Third World country attempts to claw back a geographic term which may be significant to a diaspora population, which is not the core focus of legal reasoning in First World jurisdictions. In other words, the reasoning of the Court privileges First World knowledge and continues to marginalise Third World knowledge in international law. The Court, in this instance, could be theorised as a vestige of informal imperialism which serves to widen the gap between the First and Third Worlds. This analysis suggests that the misleading-the-public test, in this case, functions according to a 'dynamic of difference' by obfuscating the relevant diaspora public.[44] It misses the opportunity to foreground the 'commensurability of difference' and sensitise the wider Canadian public.

This issue of diaspora knowledge and general third-party consumers' knowledge comes into play with the misleading-of-the-public test. Additionally, it is also related to the burden of proof of the state, which must demonstrate that the GI is recognised nationally as a precondition for protection internationally, as set out in Article 24.9 TRIPS.[45] The lack of evidence provided by

[41] *Guysuco v Bedessee* (n 5) [19].

[42] Gangjee, 'Demerara Sugar' (n 14) 12.

[43] ibid 14.

[44] See ch 1 (n 29). Anthony Anghie, *Imperialism, Sovereignty and the making of International Law* (CUP, 2014) 4.

[45] 'There shall be no obligation under this Agreement to protect geographical indications which are not or cease to be protected in their country of origin, or which have fallen into disuse in that country.' (art 24.9 TRIPS).

Guysuco reinforces Gangjee's overall advice that 'it makes strategic sense to rebrand while attempting to gradually re-establish origin specific meaning over time'.[46] Moreover, further research demonstrates that Bedessee Inc. owns at least 35 trademarks.[47] The Bedessee Brands website displays visualisations of all these trademarks with the accompanying text, 'we're in your kitchen more than you think'.[48] Besides 'Demerara Gold', there are trademarks which refer to territories, although not (de jure) GIs, since they are not registered as such: 'African pride', 'Asian pride', 'Australian pride', 'Bajan pride' (referring to Barbados), 'Dutch lady', and 'Dutch baby'. Bedessee also has several trademarks which refer to locations in Guyana, such as 'Berbice', 'Black River', and 'Courantyne'.[49] Meanwhile, Guysuco has a pending trademark application for 'Berbice Gold' in Canada.[50] This may be an indication that the saga between Bedessee and the Guyanese government may still be brewing. As such, Third World countries are challenged in their attempt to keep the law grounded in their local realities, for the law to function as an emancipatory 'global-local law'.[51]

This case is also an example of whether GI protection could help against 'genericide'[52] – the phenomenon of regional names becoming 'generic' and losing their profitable communicative link to their original place of production. As Advocate General Colomer stated, 'The process of genericide is fatal because the sign no longer functions to indicate geographical origin.'[53] A key question in this regard is whether the consumer understands Demerara as a geographical region in Guyana, or whether the term has become generic in usage without a link to its geographical location. Hence, consumer perception is vital when such issues come before the courts. According to an Australian delegate at the WTO, clawback can also be considered a form of 'reappropriation of generic terms'.[54] When the tables are turned, however, and it is a Third World country reappropriating their 'origin terms' that may have become generic through use in the First World, there is a somewhat different sentiment linked with the phenomenon of clawback. After all, it refers to a country which has undergone a

[46] Gangjee, 'Demerara Sugar' (n 14) 14.

[47] 'Bedessee Brands', https://bedesseebrands.com/.

[48] ibid.

[49] ibid.

[50] United Nations Conference for Trade and Development (UNCTAD), 'Guyana, A National Trade Strategy' (2020) 43, https://unctad.org/system/files/official-document/ditctncd2020d3_en.pdf.

[51] Phillips, 'Indigenous Peoples and the Role of the Nation State' (n 4). See also Eslava, *Local Space, Global Life* (n 4).

[52] Dev Gangjee, 'Genericide: The Death of a Geographical Indication?' in Dev Gangjee (ed), *Research Handbook on Intellectual Property and Geographical Indications* (Edward Elgar, 2016) 509.

[53] ibid. See also 'Parmesan', Case C-132/05 *Commission of the European Communities v Federal Republic of Germany* [2008] ECR I-00957; see Advocate General Colomer's opinion in 'Feta', Joint Cases C-465/02 and C-466/02 *Federal Republic of Germany and Kingdom of Denmark v Commission of the European Communities* [2005] ECR I-09115.

[54] Tegan Brink, 'Perspectives on Geographical Indications: Prospects for the Development of the International Legal Framework' (*WIPO*, 26–28 June 2007), https://wipo.int/edocs/mdocs/geoind/en/wipo_geo_bei_07/wipo_geo_bei_07_ibid_81778.pdf.

period of colonisation and exploitation, and whose land has been developed as a plantation economy for the benefit of the First World coloniser – in this regard, clawback seems somewhat more permissible as a form of trade justice. As such, clawback for Third World countries can offer a form of economic reparation.

The problem identified was also apparent in the precedent of the *Anderson v Britcher* case. That case, again, it concerned a First World Court deciding on the fate of a GI from the Third World that had essentially only been traded colonially. Hence, the judgment represents the (colonial) period within which it was made. Today, in a post-colonial period, deeper questions need to be asked about the co-existence of regimes and legal precedents which nevertheless stem from the colonial period and the quest by Third World countries to use GIs as tools for their own development.[55] While Demerara sugar is protected by GI laws in Guyana today, this broader overview has shown that attempted clawback of GI names may be ineffective in countries of the First World. Here again, only when countries of the Third World file for GI protection in First World countries would the fate of their GI really be tested. A case in point, given that the UK has left the EU, is how a 'Demerara' product would be protected in that territory, given that Demerara trademarks relating to rum exist.[56] A consideration of the Demerara Mauritius GI feasibility study adds an additional layer of complexity to this GI issue.

Despite Guyana's national GI registrations of 'Demerara sugar' and its EU GI registration of 'Demerara Rum' (2021), the 'Demerara Mauritius' trademark study demonstrates the classical problems facing competing GI names. This time, the competition comes from another country in the Third World that has equally been the subject of colonial plantation economy development.[57] There is some irony that the shared history of these countries means that they are also now both competitors in the same declining sugar market, effectively both attempting to retain some market share through the promotion of their Demerara sugars as GIs. This section will provide an overview of the ACP report's findings on the feasibility of 'Demerara sugar' as a GI for Mauritius.[58]

[55] International Labour Organization (ILO), 'Guyana Launches Study of the Socio-Economic Impact of the Closure of GUYSUCO Sugar Estates on Workers' (17 June 2021), http://ilo.org/caribbean/newsroom/WCMS_803904/lang--en/index.htm; 'National Development Strategy (Guyana) – Chapters 9–20' (*SICE*), http://ctrc.sice.oas.org/TRC/Articles/Guyana/NDS_Ch9_20.pdf.

[56] For example, 'DEMERARA RUM OVD GEORGE MORTON LIMITED DUNDEE' has been registered by William Grant & Sons Limited since 1957 and is due for renewal in 2026. See 'DEMERARA RUM OVD GEORGE MORTON LIMITED DUNDEE' (*Trademark Elite*), https://trademarkelite.com/uk/trademark/trademark-detail/UK00000763011/DEMERARA-RUM-OVD-GEORGE-MORTON-LIMITED-DUNDEE.

[57] George Beckford, *Persistent Poverty: Underdevelopment in Plantation Economies of the Third World* (first published OUP, 1972; Zed Books, 1983).

[58] Michael Blakeney and Thierry Coulet, 'The Protection of Geographical Indications (GI): Generating Empirical Evidence at Country and Product Level to Support African ACP Country Engagement in the Doha Round Negotiations' (*ACP*, 2011), http://acp.int/fr/content/protection-geographical-indications-gi-generating-empirical-evidence-country-and-product-lev.

The ACP 2011 report was conducted with the aim to ascertain the potential of the Demerara sugar GI to bolster Mauritius' market share in a declining sugar market.[59] The report explains that

> Demerara sugar is made by partially refining sugar cane extract, whereas most brown sugar is made by adding molasses to fully refined sugar. Of the special sugars, which are brown unrefined sugars, Demerara predominates, but there are no statistics on the production of Demerara sugar as a specific category.[60]

This description describes Demerara sugar as a style of brown unrefined sugar made in Mauritius. According to the Mauritius Sugar Syndicate, which has filed for the collective trademark and collective Community mark for 'Demerara Mauritius' (2008), an individual stand-alone trademark was deemed too descriptive.[61] The study draws pertinent conclusions which are summarised herein.[62] First, there has been no economic return following the registration of the collective mark, in part due to a lack of effective branding. Second, there is a perception by the Mauritius Sugar Syndicate that economic returns will be high with a GI. Third, the drawbacks of a GI relate to identifying the specific characteristics of the product; the legal and administrative complexity of the system, including implementation and management; and the shortfall of resources, including human and financial resources. Fourth, the exclusionary impacts on small producers stemming from compliance and costs were considered. In terms of the cost and management of the GI system, important institutional issues were raised.[63] The Ministry of Foreign Affairs and Trade currently manages such IP issues, although three other ministries are vying for a stake in the system. The Trade Marks Office considers that it could take on the responsibility with little extra cost; the Ministry of Industry and Science is interested in the portfolio; and the Ministry of Agriculture wants to house the GI registry and manage the system.

Competing Third World GIs may well be an issue that will be grappled with in the future. For now, it seems that composite terms may be a viable avenue for GI protection. The consideration of a Demerara Mauritius sugar clearly complicates the discussion of Demerara sugar having its origins in the eponymous region in Guyana. Meanwhile, it does, however, support international legal precedent that recognises Demerara as a style of sugar.

With regard to the libel claim, Gangjee has highlighted, in the literature, how Minister Persaud's statements could either be viewed as having a public policy orientation in their promotion of Guyanese goods or perceived as a 'public relations onslaught' against Bedessee's business.[64] While the court interpreted the

[59] ibid.
[60] ibid.
[61] ibid.
[62] ibid.
[63] ibid.
[64] Gangjee, 'Demerara Sugar' (n 14) 3.

statements to be the latter, the juxtaposition of these interpretative options is important in this analysis. At the end of chapter three, it was argued that failing to recognise the beneficiaries of the GI provisions in the CARIFORUM EPA could be seen as a missed opportunity. It is precisely in a dispute such as this one that the contextualising of GIs as having a public policy orientation may have bolstered Guysuco's claims. A reference to public policy refers to:

> a politico-administrative process of articulating and matching government goals with the means available to achieve them. Public policies thus are government actions which contain . . . justified and formulated, goal(s) or aims and some means or tools . . . which are expected to achieve them.[65]

In other words, public policies may be laws (a GI regime) adopted by governments in pursuit of a given societal outcome (to achieve sustainable development). This is consistent with the claim of this book that GIs can be normatively reconstructed as tools for sustainable development, and thus contribute to poverty eradication.

While the CARIFORUM EPA does not have an explicit public policy reference in its section on GIs, the Japan–EU EPA does refer to the 'end user' in the context of the obligation to consider public policy objectives (Article 14(2)).[66] In particular, it links the end user as a beneficiary of a public policy-oriented GI to the pursuit of innovation, creativity, and competition via intellectual property rights (IPRs), inter alia via the sharing of knowledge and culture, technology and art (Article 14(2)).[67] The provision also underlines the imperative of taking 'into account the interests of relevant stakeholders including rightsholders and users' (Article 14(2)). Although Liam Sunner, writing on the Japan Agreement, notes that the end is still commercial,[68] the primary importance placed on the end user in this provision could bolster the public policy orientation of GI claims. Nonetheless, *stricto sensu*, according to the State Immunity Act, as Sunner pointed out, the end is still commercial. This underlines the grey areas in the quest of Third World states attempting to claw back geographical names that have been trademarked in foreign jurisdictions. It also suggests that Third World countries need to be more strategic in reclaiming their GI names, and perhaps that lessons can be learnt from European precedents. For example, Gangjee suggests rebranding around a composite mark such as 'Guyanese Demerara', similarly to how 'Camembert de Normandie' is legally protected

[65] Michael Howlett and Benjamin Cashore, 'Public Policy: Definitions and Approaches' in Gilberto Capano and Michael Howlett (eds), *A Modern Guide to Public Policy* (Edward Elgar, 2020).

[66] Agreement between the European Union and Japan for an Economic Partnership [2018] OJ L330, 3–899. See ch 3.

[67] ibid.

[68] Liam Sunner, 'How the European Union is Expanding the Protection Levels Afforded to Geographical Indications as part of its Global Trade Policy' (2021) 16(4-5) *Journal of Intellectual Property Law & Practice* 346.

in France and the EU (as opposed to the generic 'Camembert');[69] in that case, ensuring that GI names are clawed back within the process of bilateral/international trade agreements. In the absence of this formal route via negotiating trade agreements, it seems that states would otherwise have to rely on infringement claims, for which the clawing back of names would be a remedy.[70]

Following on from the issues of clawing back geographic terms and the threat of genericide, the next section considers Ethiopia's decision to use trademark protection for their GI coffee as a case in point that demonstrates, at this stage, a preference for trademarks over the GI system.

5.3 LESSONS FROM ETHIOPIAN COFFEE

Understanding and unpacking the Ethiopia–Starbucks dispute is of vital importance for countries of the Third World seeking to protect their GI products.[71] This section discusses Ethiopia's choice to protect its coffee GIs for Sidamo, Yirgacheffe, and Harar coffees with *regular* trademarks. It demonstrates that, without the prerequisite legal structures already in place, a *sui generis* GI system can be considered onerous both institutionally and cognitively. As a result, and as indicated by the Ethiopian example, trademarks remain a viable legal regime that can effectively protect origin products while fostering 'development from within' according to Third World producer country preferences. It concludes by suggesting that Third World countries find it challenging to adopt *sui generis* GI regimes outright and, therefore, they may legitimately adopt other legal regimes to protect their valuable origin names.

Ethiopia is widely considered to be the birthplace of coffee, derived from 'Kafa' – referring to 'land or plant of the Gods'. Coffee as an internationally traded commodity has a long history,[72] although the focus here will be on the more recent history of GI protection.[73] At the multilateral level, the International Coffee Agreement was established in 1982 to regulate the global prices of coffee.[74] The Agreement collapsed in 1989 and left the industry in a

[69] See examples in ch 3. Gangjee, 'Demerara Sugar' (n 14) 14.

[70] This is the third of three possible scenarios highlighted in Yentyl Williams, 'Post-Cotonou and Innovation? Lessons Learned from Intellectual Property provisions on Geographical Indications in the EU-ACP Economic Partnership Agreements' (*Afronomicslaw*, 31 May 2019), https://afronomicslaw.org/2019/05/31/post-cotonou-and-innovation-lessons-learned-from-intellectual-property-ip-provisions-on-geographical-indications-gi-in-the-eu-acp-economic-partnership-agreements-epas.

[71] USPTO, 'Response to Office Action, Serial Number 78589307' (n 6).

[72] Four waves of coffee, based on its production, consumption, and industry have been identified: 1800–1960 (growing consumption); 1960–1990s (quality and social experience); 1990s–2015 (emphasis on origin); 2015 to today (specialty coffees). See International Trade Centre, *The Coffee Guide*, 4th edn (ITC, 2021) 13–20, https://intracen.org/resources/publications/the-coffee-guide-fourth-edition.

[73] For an overview, see Ramona Teuber, 'Geographical Indications of Origin as a Tool of Product Differentiation: The Case of Coffee' (2010) 22 (3-4) *Journal of International Food & Agribusiness Marketing* 1–28.

[74] International Coffee Agreement 1983 (adopted 16 September 1982) 1546 UNTS 347 (ICA).

crisis, and this has also been compounded by other factors, such as environmental (drought) and regulatory (national conflicts) issues.[75] It is recognised that this has resulted in the overproduction of coffee and, consequently, historically low prices.[76] The 2003 World Bank study on the crisis had proposed GIs as a strategy for recovery.[77]

Additionally, there seems to be value in protecting a product such as coffee through GI laws that safeguard the origin–quality link, since coffee has between 700 to 850 different substances that influence its taste profile.[78] In other words, coffee has double the number of substances found in wines, the archetypal *European* GI. For this reason, countries of the Third World could seek GI protection for their coffee products as lucrative origin-linked exports.[79]

5.3.1 Coffee and Trademark Licensing

In 2003, Ethiopia founded its Intellectual Property Office (IPO), and its single-origin coffee industry was identified as one of its IP assets. By 2004, Ethiopia had launched the Trademarking and Licensing Initiative (hereafter 'the Initiative'), with the aim of ensuring that premiums from its globally recognised coffees could be reaped closer to home.[80] The Overseas Development Institute (ODI) report explains:

> The Ethiopian Trademarking and Licensing Initiative is an Aid for Trade initiative that has strong trade development and poverty reduction foundations: it aims to increase Ethiopia's coffee export income while ensuring a higher and more predictable income for Ethiopian coffee farmers and their households, by enabling them to capture a larger share of the final retail value of their coffee and more stable and predictable prices for their coffee.[81]

The case study on the Initiative has been drawn up according to an 'inclusive trade and poverty reduction perspective',[82] which aligns with the methodological

[75] Mary O'Kicki, 'Lessons Learned from Ethiopia's Trademarking and Licensing Initiative: Is the European Union's Position on Geographical Indications Really Beneficial for Developing Nations' (2008) 6 *Loyola University of Chicago International Law Review* 315.

[76] ibid.

[77] The full suggestion is 'Use the internet for more than just traditional marketing including sharing information regarding certification, land use and Geographic Indications of Origin.' See Varangis et al, 'Dealing with the Coffee Crisis in Central America: Impacts and Strategies' (World Bank Policy Research Working Paper No 2993) 42–44, available at http://ssrn.com/abstract=636355, in ibid 315.

[78] O'Kicki, 'Lessons Learned from Ethiopia's Trademarking and Licensing Initiative' (n 75).

[79] See Teuber, 'Geographical Indications of Origin' (n 73).

[80] Kate Bird, Tali Diamant, Ursula Grant, Kate Higgins, Rainer Quiztow, Liz Turner, and Milo Vandemoortele, 'Ethiopia Trademarking and Licensing Initiative: Supporting a Better Deal for Coffee Producers through Aid for Trade' (ODI, 2009), https://cdn.odi.org/media/documents/5946.pdf.

[81] ibid 1.

[82] ibid 2.

approach of this book – to understand how the law can contribute to poverty reduction. Once contributing to almost half of the GDP of Ethiopia, agriculture now contributes to just over a third.[83] With over 90 per cent of the farmers working in coffee being smallholder farmers,[84] and Ethiopia being the second-most populous nation on the African continent, the sector clearly has a vital role to play in supporting the socioeconomic fabric of the Ethiopian nation.

Accordingly, the Ethiopian government is the legal owner of the specialty coffee trademarks, which are managed by the Ethiopian IPO.[85] The Ethiopian IPO co-ordinates with stakeholders – exporters, co-operatives, and government agencies – via the Ethiopian Fine Coffee Stakeholder Committee.[86] The Committee has set up a network of licensed roasters, retailers, exporters, and importers who contribute to brand promotion and management strategy. Over 80 companies have signed up to be licensees, and thus to benefit from using the trademark label of 'Sidamo', 'Harar', or 'Yirgacheffe'.[87] Under the new initiative, farmers deliver and sell their beans directly to the Ethiopian Commodity Exchange (ECX) warehouses, where they are sorted, graded, and registered in an inventory.[88] This process is intended to assure quality and traceability, and to increase farmers' knowledge about the retail price of their beans, since it is set by the ECX, and no longer the New York Stock Exchange (NYSE).

The next section discusses the process in which Ethiopian coffee attained legal protection in the US, inter alia, as a result of the Ethiopia–Starbucks dispute.

5.3.2 Ethiopia–Starbucks Dispute

In 2004, the Starbucks Coffee Company – the largest buyer of Ethiopian coffee – filed to register 'Shirkina Sun-Dried Sidamo' at the United States Patent and Trademark Office (USPTO). It subsequently withdrew its application.[89] Initially, Starbucks refused to withdraw the application and cited that the Ethiopian government should opt for a certification trademark, which in its perspective was more appropriate to monitor the standards and quality of the coffees, as opposed to the regular trademark scheme (more akin to 'labelling'). Although

[83] World Bank, 'Agriculture, Forestry, and Fishing, Value Added (% of GDP) - Ethiopia', https://data.worldbank.org/indicator/NV.AGR.TOTL.ZS?locations=ET.

[84] Bird et al, 'Ethiopia Trademarking and Licensing Initiative' (n 80) 3.

[85] ibid 8.

[86] Committee membership includes the Ethiopian Coffee Exporters Association Board, Ethiopian IPO, Federal Cooperative Agency, Ministry of Agriculture and Rural Areas Development, Ministry of Foreign Affairs, Ministry of Trade and Industry, and the Sidamo, Oromia and Yirgacheffe Coffee Farmers' Cooperative Unions (ibid 8).

[87] ibid 9.

[88] ibid.

[89] Application No 78,431,410 (abandoned 8 July 2006). See 'Shirkina Sun-Dried Sidamo' (*USPTO*), https://www.uspto.gov/main/trademarks.htm.

it withdrew the application, Starbucks is nevertheless a member of the US National Coffee Association, which later filed an objection to the Ethiopian application to trademark 'Sidamo'.

In 2005, the Ethiopian government filed regular trademark applications for 'Harar', 'Sidamo', and 'Yirgacheffe' coffees at the USPTO. While those three names refer to heritage coffees of Ethiopia, the application received an objection by the US National Coffee Association, for the 'Sidamo' registration, on the grounds that it was considered a generic name used over several centuries in the US.[90] The Court of Appeal of the Federal Circuit relied on the two-step test: 'First, what is the genus of goods or services at issue? Second, is the term sought to be registered or retained on the register understood by the relevant public primarily to refer to that genus of goods or services?'[91] In its response, the government of Ethiopia presented that

> [t]he relevant public does not understand the term 'SIDAMO' to mean coffee without regard to the source or geographic origin of the coffee or the qualities associated with 'SIDAMO' coffee. 'SIDAMO' is not synonymous with the broad class of coffee.[92]

The Association supported their objection with over 600 documents to support the claim that Sidamo was generic and, therefore, should not be protected under US law. However, the USPTO agreed that the term 'SIDAMO' passed the two-step test, since its genus is Ethiopian and it is recognised as a signifier of a coffee coming from that territory. As such, Sidamo was not deemed generic, and was protected via its trademark registration, granted in February 2008.

The USPTO granted trademark protection to all three terms, although the term 'Sidamo' was only protected upon appeal by the Ethiopian government.[93] This shows the power of objections supported by substantial documentation, but also how the verdict can be appealed – and rightly so, in this case – in favour of the Ethiopian government, to protect and use its IP assets as it so chooses. These terms are equally protected in the EU, Japan, Canada, and Australia.

5.3.3 To GI or Not to GI? Interpretative Variations of the Ethiopia–Starbucks Dispute

There are generally two interpretative variations on the Ethiopia–Starbucks dispute. One recognises that, de jure, trademarks offer direct protection for the owner of the trademark – the Ethiopian government – who, therefore, have the right to exploit, license, and use the name, including the right to exclude others from using the name in trade. On the other hand, there are those that

[90] USPTO, 'Response to Office Action, Serial Number 78589307' (n 6).
[91] *Marvin Ginn Corp. v Int'l Ass'n of Fire Chiefs, Inc.* [1986] FC 782 (F.2d 987) 990.
[92] USPTO, 'Response to Office Action, Serial Number 78589307' (n 6).
[93] US Trademark No 3,381,739 (filed 17 March 2005).

are critical of the Ethiopian government's choice of trademark protection, for several reasons, which shall be discussed below.

Amongst the critics, Christopher Heath is critical about the government of Ethiopia's choice to use trademark protections for its specialty coffees, on the ground that these terms risk being descriptive or deceptive in practice. Quoting WIPO's coverage of the Ethiopia Starbucks dispute – which recognises that, contrary to GI protection, trademarks do not need to have a specific link to a geographic region or a quality associated with that territory – he claims, '[t]his summarises about everything that is legally wrong with registering geographical names as trademarks'.[94] This is an issue picked up by Justin Hughes in his work on how GIs can help developing countries, and particularly their smallholder farmers. Hughes sets out the advantage of locating GI rights firmly with farmers precisely because of the lack of transparent public institutions.[95] In reference to public statements by the Ethiopian government and the UK NGO Light Years, who assisted in the trademark licensing initiative, Hughes summarises that '[a] benign interpretation of all these statements is that officials in Addis Ababa realize that they cannot establish an effective, dependable system for geographical certification, let alone additional quality controls that EU officials associate with true GIs'.[96] In this regard, Hughes does not see the value in trademark registration, since farmers, the producers of this commodity, do not benefit from such a system. Rather, Hughes presents the challenge that the Ethiopian government should invest the resources to establish a GI system, in which farmers are beneficiaries and the state is transparent in its processes. Overall, there is consensus among scholars that the Ethiopian government does not currently have the resources or infrastructure to put a GI certification or *sui generis* system in place.

Maria Brownell, on the other hand, offers a more nuanced perspective on Ethiopia's trademark licensing initiative: 'the Ethiopian licensing model is a model for any farmer who wants to capitalize on the value of commodity export products', and '[it] will be more successful at achieving that goal when coffee farmers are informed of and participate in the plan'.[97] As such, Brownell's text is rooted in a legal analysis which demonstrates that trademark protection provides the Ethiopian government, as the sole owner, with the exclusive right, as duty-bearer, to control the specialty coffee sold. This text also contextualises the high cost of one of the alternative routes of certification, for which Brownell underscores that the primary aim would be to prevent misuse and imitation. Trademarks, her text underscores, fulfil the prevention-of-misuse function of

[94] Christopher Heath, 'How Would Geographical Indications from Asia Fare in Europe?' in Irene Calboli and Ng-Loy Wee Loon (eds), *Geographical Indications at the Crossroads of Trade, Development and Culture* (CUP, 2017) 200.

[95] Hughes, 'Coffee and Chocolate' (n 1).

[96] ibid 79.

[97] Maria Brownell, 'Coffee Trademark Licensing for Farmers: Brewing a Farmer-Owned Brand' (2009) 14 *Drake Journal of Agricultural Law* 294.

a certification mark while also providing the owner with the right of exclusive usage to control the use and the right to use of the product.[98] In other words, the absolute control that can be exercised to manage the brand and its value is not paramount in a certification mark system, where any company can use the given mark. Furthermore, Brownell recognises that even a European GI for Ethiopian specialty coffees would only be valid in the EU, and thus, in the context of securing Ethiopia's market interests vis-à-vis the US, trademarks offer the most secure means of controlling that market.[99] Brownell's analysis is pertinent and relevant to this study, since CARIFORUM countries are struggling to establish GIs in their territories, even though the laws have been introduced, in the early 2000s. It suggests that, in the absence of implementation, some countries and companies may, like Ethiopia, wish to opt for trademark protections if the requisite support for practically implementing GIs is unavailable. This does not undermine the claim of this book that GIs can be tools for sustainable development; rather, it reinforces the de jure reality that there are legal options for Third World countries to protect their origin products.

In relation to farmers' interests, Brownell maintains a nuanced analysis in recognition that farmers will benefit when consumer demand translates to an increase in price, especially since the Ethiopian government's initiative to regulate the price of coffee via the ECX and not via the NYSE, as had been the case.[100] This latter fact is an important demonstration of the government of Ethiopia reclaiming control over its commodity pricing, and is in line with the control it seeks over the coffee sector via its trademark licensing initiative.

Mary O'Kicki similarly opines that the Ethiopian government's choice of trademark protection for their specialty coffees is in line with the 'political, economic and cultural needs of its people'.[101] O'Kicki contextualises that GI systems, certification, or *sui generis* systems are better suited to countries who have a long history of GI usage and, therefore, the infrastructure in place to operate such systems. Rather, she argues that GI protection puts an undue burden on developing countries to have a market presence for their traditional goods.[102]

The critical analyses of both camps, however, converge in consideration of smallholder farmers, who are cited as beneficiaries of the licensing initiative. The licence agreement states:

> *The purpose of these filings is to seek to maximise the benefits to farmers* of the use of the Marks and the Goodwill symbolized by the Marks Worldwide, and to prevent misuse . . .
>
> Licensor has committed itself to securing, enhancing and managing the rights associated with use of the marks, including all right, title and interest in and to the marks,

[98] ibid 305.
[99] ibid 307.
[100] ibid 308.
[101] O'Kicki, 'Lessons Learned' (n 75) 335.
[102] ibid 331.

> *for the benefit of, and in collaboration with, up to 4 million Ethiopians engaged in the production and supply of coffees covered by the marks as represented by farmer cooperatives and other organized stakeholder organisations* in the Ethiopian coffee sector (emphasis added).

Both Hughes' and Brownell's texts consider the current levels of poverty alongside corruption claims, while putting forth the recommendation that farmers must be informed participants in the process of protecting specialty coffees.[103] For Brownell, this can be done within the trademark framework, whereas for Hughes, this could have been done via a certification scheme, which is the common means for protecting GIs in non-*sui generis* GI systems. For Philip Matthews, the relative impersonality of the GI system offers a greater opportunity for producers to control the specialty coffee product and profits,[104] albeit in markets that recognise *sui generis* GI protection. In the same vein as Hughes' argument, the control would be with the smallholder coffee farmers as right-holders, as opposed to the government of Ethiopia. Additionally, the Overseas Development Institute (ODI)'s case study also suggests that producers need to be equipped to take advantage of the opportunities of the scheme, both in terms of legal and business expertise, as well as inclusion of farmers who are not yet in co-operatives. The latter is an issue that the ODI recognises as a concern from a pro-poor approach, since only 15 per cent of farmers were in co-operative organisations at the time of writing, and hence the rate of exclusion, particularly of the most marginalised, is high.[105]

Overall, the analysis suggests that the trademark system has enabled the Ethiopian government to begin a process of cataloguing its (coffee) IP assets, and it does not close the door to future GI (certification or *sui generis*) protection.[106] This suggestion contextualises the debate on trademark protection for Ethiopian specialty coffees in the reality that setting up IP systems where they did not previously exist is extremely challenging; that is, even where Third World countries can access IPs, their formalisation can be a practical impediment. As such, it highlights the specific hurdles that developing countries can face when attempting to adopt the most relevant protection for their GI products. It shows that, although a GI system may be effective in theory, its effectiveness is inherently linked to the ability to implement the system in practice, and this is linked to having the requisite resources to do so. Rather, in this case, it seems that the roots have been planted for IP protection for Ethiopia's specialty coffees, and it is not far-fetched to imagine that, within jurisdictions where *sui generis* protection is commonplace, Ethiopian GIs may be protected as such in due course. What

[103] Brownell, 'Coffee Trademark Licensing for Farmers' (n 97) 312.

[104] Philip Matthews, 'Increasing Revenue in Developing Nations through Intellectual Property Rights: Why a Diversified Approach to Intellectual Property Protection with a Focus on Geographical Indications is the Best Method' (2010) 7 *Buffalo Intellectual Property Law* 217.

[105] Bird et al, 'Ethiopia Trademarking and Licensing Initiative' (n 80) 12–13.

[106] See ch 2.

this case does demonstrate is that options remain open to developing country governments to use the IP system of protection as they see fit, based on their own socioeconomic, political, and cultural realities. There is the need for flexibility in legal regimes – the need to allow countries (and especially those in the Third World) the opportunity to use the trademarks or *sui generis* GI system that best suit their economic, social, and cultural needs.

A key lesson from the Ethiopian case is that, while IPRs can increase the retail value of Ethiopian coffee for its producers, this must be accompanied by an effective branding management strategy.[107] Under the trademark licensing agreement, licensees agree to advertising, marketing, and promotion of the mark to enhance its value, including via its sub-licensees.[108] This is where the literature has underscored the importance of a participatory and inclusive approach to implementing the Initiative, since the smallholder farmers are intended to be a key beneficiaries of such an initiative and not merely co-opted to facilitate attracting premium prices for consumers.[109] On this backdrop, the chapter turns to look at the case of Café de Colombia, considered a success story for GI protection coming from the Third World.

5.4 SUCCESS STORIES OF THIRD WORLD GIS

5.4.1 An Insight from Café de Colombia

Café de Colombia was the first non-EU GI registered in the EU, in 2007,[110] and it is significant for the analysis in this book because it represents the first non-EU GI registered in the EU's *sui generis* GI protection system. The labelling of Café de Colombia started in the early 1900s, and a wide-scale government-led marketing campaign followed in the 1960s. Although the initiative began in response to a thriving (US) export market, the origin of coffee was not well known to US consumers.[111] The campaign focused on the fictional character of 'Juan Valdez', who was designed to be representative of the average Colombian coffee farmer. Prior to the Protected GI (PGI) status in the EU, 'Juan Valdez' and 'Café de Colombia' were protected as trademarks,[112] as well as through a Community

[107] The report also adds that the following are needed: legal and business expertise; co-ordination, including institutional mechanisms established between national stakeholders and producers; and transparency in the supply chain. Bird et al, 'Ethiopia Trademarking and Licensing Initiative' (n 80) 11–13.

[108] Ethiopian Trademark Licensing Agreement, s 10.

[109] Brownell, 'Coffee Trademark Licensing for Farmers' (n 97) 310–14.

[110] European Commission, Publication of an Application Pursuant to Article 6(2) of Council Regulation (EC) No 510/2006 on the Protection of Geographical Indications and Designations of Origin for Agricultural Products and Foodstuffs [2006] OJ C 320, 17.

[111] A survey taken in 1950 revealed that only 4% of consumers were aware of the origin: Hughes, 'Coffee and Chocolate' (n 1) 82, fn 265.

[112] See Juan Valdez (n 7).

trademark for 'Café de Colombia' in 2001. Additionally, 'Juan Valdez' coffee of Colombia was registered as a trademark in 1963, as well as a US trademark for '100% Colombian Coffee', linked to the Juan Valdez character. By 1973, the Colombian government had registered the Colombian certification mark, which showed that the coffee originated in Colombia, was subject to standards inspection, and was approved for export.[113] Today, there exists a successful chain of coffee shops named 'Juan Valdez', owned by the non-profit producers' organisation Federación Nacional de Cafeteros de Colombia. The motto or branding of this chain is 'JUAN VALDEZ CAFES make it possible for our farmers to obtain a fair revenue for their work'.[114] This example shows that Colombian coffee producers, supported by the Colombian government, are using a combination of all the legal protections required to protect their origin coffee. Furthermore, this illustrates a participatory, inclusive, farmer-integrated approach of the type that the above-mentioned authors allude to.

In Hughes' opinion, 'There is no more successful example of the creation of a globally valuable geographical indication from a developing country than COLOMBIAN coffee.'[115] Despite critical acclaim of the Café de Colombia branding case, Hughes does, however, warn that '[t]he strength of the overall COLOMBIAN brand may now limit the ability of Colombia or others to develop more specific, more high-end, niche geographical brands for Colombian coffees'.[116] In other words, the Café de Colombia brand may over-represent Colombian coffee generally, as opposed to providing a springboard from which other local regional brands may be developed. However, given that consumers link the country to having the reputation of a quality coffee producer, it could equally be argued that consumers would also be willing to pay a higher premium price for local niche brands. Indeed, the Colombian Coffee Growers' Federation (FNC) has held six editions of a national quality competition for its reputed coffees, under the banner of 'Colombia, Land of Diversity'.[117] This is evidence that the producers themselves are involved in showcasing and supporting the diversity of coffees that make up the renowned (national) brand 'Café de Colombia'.

This is precisely the issue of country-GI protections that is important to consider in the development of country-name GIs in developing-country contexts. Yet, it is also recognised that some of the most successful geographic names are based on country names. Take, for example, Scotch whisky, Swiss or

[113] Hughes, 'Coffee and Chocolate' (n 1) 82.
[114] ibid 121–22.
[115] ibid 81.
[116] ibid 85.
[117] Antioquia, Cauca, Cundinamarca, and Norte de Santander were the 2021 winners: 'Coffees from Antioquia, Cauca, C/marca and N. de Santander win 6th competition "Colombia, Land of Diversity"' (*Federacion de Cafeteros*, 15 April 2021), https://federaciondecafeteros.org/wp/listado-noticias/coffees-from-antioquia-cauca-c-marca-and-n-de-santander-win-6th-competition-colombia-land-of-diversity/?lang=en.

Belgian chocolate, and Kenyan coffee.[118] This will be an important element to consider as Caribbean countries develop their GI schemes as a means of protecting and regulating the usage of their IP assets.[119]

5.4.2 An Insight from Indian Basmati Rice

In the Basmati case,[120] Rice Tec, a Texan (US) company, attempted to register trademarks for 'Texmati' and 'Kasmati' in the UK. Rice Tec unsuccessfully claimed that the cross-bred Indian basmati rice and Texan dwarfed rice could be protected, since, in their view, 'basmati' merely referred to an aromatic rice and there was no GI link to India. However, their 'Kasmati' packaging did include the phrasing 'Indian Style Basmati Rice', as well as the graphic reproduction of one of India's most iconic buildings, the Taj Mahal.[121] The Indian government successfully defended 'Basmati' as an Indian GI in the UK. Meanwhile, the US Federal Trade Commission responded to Indian NGO complaints on the issue by stating that basmati was, in their perspective, generic.[122] Today, 'Texmati' is permitted under US law.[123] The dynamics surrounding this case are of threefold interest to this book. Firstly, the case propelled a multi-stakeholder outcry globally, one which scholars have suggested was akin to 'defending the Indian flag against a foreign invasion and neocolonialism'.[124] It provides a strong indication that both national and diasporic responses to actions perceived to be to neocolonial,[125] effectively perpetuating

[118] Hughes, 'Coffee and Chocolate' (n 1) 87.

[119] See ch 6.

[120] Trademarks (n 8).

[121] Delphine Marie-Vivien, 'From Plant Variety Definition to Geographical Indication Protection: A Search for the Link Between Basmati Rice and India/Pakistan' (2008) 11(4) *Journal of World Intellectual Property* 322.

[122] ibid.

[123] For an overview of the US case, see Bernard O'Connor, *The Law of Geographical Indications* (Cameron May, 2004) 307, 368.

[124] Denis Vidal, 'In Search of "Basmatisthan": Agro-nationalism and Globalisation' in Jackie Assayag and CJ Fuller (eds), *Globalizing India: Perspectives from Below* (Anthem Press, 2005), in Estelle Bienabe and Delphine Marie-Vivien, 'Institutionalizing Geographical Indications in Southern Countries: Lessons Learned from Basmati and Rooibos' (2017) 98 *World Development* 58–67, 60.

[125] ibid. The continuation between the colonial and post-colonial period is what a number of authors regard as the continuation of colonialism by other means, or rather, neo-colonialism. For Rahmatian, neo-colonialism and IP concerns precisely with how law functions as a tool to facilitate economic neo-colonialism through the system of international trade: Andreas Rahmatian, 'Neo-Colonial Aspects of Intellectual Property Protection' (2009) 12(1) *Journal of World Intellectual Property* 41. Within a post-colonial context, Kwame Nkrumah, the first president of independent Ghana explained, 'it is this sum total of these modern attempts to perpetuate colonialism while at the same time talking about "freedom" which has come to be known as neo-colonialism'. See Kwame Nkrumah, *Neo-Colonialism, The Last Stage of Imperialism* (International Publishers Co, 1965) 239. The authors converge on this definition that economic penetration and extraction is the key tenet of neo-colonialism, which serves as a key reflective point in my investigation.

underdevelopment due to the lack of recognition for a pre-existing GI product, can wield significant power to lead to national policy change.[126] Similar reactions have been seen with 'Jamaica Jerk', which is a registered GI in Jamaica, and against the J'ouvert rum.[127]

Secondly, scholars have recognised that a *sui generis* GI system requires more public intervention than a trademark system, particularly requiring rigorous examination to establish the collective reputation *and* origin link,[128] which is a requirement of establishing a GI specification.[129] In this case, it appears that the establishment of a separate body of *sui generis* GI law is deemed necessary to go beyond the bureaucratic strictures of the trademark system, in order to embed a more thorough system of public oversight that is capable of recognising a GI as a heritage-based product.[130] This is linked to the secondary rural development aspect of the economic rationale for protecting GIs, and thus, subsequently, it is expected that this will have rural-development-related effects.[131]

Thirdly, there is evidence that the Indian state is using GIs as a means to protect their local, cultural, and national heritage-based products in the absence

[126] This contrasts with the South African Rooibos case, which, while having similar reactions, did not lead to the enactment of a separate *sui generis* GI law. See Bienabe and Marie-Vivien, 'Institutionalizing Geographical Indications' (n 124) 60.

[127] The issues summarised: 'The decision to label the microwavable rice "jerk" has been criticised, because the product doesn't contain many of the ingredients traditionally used in a Jamaican jerk marinade.' ('Jamie Oliver's "Jerk Rice" Accused of Cultural Appropriation' (*BBC Newsbeat*, 21 August 2018), https://bbc.co.uk/news/newsbeat-45246009. See also Zoe Williams, 'Here's the Main Issue Behind the Jamie Oliver Jerk Rice Row – and it's Not Cultural Appropriation' *The Guardian* (London, 22 August 2018), https://theguardian.com/commentisfree/2018/aug/22/heres-the-main-issue-behind-the-jamie-oliver-jerk-rice-row-and-its-not-cultural-appropriation; Verdel Bishop 'J'Ouvert Rum Angers Trinis' *Trinidad Express* (Port of Spain, 21 June 2021), https://trinidadexpress.com/news/local/j-ouvert-rum-angers-trinis/article_8a4092ac-d227-11eb-9254-936fbfb2e932.html.

[128] This is not a new debate. The institutional differences between the TM and GI legal systems have been recognised since the inception of multilateral negotiations on industrial policy: 'recognising a collective interest in a geographical term proved difficult for registration systems that only recognise signs indicating distinctiveness of individual trade sources'. See Dev Gangjee, *Relocating the Law on Geographical Indications* (CUP, 2012) 60.

[129] This has been recognised by Audier, 1999; Hughes, 2006; Marie-Vivien, 2010; Bramley, Marie-Vivien, and Bienabe, 2013, in Bienabe and Marie-Vivien, 'Institutionalizing Geographical Indications' (n 124) 58.

[130] Balganesh, 2003, in Bienabe and Marie-Vivien, 'Institutionalizing Geographical Indications' (n 124) 60. Also, Bienabe and Marie Vivien, in particular, put forth: 'we argue that heritage-based reputation should per se constitute an essential criterion for the decision to grant a GI and that this effectively defines GIs as a specific IPR': Bienabe and Marie-Vivien (ibid) 64. Gangjee also noted that GIs' heritage (and rural development) aspect has gained importance: Gangjee, *Relocating the Law on Geographical Indications* (n 128) 8.

[131] Delphine Marie-Vivien considers conservation, biological resources, biodiversity, and cultural diversity aspects of GI protection: 'Protection of Geographical Indications in ASEAN countries: Convergences and Challenges to Awakening Sleeping Geographical Indications' (2020) 23(3-4) *Journal of World Intellectual Property* 328.

of any export potential.[132] This is interesting since it suggests an 'inventory usage' of GIs,[133] which challenges the link with GIs as IPRs applied traditionally to export commodities.[134] An inventory list means that GIs are registered (somewhat) as a heuristic tool of the state in order to 'map' which GIs exist, irrespective of their export potential, but rather due to their cultural, local market heritage. The Indian state has the capacity to roll out such a system. By contrast, the Caribbean is taking a piecemeal, step-by-step approach, incrementally registering its GIs, which also have substantial export market value. A case in point is that the majority of GIs being considered are historically exported commodities, such as (Demerara) sugar and molasses, or (Barbados or Jamaica) rums. Essentially, the Indian precedent challenges the economic rationales linked to GI development, namely that GIs' protection has an impact on product differentiation and market access. Rather, the emphasis seems to be more on the secondary effects linked to rural development.

Together, these three aspects – the infringement-reactionary approach to GI development; the need for a more responsive *sui generis* legal system; and the heritage-based 'inventory usage' of the law – provide an interesting backdrop, since several developing-country cases also demonstrate similar features. For example, Demerara sugar/Gold and the Ethiopian coffee cases both had elements of the infringement-reactionary approach, which catalysed to some extent the GI protection sought; apart from the current status quo in Ethiopia, both the Guyanese government and the Jamaican government are enacting *sui generis* GI protections; India is somewhat an outlier in its inventory usage approach, which reflects the state's capabilities and resources to enact and enforce GI laws (in contrast to Ethiopia, for example). This, however, is not the end of this tale, as the results are bittersweet for some producers. Despite the Indian government's

[132] This is referred to as inventorying local products or protecting via the GI registry as a type of inventory usage. From a critical point of view, Gramsci suggests amassing the 'infinity of traces' to build our very own 'inventory'. Caribbean scholars, such as Barry Chevannes and George Lamming, have heeded this advice, since it contributes to reviving subjugated knowledges. See discussion in Yentyl Williams, '"Doing and knowing" IEL through the lens of Caribbean Rastafari philosophy (IEL Collective Symposium II)' (*University of Bristol Legal Research blog*, 26 March 2020), https://legalresearch.blogs.bris.ac.uk/tag/barry-chevannes/. See also Pooja Parmar, 'TWAIL: An Epistemological Inquiry' (2008) 10(4) *International Community Law Review* 363–70. For reference to Indian usage of GIs, see Bienabe and Marie-Vivien, 'Institutionalizing Geographical Indications' (n 124) 60.

[133] This is the term that I give to this type of usage of GIs.

[134] The total world demand for Basmati rice is around 1.18 million tons and is valued at USD 700 million (Padmanabhan, 2003). The majority of the exports are to the Middle East, while a small percentage of basmati is exported to Europe and North America. Saudi Arabia is the largest importer of basmati rice (65% of Indian exports), followed by the UK (15% of Indian exports), Kuwait (10%), UAE (5%), and other countries (5%) (ITCIBD, 2003). See Kranti Mulik and John M Crespi, 'Geographical Indications and the Trade Related Property Rights Agreement: A Case Study of Basmati Rice Exports' (American Agricultural Economics Association Annual meeting, Denver, 1–4 August 2004) (New Name, 2008: 'Agricultural and Applied Economics Association') 10. Another academic text states that the export value is in the region of USD 350 million for India. See Harsh Chandola, 'Basmati Rice: Geographical Indication or Mis‐Indication' (2006) 9(2) *Journal of World Intellectual Property* 166–88.

best efforts to protect basmati, Texmati and Jasmati rice are protected in the US, as they are not deemed to confuse the US consumer.[135] There is also discontent locally, as some rice producers claim to be excluded from the GI specification's basmati-growing region, including those from neighbouring Pakistan.[136]

5.5 CONCLUSION

This chapter has discussed Guysuco's opposition proceedings against Bedessee's trademark application for Demerara Gold and the libel claim launched by Bedessee, and Minister Persaud's unsuccessful recourse to the state immunity defence. Overall, it demonstrates that not only are GIs part of the trademark melting pot in the absence of a *sui generis* GI system, but that prior trademarks, in the absence of effective infringement claims, are shielded by the 'first in time, first in right' (FITFIR) principle.[137] Moreover, attempts of GI-producing governments to claim that prior trademarks may be deceptively misdescriptive could be open to libel claims, given the commercial nature of the trade in GIs, which prevents the exception that could be granted as part of state immunity.

The chapter also discussed how Ethiopia sought to protect its GIs nationally and internationally. The government of Ethiopia, however, chose the trademark route, effectively demonstrating that a *sui generis* GI system may not be a short-term or immediate solution for protecting Third World GI products, especially when implementing IP protection for the first time. Rather, protecting IP assets as GIs, as opposed to trademarks, has a qualitative difference, and requires the administrative, bureaucratic, and financial means to implement such a system, which Third World countries may struggle with.

Insights provided from the first non-EU GI registered in the EU in 2007, for 'Café de Colombia' demonstrated the success of a participatory, inclusive, farmer-integrated approach to marketing Colombian coffee. A consistent and strategic approach to protecting the Colombian coffee GI, notwithstanding the registration system, allowed Café de Colombia to establish its reputation. With reference to the process which began in the 1990s, an overview was given on how the Colombian government and coffee producer associations adopted a strategy to ensure that sales of Colombian coffee as trademarks in the US context, represented by the symbolic figure of 'Juan Valdez', would provide fair revenues for Colombian farmers.

The basmati rice case in the UK demonstrated the impact of the government of India and its diaspora, rallying to protect their basmati rice. However,

[135] Chandola, 'Basmati Rice' (n 134) 166.

[136] Christine Haight Farley, 'Looking Beyond the Known Story: How the Prehistory of Protection of Geographical Indications in the Americas Provides an Alternate Approach' in Calboli and Wee Loon (n 94) 230–32.

[137] See Gangjee, *Relocating the Law on Geographical Indications* (n 128) 225.

it also demonstrated that a success in one jurisdiction that protects GI rights is not a win in all jurisdictions, as basmati rice legal cases ensued in the US, and Texmati and Jasmati are permitted trademarks which nevertheless evoke a link to basmati.[138] Read alongside the Café de Colombia case, this suggests that there is room yet for more strategic engagement to protect basmati in jurisdictions that do not have stand-alone *sui generis* GI laws. Yet, this case perhaps most insightfully sheds light on how the Indian government is implementing its *sui generis* GI laws within India as a form of inventory of origin-heritage products. Notwithstanding challenges that Indian GI products may face abroad, the registration in their home territory is evidence of the priority the government has given to protecting Indian GI products. Furthermore, the capacity of the state to do so reflects India's ability – in contrast to Ethiopia, for example – to use GIs as emancipatory legal tools distinct from the private rights of trademarks, to foster sustainable development in Third World contexts. The lessons drawn are meant to serve as analytically valuable tools for CARIFORUM countries as they seek to protect their IP assets via a *sui generis* GI system for the first time.

In the next chapter, GI protection for Demerara and Barbados Rum is discussed alongside insights from Mexico's tequila GI industry, to assess to what extent reputable GIs have an emancipatory potential for GI communities, as such, contributing to a 'development from within' in their local contexts.

[138] On evocation, see ch 3, n 40, and also ch 4 discussions.

6

Can Caribbean Rum GIs Learn Lessons from Mexico's Tequila GI? Insights from Demerara and Barbados

Demerara Rums are celebrated for more than 300 years of artisanal rum production in the original Double Wooden Pot and the Coffey stills invented in Guyana. Rums from Demerara have been exported for more than 200 years including historical supply to the British Royal Navy for the daily ration to sailors. Some of these original stills have survived and are in operation to this day.

The confluence of heritage, natural factors, and the art and science of distillation by traditional methods, equipment and human expertise has immeasurably maintained the character and quality of Demerara Rums as well as their reputation.[1]

Demerara Rum GI (2021).

6.1 INTRODUCTION

THIS CHAPTER PROVIDES AN overview of the GIs for rums in the Caribbean, particularly interrogating the substantive elements of the Demerara Rum GI, the first Caribbean rum GI protected within the EU,[2] and the tensions stalling the registration of a Barbados Rum GI. The analysis draws on lessons from the oldest (subaltern) GI in the Third World, Mexico's Tequila GI, to assess how GIs can foster 'development from within' for Third World states in a post-colonial era.[3] The chapter also considers that CARIFORUM states, as Small Island Developing States (SIDS), face unique challenges linked to their limited

[1] 'DEMERARA RUM' (File number: PGI-GY-02423 – 28.6.2018). Publication of an Application Pursuant to Article 17(6) of Regulation (EC) No 110/2008 of the European Parliament and of the Council on the Definition, Description, Presentation, Labelling and the Protection of Geographical Indications of Spirit Drinks and Repealing Council Regulation (EEC) No 1576/89 [2021] OJ C120/7, 11.

[2] ibid.

[3] Sarah Bowen, 'Development from Within? The Potential for Geographical Indications in the Global South' (2010) 13(2) *Journal of World Intellectual Property* 231, 232. See ch 1.

geographic scope, which may impact on how the law can function inclusively, as a global-local law.[4] However, it is also demonstrated that the geographic delimitations of CARIFORUM territories can be harnessed as an opportunity to strategically co-brand GIs with the government, in order to foster sustainable development. This chapter is concerned with addressing the following question: *to what extent are country name GIs optimal in the Third World CARIFORUM countries?* It also poses the question, *what lessons can be gleaned for framing GIs as emancipatory legal tools from the Mexican Tequila GI case study of 'development from within'?* The chapter demonstrates that national rum GIs have proven difficult to achieve in the region, due to ineffective and inefficient dialogical manoeuvres from the different rum producers based on their different preferences – related to water inputs and cask ageing, for example – when drawing up draft GI specifications.

The chapter discusses the current deadlock to achieving a Barbados Rum GI with reference to the West Indies Rum Distillery (WIRD) (the largest rum distiller) and Mount Gay, Foursquare, and St Nicholas Abbey (three smaller producers). The rationale for protection sought, therefore, differs not only legally – in the absence of Protected Designation of Origin (PDO) and Protected Geographical Indication (PGI) distinctions de jure[5] – but has implications substantively on whether the GI is produced and protected according to the 'dynamic of difference' or the 'commensurability of difference'.[6] The chapter also draws on the case study of the Ron Dominicano GI to demonstrate how to overcome some of the challenges facing GI regulatory bodies in the process of registering a GI specification, the legal document outlining GI protection. It demonstrates that 'development from within' must be strategically embedded in the entire process of protecting a GI, as part of a process of reconceptualising the GI as an emancipatory legal tool, from drafting the registration and establishing regulatory bodies, to its functioning once implemented.

The chapter begins by introducing the concept of 'development from within' and outlines the substantive and institutional issues that have emerged from Sarah Bowen's analysis of the Tequila GI. Section 6.1 presents an overview of the Demerara Rum GI, which represents the first Caribbean GI to be protected in the EU, and the Barbados Rum case studies. Section 6.2 applies the concept of 'development from within' and the corollary substantive and institutional issues to the process of GI development in the Caribbean, with reference to the two rum GI case studies: the case study of the Barbados Rum, and the Ron

[4] See Valerie Phillips, 'Indigenous Peoples and the Role of the Nation State' (2007) 101 *American Society of International Law* 319. See also Luis Eslava, *Local Space, Global Life: The Everyday Operation of International Law and Development* (CUP, 2015).

[5] See ch 6.

[6] On 'dynamic of difference' see ch 1 (n 29); Anthony Anghie, *Imperialism, Sovereignty and the Making of International Law* (CUP, 2014) 4. On 'commensurability of difference' (own usage), see ch 1 (n 23).

Dominicano GI.[7] The Conclusion (section 6.3) summarises that GIs drawing on country names can engage in a co-branding strategy so that the GI can foster 'development from within' for producers and producing territories alike. In particular, the chapter suggests that heritage can be added to the traditional triptych – quality, reputation, and characteristics – that defines the origin link. In this way, Caribbean producers, through recontextualising the GI as an emancipatory global-local legal tool, can see themselves as collaborators and not competitors of GI products.

6.1.1 GIs as 'Development from Within': A Case Study of the Tequila Industry

This section introduces the concept of 'development from within' and demonstrates how GIs can serve as sustainable developmental tools. 'Development from within', according to Sarah Bowen, refers to the capacity of a GI to not simply reap economic returns, but to spill over to provide community-wide development.[8] These spillover effects may include, inter alia, the protection of 'traditional heritage, farmer knowledge, and environmental resources associated with typical products'.[9] Bowen also does not refute the European normative conception of GIs as contributing to the quality, cultural preservation, and development of the local community from which the GI emanates.[10] For example, up to 70 per cent of GIs in the EU come from local contexts considered economically deprived.[11] In the case of the Comté GI, farmers producing the renowned cheese reaped a 20 per cent premium for the milk supplied, as a result of the GI.[12] The economic return, therefore, can contribute in real-life terms to

[7] While there are many more examples – Jamaica Rum GI, Ron Cubano GI, Ron Venezuelano GI – the case studies were practically delimited to focus on the present issues facing GI producers seeking registrations, although it is recognised that there is a wealth of lessons to be learnt from other Third World GIs. There is already some literature addressing Jamaica rum; although the application has been filed, there is evidence that producers are not focused on setting up a Regulatory Council but instead want to rewrite the GI specification. Given the limbo that this GI was in, it was excluded. For a general overview, see Enrico Bonadio and Chauntina Poyser, 'Protecting Jamaican Geographical Indications: The Cases of "Jamaica Jerk", "Jamaica Rum" and "Blue Mountain Coffee"' (2021) 5 *European Intellectual Property Review*. Ron Dominicano GI was chosen from the Spanish-speaking Caribbean as the example to be drawn on for this chapter. Indeed, the Dominican Rum Producers' Association (Asociacion Dominicana de Prodoctores de Ron, Inc, or ADOPRON) made reference to the Ron Venezuelano GI in their defence.

[8] Bowen, 'Development from Within?' (n 3).

[9] ibid.

[10] ibid 231.

[11] Nicholas Parrott, Natasha Wilson, and Jonathan Murdoch, 'Spatializing Quality: Regional Protection and the Alternative Geography of Food' (2002) 9(3) *European Urban and Regional Studies* 241–61, in ibid 234.

[12] Pierre Colinet, Marion Desquilbet, Daniel Hassan, Sylvette Monier Dilhan, Valérie Orozco, and Vincent V Requillart, 'Case Study: Comté Cheese in France' (2006) Institut Nationale de la Recherche Agronomique, Toulouse, in ibid.

sustainable development in rural areas and benefit farmer livelihoods.[13] In the Third World context, where premiums for raw commodities are often reaped in the value added abroad, a GI can be a valuable tool to lock in premiums closer to the farm gate. This can positively impact on farmers' lives, increase human development indicators (HDIs), and allow producer communities to live in dignity, in line with the Sustainable Development Goals (SDGs).[14] As such, 'development from within' denotes an alternative type of development that is rooted in the community of producers as the locus of where development starts, emanates from, and returns to. This implies that GIs have a precedent of functioning as emancipatory legal tools, fostering 'development from within' based on a localised understanding of sustainable development. This is in direct contrast to the model of plantation economy during the colonial period, which locked the Caribbean (and colonised nations all over the world) in a dialectic of development–underdevelopment.[15] As emancipatory legal tools capable of fostering 'development from within', GIs appear to offer an opportunity for a break with the past, where colonial masters and empire were being enriched and producer communities were quite literally enslaved for colonial development. Yet, Bowen's analysis of the unfulfilled potential of the Tequila GI to contribute to 'development from within' in the Mexican context offers a cautionary tale for all countries of the Third World implementing GIs.

The Tequila GI is a unique GI in the Third World context, for at least three reasons, outlined by Bowen: it is the oldest GI in the Third World, having been registered as a '*denominacion de origen*' in 1974; it has a globally renowned reputation; and the GI system in Mexico is considered a model in the region.[16] *Agave tequilana Weber* has been distilled and fermented to make tequila liquor since the 1500s, with its commercialisation in the 1700s and 1800s with the Cuervo, Sauza, and Herradura brands.[17] Although smallholder farmers used to grow the mature blue agave for between six and eight years before selling it on to the companies, the commercial power of tequila brands has changed the supply chain, and they are increasingly self-sufficient (discussed further below). Bowen's field research demonstrates how tequila farmers have been progressively marginalised by the commercial powers of both tequila companies/distillers, and the bottlers and distributors. Moreover, the government of Mexico, which owns

[13] ibid.

[14] There are 17 SDGs in the international framework for development, 2020–2030, agreed to by the international community at the UN. See United Nations, 'Sustainable Development Goals: 17 Goals to Transform our World', https://www.un.org/en/exhibits/page/sdgs-17-goals-transform-world#:~:text=GOAL%201%3A%20No%20Poverty%20GOAL,10%3A%20Reduced%20Inequalities%20GOAL%2011.

[15] See George Beckford, Persistent Poverty, *Underdevelopment in Plantation Economies of the Third World* (first published OUP, 1972; Zed Books, 1983); and Walter Rodney, *How Europe Underdeveloped Africa* (first published Bogle-L'Ouverture Publications, 1962; Pambazuka Press, 2012).

[16] Bowen, 'Development from Within?' (n 3) 235.

[17] Enrique Martinez, *Tequila: The Spirit of Mexico* (Abbeville Press, 2000), in ibid.

the GI, is critiqued for not ensuring that the GI regulatory body is transparent in its functioning and inclusive in its stakeholder engagement in the process of redefining GI norms. And extra-local actors – foreign multinationals that own the tequila brands,[18] and buying countries, in this case the United States (US) – can impact on GI norms and practice.

Bowen warns that, 'the tequila case demonstrates that GI protection in and of itself is not beneficial; the way that the GI legislation is designed, and, in particular, how it is enforced on the ground, is what is determinant'.[19] Although contextualising the analysis of the Tequila GI within the framework of the EU's promotion of GIs at the World Trade Organization (WTO), and for developing countries, Bowen challenges the notion that GIs can be implemented successfully in both contexts. Drawing on Peter Evans' 'institutional monocropping' concept, Bowen makes the case against the copy-pasting of rules and regulations from developed countries into developing-country contexts.[20] This is further bolstered by references to the World Bank's Commission on Growth and Development, which calls for country- and context-specific goal setting for development purposes.[21] Bowen puts aside the success of a GI based solely in economic terms and claims that, on the basis of returns for the local population and environment, the Tequila GI has failed.[22] As such, the implementation of the Tequila GI, according to her analysis, has departed from the theoretical underpinnings of GIs, and this has contributed to the dilution of the traditional quality inherent in tequila. A large part of this, according to her assessment, is due to powerful and extra-local actors influencing the tequila production standards in four substantive ways, discussed below. Additionally, the propensity of such exogenous forces to influence the implementation of GIs is also the result of four institutional issues, which are considered in the next section. These factors impact on the propensity of GIs to function as emancipatory legal tools that contribute to 'development from within' for Third World countries.

Bowen points to four substantive examples to underline the issues of changing (or loosening) standards relating to the Tequila GI, meaning that 'development from within' has not fulfilled its potential to manifest itself in the Mexican context: first, the reduction in the required quantity of blue agave sugars;[23]

[18] The four firms Cuervo, Sauza, Herradura, and Cazadores control 67% of the market, and are now owned by Fortune Brands, Brown-Forman, and Diageo; Bowen, 'Development from Within?' (n 3) 238.

[19] ibid 245.

[20] Peter Evans, 'Development as Institutional Change: The Pitfalls of Monocropping and the Potentials of Deliberation' (2004) 38(4) *Studies in Comparative International Development* 30–52, in ibid.

[21] Commission on Growth and Development, 'The Growth Report: Strategies for Sustained Growth and Inclusive Development' (2008) IBRD/WB, in ibid.

[22] ibid 231.

[23] The Tequila GI states that there are generally two types of tequila: 100% blue agave tequila and *tequila mixto* (51% blue agave and 49% sugar-based alcohol). Additionally, there are four age categories: *blanco/joven* (aged 2 months or less); *reposado* (aged 2 months and more); old/*anejo* (aged for 1 year and more); and extra old/*extra anejo* (aged 3 years and more): ibid 237.

second, the continued export of bulk *tequila mixto*; third, the innovation of flavoured tequila; and fourth, the definition of what constitutes 'mature' agave to be used in tequila production.[24] These four substantive examples demonstrate the challenges of achieving a truly endogenous and local 'development from within', since global influences, power, and preferences have a loop-back effect in GI production, as demonstrated in the case of tequila. These four substantive examples reinforce the points Bowen is making about 'development from within': the tradition associated with tequila production is being lost with the changing standards of the industry, and this does not benefit tequila farmers, who are at the foundation of the supply chain. Rather, the evidence points to the fact that the evolution of the tequila-producing standards undermines the ability of the GI to function as a tool for 'development from within' for farmer communities. As such, according to Bowen's analysis, and through a Third World Approaches to International Law (TWAIL) lens, a GI subjected to these challenges fails, in its Third World context, to function as an emancipatory tool, a precondition for achieving sustainable development and poverty eradication.

Bowen has also identified four institutional gaps in the management of the Tequila GI in Mexico that can serve as pertinent reflective points for Caribbean countries and producer associations as they engage in developing GIs across the region. These four issues relate to the institutional regulation of the GI. First, there is no specific institution that regulates GIs; second, GIs are used by the government and producer communities as a form of protection against foreign imitations without a broader consideration of other sustainability objectives that can be pursued as part of a wider development strategy; third, the Mexican government, as legal owner, does not play a significant role in GI management; and fourth, the Mexican government's autonomy is put into question due to the economic influence of the US.[25] Generally, these substantial and institutional issues chime alongside the very same issues Caribbean rum producers are grappling with, from the process of drawing up GI specifications to the practical management of the GI. Moreover, these institutional issues point to how 'development from within' can be undermined, both *from within* – weak regulatory oversight and lack of inclusion of all stakeholders – *and outside*, through commercial pressures from foreign buying governments. Outlining these challenges can serve as lessons and point to areas where support is needed for a GI in a Third World context to fulfil its broader potential to contribute to 'development from within'.

Bowen's account of the specific challenges that Third World countries face represents a cautionary tale for the implementation of GIs in the Caribbean and their potential to function as emancipatory legal tools in practice. Bowen's analysis, while substantively different in its focus on the single large territory of Mexico (and the external influence of the US), has parallels with the Caribbean

[24] ibid 238.
[25] Bowen, 'Development from Within?' (n 3).

rum industry in SIDS territories and the influence of foreign ownership, notably by European companies, Campari (Appleton, Jamaica), Maison Ferrand (West Indian Rum Distillery, Barbados), and Remi Martin (Mount Gay, Barbados). Each of the above-mentioned substantive and institutional issues will be dealt with in turn, with reference to the concomitant issue impacting on Caribbean rum producers.

6.1.2 The (Guyana) Demerara Rum GI: Charting the Success of the First CARIFORUM GI in the EU

This section will analyse the Demerara Rum GI in relation to the concept of 'development from within', while discussing its sociopolitical, cultural, and economic context. The technical file that contains the main specifications for the 'Demerara Rum' GI was submitted by Demerara Distilleries Ltd, and this was published in the official journal of the EU on 28 June 2018.[26] There was no opposition to its application, and it was registered on the same date of publication. The specification of the Demerara Rum GI outlines the description of the rum, its chemical and organoleptic requirements, and its specific characteristics which distinguish it from other spirits.[27] The Demerara Rum GI is described as 'a spirit drink with discernible sugar cane organoleptic characteristics (appearance, colour, aroma, flavour), which is produced exclusively by fermentation and distillation of molasses or sugar-cane based substrate'.[28]

Importantly, the Demerara Rum GI specification indicates that the rum can be produced with molasses or sugar cane, and does not restrict production to one or the other. It must contain no less than 40 per cent alcohol and the rum must not be coloured unless this is the result of the maturation process in the wooden casks or naturally occurring from the sugars.[29] Demerara Rum is distinguished from other spirits in the same category due to its complexity of flavours, which the specification identifies as being linked to the traditional processes used, as well as the mineral content of the Demerara waters of the region.[30] The geographical area is specifically delimited to the low coastal plains of the Demerara county in Guyana, between the Boeraserie River to the west and Abary Creek to the east. The Demerara region is historically a significant sugar-growing region, with approximately 300 plantations in the late 1700s. Today, Demerara Rum Distilleries LLC is the only remaining sugar and rum producer in the area.

[26] Demerara Rum (n 1).
[27] Although, according to its title, the specification details 'the definition, description, presentation, labelling and the protection of geographical indications of spirit drinks', 11 of the 12 pages outline the description (ibid 1–11).
[28] ibid 1.
[29] ibid 1–2.
[30] ibid 2.

The specification outlines the link to the Demerara region as being related to the agroecology of the region and the production process, which connects 'nature, tradition, art and science'.[31] It specifies the environmental and climatic conditions, the water quality, human and process-related factors, and historical origins, as well as the reputation, which links the quartet of factors of 'quality, characteristics, reputation and heritage' of Demerara Rum to the Demerara region.[32] These are all of key importance for understanding what is protected, how it is protected through the GI, and issues that may arise in the future, not only for the Demerara Rum GI but also for other rum GIs in the region. This latter element of the Demerara Rum GI specification proves a point of this book: GIs in the Third World must be firmly rooted in new normative grounds which consider the specificity of the producing community's sustainable development needs. The Demerara Rum GI considers not only the traditional triptych of 'quality, characteristics and reputation' linked to a geographic origin, but, importantly, it also considers 'heritage'.[33] This fourth additional link to the GI territory represents the added value of a GI to a localised form of sustainable development – a 'development from within' for Third World countries. As such, a GI can function as an emancipatory legal tool, which benefits Third World producer communities harnessing heritage for 'development from within'.

The Demerara Rum GI specification makes three explicit linkages between the traditional methods of production and the triptych of quality, characteristics, and reputation linked to Demerara Rums. In two of these references, heritage is also cited.[34] For example, the 'authentic character of the production process' is due to the combination of 'nature, tradition, art and science',[35] and this underpins the origin link of this GI. The traditional production processes also contribute, inter alia, to the complexity of flavours found in Demerara Rums.[36] The specification also provides a historic origins overview of the GI, in which it is explained that 'traditional methods, equipment and human expertise has immeasurably maintained the character and quality of Demerara Rums, as well as their reputation'.[37] It also specifically refers to the artisan Double Wooden pot and the Coffey stills made in Guyana, some of which have survived and are still used in distilling today.[38] However, there is no further explicit reference regarding which stills are used for the Cask Aged, Special, or Grand Special Reserve Demerara Rums, since this may amount to sharing the traditional recipes or trade secrets of these renowned rums. Overall, the linkage between producing

[31] Demerara Rum (n 1).
[32] ibid 4–5.
[33] ibid 3.
[34] ibid 3, 5.
[35] ibid 3.
[36] ibid 2.
[37] ibid 5.
[38] ibid.

rum traditionally and the influence this has on the resultant GI origin link is strongly emphasised. The methods, equipment, and expertise outlined in the GI specification represent the key ingredients of not only what is protected within the GI law but the value of what the concept of 'development from within' seeks to preserve and sustainably reinvest into. As such, a GI is not merely for a product, but it serves the community's sustainable development goals through fostering 'development from within'.

The references to traditional methods are significant in a post-colonial Third World context. Formerly colonial territories engineered for plantation economies and cash crop production, the GI territories of Third World nations today offer an opportunity for post-colonial states to reap the sustainable development returns from GI products. Nonetheless, it is a point of interest, from a critical approach, to discern precisely what traditional methods refer to. From this perspective, a key factor to consider is who developed these traditional methods in a colonial context wrought with structural hierarchies. In other words, were methods imposed top-down by colonial masters or developed by the indigenous population who were enslaved?[39] Indeed, in historic sources, there is evidence that enslaved populations contributed to rum production.[40] Such an interrogation can shed light on the fact that the formalisation and technocratisation involved in the GI registration process can exclude significant historical and normative aspects of GI development. It represents an omission of a less palatable ingredient of rum-making across the entire Caribbean region – the extractive industry of enslavement. More broadly, it frames GIs in the Caribbean as post-colonial by-products of an extractive and structurally oppressive past regime of colonial exploitation. Notwithstanding this, GIs have the transformative potential to contribute to poverty eradication in post-colonial contexts: grappling with historical, traditional, and heritage aspects, Third World GIs can seek to respond to the development challenges that countries have inherited from their colonial past rather than overlooking them.

In relation to the Demerara Rum GI, for example, if the GI spearheaded by Demerara Rum Distillers has the capacity to include the local community of producers along the rum value chain, it could fulfil Bowen's concept of 'development from within' and the TWAIL analysis – that the GI functions as an emancipatory legal tool. This includes, and is not limited to, the references of

[39] Small 'i' indigenous refers not to the Indigenous communities of the Caribbean that were largely subject to genocide, but to populations imported for the purpose of plantation economy. This is discussed in literature by Yentyl Williams, Aleema Gray, and Chevy Eugene, 'Groundings and Rastafari: Re-territorializing Indigenous Knowledges' in Camille Nakhid, Margaret Nakhid-Chatoor, Anabel Fernandez Santana, and Shakeisha Wilson-Scott (eds), *Affirming Methodologies: Research and Education in the Caribbean* (Routledge, 2022) 162–65.

[40] Anthony Dias Blue, *The Complete Book of Spirits: A Guide to Their History, Production, and Enjoyment* (HarperCollins, 2004). Additionally, there is a photograph of an enslaved or indentured 'artisanal' worker making a cask for rum storage at Appleton Distillery, St Elizabeth, Jamaica. This picture does not feature on the official tour but was found by the author after enquiring further about the silences around the rum history and colonialism.

local heritage, knowledge, and environmental resources, which are all mentioned in the GI specification.[41] The obvious challenge in the Demerara case is that the company Demerara Distillers are the sole owner of the GI, although historically there were up to 300 sugar plantations, each producing molasses and rum, along the Demerara River.[42] It is not clear from Bowen's conceptual framework whether 'development from within' can still occur in the context where there is only one producer, a private company, operating in the given geographic territory. Or perhaps the company, in co-ordination with the local community, can put in place processes for ensuring community-wide development where a GI can serve as an emancipatory legal tool and function as a public good.[43] Bowen has distinguished a trademark as a private right which can be monopolised and co-opted,[44] but it remains unclear whether this monopolisation and co-optation may occur where there is only one producer of a GI. A TWAIL *sensibility* would seek to clarify this by understanding whether the GI benefits the transnational capitalist class or the historically oppressed producer/enslaved class.[45] It further raises the question of whether the public good element should be explicitly referenced within GI specifications. As such, explicitly stating the public good impact of the GI can establish a new normative ground for GIs based on the concept of 'development from within'. While the answers may be beyond the analysis of this chapter, the overview of the Tequila GI case study is intended to demonstrate more about the capacity for a GI to contribute (or not) to 'development from within' and to function as a public good.

6.1.3 Barbados Rum GI(s): Tensions and Way Forward?

This section outlines the status quo of the Barbados Rum GI discussions. It sheds light on the tensions around the four distilleries' (dis)agreements on the Barbados Rum GI. Globally, the island of Barbados, just 430 km^2 in size and with a population of around 287,000,[46] has exported USD 39 million of rum, equivalent to 3 per cent of the global rum trade.[47] In the UK, for example, half

[41] Bowen, 'Development from Within?' (n 3); Demerara Rum (n 1).

[42] Jack notes that 'a process of amalgamation over the centuries saw various plantations combine - by the 1930s there were 230 operating sugar plantations and in 1958, only 18'. See Eilidh Jack, 'Demerara Rum: History of the Versailles Still' (*Rum Auctioneer*, 5 November 2019), https://rumauctioneer.com/news/history-of-the-versailles-still.

[43] This can be considered alongside the option of co-branding, as referenced in relation to Natalie Corthésy's work below. Note that this is an area of future research outlined in ch 7.

[44] Bowen, 'Development from Within?' (n 3).

[45] BS Chimni, 'Third World Approaches to International Law: A Manifesto' (2006) 8 *International Community Law Review* 3–27, 29.

[46] Population, Total – Barbados, (*World Bank*, 2023), https://data.worldbank.org/indicator/SP.POP.TOTL?locations=BB.

[47] Danny Hamrick and Karina Fernandez-Stark, 'Barbados in the Rum Global Value Chain' (*Duke Global Value Chain Centre*, August 2017), https://gvcc.duke.edu/wp-content/uploads/2018.01.11_The-Rum-Global-Value-Chain_PUBLIC-1.pdf.

of the top 10 brands are Caribbean rum brands,[48] with Barbados' Mount Gay being widely consumed. Earlier on in the chapter, it was discussed briefly that Demerara Distilleries LLC is the only producer of Demerara Rum, and hence writing the GI specification was relatively unproblematic. In contrast, Barbados has four rum producers, and the distribution of production differs substantially. The biggest rum producer – the West Indian Rum Distillery (WIRD) – dominates 85 per cent of the market, while three smaller producers account for the remaining 15 per cent: Mount Gay, Four Square, and St Nicholas Abbey.[49] Indeed, Mount Gay, Four Square, and St Nicholas Abbey have submitted a Barbados Rum GI application to the government of Barbados, yet none of the draft GI specifications are publicly available.[50] This section aims to elucidate where a key challenge may apply in the implementation of the GI in a SIDS territory such as Barbados. It will contrast the Barbados GI Act with the EU GI models, with the objective of demonstrating where the tension may lie, to later offer some solutions in the Conclusion.

The Barbados GI Act defines the GI as follows:

> 'geographical indication' means an indication which identifies a good as originating in the territory of a country, or a region or locality in that territory, where a given quality, reputation or other characteristic of the good is essentially attributable to its geographical origin.[51]

This definition adheres to the requirements of a GI as established under the TRIPS Agreement (art 22) at the WTO.[52] Indeed, it directly copies from the legal definition under TRIPS, and therefore represents a seamless transfer of law from the international level to the national level, to ensure TRIPS compliance.

According to the EU model of origin protection,[53] the PDO is defined in Article 5.1 of Regulation (EU) No 1151/2012 as referring to a product:

> (a) originating in a specific place, region or, *in exceptional cases, a country*; (b) whose quality or characteristics are *essentially or exclusively due to a particular geographical environment* with its inherent natural and human factors; and (c) the production

[48] Caribbean Export, 'Caribbean Export Report – Unlocking the Profit Potential of the Caribbean highlights growing trend for Caribbean rums across Europe' (12 November 2020), https://carib-export.com/news/caribbean-export-report-unlocking-the-profit-potential-of-the-caribbean-highlights-growing-trend-for-caribbean-rums-across-europe/.

[49] West Indian Rum Distillery (WIRD) Tour (Barbados, 9 May 2022).

[50] Access to Information Acts allow for the public to access GI specifications via the relevant Intellectual Property Offices (IPOs). However, there is a knowledge gap in this process, since some producers are unaware of this, although the IPOs have confirmed that a search can be conducted in person or online, subject to a fee: The Organization for an International Geographical Indications Network (oriGIn)/West Indies Rum and Spirits Producers' Association (WIRSPA), International Online Forum on Spirits GIs: Trends & Opportunities of Cooperation' (Zoom conference, 19 October 2022).

[51] Barbados Geographical Indications Act 2002 (c 320).

[52] See ch 2.

[53] ibid.

> steps of which *all take place* in the defined geographical area[54] (italics added for emphasis).

In contrast, Article 5.2(a) provides that, within EU law, a PGI refers to a product:

> originating in a specific place, region or country; (b) whose given quality, *reputation* or other characteristic is *essentially attributable* to its geographical origin; and (c) *at least one of the production steps* of which take place in the defined geographical area (emphasis added).[55]

There are two main points of interest in respect of the development of GIs in the Caribbean. The PDO definition outlines that only in exceptional cases should the PDO be a country name. Further, the PDO requires the quality and characteristics to be essentially or exclusively linked to the geographical area of origin, and all the production should, equally, take place therein. In contrast, the PGI is less strict, since the quality, characteristics, and reputation only need to be essentially (not exclusively) linked to the geographic territory, and not all steps of production need take place therein. A PGI, in contrast to a PDO, allows for some of the production process to happen outside the given territory. This is important for rum, since it has been exported in bulk, over centuries, from the Caribbean region. This trade has not stopped today, nor will it stop. Therefore, a Caribbean Rum GI that contributes to 'development from within' would be one which considers the existing bulk export trade and the need to prevent imitation while striking the balance with preserving the rich local heritage around rum production. This is what Demerara Distillers have done with their PGI in the EU. Barbados Rum producers would benefit from following this PGI model. After all, the current tensions around the smaller and larger producers can be summarised as arguments in favour of a PDO model *and* a PGI model, respectively. However, producers are forced to establish a middle ground, since GI laws in Barbados do not have a PDO and PGI distinction.

The issues discussed in this section will be elaborated further in reference to the substantive and institutional issues related to 'development from within', in the following section.

6.2 'DEVELOPMENT FROM WITHIN' AND CARIBBEAN RUM GIS

This section contrasts the substantive and institutional issues of Bowen's concept of 'development from within' with the two case studies on the first EU-registered Demerara Rum GI and the Barbados Rum GI status quo.

[54] Regulation (EU) No 1151/2012 of the European Parliament and of the Council of 21 November 2012 on Quality Schemes for Agricultural Products and Foodstuffs [2012] OJ L343.

[55] ibid. See the discussion of this in 'Turron de Jijona' C-3/91 *Exportur SA v LOR SA* 1992 ECR I-5529, I-5535; and Dev Gangjee, 'Melton Mowbray and the GI Pie in the Sky: Exploring Cartographies of Protection' (2006) 3 *Intellectual Property Quarterly* 291-306.

6.2.1 Substantive Issues: Sugars, Bottling, Flavours, and Casks

This section considers the four substantive issues that undermine the Tequila GI's ability to contribute to 'development from within'. These are: the reduction in the required quantity of blue agave sugars; the continued export of bulk *tequila mixto*; the innovation of flavoured tequila; and the definition of what constitutes 'mature' agave to be used in tequila production.[56] For the purposes of a comparative analysis with the issues impacting on the Caribbean rum GI development, these are summarised as issues concerning sugars, bottling, flavours, and casks. A comparison will be drawn with the Scotch Whisky GI, to demonstrate how GI regulations can be drawn up to allow for flexibility in implementation – a lesson that Caribbean rum GIs can consider.

6.2.1.1 Sugars

The issue of whether rum is to be made from molasses or cane sugar is one that divides Caribbean rum producers. To summarise, French producers of rum, known as *rhum agricole*, traditionally use sugar cane juice, while the anglophone Caribbean producers use molasses. It is important to note that rum produced by anglophone Caribbean producers accounts for 97 per cent of rum produced in the region.[57] Given the presence of some French rum producers in the Caribbean rum market, this therefore becomes a thorny issue when attempting to define a GI that will effectively lock in GI production standards for all producers in the given territory. In the Mexican case, the regulations around tequila production implemented a reduction in the input of blue agave sugars required, from 70 per cent in 1964 to 51 per cent in 1970. This has been critiqued as watering down tequila to a product which is essentially half rum, half tequila, since it allows for almost half of the sugar inputs to come from generic sugars. The sugar inputs for the Caribbean rum industry are an important issue for rum production. Sugar has been in decline in production in the region since the end of colonialism. It is well documented that Europe went from a net importer of sugar during the colonial period, when sugar plantations were the backbone of colonial plantation economies, to a net producer of beet sugars in the post-colonial period.[58] As a result of the decline in sugar in the region, rum producers have increasingly relied on sugar imports for their rum production. However, not all rum producers import their sugar inputs. Guyana is just one of three CARIFORUM countries that produce over 50 per cent of the food they consume, while in all other CARICOM economies, it is commonplace that between 60 and 80 per cent,

[56] Bowen, 'Development from Within?' (n 3) 238.

[57] The Rum Authority, 'The Molasses vs Sugar Cane Juice Issue', http://ibid.therumauthority.com/rum-101/the-molasses-vs-sugarcane-juice-issue/.

[58] Ben Richardson, *Sugar: Refined Power in a Global Regime* (Palgrave Macmillan, 2009).

or even 90 per cent, of food is imported.[59] In this case, it is clear that the Demerara region can produce enough of its sugar inputs, as the Demerara Rum GI specification obliges that the sugar used must come from the region.

There are a number of interesting points in relation to the method of production of Demerara Rum outlined in the specification. First, it states that all sugar used in the production of Demerara Rum must come from the same geographic region. Second, water must come exclusively from Demerara artesian wells, and the specific qualities of that water are outlined.[60] For example, it is noted to be low in calcium in relation to other Caribbean islands, and to contain moderate levels of sodium and iron due to the geographic substrate of the region with marine and fluvio-marine deposits, with high mineral content.[61] The varying levels of mineral content, sodium, and iron, as well as the use of water at different stages of rum production, are some of the factors that some stakeholders deem to influence the characteristics of the rum.[62] Further on in the Demerara Rum GI specification, the link to the region is further emphasised as one of the environmental factors that contribute to the GI:

> The high retention of minerals and organic content in these clay soils redound to high yields in the local sugar cane crop, which lead to rich sugar content in the substrate for fermentation. . . . Owing to the manual/semi-mechanical method of harvesting the sugar cane, there is much interaction of the sugar cane stalks with the soil, some of which survives the journey to the factory and end up in the molasses by-product that is primarily fermented to produce Demerara Rum.[63]

Here, it has been emphasised that the clay soil contributes to the sugar cane crop (natural factors), and that the heritage of manual and semi-mechanical harvesting (human factors) contribute to the specific factors that not only link the rum product with its region but, importantly, distinguish it from other rum GIs. This combination of human and natural factors are elements that have been highlighted by the drafters of the legal specification of the GI. In relation to

[59] Guyana, Belize, and Haiti all produce over 50% of their food consumption. See 'Guyana Amongst Three Caribbean Countries Producing More Thank 50% of its Own Food' *Kaiteur News* (Georgetown, 21 June 2022), https://kaieteurnewsonline.com/2022/06/21/guyana-among-three-caribbean-countries-producing-more-than-50-of-its-own-food/. See also Deodat Maharaj, 'Building Caribbean Food Security via Technology – A Caribbean Export Perspective' *CARICOM Today* (Georgetown, 10 April 2021), https://today.caricom.org/2021/10/04/building-caribbean-food-security-via-technology-a-caribbean-export-perspective/. 'It has long been the case that between 80 and 90 per cent of all food consumed in the region (in the amount of about $6 billion according to the latest numbers) originates from foreign countries', writes Daphne Ewin-Chow, 'Five Ways That COVID-19 Has Changed What Food Insecurity Looks Like In The Caribbean' (*Forbes*, 31 March 2020), https://forbes.com/sites/daphneewingchow/2020/03/31/five-ways-that-covid-19-has-changed-what-food-insecurity-looks-like-in-the-caribbean/?sh=34d69519143e.

[60] Demerara Rum (n 1) 2–3.

[61] ibid 3.

[62] Although there is no consensus on the issue, see Josh Miller, 'How Does Water Quality Affect Rum Production?' (*Inuakena*), https://inuakena.com/misc/how-does-water-quality-affect-rum-production/. See also 'The Stages of Rum Making' (*Mount Gay Rum*, 2023), https://mountgayrum.com/rum-making/.

[63] Demerara Rum (n 1).

the human and process factors, the specification also highlights the traditional heritage of knowledge, skills, and expertise in the making of the GI-protected rum. The specification states that:

> *Knowledge/skills/expertise* in the production processes that were developed in Demerara were *handed down over the centuries*, including the *philosophical approach* to distilling where complex flavour profiles are pursued directly through fermentation and distillation, which have *remained largely unchanged from the original methods*.[64]

This excerpt highlights how traditional know-how related to fermentation and distillation processes has been safeguarded to the extent that it influences the philosophical approach to rum production today, which is largely unchanged. It is striking that, despite technological innovation, this industry relies on the original methods that have been used over centuries. Yet, as alluded to above, given the colonial context of centuries gone by, it is ambiguous as to which knowledge, skills, and expertise the specification refers to. Despite its origins from a colonial cash crop, the resulting rum product can be a valuable tool for development in today's post-colonial period. Herein lies the interest in exploring the emancipatory potential of GIs as a legal tool with the capacity to contribute to 'development from within' in today's post-colonial period, where the need to eradicate poverty is acute. By extension, it becomes apparent that the silences of the GI specifications clearly do leave food for thought.

6.2.1.2 (Local) Bottling

The decision to bottle Caribbean rums locally or to allow for some rum to be bulk exported is a divisive one amongst the smaller and bigger producers in the Caribbean rum industry.[65] Some smaller producers share the perspective that managing all aspects of the rum production locally is what constitutes a Caribbean rum.[66] By contrast, other producers, with a history of bulk rum production, believe that Caribbean rums can still be exported and not lose their geographical link to their place of production.[67] The tequila industry grapples with this issue, since 100 per cent blue agave tequila must be bottled locally, while *tequila mixto* is bulk exported. This blended approach to protection may be a middle ground which Caribbean rum producers seeking a GI may pragmatically agree on. Scotch Whisky, for example, is protected as a PGI in the EU, which allows for a blend of a strict (in-country bottling requirements, for example) and

[64] ibid, emphasis added.
[65] See, e.g. Melita Kieley, 'How Important is a GI for Barbados Rum?' (*The Spirits Business*, 26 June 2020), https://thespiritsbusiness.com/2020/06/producers-clash-over-a-gi-for-barbados-rum/.
[66] ibid.
[67] ibid.

loose approach (bulk export permitted) to GI protection.[68] In other words, a PGI allows for inputs to come from elsewhere, or in this case, for blends. For example, the Scotch whisky specification explains that Single Malt Scotch Whisky cannot be exported in bulk, while Scotch Whisky can. This difference is akin to the Cask Aged, Special Reserve and Grand Special Reserve Demerara Rums, which cannot be exported in bulk. However, the fact that 70 per cent of tequila is exported in bulk, according to industry stakeholders, reduces the ability of the region to contribute to 'development from within' through provision of jobs, while also impacting on the quality of tequila.[69] Between 2003 and 2006, the Mexican government and the US were in conflict on this issue. The Mexican government originally proposed to bottle 100 per cent of its tequila in the territory of Mexico, but eventually signed an agreement with the US to instead allow for bulk exports while increasing its regulatory oversight on the quality of tequila in the US.[70] This agreement struck the balance between Mexico's reliance on the US as its foremost export market contributing to its gross domestic product (GDP) and the need to regulate its tequila industry to ensure that the quality and reputation linked to tequila was being maintained.

Drawing on the Prosciutto di Parma case,[71] Bowen juxtaposes the European Court of Justice ruling that the *Consorzio* producing the renowned Prosciutto di Parma had the legitimate right to restrict the packaging and slicing to the region of production, given its link to assuring the quality of the GI, with the failure to do so on the Mexican side due to the extra-local influence of the US on the tequila industry.[72] In reflecting on what this may mean for Caribbean rum producers, it does not seem that such reasoning would support the producers in the industry wanting to bottle locally, since there is a growing trend of rum production in Europe,[73] as well as a reliance on foreign exchange.

Demerara Distillers, who own the GI, took a blended approach to the issue of bottling. As mentioned above, Cask Aged, Special Reserve, and Grand Special Reserve must be produced (fermented, distilled, and aged), blended, and bottled in the region. This is outlined in the specification in order 'to safeguard the reputational and historical integrity of the premium and super-premium value,

[68] Scotch Whisky GI Specification, PGI-GB-01854, filed 12 June 1989, Ares (2013) 3005272 available via eAmbrosia, EU GI database: 'Technical File for Scotch Whisky' (*Europa*, 6 September 2013), https://ec.europa.eu/geographical-indications-register/eambrosia-public-api/api/v1/attachments/45004.

[69] Bowen, 'Development from Within?' (n 3) 239.

[70] The signing of the United States–Mexico–Canada Agreement (USMCA) ensures the continuity of tequila's protected GI status. See Anabel Ramírez, 'USMCA and its Effects on the Exportation of Tequila' (*Casa Sauza*, 17 December 2021), https://casasauza.com/en/tequila-process/usmca-effects-on-exportation-tequila#:~:text=The%20USMCA%20protects%20GI%2C%20which,the%20tequila%20industry%20as%20well.

[71] Case C-108/01 *Consorzio del Prosciutto di Parma and Salumificio S. Rita SpA v Asda Stores Ltd and Hygrade Foods Ltd* ECLI:EU:C:2003:296.

[72] Bowen, 'Development from Within?' (n 3) 239.

[73] Examples include Brixton rum in South London, or Outlaw rum company, whose motto is 'born in Trinidad, aged in Scotland'. See 'Brixton Distillery', https://brixtondistillery.com/, and ibid .outlawrum.co.uk.

which can only result from the local knowledge and techniques of the production process'.[74] Additionally, it is stated that this requirement has been introduced to avoid adulteration of Demerara Rums, since unaged Demerara Rum is exported in bulk. It notes:

> The fact of the difference between Demerara-aged and non-Demerara-aged rums could provide incentive to bottlers elsewhere to attempt to compensate for the lack of tropical aged quality by these deceptive measures . . . which gives rise to the risk of aged rums not consistent with the Demerara Rum age profile, to be bottled, sold and marketed as aged rums.[75]

By defining the difference between these two categories of aged and non-aged Demerara Rum, the producers have sought to strike a balance between its export market (for unaged rums) and the local heritage and know-how linked to Demerara rum production, when drawing up the GI. Rum producers across other Caribbean islands may want to take a similar approach to balance the interests of various rum producers; however, the case of the Demerara Rum GI is less fraught with tension for a key reason – its geography. The Demerara Rum GI is a regionally protected GI from the Demerara region, as opposed to a Guyana-wide GI. By contrast, the Barbados Rum GI is being sought for the entire territory.

Since bottles are imported into the region, this adds an environmental concern, given that imports raise carbon footprints, amongst other environmental factors linked to waste, recycling, and others. All the issues raised here impact on the decision to bottle locally or allow for some rum exports to be bottled abroad – an issue the tequila industry has also had to contend with.

6.2.1.3 *Flavour*

Flavoured rum has been on the rise, and has resulted in bitter exchanges over the rum-producing norms.[76] Tequila producers also grapple with this issue.[77] In the tequila industry, stakeholders criticise the 2006 revision of the tequila specification, which allowed for the introduction of flavoured tequilas. It was argued that this new norm is an affront to the history and quality of tequila

[74] Demerara Rum (n 1) 3.

[75] ibid.

[76] Ian Burrell, known as the Rum Ambassador, summarises, 'Every single unadulterated brand or rum company I know doesn't have a problem with spiced rum . . . What they have a problem with is the way spiced rums are allowed to market themselves as rums.' Furthermore, the article also recognises that the terms 'spiced rums' and 'flavoured rums' are often used synonymously; the issue of marketing as 'rum' remains, regardless of the term used. See Tom Bruce-Gardyne, 'Flavoured Rum: Surfing the Wave' (*The Spirits Business*, 14 September 2022), https://thespiritsbusiness.com/2022/09/flavoured-rum-surfing-the-wave/. On authentic rum, see WIRSPA, 'Unlocking the Potential of Authentic Caribbean Rums, Rum Market Report', https://wirspa.com/wp-content/uploads/ACR%20Publications/Rum-Market-Report.pdf.

[77] Bowen, 'Development from Within?' (n 3).

as a traditional Mexican product.[78] In the Demerara case, Demerara Rums, labelled as such, cannot be blended. However, unaged Demerara Rums that are exported are likely to be flavoured. The specification outlines the importance of distinguishing Demerara-aged Rums from unaged Demerara Rums, based on the premium that consumers associate with the high-value aged Demerara Rum product protected through the GI.[79] Given that unaged Demerara Rums are likely used in flavoured rum products in foreign export markets, it is of high importance that the final flavoured end product is not confused with the origin of the rum in the Demerara region, and specifically the heritage and reputation of Demerara-aged Rums.

Demerara Rum cannot be blended with other rums outside the region of Demerara, nor can it be flavoured. The specification does state, however, that it can be 'only sweetened to round off the final taste of the product up to a maximum of 20 grams per litre'.[80] 'Demerara Rum' can be blended with 'Old Demerara Rum' (aged a minimum of two years) and still be labelled as such, although the 'Cask Aged Demerara Rum', 'Special Reserve Demerara Rum', and 'Grand Special Reserve Demerara Rum' (aged a minimum of 3, 12, and 25 years, respectively) must be bottled in the region. This bottling requirement, according to the specification, fulfils two objectives related to the GI status of the rum.[81] First, it is stated that this bottling requirement protects both the reputation and the historical integrity of the rum as a premium and super-premium value product. Second, this deters the adulteration of Demerara-aged Rum, since unaged rums are exported in bulk.

6.2.1.4 Casks

The issue of which casks are used to age rum has arisen in stakeholder discussion on the rum GIs.[82] In the case of tequila, a similar issue was raised in relation to the change introduced in 1995, which no longer requires 'mature' blue agave to be used in tequila production. According to the smallholder farmers who produced this, such a change favours the commercial producers of tequila, since it allows them to use immature heads of agave produced on their land, as written into the 1995 law, as opposed to buying directly from smallholders who produce the mature heads. This demonstrates the cleavage that can exist between smallholder producers and more commercial players in GI industries. The same issues are emerging in different areas across (potential) GI producers in the Caribbean.

The Caribbean rum industry is also grappling with the issue of casks. In response to the US law which does not allow bourbon casks to be reused for

[78] ibid 240.
[79] Demerara Rum (n 1) 3.
[80] ibid.
[81] ibid.
[82] WIRD (n 49).

the purpose of producing bourbon whisky,[83] the Caribbean rum industry benefits from importing these casks and using them in the maturation process. For example, the Demerara Rum specification outlines that maturation takes place in 'American white oak casks . . . or other casks as required'.[84] Indeed, several casks are used in the rum-blending process. Some producers wish to limit the types of casks used to age rum within a GI specification,[85] while other producers have found historic evidence which shows that the types of casks used for ageing were, in fact, more diverse than today.[86] For example, in Barbados, local woods have been used in rum production: hog plum, mango, sweet-wood, clammy cherry, broad leaf, West Indian birch, and wild cassada.[87] Today, however, there is a heavy reliance on imported bourbon casks. If the US bourbon industry were to change their regulations on ageing and allow for the reuse of casks, this could send the Caribbean rum industry into peril, as producers who were reliant on bourbon casks would need to find a new source. Worse yet, if a GI specification were to be enacted with a limited type of cask, this could prove stifling for producers and impact on the ability to contribute to 'development from within'. This is one key element that deserves particular attention, and careful consideration is required so as not to draw up a GI specification that is so restrictive that it cannot respond to market forces, innovation in casks used, or recognition of heritage in the rum-making processes. The ability of the GI to be successful in its marketplace is paramount to the success of the GI itself. When this is linked to 'development from within', it creates a linkage of the GI's market value with its potential to contribute to sustainable development of the given GI territory, and the ability of the GI to function as an emancipatory legal tool.

6.2.2 Institutional Issues: Management and Regulation, Protectionism, and Exogenous Forces

Bowen identified four issues related to the institutional establishment of the Tequila GI in Mexico which are relevant for the development of GIs in the Caribbean context. The institutional regulation of the GI and its management by the government were the first two issues highlighted. The third issue was that the fact that GIs can be used as protectionist measures can impact on the ability of the GI to fulfil sustainable (social, economic, and environmental) objectives. Lastly, the impact of the dependency of exports and the resulting commercial power the US exercises in its relationship with the Mexican government was perceived as a threat to the Mexican government's autonomy. These institutional

[83] US Federal Alcohol Administration Act of 1935.
[84] Demerara Rum (n 1) 3.
[85] Kieley, 'How Important is a GI for Barbados Rum?' (n 65).
[86] WIRD (n 49).
[87] ibid.

issues can provide critical reflective points for the development and management of GIs in the Caribbean context and serve as launch pads for critical engagement in the process of developing GIs that are emancipatory, and thus capable of serving local developmental needs.

6.2.2.1 *Institutional Management – A Regulatory Body for GIs*

This section considers the issue of the institutional management of GIs, particularly the role of GI regulatory bodies. This is framed in the context of the GI products as the contemporary evolution of former colonial cash crops of extractive plantation economies in a post-colonial setting.[88] The conundrum posed by GIs is to make digestible how GIs can serve the post-colonial sustainable development aspirations of Caribbean states today; or, how the GIs can serve as emancipatory legal tools capable of fostering 'development from within', a form of development that prioritises producer groups and countries formerly disenfranchised from the process of development under former imperial and colonial models. Implicated within this is the role that institutions, particularly GI regulatory bodies, can play to enforce the emancipatory potential of GIs as legal tools to contribute to 'development from within'. To gain a further insight into precedent in the region, this section considers the case of Dominican Republic rum ('Ron Dominicano').

The Dominican Association of Rum Producers (Asociacion Dominicana de Prodoctores de Ron, Inc, or ADOPRON) filed for the Ron Dominicano GI and its corresponding logo on 15 August 2014 in the Dominican Republic.[89] ADOPRON produces 90 per cent of rum nationally, exports 95 per cent of total rums exported, and contributes to 97 per cent of sales taxes from the rum industry in the Dominican Republic. By the following month, an opposition had been filed by six companies in the rum industry (Bodegas Pedro Oliver SRL, Rones del Caribe, Oliver & Oliver International Inc, Alebrand Spirits Company LLC, Asociacion de Roneros Dominicanos (ARD), and IMEX Spirits).

The Trade Marks Opposition (TMO) board considered the opposition to the application, relating to three issues. First, the plaintiffs questioned the rum's characteristics and quality, claiming that they were different to those indicated in ADOPRON's application. Second, the six plaintiffs wanted their own rum interests represented. Third, they also held the trademark for 'Ron Dominicana' in both the national territory of the Dominican Republic and abroad, at the EU

[88] Beckford, *Persistent Poverty* (n 15).

[89] ADOPRON consists of Casa Brugal, Ron Barceló SRL, Vinícola del Norte, Isidro Bordas, and Yazoo Investment: Bufete Messina & Lugo IP, 'Geographical Indications: Dominican Republic View' (*IPCA*, November 2017), https://ipca.website/wp-content/uploads/2019/09/GIDominicanRepublicBufeteMessinaLugoIP.pdf. See also Cándida Acosta, 'Marca Pais de Ron Dominicano in Riesgo' *Listindario* (Santo Domingo, 14 June 2017), https://listindiario.com/economia/2017/06/14/470069/marca-pais-del-ron-dominicano-en-riesgo.

level. The plaintiffs claimed that the Regulatory Council would be biased in favour of ADOPRON in the process of managing the GI.

The TMO board's ruling refusing the GI application, at that time,[90] offers lessons on the facts of the case. First, in relation to the quality and characteristics, the board sided with the plaintiffs that the sugar inputs must come from the territory of the Dominican Republic, in accordance with the law 477 on in-country rum production.[91] Second, the board affirmed that one applicant was sufficient to register a GI.[92] However, given that the GI applied for covered the entire territory of the country, it should be as inclusive as possible. Third, the board explained that there was no conflict of interest with the prior rights for the trademark held by the plaintiffs. The board prioritised the broader policy context concerning the sourcing of the rum, deemed an integral part of the GI, while also highlighting the need for the GI to be managed inclusively.

Today, 'Ron Dominicano' is a registered GI, with four producers benefiting from the sign.[93] Members of the Regulatory Council include the rum distillers; sugar producers and processors; the Dominican Republic's Industries' Association (AIRD); Ministry of Industry, Commerce and MSMEs (MICM); and the Export and Investment Center and Quality Institute (INDOCAL). The Council manages the records on production, packaging, and use of the distinctive signs.

This section has highlighted that, in the Ron Dominicano case, the TMO board set a precedent by outlining the value of an inclusive council for strategic management of the GI. This is food for thought for both the Jamaican Rum GI that is currently the centre of a legal battle to amend the GI to stipulate that a Jamaican Rum can 'only' be aged in Jamaica,[94] and for other GI producer groups regionally that are considering registering their origin products. In line with the claims of this book, councils can strategically embed 'development from within' to secure the SDGs of poverty eradication of producer communities and effectively assist in the transition from extractive plantation economies of the colonial past.

[90] Resolution No 000279, 12 July 2016, TMO.

[91] 'Dominican Standard 477 specifies how the spirit must be made to be considered rum from the Dominican Republic. Among those commandments is that the alcoholic fermentation and distillation must be derived exclusively from molasses, syrups or cane sugar juice and that the entire process be carried out in the country. In addition, it indicates that the liquid must have at least one year of ageing in oak barrels, as well as an alcohol content of 37.3%.' See Felivia Mejía, 'Ron Dominicano Busca Denominación de Origen' (*Forbes*, 9 May 2022), https://forbes.do/editors-picks/2022-05-09/ron-dominicano-busca-denominacion-de-origen-2.

[92] ADOPRON had given other examples as precedents, also in Spanish-speaking jurisdictions: Café Barahona and Café Valdesia in the Dominican Republic, as well as Ron de Guatemala and Ron de Venezuela.

[93] See WIRSPA-CARIFORUM Intellectual Property Rights and Innovation (CarIPI) project, 'International Online Forum on Spirits GIs: Trends and Opportunities of Cooperation' (*OriGIn*, 19 October 2022), https://origin-gi.com/wp-content/uploads/2022/10/Lendor_DO_Ron_Dominicano.pdf.

[94] Stephen Jackson, 'National Rums get Temporary Relief in Industry Fight' (*Jamaica Gleaner*, 1 October 2025), https://jamaica-gleaner.com/article/business/20251001/national-rums-get-temporary-relief-industry-fight#:~:text=She%20added%20that%20the%20ruling,indication%2C%E2%80%9D%20the%20association%20stated.

6.2.2.2 *GI Management – The Role of Governments*

How the GI is managed is very important, and the role of the government and producers' organisations must be properly understood. This section specifically considers the issue of country name GIs and the key issue impacting on the registration of a Barbados Rum GI, by drawing on the work of Caribbean IP scholar Natalie Corthésy. Corthésy proposes that country names can serve the following purposes: they can inform consumers about the origin of a product, be part of a valuable co-branding strategy for goods or services, and serve as a national competitive identity of a state.[95] She posits that country names currently sit at the intersection of unfair competition, trademarks, and GI laws and explains that there is enhanced interest in creating a *sui generis* protection regime for country names.[96] In the same way that GIs are manifested as *sui generis* stand-alone legal regimes, the Corthésy model of country name protection proposes a stand-alone legal regime for their protection.[97] However, the interest in this section relates to the intersection of the country name and GIs, as it is most relevant to the ongoing tensions around GI registrations in various Caribbean countries, most notably in the case of the Barbados Rum GI.

In considering the composite term of a state alongside a product such as rum – the Barbados Rum GI is a case in point – the approach to enacting GI protection could also be considered as one of nation branding. This refers to the ability of a state, through private–public partnerships, to construct and portray a certain image of itself, such that the competitive identity of the state becomes embedded in the brand.[98] Understanding how the country name can function as a nation brand is key to understanding the tensions that arise in the development of GI laws in SIDS territories when producers opt for a country name in an exclusionary fashion. This is precisely what is being played out in the Barbados Rum GI case since the introduction of the GI Act in Barbados.[99] The Act stipulates that GIs in Barbados are protected whether registered or not (section 3.1). While there is much ambiguity over unregistered GIs, the registration procedure of GIs is set out under section 8 of the Barbados GI Act:

> The following may make an application to the Director for the registration of a geographical indication:
>
> (a) persons carrying on an activity as producers in the geographical area specified in the application, with respect to the goods specified in the application;

[95] Natalie Corthésy, 'Trade Marks Country Names and Misappropriation of National Identity' (2017) 12(4) *Journal of Intellectual Property Law and Practice* 297.

[96] See Natalie Corthésy, 'Country Name Designation and International IP Protection of National Competitive Identities' (2021) 16(4-5) *Journal of Intellectual Property Law and Practice* 357, figs 1 and 2.

[97] ibid.

[98] ibid 3–4.

[99] Barbados GI Act (n 53).

(b) consumers and groups of consumers; or
(c) any marketing organisation incorporated under the Companies Act, Cap. 308 or established under any enactment.

Of particular relevance, it states that the registration must be submitted to the Director of GI registration by 'persons carrying on an activity as producers in the geographic area specified in the application, with respect to the goods specified in the application' (s 8.1.a GI Act).[100] Within the meaning of this section, it is debatable as to whether three of the four producers of rum in Barbados possess the right to register a GI, as they are not *all* the producers within the given geographical area.[101] Although the section does not *verbis expressis* require *all* producers to make the application, it is implied that, given the small territory and limited number of producers, they would unite for such a registration (especially in light of the case of nation state names and a co-branding strategy). It may also be considered optimal that four as opposed to three producers align their interests in a GI within the process of GI registration, from drawing up the GI specification and code of practice to the application and management of the GI. Additionally, naturally, as WIRD is the largest distillery and producer of labels now owned by the other distilleries, its de facto exclusion from the application for a Barbados Rum GI by the three smaller producers – Mount Gay, Four Square, and St Nicholas Abbey distilleries – is sub-optimal from a sustainability perspective. In other words, 'development from within' and the ability for a GI to serve as an emancipatory legal tool for the entire community is enhanced if WIRD is included in the GI registration and process, precisely given the potential for sustainable developmental impacts on producing communities and Barbados at large.[102] Legally, a registration can be opposed under section 10 of the GI Act:

> Any interested person may, within the prescribed period and in the prescribed manner, give notice to the Director of an objection to the registration of the geographical indication referred to in section 8 on the grounds that it does not comply with the requirements of section 5 or 8, or the regulations (Section 10.1 GI Act).

Within the meaning of this section, and drawing on Corthésy's work on nation branding – where a nation's name is invoked in a co-branding private–public partnership – it can be expected that the GI should serve 'development from within' objectives. From this optic, and in consideration of the potential of the

[100] Consumer groups and marketing organisations are also mentioned in Articles 8.1.b and c respectively, ibid.

[101] 'Big 3 in Barbados Rum Apply for GI - Geographical Indication,' *Barbados Loop* (Bridgetown, 21 July 2022), https://barbados.loopnews.com/content/big-3-barbados-rum-apply-gi.

[102] Recall the principle of integration embedded in the concept of sustainable development – inter and intra generational equity and inclusive dialogue – as set out by Ortino in ch 1. See Federico Ortino, 'Investment Treaties, Sustainable Development and Reasonableness Review: A Case Against Strict Proportionality Balancing' (2017) 30 LJIL 1, 83.

public policy orientation of a GI, it could be plausibly argued that three of four producers do not fall into the intention of section 8's requirement of producers within the geographic territory registering a GI. Rather, three out of four producers cannot claim a GI that 'identifies a good as originating in the territory *of a country*'[103] – Barbados. This claim is even weaker when considering that these three rum producers only represent a 15 per cent share of foreign exchange earnings from rum sales.[104] Although literally following the ADOPRON ruling demonstrates that one producer can register the GI, albeit in line with existing policy requirements, and given that the GI remains inclusive to all producers in the territory, the main difference, however, is that ADOPRON's position is akin to WIRD in terms of economic power within the industry (recall that the former produces 90 per cent of rum in the territory and the latter receives over 80 per cent of foreign exchange earnings in the industry). That said, it would be of interest to all four rum GI stakeholders in Barbados to collaborate to draft an inclusive GI.

The attempt to obtain a Barbados Rum GI by the three smaller distilleries poses several issues that Corthésy has highlighted in her work on country names. Corthésy has coined the term 'argotisation', 'to denote both the informal unregulated appropriation of country names in commerce, and the corresponding "swift" accumulation of goodwill and reputation that this can engender'.[105] This case of the attempted registration of a Barbados Rum GI by three distilleries is evidence of the latter. Although having a legitimate right to claim to use the label 'Barbados Rum', the three distilleries would be, in part, attempting to benefit from the goodwill and reputation that WIRD has *also* built up with regard to the Barbados Rum designation. As such, it could be assessed that the three distilleries are engaging in a form of *parasitisme economique* (economic free riding), since they are all competitors within the Barbados and global rum industry.[106] Their attempt to obtain a Barbados GI can, therefore, be considered 'argotisation', albeit not (only) perpetrated by foreigners but, in fact, locally owned businesses ('argotisation' from within). The ability to use the country name, or its abuse, through its attempted appropriation has direct implications for 'development from within'. The economic argument can be raised that drawing on the goodwill and reputation associated with Barbados Rum, albeit excluding the largest producer and foreign exchange earner, weakens the possibility to contribute to 'development from within'. The economic case would emphasise the necessity of including all producers, especially WIRD, given its economic contributions to the state of Barbados currently, as well as the

[103] Barbados GI Act (n 53). Emphasis added.

[104] WIRD (n 49).

[105] Natalie Corthésy, 'Brand New IP: "Country Name Designation" – from France with Love' in Daniel Gervais (eds), *The Future of Intellectual Property* (Edward Elgar, 2021) 325.

[106] Corthésy notes that, in the French conception of free riding, there was a distinction between *parasitisme économique* and *concurrence parasitisme* whereby the latter denotes that the competitors are unaware of each other. See the debate on argotisation (ibid 324–26).

collective potential to further impact on sustainable development through an inclusive GI scheme.

The attempted registration of the Barbados Rum GI by three of the distilleries implicates the government of Barbados. Yet, an approach which makes the producers overcome their differences to draft and implement a country GI for Barbados Rum would be akin to retrieving the distinctiveness of Barbados Rum.[107] Barbados, as a state, therefore has both a positive right to control the exclusive use of the nation's name in commerce as well as the negative right to prevent abuses against it.[108] In essence, the government of Barbados ought to recognise its inalienable property right of the Barbados country name designation. After all, the country name has a communicative function indicating the source of rum and preventing unfair competition, as an appellation of origin denoting the quality–place linkage, and as a GI wherein the evocative value of the geographic name is protected. Yet, in practice, what the government exercises when it instructs the four distilleries on the island to co-operate in the establishment of a GI is, at its core, an expression of its national competitive identity. As such, the Barbados Rum GI may in fact be a springboard to enhanced protection of the Barbados country name as a competitive identity. It may be considered also as laying the path for further momentum of a *sui generis* protection regime for states' country names in the future. This chapter proposes that GIs can offer an opportunity to leverage nation brands in international trade, in the absence of Corthésy's proposed stand-alone or *sui generis* body of law for country name protection.[109]

Corthésy argues that protecting country names ought to be done on both economic and moral grounds, and that this protection is a *sine qua non* for determining the success of a branding scheme.[110] One of the claims of this chapter is that GI laws offer such protection. Moreover, protection of origin products using country names via GIs, applied to SIDS and territories where the entire state is referred to in the GI, represents the new normative ground on which GIs can be developed, especially for Caribbean SIDS. Corthésy also boldly asserts that the current IP regimes offer insufficient protection and incentives for Third World countries to consider national branding as a development tool.[111] This therefore underlines that IP tools are not being effectively mobilised to contribute to 'development from within' in the region. In part, this is due to the history of IP regimes drawn up by imperial and colonial powers and embedded with their normative preferences. From a historical perspective, at the time that Article 6*ter* of the Paris Convention of 1886 was drafted, there were only a handful of states, who were colonial masters.[112] Independent states today

[107] The remedy of argotisation (ibid 325).
[108] ibid 326.
[109] Corthésy, 'Country Name Designation' (n 96) fig 1, 8–10.
[110] Corthésy, 'Brand New IP' (n 105) 336.
[111] ibid 340.
[112] See ch 2. Art 6*ter* concerns 'Marks: Prohibitions concerning State Emblems, Official Hallmarks, and Emblems of Intergovernmental Organisations'.

that were formerly colonies did not contribute to the drafting of formative IP agreements, yet they were, and still are, subject to their provisions, albeit they have contributed to later amendments post-independence. The new states are all smaller, and there was no thought about the competitive identity of smaller (former colonial) states. In this light, the reclaiming or co-branding of country names can be perceived as an attempt by post-colonial Third World SIDS, such as Caribbean states, to reclaim their competitive identity in the global economy. Nation branding today, therefore, can be leveraged as an invaluable tool to contribute to societal development in a post-colonial context or, put differently, to foster 'development from within' insofar as GIs function as emancipatory legal tools for GI-producing communities in the Third World; that is, notwithstanding, as Corthésy recognises, the challenges of setting up GI schemes in the first place, from the administrative undertakings of registering the GI to fighting legal battles over infringements.[113]

This case study echoes Corthésy's claim that '[m]onopoly is not the problem. The issue is, monopolised by whom?'[114] Applied to the case of the Barbados Rum GI, it is plausible that an attempted registration by three of the four distilleries on the given territory, without majority shares in the rum production or foreign exchange earnings, would be considered an abusive act to monopolise the Barbados Rum name, and thus the state would resort to defending its national competitive identity. As Corthésy has pointed out, this becomes all the more problematic when such 'argotisation' appears via the registration of domain names.[115] Yet, the CARIFORUM–EU EPA is avant-garde in this regard, since there is a provision for the protection of GIs on the Internet and in e-commerce.[116] As such, a co-branding strategy with the government and GI producers can contribute, if effectively designed, as a tool for 'development from within'. Tangibly, it can encourage reinvestment into the country, based on how the GI specification is not only drawn up to strike the balance between the needs of smaller and larger producers but, crucially, co-managed. To this end, drawing on Corthésy's work demonstrates how co-branding the national competitive identity of states, especially for Third World Caribbean SIDS, can foster sustainable development of GI producer communities. As such, the country name can be leveraged as part of a strategic approach to GIs as an emancipatory legal tool contributing to 'development from within'.

6.2.2.3 *Trade Protection Tools?*

This section considers how GI specifications can be drawn up in an exclusionary manner or in such a way that they may be considered tools for trade

[113] Corthésy, 'Brand New IP' (n 105) 341. See also ch 5.
[114] Corthésy, 'Brand New IP' (n 105) 343.
[115] ibid.
[116] Art 145.F; see discussion in ch 4.

protectionism. It considers three examples of cask-ageing, water, and sugar input requirements. These examples shed light on how 'development from within' may be undermined, thus inhibiting the GI to function in an emancipatory way for producer communities.

Cask-ageing is an issue that is prevalent in the current deadlock of the Barbados Rum GI. The three relatively small producers (Mount Gay, Foursquare, and St Nicholas Abbey) have a preference for restricting cask-ageing requirements to specific wooden casks. In contrast, the largest producer (WIRD) has shown an interest in rebirthing a heritage of ageing in different casks.[117] Restricting cask-ageing to imported oak casks, for example, would strengthen a reliance on such imports from the US and create a vulnerability in a scenario where the US bourbon industry were to change its regulations on the non-reuse of casks. In contrast, in WIRD's perspective, ageing requirements should not be restricted to what is currently used, and as such the specification should be written in such a way that allows for innovation and recognition of past practices with more diverse woods.[118] Yet, for the other three, WIRD's acquiescence to allowing the practice of 'double ageing', both in Barbados and abroad, waters down the pertinent geographic link of a Barbados Rum to its territory of origin.

Mount Gay's managing director has pertinently posed the question, 'If you asked a Scotsman tomorrow, I don't think he would accept Scotch Whisky *aged* in Poland – I don't think anybody would.'[119] This concern relates to the issue of the origin link to the GI, and also, pertinently, the PDO or PGI model adopted, outlined above.[120] The deadlock around the Barbados Rum GI seems to be concentrated in attempts to serve private interest linked to commercial supply, as opposed to seeing the public-good potential a GI can serve. In this regard, despite the differences, WIRD has aptly stated, 'It is important that the GI is not to be used as a competitive tool by one interested party over another.'[121] One way to ensure this may indeed be to allow ageing in a variety of casks, which also leaves the door open to innovation, research, and development, as WIRD advocates.

WIRD's 'field to bottle' model can be seen as trialling a development-from-within approach, since it is focused on community-based sustainable development. The model is based on working with local farmers and the Barbados government to have a positive impact on the Barbados sugar cane industry.[122] WIRD aims to purchase locally produced molasses at a 20 per cent premium. Additionally, there is an educational aspect that links the history of rum and

[117] Reference to mango wood casks here: Jacopo Mazzeo, 'Will Barbados Rum Get its Own GI?' (*Wine Mag*, 25 October 2022, https://winemag.com/2022/10/25/barbados-rum-get-own-gi/.

[118] Kieley, 'How Important is a GI for Barbados Rum?' (n 65).

[119] ibid, emphasis added.

[120] Regulation (EU) No 1151/2012 (n 54).

[121] ibid.

[122] WIRD (n 49).

sugar to tourism via the establishment of a Barbados and Caribbean Rum Trail. WIRD describes the 'field to bottle' mission as a sustainable one, which is championed by its owner Maison Ferrand for the benefit of the staff, the distillery, and Barbados. Given that WIRD is the largest rum producer in Barbados (85% of all rum on the island) and largest foreign exchange earner,[123] this initiative has considerable potential to positively impact sustainable development outcomes.

Water is a key ingredient in the production of rum. Yet, requirements to only source water from artisanal wells, if written into a Barbados Rum GI specification, may be perceived as a trade protectionist measure. For example, such a requirement could inhibit newcomer producers who may wish to benefit from GI protection, if they cannot source artisanal well water. Moreover, historic evidence has been found which shows that sea water was used in rum production in the early 1900s.[124] In other words, the use of artisanal well water could, in effect, be a protectionist measure designed to benefit particular stakeholders with access to artisanal well water and, in effect, lock out others without such access. Such an approach also ignores the fact that, historically, sea water or other water sources have been used in rum production. The choice of how a GI specification is drawn up is, therefore, critical, since it has the power to be inclusive or exclusive to new entrants in the market.

The issue of sourcing sugar is also a prominent factor that can be perceived as a trade protectionist measure. Whether sugar is produced locally or imported, and the quantity of such inputs, is a point of consideration for rum GIs. Yet, sugar does not need to come exclusively from the given geographic territory, as a PDO model would presuppose. Rather, sugar can be imported. Additionally, there is historic evidence of molasses being imported to make rum in the late 1800s.[125] In this regard, it is advisable that GI specifications remain open to (sugar) inputs outside the GI territory, along the lines of a PGI model, given the contemporary structure of the industries and the current realities and interdependencies of globalised trade.

GI rules which would prevent new entrants to the market would be restrictive. For example, the Ten to One Rum[126] is one of the newest entrants in the rum market, and the choice of name can be considered as an ode to the Caribbean's divisive past. Indeed, a key lesson can be gleaned from the choice of name of this new rum. In 1962, Eric Williams, the first post-independence prime minister of Trinidad and Tobago, criticised Jamaica's decision to leave the West Indian Federation and famously claimed that 'one from ten equals naught'.[127]

[123] M Pietrek, 'Barbados Rum Cheat Sheet' (*CocktailWonk*, 4 December 2018), https://cocktailwonk.com/2018/12/barbados-rum-cheat-sheet.html.

[124] ibid.

[125] WIRD (n 49).

[126] 'Ten to One', https://tentoonerum.com/.

[127] 'One from Ten Equals 0' *The Tribune* (Nassau, 6 May 2019), http://tribune242.com/news/2019/may/06/one-10-equals-0/.

Regionally, this story is well known and depicts how the Caribbean region was divided against taking a united approach to socioeconomic and political development. And, indeed, younger generations are reminded of this story as to how the region has never overcome its divided history at a critical post-colonial juncture after independences. This does, indeed, offer lessons to the burgeoning GI community in the region – the goal of GIs can be larger than the territory it serves.

6.2.2.4 *Exogenous Influences?*

The issue of exogenous forces influencing the GI process is a considerable one. In the Mexican case, it was shown that the Mexican government was not only criticised for its management of the GI, but was shown to have been influenced by the US in amending the regulations of the tequila industry.[128] Management of the GI will be a litmus test for Caribbean producers. The role of exogenous forces is somewhat more of a dark and stormy issue in the Caribbean, due in part to its intertwined colonial history with Europe, as well as the aftermath of colonialism, which has left Caribbean societies not only divided but also underdeveloped.[129] In Barbados, three of the four producers are of European heritage, while the largest bulk producer is French-owned. In Jamaica, the renowned Appleton rum is owned by the Italian Campari Group. Historically, Appleton, an Englishman, received the land as an award from the colonial British administration after having won a battle against the indigenous Jamaican maroons; this is the land where the Appleton factory is still based in St Elizabeth parish, and it has expanded its land ownership ever since.[130] Meanwhile, the local white rum favourite Wray and Nephew is also owned by Campari Group. While the origins of the owners of the rum may be an interesting addition to GI stories in the Caribbean, this book argues that the ability of the GI to contribute to 'development from within', as an emancipatory legal tool, is crucial. Thus far, there is no indication from the Demerara Rum GI specification that there will be management issues, or that there are external threats from foreign interests. Rather, as the first GI registered from a CARIFORUM country in the EU, it offers

[128] Bowen, 'Development from Within?' (n 3) 238–41.

[129] Beckford, *Persistent Poverty* (n 15).

[130] Land or the plantation economy was a central element in colonial rule, and this has been widely written on by Caribbean scholars. See Eric Williams, *Capital and Slavery* (University of North Carolina Press, 1944) and Beckford, *Persistent Poverty* (n 15). Kidd recognises the conquest for Jamaica and how land was used as a reward, albeit not explicitly stating the details of that history on this website: 'The first known documentation of rum production on the Appleton Estate is dated 1749. However, it is believed that the origins of the Estate date back to 1655, when England captured Jamaica from Spain. Frances Dickinson, whose grandsons Caleb and Ezekiel are the earliest known owners of Appleton Estate, *took part in that conquest of Jamaica*. It is believed that Appleton Estate was part of the land grant that Frances Dickinson received as *a reward for his services*' (italics added): Hope Kidd, 'Appleton Estate' (*Jamaican Products*, 10 June 2018), https://jamaicanproducts.com.au/2018/06/10/appleton-estate/.

hope that, in defining the characteristics, qualities, reputation, and heritage of Caribbean GI products, the region can take a step in positively contributing to GI protection, which can have manifold 'development from within' impacts for the region.

6.3 CONCLUSION

This chapter has considered the heuristic concept of 'development from within', and how the GI can be an emancipatory legal tool for sustainable development, by drawing on Bowen's case study of the oldest Third World GI, for tequila. A discussion of both the substantive and institutional issues related to drafting and managing the GI were examined, which could provide important lessons for Caribbean rum GIs. This chapter also provided an overview of the first Caribbean GI to be registered in the EU, the Demerara Rum GI, and explained the tensions around achieving a Barbados Rum GI. In the case of the Demerara Rum GI, it was demonstrated that the drafters of the GI took into consideration the typical triptych of GI factors – quality, reputation, and characteristics – and, importantly, added a fourth issue, heritage.

This chapter proposed that 'heritage' can be an explicitly linked new normative ground for GIs in the post-colonial context; as such, references to heritage would be included alongside the GI triptych of quality, characteristics, and reputation of the GI product. However, the chapter has also highlighted that GIs must not be weaponised as a protectionist measure; rather, it must strike the balance between recognising the cultural history embedded in the GI product and innovation required for the product to remain relevant in its given marketplace. As a way forward for Barbados rum producers, this chapter puts forward the recommendation that producers can add the fourth missing link – heritage – and put the points of contention behind them to agree on a GI that foregrounds the GI as an emancipatory legal tool that promotes sustainable development in the region – a 'development from within' for Barbados. This would draw on the precedent of the Demerara Distillers' GI, which recognises heritage, alongside the quality–characteristics–reputation origin link. Additionally, it would demonstrate how GIs are being implemented to account for context specificity, along the lines of Bowen's recommendation that 'GI schemes . . . be adapted to the specific resources, objectives, and challenges of each context, in order truly to lead a process of "development from within"'.[131]

The chapter also considered how heritage and history are included in the GI and its co-branding with the country name. Strategic co-branding would aim to harness the national competitive identity of Third World Caribbean SIDS, rather than being used as a trade protectionist tool that may inhibit new entrants to the rum market. Indeed, today there are local and diaspora producers who

[131] Bowen, 'Development from Within?' (n 3) 245.

are new entrants to the rum market who would also benefit from GIs, whether co-branded or not. For Third World SIDS of the Caribbean, GIs can foster sustainable development at a crucial moment, when the Caribbean remains vulnerable to external shocks and inflation.[132]

In the next chapter, the Conclusion summarises the main findings of this book. It concludes that GIs are sites of contestation between First and Third World knowledges, and therefore their ability to function as global-local laws remains a challenge to ensure that *all* nations can benefit from the sustainable development potential inherent in these legal tools.

[132] Vulnerability of SIDS is particularly acute, according to several key factors: 'limited ability to exploit economies of scale; their lack of natural resource endowments; their inability to influence external prices and their lack of environmental and social resilience'. See Economic Commission for Latin America and the Caribbean (ECLAC), 'Study on the vulnerability and resilience of Caribbean Small Island Developing States (SIDS)' (*CEPAL*, 7 December 2011), https://cepal.org/sites/default/files/publication/files/38568/LCCARL354_en.pdf.

7

Conclusion

> GI protection in and of itself is not beneficial; the way that the GI legislation is designed, and, in particular, how it is enforced on the ground, is what is determinant.[1]
>
> Sarah Bowen (2010).

THE PRIMARY AIM OF this book has been to shed light on Geographical Indications (GIs) in the Third World context, with a focus on the implementation of GI laws in the Caribbean. The purpose of this book was to consider three distinct and interrelated themes.[2] First, this book explained how GIs were colonial constructs by tracing their historical origins in law and policy. Second, this book considered whether GIs could foster sustainable development in Third World GI-producer territories, irrespective of their colonial origins. Third, this book assessed to what extent GIs could function as emancipatory legal tools to foster 'development from within',[3] for GI producing communities in the Caribbean. In doing so, this book has provided an original contribution to the scholarship on GIs, with a substantive focus on the Third World Small Island Developing States (SIDS) context of Caribbean nations.[4] There is very little literature that focuses on the sustainable development potential of GIs in the Caribbean, and this book fills this knowledge gap. It offers a new

[1] Sarah Bowen, 'Development from Within? The Potential for Geographical Indications in the Global South' (2010) 13(2) *Journal of World Intellectual Property* 231.

[2] To what extent are GIs colonial constructs? To what extent are GIs tools for sustainable development, especially for Third World countries? To what extent can GIs contribute to 'development from within' in the Caribbean?

[3] Bowen, 'Development from Within?' (n 1).

[4] There is only one article that predates my investigation and was not known to me at the time of my initial publication setting out a culturally relevant approach (Yentyl Williams, '"Doing and knowing" IEL through the lens of Caribbean Rastafari philosophy (IEL Collective Symposium II)' (*University of Bristol Law School Blog, Legal Research*, 26 March 2020), https://legalresearch.blogs.bris.ac.uk/2020/03/doing-and-knowing-iel-through-the-lens-of-caribbean-rastafarian-philosophy-iel-collective-symposium-ii/). See Marsha S Cadogan, 'A TWAIL-Constructivist Critique of the IP and Development Divide in the Age of Innovation – Has the Protection of Place-based Goods Changed the Narrative for the Caribbean?' in Susy Frankel (ed), *The Object and Purpose of Intellectual Property* (Edward Elgar, 2019) 57–89. Besides Cadogan's work, which is both on TWAIL and the Caribbean and GIs, there are two other text that connects TWAIL and the Caribbean in the area of human rights: see H Patrick Wells, 'A Leap of Faith: TWAIL Meets Caribbean Queer Rights Jurisprudence—Intersections with International Human Rights Law' (2020) 43(1) *Dalhousie Law Journal* 397 and R Biholar, 'Reparations for Chattel Slavery: A Call From the 'Periphery' to Decolonise International (Human Rights) Law' (2022) 40(1) *Nordic Journal of Human Rights* 64.

critical approach to a legal question concerning the Caribbean context, and it is intended to offer a new critical methodological approach to assessing laws in the post-colonial context of Caribbean SIDS. With a focus on two prominent aspects of GI laws which remain under-researched – the history of GIs as a colonial construct of IP law and the contribution GIs can make to sustainable development in Third World countries – this book offers a new and timely intervention into the scholarship that will benefit academics and policy-makers.

One of the primary findings of this book is that GIs are colonial constructs but have emancipatory potential as legal tools to contribute to sustainable development in Third World contexts. An objective of this book was to analyse the extent to which the specific provisions on GIs as a subset of intellectual property (IP) can contribute to sustainable development in the CARIFORUM region.[5] It has critically interrogated GIs and used case studies from the Third World to explore whether GIs can promote 'development from within': a holistic concept of community-based development rooted in the collective territory of GI producers, as the locus of where development starts, emanates from, and returns to.[6] In the specific context of the Caribbean, this book has examined the commitments and obligations relating to GIs set out in the EU–CARIFORUM Economic Partnership Agreement (EPA),[7] which provides the legal architecture for GI governance between the two regions.[8] In part, this book has assessed whether and to what extent the historical and colonial legacy of the legal framework will influence the creation of GIs in the Caribbean in the future. To this end, this book has demonstrated that free trade agreements (FTAs) can bring about structural changes that can result in both challenges and opportunities for their signatory parties, and especially those in the Caribbean.

Chapter one of this book outlined how this research offers an original contribution to the broad scholarship on IP and the more specialised scholarship of GIs by critically examining the origins of GIs and their development potential for Caribbean nations. The chapter contextualised the focus on GIs in the Caribbean and the framework of the EU–CARIFORUM EPA based on the potential of the laws to contribute to sustainable development in the post-colonial Caribbean territories, the historic development of these laws by European countries, and the ongoing EU–Caribbean relations, which influence development in the Caribbean region from the colonial epoch to present day. Departing from extractive colonial relations and non-reciprocal post-colonial relations, the shift towards reciprocal trade relations between the EU and CARIFORUM states

[5] There are several references in the preamble of the EPA, and in the framing of the objective of the EPA as outlined in art 1 (a), 'contributing to the reduction and eventual eradication of poverty through the establishment of a trade partnership consistent with the objective of sustainable development'. Additionally, art 3 explains sustainable development. See 'Economic Partnership Agreement between the CARIFORUM States, of the one part, and the European Community and its Member States, of the other part' [2008] OJ L289/I/3 (hereinafter 'EU–CARIFORUM EPA').

[6] Bowen, 'Development from Within?' (n 1).

[7] EU–CARIFORUM EPA (n 5).

[8] See ch 4 in particular.

within the signing of the EPA in October 2008 was discussed, to demonstrate how the potential of GIs to serve as emancipatory legal tools must be tested, in light of changing trade rules.[9] The EPAs extend the EU's long-standing relationship with the ACP group, now rebranded as the Organisation of ACP States (OACPS),[10] and foreground that reciprocal trade between these historic partners can achieve sustainable development, notwithstanding previously disadvantageous colonial and post-colonial trade relations. This book demonstrated that there is potential for these provisions on GIs to promote sustainability in Third World countries,[11] insofar as the law functions to liberate producer communities and spur sustainable development in communities that were historically deprived of the opportunity to develop on their own terms. Therein, GIs can function as emancipatory legal tools for GI-producer communities in Third World contexts.

Chapter two provided a legal analysis of the origins of GIs and confirmed their roots in the epoch of colonialism and imperialism. The analysis was framed around the three waves of IP multilateralism advanced by Ruth Okediji,[12] as a heuristic tool for conceptualising the developments of the legal regimes from the fifteenth century up until today. It was shown that the law was developed according to a 'dynamic of difference',[13] thus privileging First World knowledge and ways of thinking, doing, and being over Third World realities across key IP treaties internationally: (i) the Paris Convention; (ii) the Madrid Agreement; (iii) the Lisbon Agreement, including the Geneva Act; and (iv) the TRIPS Agreement of the WTO.[14] The legal analysis in this chapter demonstrated that the legal provisions of IP functioned as colonial strategies whose rationale was aimed at assimilating, incorporating, and controlling colonial Third World territories and subjects.[15] Through the process of deconstructing the law, the neutral façade of the law was exposed: the universalism upon which this (colonial) law is based risks reproducing bygone structures of the colonial epoch that, as vestiges of

[9] EU–CARIFORUM EPA (n 5).

[10] See OACPS, https://www.oacps.org/.

[11] See the chapters that addressed the reconstructive and emancipatory potential of GI laws: chs 3, 4, 5, and 6.

[12] This refers to the unequal trading relations characterised by domination, dispossession, and accumulation, of the 1500s–1945; extension of international law doctrines such as sovereignty 1945–1990s; and the establishment of the WTO from 1990 to today. See Ruth Okediji, 'The International Relations of Intellectual Property: Narratives of developing country participation in the global intellectual property system' (2003) 7 *Singapore Journal of International & Comparative Law* 315.

[13] Anthony Anghie, *Imperialism, Sovereignty and the Making of International Law* (CUP, 2014) 4. See also Antony Anghie and BS Chimni, 'Third World Approaches to International Law and Individual Responsibility in Internal Conflicts' (2003) 2(1) *Chinese Journal of International Law* 33–34.

[14] Post-colonial Third World nations acceded to these agreements after the majority of Acts had been passed, with the exception of TRIPS. The Paris Convention for the Protection of Industrial Property (1883); the Madrid Agreement for the Repression of False and Deceptive Indications of Source (1891); the Lisbon Agreement for the Protection of Appellations of Origin and Their International Registration (1958), including the Geneva Act (2015); and the WTO Agreement on Trade-Related aspects of Intellectual Property Rights concluded in 1995 (hereafter 'TRIPS'). See ch 3.

[15] Okediji, 'The International Relations of Intellectual Property' (n 12) 325.

formal empire, serve to keep Third World peoples marginalised.[16] As such, it maintains the gap between the First and Third Worlds, continuing the colonial strategy to attain and maintain commercial superiority,[17] a case in point being the low number of GI registrations from Third World countries, many of whom acceded to the treaties referenced after the Acts had been passed, with the exception of TRIPs.[18] Nonetheless, the chapter also outlines that Third World countries, albeit latecomers to the GI debate, can choose to strategically engage with these legal tools for their own sustainable development: engaging with and interpreting the law in an emancipatory and transformational approach,[19] to derive benefits from a system that was not initially conceived for their inclusion.

Chapter three examined the role played by the EU as a norm exporter of GIs globally, through an assessment of the GI provisions in the EU–CARIFORUM EPA and EU FTAs with Vietnam,[20] Singapore,[21] Canada,[22] Japan,[23] and Columbia/Peru.[24] An assessment of the substantive provisions relating to the terms of protection, generic terms, the relationship between GIs and trademarks, future agreements, and Internet protection was presented. The analysis confirmed that the EU's own universality of the norms and practice of GIs has been given sanction though international law,[25] and that, via its FTAs, the EU continues to play a role shaping international trade and its corresponding norms, including with countries that do not have existing *sui generis* GI regimes. As a result, the enquiry on whether the inclusion of GIs was based on a 'dynamic of difference' or the 'commensurability of difference'[26] was central to the methodological approach to reconstruct the law as an emancipatory legal tool that can serve the interests of Third World nations. Notwithstanding the type of inclusion of GIs in FTAs, given the power asymmetries evidenced in the number of GI products listed and protected between the parties to the Agreements, it was argued these FTAs are sites where dialogical manoeuvres can take place to reconceptualise parts of

[16] Anghie, *Imperialism, Sovereignty and the Making of International Law* (n 13).

[17] Okediji, 'The International Relations of Intellectual Property' (n 12) 324.

[18] See the interactive map of registrations of AOs: WIPO, 'Appellations of Origin', https://wipo.int/ipdl/en/lisbon/lisbon-map.jsp.

[19] See chs 5 and 6..

[20] Free Trade Agreement between the European Union and the Socialist Republic of Viet Nam [2020] OJ L186.

[21] Free Trade Agreement between the European Union and the Republic of Singapore [2019] OJ L294.

[22] Comprehensive Economic and Trade Agreement (CETA) between Canada, of the one part, and the European Union and its Member States, of the other part [2017] OJ L11.

[23] Agreement between the European Union and Japan for an Economic Partnership [2019] OJ L330.

[24] Trade Agreement between the European Union and its Member States, of the one part, and Colombia and Peru, of the other part [2012] OJ L354.

[25] Makau Mutua, 'What is TWAIL?' (2000) *Proceedings of the ASIL Annual Meeting* 17.

[26] I put the emphasis on the reconceptualisation of the law to serve Third World communities, and hence refer to the 'commensurability of difference' that is an aspiration in today's post-colonial context. On the original usage of the term 'incommensurability of difference', see Dianne Otto, 'Subalternity and International Law: The Problems of Global Community and the Incommensurability of Difference' (1996) 5(3) *Socio-Legal Studies* 337, 360.

the law as 'global-local' laws serving Third World developmental ends.[27] One such strategy to reduce power asymmetries is that GIs and trademarks can be used cumulatively to protect origin products while also reducing or attempting to balance power asymmetries that exist. Comparatively, it was also shown that the failure to include a de jure reference to the beneficiaries or end users of the Agreement, as outlined in other FTAs, was a missed opportunity. However, and in keeping with the transformational intention of the methodological approach of this book, the analysis of the text revealed that the promotion of sustainable development through GIs can nevertheless be inferred and implemented de facto through the outstanding provisions, inter alia, outlined in the EU–CARIFORUM EPA preamble and Article 3 on 'sustainable development'.

Chapter four examined the institutions of the EU–CARIFORUM EPA and assessed their potential to promote dialogical manoeuvres to frame GIs as emancipatory legal tools for the CARIFORUM countries. Drawing on the five- and ten-year reviews of the trade agreement,[28] this chapter drew on the theory-of-change approach to monitoring the EPA, which privileges assessing the sustainable development potential of the EPA to attain the post-colonial guarantees sought through law, namely that the EPA implementation is the intervention that is expected to bring about the objectives of the EPA, which is the change sought by both parties. However, the chapter put forth that, in the absence of a dedicated monitoring mechanism, the potential emancipatory elements of the EPA are not being realised, and that GI laws may not be being challenged to function as emancipatory tools contributing to an inclusive global-local law. In other words, the law would not function according to a language of emancipation unless challenged to do so through processes of dialogical engagement involving education, sensitisation and motivating stakeholders' buy-in to the agreement. The risk was exposed that, without effective monitoring aligned with the theory of change sought – namely fulfilment of the objectives of the EPA – this would threaten the shift from a 'dynamic of difference' to the 'commensurability of difference' that arises out of framing alternative GI norms based on dialogical manoeuvres within these institutions.[29] It found that, if the EU is the only benefactor, this is contrary to the spirit of agreement – contrary to Article 1 of the EPA that outlines that Caribbean

[27] See Valerie Phillips, 'Indigenous Peoples and the Role of the Nation State' (2007) *Proceedings of the ASIL Annual Meeting* 101, 319. See also Luis Eslava, *Local Space, Global Life, The Everyday Operation of International Law and Development* (CUP, 2015)..

[28] See the five-year review: European Commission, Directorate-General for Trade, Sacha Peter Silva, Ranjit Singh, Keisha-Ann Thompson and Paul Hare, *Monitoring the Implementation and Results of the Cariforum-EU EPA: Final Report* (Publications Office, 2015). See the EU's ten-year review: European Commission, Directorate-General for Trade, Nora Plaisier, Tahmina Shafique, Michael Fuenfzig, David Luff and Simone Snoeijenbos, *Ex-post Evaluation of the EPA between the EU and its Member States and the CARIFORUM Member States: Final Report* (Publications Office, 2021). See the CARIFORUM's ten-year review: Audel Cunningham, 'Consultancy to Prepare Technical Position Paper on CARIFORUM's priorities for the Second Five Year Review of the CARIFORUM-EU EPA' (Final Report, 13 December 2020).

[29] Anghie, *Imperialism, Sovereignty and the Making of International Law* (n 13) and own usage ch 1 (n 29).

peoples would be beneficiaries of the post-colonial guarantees of the Agreement. The chapter demonstrated that existing power imbalances threaten the ability of the agreement to contribute to sustainable development generally, and 'development from within' for Third World GI producing communities in particular. The continued reliance on EU funding to support GI and EPA implementation, therefore, functions as a litmus test of successful implementation of the de jure provisions, while also reflecting the EU's post-colonial interests in the region.[30]

Chapter five provided evidence of the gap between the development promise and the reality of GIs, through its assessment of four case studies on Third World GIs: Guyana Demerara Gold,[31] the Ethiopia–Starbucks dispute,[32] the Café de Colombia GI,[33] and the Indian basmati rice GI.[34] The purpose of the analysis in this chapter was to demonstrate that, in spite of the development potential of GIs, Third World countries are not always successful in clawing back their origin names. However, this chapter demonstrated that reclaiming origin-linked names (most common in European cases, such as port or sherry, feta, and Parmigiano Reggiano)[35] is one means to attempt to keep GI laws grounded in local realities. Nevertheless, this chapter underlined that the vestiges of informal imperialism may continue to marginalise the Third World insofar as international law continues to privilege First World knowledge. For example, while Café de Colombia has a successful strategy of GI protection in both the US, using trademarks, and the EU, via its *sui generis* system, the Indian government faces challenges to protect its basmati rice as a GI in the US. The Guyanese government faces similar challenges in both the US and Canada, as its Demerara sugar, although protected as a GI in Guyana, is considered generic in those territories. While the case of Café de Colombia appears as an outlier in contrast to the Indian basmati rice GI and Guyana Demerara sugar GI cases, Third World countries that seek to protect their origin products for the first time through IP strategies are not all taking the *sui generis* GI route. The case of the protection of Ethiopian coffee is a case in point. Without the prerequisite legal structures already in place, GI laws can be considered onerous – institutionally

[30] On CarIPI, see ch 3 (n 116).

[31] *Guyana Sugar Corporation (Guysuco) v Bedessee Imports Ltd* [2011] TMOB 102, 11 (CanLII), https://canlii.ca/t/fm8w7.

[32] USPTO, Response to Office Action, Serial Number 78589307, US Patent and Trademark Office (Jan 17, 2007), Application No 78589307, http://tmportal.uspto.gov/extemal/portal/tow?SRCH=&isSubmitted=true&details=&SELECT=U S+Serial+No&TEXT=78589307#.

[33] Café de Colombia and Juan Valdez have been protected as trademarks since 1967 – Denmark; 1975 – UK; 1988 – Poland, Slovenia; 1989 – Italy, Slovakia, Czech Republic; 1990 – Germany; 1992 – Portugal; and 1999 – Greece. Café de Colombia was the first non-EU GI registered in the EU, in 2007. See European Commission, Publication of an Application Pursuant to Article 6(2) of Council Regulation (EC) No 510/2006 on the Protection of Geographical Indications and Designations of Origin for Agricultural Products and Foodstuffs [2006] OJ C 320, 17.

[34] See Trade Mark application no UK00001081589, https://trademarks.ipo.gov.uk/ipo-tmcase/page/Results/1/UK00001081589.

[35] See Commission, 'WTO Talks: EU Steps up Bid for Better Protection of Regional Quality Products' (*Europa*, 28 August 2003, https://ec.europa.eu/commission/presscorner/detail/en/IP_03_1178.

and cognitively – for Third World countries. As such, this latter case suggests that *sui generis* GI systems are not the only choice for protecting origin products from Third World nations – a point that supports the comparative analysis of GI usage in chapter three. In other words, Third World countries may opt to pursue protecting their origin products via IP strategies that promote sustainable development via GIs, whether they are *sui generis* GI systems or not.

Chapter six examined the first CARIFORUM GI to be registered in the EU, for (Guyana) Demerara Rum,[36] and the tensions preventing the registration of a national Barbados Rum GI. It drew on the analysis of 'development from within' within the literature for the oldest Third World GI, for Tequila (Mexico), to explore the extent to which GIs in the Third World context are functioning – or have the potential to function – as emancipatory developmental tools that contribute to a global-local law, in practice. It demonstrated the challenges to shape the law – in relation to rum casking, ageing, and water inputs requirements within the GI specification process – and to define what an inclusive GI process grounded in local realities means in practice. This chapter showed that GIs in the Third World context risk replicating colonial structures wherein transnational capitalist classes who own GIs continue to reap the benefits of these legal tools.[37] As such, 'development from within' is not guaranteed, and it follows that there is no guarantee for Third World GIs to function as a form of 'global-local law' that benefits GI-producer communities. Rather, in the Third World context, GIs are sites of contestation between First and Third World knowledges.

Yet the chapter outlined two areas in which opportunities can be reaped to foster sustainable development by contributing to 'development from within' for GI-producer communities. First, drawing on the case of the Demerara Rum GI, it was demonstrated that heritage can be added to the traditional triptych – quality, reputation, and characteristics – that define the origin link, by establishing new normative grounds for GIs in the Third World post-colonial context. Second, strategic co-branding between CARIFORUM governments and producers would aim to harness the national competitive identity of Third World Caribbean SIDS[38] while establishing a new normative basis for GIs. While, in the EU, GI norms consider country names an exception rather than a rule, for Caribbean SIDS, country names are not only culturally relevant but strategically valuable, given the economies of scale of Caribbean SIDS. Together, both these opportunities to ground GIs in the local realities that emphasise both

[36] 'DEMERARA RUM' (File number: PGI-GY-02423 – 28.6.2018), Publication of an Application Pursuant to Article 17(6) of Regulation (EC) No 110/2008 of the European Parliament and of the Council on the Definition, Description, Presentation, Labelling and the Protection of Geographical Indications of Spirit Drinks and Repealing Council Regulation (EEC) No 1576/89' [2018] OJ C120/7.

[37] BS Chimni, 'Third World Approaches to International Law: A Manifesto' (2006) 8 *International Community Law Review* 29.

[38] See Natalie Corthésy, 'Trade Marks Country Names and Misappropriation of National Identity' (2017) 12(4) *Journal of Intellectual Property Law and Practice* 297. See also other texts cited in ch 6.

heritage and country name co-branding can assist in overcoming inefficient dialogical manoeuvres that prevent GI registrations. It offers an opportunity to change the narrative for GI producers to see themselves as collaborators and not competitors of GI products. The current deadlock for the Barbados Rum GI and the challenges to the Jamaican Rum GI revolve around distinctions between Protected Designation of Origin (PDO) and Protected Geographical Indication (PGI) statuses which are de jure absent in CARIFORUM countries.[39] Placing the emphasis on heritage overcomes dichotomous debates by striking the balance between the cultural history embedded in the GI product and innovation required for the product in the GI marketplace. The approach set out in this chapter promotes that 'development from within' must be strategically embedded in the entire process of protecting a GI, as part of a process of reconceptualising the GI as an emancipatory legal tool, from drafting the GI specification for registration and establishing regulatory bodies,[40] to its functioning once implemented.

Both chapters five and six demonstrated that there are practical issues relating to institutional and knowledge gaps that proscribe the ability of GIs to serve as emancipatory tools that will promote 'development from within'.[41] In other words, even if, in theory, EU FTAs and international law provide the grounds for reconceptualising GIs as inclusive legal tools, the reality is that the vestiges of informal imperialism continue to privilege only First World knowledge and maintain the gap between the First and Third Worlds. Third World countries sit between a theoretical rock and a practical hard place in the process of attempting to reconstruct not only GI laws but the entire GI marketplace to be inclusive, and to function as a global-local law with emancipatory potential. Yet, foregrounding the 'commensurability of difference' offers a launch pad from which Third World nations can transition from a place of marginalisation to one of inclusion, upon which emancipation, sustainable development, and poverty eradication in our post-colonial context is based. In this way, Third World countries, through mobilising GIs as emancipatory legal tools protecting Third World products in post-colonial trade, continue to challenge international law to serve *all* nations and realise the global-local potential upon which it was developed. GIs can function as emancipatory legal tools capable of fostering sustainable development in Third World communities; however, the assessments throughout this book have shown that 'development from within' should be foregrounded in both the conceptualisation and implementation of GIs. In other words, to overcome the colonial origins of GIs as tools developed to serve First World

[39] See ch 6.

[40] See ch 6 insights from the Ron Dominicano GI and Scotch Whisky GI.

[41] See the author's co-authored piece on the institutional and knowledge gaps identified in the case study of GI implementation in Jamaica: Enrico Bonadio, Natalie Corthésy, Marc Mimler, Dianne Daley McClure, Yentyl Williams, and Shadae Deslandes, 'Maximizing the Benefits of Origin Products in An Emerging Economy - the Impact of Geographical Indication Protection in Jamaica' (2023) 5 *European Intellectual Property Review* 1–16 (available at https://ssrn.com/abstract id=4368537).

nations,[42] GIs must be explicitly 'development from within'-oriented to serve the needs of Third World GI-producer communities and offer them the opportunity to benefit from the potential of GIs as emancipatory legal tools today.[43]

7.1 FUTURE RESEARCH

This book sets out an original contribution to the scholarship by offering an analysis of the potential for GIs as strategic tools for development in the Caribbean. Yet, throughout the course of researching the work for this book, it became apparent that there are areas beyond the scope of this book that merit further research. There are six such areas that will be discussed below.

The first area that merits further research relates to *methodological analyses of IP*, generally, and GIs, specifically. This author has considered the relevance of Rastafari philosophy, which was born in the Caribbean, and its theoretical convergences with international economic law and TWAIL scholarship.[44] Deeper insights into such culturally relevant indigenous/Indigenous approaches can serve to better interrogate the legal structure of the law, to unpack elements where the 'dynamic of difference' may be present, and, importantly, highlight how the law can be reconceptualised to serve Third World country needs.[45] For example, an analytical inquiry could focus on the heritage aspect of GIs as highlighted in reference to the Guyana Demerara Rum GI legal specification.[46] The use of home-grown methodological and culturally relevant approaches and philosophies *within* the territories where GIs are sought can add a new level of richness to the discussion on how GIs can serve as emancipatory legal tools for Third World GI-producer communities.

The second area, which is linked to the first, is related to the *knowledge and institutional gaps* in relation to GIs in the Caribbean, and more broadly in the

[42] See chs 2 and 3 in relation to research question 1: 'To what extent are GIs colonial constructs?' This relates to the first claim of the book that GIs are colonial constructs. Ch 2 set out the methodological framing under which the second claim is explored, namely that GIs can promote 'development from within' through a reconceptualisation of the GI law.

[43] See chs 3, 4, 5 and 6 in relation to research questions 2 and 3 (n 2). This relates to claims three and four that Third World countries have not been involved in the conceptualisation of GIs and, therefore, transnational capital classes from the colonial to post-colonial epochs continue to dominate and capitalise on GI developments, muting their broader development potential for Third World producers.

[44] Williams, 'Doing and knowing' (n 4).

[45] See Marcus Goffe and Yentyl Williams, 'Rastafari as Religious and Indigenous Rights-Holders: Exploring Intellectual Property and Traditional Knowledge Frameworks' in Enrico Bonadio, Bryan Khan, and Nicola Luchi, *Religion and Intellectual Property* (forthcoming, 2026). See also ch 6 and Yentyl Williams, Aleema Gray, and Chevy Eugene, 'Groundings and Rastafari: Re-territorializing Indigenous Knowledges' in Camille Nakhid, Margaret Nakhid-Chatoor, Anabel Fernandez Santana, and Shakeisha Wilson-Scott (eds), *Affirming Methodologies: Research and Education in the Caribbean* (Routledge, 2023) 162–65. On the Fourth World of Indigenous peoples, see Usha Natarajan, John Reynolds, Amar Bhatia, and Sujith Xavier, 'Introduction: TWAIL: on praxis and the intellectual' (2016) 37(11) *Third World Quarterly* 1946, 1953.

[46] See ch 6.

Third World country context. While there has been one research project that assessed GI developments in Jamaica that outlined these gaps,[47] similar projects must be conducted across the Caribbean. For example, several Caribbean countries have recognised that their cocoa can benefit from GI status, and peer learning can be done with the first cocoa GI, for Montserrat Hills Cocoa in Trinidad and Tobago.[48] Such projects would aim to map existing and potential GIs, as well as the capacity-building needed for the implementation of the GI beyond its mere de jure existence. This logic of peer-to-peer learning to fill knowledge and institutional gaps can also extend to other Third World territories which are seeking protection for similar products for the first time in their history.[49] This is needed in order to mobilise GIs as emancipatory legal tools that can fulfil the sustainable development aspirations and the poverty eradication sought by Caribbean SIDS in today's post-colonial setting, and in the context of the EPA.[50]

The third area for further research relates to sustainable development and the need to distinguish between the *theory and the practice of sustainable development* while also outlining how the tensions between both can forge a new context-specific understanding, whether qualified as 'development from within' or poverty eradication. As alluded to by the epigraph in this section, and those selected for every new chapter of this book, context specificity is key. Just as a GI connects qualities, characteristics, and reputation with a given territory, the goal

[47] See Enrico Bonadio and Chauntina Poyser, 'Protecting Jamaican Geographical Indications: The Cases of "Jamaica Jerk", "Jamaica Rum" and "Blue Mountain Coffee"' (2021) 5 European Intellectual Property Review

[48] Examples include Belize Cocoa and Cocoa products (Toledo Mayan Cocoa); Grenada cocoa/chocolate; Guyana cocoa and cocoa products; Jamaican cocoa; and St Lucia Cocoa and cocoa products. For the list, see Caribbean GI list appended to, Saltwater Reasonings – Dr Tracie Rogers Episode 1 with Dr Yentyl Williams, 'Reasoning as Method: Caribbean Epistemologies in Practice' (*Tracie Rogers*), https://www.tracierogers.com/episodes/yentyl-williams-reasoning-as-method. Note that there are, in fact, seven fine cocoa producing countries in the CARIFORUM region: Belize, Commonwealth of Dominica, Dominican Republic, Haiti, Jamaica, Grenada, and Trinidad and Tobago. However, Haiti and Dominica did not list cocoa as a possible GI. Nonetheless, they can be considered for those countries, and revision of the lists to add new products is recommended. See also UWI MonaMedia, 'Geographical Indications in the Global Market | MonaLaw Master Class Series' (*UWIMonaMedia*), https://www.youtube.com/live/-dA9V1SaGnc.

[49] For example, in the African context, the Ghanaian Kente cloth GI has been registered in 2025. For an overview, see Michelle Okyere and Janice Denoncourt, 'Protecting Ghana's Intellectual Property Rights in Kente Textiles: The Case for Geographical Indications' (2021) 16(4-5) *Journal of Intellectual Property Law & Practice* 415 (April–May 2021). Also in anglophone West Africa, there has been a Coffee Kenya certification mark since 2010, and a GI Bill has been under consideration. See Catherine W Ng, Titilayo Adebola, and Abbe EL Brown, 'Place-Branding Experiences – Perspectives From Three Case Studies' in Catherine W Ng, Titilayo Adebola, and Abbe EL Brown (eds), *Place-Branding Experiences: Perspectives from Intellectual Property Owners, Users and Lawyers* (Edward Elgar, 2024).

[50] The interdisciplinary linkages with GIs are expanding and peer-to-peer learning can also assist with understanding how GIs support gender equity, decolonial racial labour standards, and agroecology, amongst others. See Rosemary J Coombe and S Ali Malik, 'Transforming the Work of Geographical Indications to Decolonize Racialized Labor and Support Agroecology' (2018) 8(3) *UC Irvine Law Review* 363–412. See also Rosemary J Coombe and S Ali Malik, 'Rethinking the Work of Geographical Indications in Asia: Addressing Hidden Geographies of Gendered Labor' in Irene Calboli and Ng-Loy Wee Loon (eds), *Geographical Indications at the Crossroads of Trade, Development, and Culture: Focus on Asia-Pacific* (CUP, 2017).

of sustainable development must also be linked to that sought by GI-producer communities. In other words, a blanket approach to GI implementation will not work: even where de jure the GI laws are identical from one Caribbean SIDS to another, each must be assessed on a case-by-case basis. The Introduction outlined that, while sustainable development is a contested concept, for dialogical engagement to attain developmental needs, it must be inclusive and based on the principle of integration – meaning that it is inter-generational, intra-generational, and based on equitable dialogue.[51]

Sustainable development is not only a theory but also a practice. Further research on GIs in a Third World context can focus on how the practice of sustainable development implicates environmental and technological issues. Further research into the multiple aspects of the numerous basmati cases shows that there are ongoing sustainable development questions around basmati breeding and standards. This raises questions around GI products, their quality, characteristics, and reputation, and thereafter their intersection with sustainability development, notwithstanding their geographic linkage. For example, if technology can enhance the environmental aspects of basmati rice production through becoming more drought resistant and less water intensive in its production, can they still be authentic GI products?[52] Or, in other words, how will technological developments and environmental concerns challenge GI products? The opening quote of this book drew on the Brundtland Report, which alluded to this.[53] For some commentators on the Basmati case, 'It's an interesting case study in how cutting-edge technology and the right regulation can ensure that an ancient industry remains fit for purpose in the 21st century.'[54] For others, it may raise questions that connect IP with ecological and ethical questions. A consideration into the public policy aspect of GI can also bridge both the theory and practice elements of sustainable development related to GIs while developing interdisciplinary research on the topic.[55]

[51] See ch 1. Federico Ortino, 'Investment Treaties, Sustainable Development and Reasonableness Review: A Case Against Strict Proportionality Balancing' (2017) 30(1) *Leiden Journal of International Law* 71–91.

[52] Katherine Steele, 'Basmati Rice: The New Authenticity Rules Aiming to Remove Sub-standard Varieties from the Market' (*The Conversation*, 29 December 2022), https://theconversation.com/basmati-rice-the-new-authenticity-rules-aiming-to-remove-sub-standard-varieties2-from-the-market-196818.

[53] See ch 1.

[54] Steele, 'Basmati Rice' (n 53).

[55] While Bowen does discuss the public good element of GIs, other non-legal texts consider the issue in more depth. See Maria Cecilia Mancini, Marianna Guareschi, Valentin Bellassen, and Filippo Arfini, 'Geographical Indications and Public Good Relationships: Evidence and Policy Implications' (2022) 21(2) *EuroChoices* 66–71; Giovanni Belletti, Andrea Marescotti, and Jean-Marc Touzard, 'Geographical Indications, Public Goods, and Sustainable Development: The Roles of Actors' Strategies and Public Policies (2017) 98 *World Development* 45–57; Bertil Sylvander, Anne Isla, and Frédéric Wallet, 'Under What Conditions Geographical Indications Protection Schemes Can Be Considered as Public Goods for Sustainable Development?' in André Torre and Jean-Baptiste Traversac, *Territorial Governance: Local Development, Rural Areas and Agrofood Systems* (Physica-Verlag, 2011) 185–202.

Fourth, further research is needed into the prevalence of the same *GI names*, or even *homonymous names*, across different territories. There is already some limited research on the issue concerning basmati rice, as it has been produced in at least three territories historically: India, Pakistan, and Nepal.[56] Additionally, a GI registration by one of these countries in a third territory is always followed by an opposition from another producing territory.[57] This could arise in the Caribbean, especially given the shared linguistic and colonial history, which translates into many shared names across different territories. For example, could the Montserrat Hills Cocoa from Trinidad cause confusion with the island territory of Montserrat, a CARICOM observer? The issue of homonymous names across Caribbean SIDS, and more broadly across Third World countries, subject to the same or similar colonial history can unearth more about the colonial implications of GIs in a post-colonial epoch and set out some of the challenges Third World GIs may face when attempting registration. The multiple Demerara sugars – Guyana Demerara GI, Mauritius Demerara, and the generic Demerara[58] – is a case in point that underscores how the colonial past can linger in the post-colonial context and undermine the emancipatory potential of GIs to contribute to sustainable development of Third World producer communities.

The fifth research area considers *GIs as strategic recovery tools post-disaster*, specifically where Third World countries are impacted by *climate disasters*. Jamaica experienced its first Category 5 hurricane, 'Melissa', in October 2025, and scientists confirmed that 'human-induced climate change made Hurricane Melissa more intense and destructive'.[59] The colonial linkage – the legacy of plantation economies and underdevelopment that exposed communities in the path of the hurricane – was evidenced in the aftermath of the destruction of the Western bread basket of the island.[60] This has encouraged a new framing of GIs as strategic tools for rebuilding producer communities in the Third World context.[61] It reinforces the linkages to the aforementioned research areas to fill

[56] Pratyush Upreti, 'The Battle for Geographical Indication Protection of Basmati Rice: A View from Nepal' (2023) 54 *International Review of Intellectual Property and Competition Law* 710–31.

[57] ibid.

[58] See ch 6.

[59] See Global Campus, 'UWI Scientists Co-Author Study That Finds Climate Change Enhanced Hurricane Melissa's Intensity' (*UWI*, November 2025), https://global.uwi.edu/media/news/uwi-scientists-co-author-study-finds-climate-change-enhanced-hurricane-melissas. See also WWA, 'Climate change enhanced intensity of Hurricane Melissa, testing limits of adaptation in Jamaica and eastern Cuba' (*WorldWeatherAttribution*, 6 November 2025), https://www.worldweatherattribution.org/climate-change-enhanced-intensity-of-hurricane-melissa-testing-limits-of-adaptation-in-jamaica-and-eastern-cuba/.

[60] Marcus Goffe, Yentyl Williams, and Dane Malcolm-Buchanan, 'A Reparatory Justice Approach to Land Reform for Climate Resilience Post-Hurricane Melissa,' UWI Policy Brief no 10, 11 December 2025.

[61] As discussed in the University of the West Indies webinar, 'GIs in the Caribbean: Institutional Perspectives on GIs Recovery Post-Hurricane Melissa' with the Jamaican Intellectual Property Office (JIPO) and the Jamaican Agricultural Commodities Regulatory Authority (JACRA): UWI MonaMedia (n 48).

knowledge and institutional gaps while fostering peer-to-peer learning to implement sustainable development through GIs for all potential GI communities affected: St Elizabeth thyme, St Elizabeth scallion, Middle Quarters shrimp, and Orange Hill cannabis, to name a few. Lessons may be learnt from other linguistic jurisdictions,[62] and non-traditional case studies such as cannabis,[63] and critical reparatory justice lenses can be applied to catalyse the transformative potential of GIs in a post-disaster recovery process.[64]

The sixth and final research area relates to the issues of *overseas territories of developed countries* and their continued post-colonial relations that shape the laws in Third World country contexts. This final story sheds light on the fact that, often, colonial and post-colonial realities are quite literally blended, by drawing on the case of the British Overseas Territory of Bermuda, the Gosling Brothers Limited Bermuda Rum, and their trademarking initiative of the Dark 'n Stormy cocktail. In the 1800s, the Gosling family, originally British wine merchants, began blending Caribbean rums to make the reputable Gosling's Bermuda Rum.[65] In the late twentieth century, two factors contributed to their unique IP story of trademarking their Gosling's Rum 'Dark 'n Stormy' cocktail. First, they started canning pre-mixed Dark 'n Stormy cocktails, and second, they started exporting their product for the first time.[66] Both these events led to the use of IP to protect the integrity of their cocktail, while harnessing technology and market opportunities to can and export their product. Besides promotion at international cocktail meetings, which serve as educational platforms to learn more about the history of the product,[67] they are also promoting their brand and spreading awareness through the Dark 'n Story Day, celebrated on 9 June annually.[68] Although not a GI, there is a strong origin story here which demonstrates the power of IP to protect a rum product made of Caribbean rums (Barbados, Guyana, Jamaica, and Trinidad and Tobago) blended in the subtropical British territory of Bermuda.

This example demonstrates that Caribbean–British post-colonial ties are not only prominent procedurally, but also prominent substantively, in the consideration

[62] Enrico Bonadio, Yentyl Williams, and Bryan Khan, 'Protecting Geographical Indications in the English, French and Spanish-Speaking Caribbean' in Andre Zappalaglio and Enrico Bonadio (eds), *The Future of Geographical Indications: European and Global Perspectives* (Edward Elgar, 2025).

[63] Yentyl Williams, 'Geographical Indications and Cannabis' in Natalie Corthésy, Enrico Bonadio, and Yentyl Williams (eds), *Intellectual Property and Cannabis* (Edward Elgar, 2025).

[64] Yentyl Williams, Bryan Khan, and Enrico Bonadio, 'Geographical Indication Laws in the Caribbean: Towards Post-Colonial Justice for former Plantation Economy Crops? The Case of Rum' (2025) *European Intellectual Property Review* 1.

[65] 'Goslings Since 1806' (*Difford's Guide*), https://www.diffordsguide.com/producer/1122/gosling-brothers/story.

[66] Goslings Rum, 'The Story', https://www.goslingsrum.com/the-story.

[67] T Cole Newton, 'Intellectual Property and Cocktails: What Everyone Should Know About Protecting Their Cocktail Creations' (*Tales of the Cocktail*, 30 August 2017), https://talesofthecocktail.org/behind-bar/intellectual-property-and-cocktails-what-everyone-should-know-about-protecting-their-cocktail-creations/.

[68] Evan Rail, '9 Reasons the Dark 'n Stormy® Will Stand the Test of Time' (*VinePair*, 23 June 2020), https://vinepair.com/articles/9-reasons-the-dark-n-stormy-will-stand-the-test-of-time/.

of sustainable development impacts and GI rum specifications. For example, any CARIFORUM country's rum GI specifications would need to ensure, procedurally and substantively, that bulk rum production is permitted.[69] As such, the rums could still be exported to the territory of Bermuda, where they are blended before being shipped off to other markets worldwide. There are sustainable development implications, whereby the economic revenues from this rum sale can support 'development from within' in these Third World rum-producing countries. This shows that the narrative of the colonial past and the linkage of colonial and post-colonial relations must neither be overlooked nor disregarded altogether. Rather, in a post-colonial epoch where sustainable development is foregrounded in an inclusive manner[70] – inter- and intra-generationally, and through equitable dialogue[71] – the new normative foundations upon which GIs are being developed through dialogical engagements and manoeuvres delivers the pièce de résistance of GIs: GIs can serve as emancipatory legal tools fostering 'development from within' in Third World GI producing communities, notwithstanding the colonial origins of GIs as a subset of IP laws.

This book set out with the aim of understanding how GI provisions within the EU–CARIFORUM EPA can be win–win for both parties to the Agreement. While the EU was able to list over 100 products to be protected within the EPA at the time of signing in 2008, the CARIFORUM countries were unable to list even one.[72] While negotiations for a stand-alone GI Agreement in which the CARIFORUM side will publicly list their GIs to be protected is ongoing, this book provides an overview of the origin of GI laws, the sustainable development potential of GIs, and specifically how they can be conceptualised as tools to foster 'development from within' for Caribbean SIDS territories. The book is intended to provide a fertile substrate of academic research that can be built upon in ways identified herein and beyond, both in law and other fields of academic and non-academic research aimed at mobilising law for emancipatory ends, namely to foster 'development from within' for communities historically deprived of this opportunity.

[69] See ch 6 on how the Demerara Rum GI specification does this, and the example of Scotch Whisky GI, which also allows for this.

[70] Tonia Novitz and Margherita Pieraccini, 'Agenda 2030 and the Sustainable Development Goals: "Responsive, Inclusive, Participatory and Representative Decision-Making?"' in Margherita Pieraccini and Tonia Novitz (eds), *Legal Perspectives on Sustainability* (Bristol University Press, 2020) 40. See also See Clair Gammage and Tonia Novitz, 'The Concept of Sustainability and its Application in International Trade, Investment and Finance' in Clair Gammage and Tonia Novitz (eds), *Sustainable Trade, Investment and Finance* (Edward Elgar, 2019) 1.

[71] Ortino, 'Investment Treaties, Sustainable Development and Reasonableness Review' (n 51) 83.

[72] See ch 5.

Bibliography

BOOKS, JOURNALS, AND REPORTS

Anghie A, *Imperialism, Sovereignty and the Making of International Law* (CUP, 2014).

Anghie A and Chimni BS, 'Third World Approaches to International Law and Individual Responsibility in Internal Conflicts' (2003) 2(1) *Chinese Journal of International Law* 77–103.

Aoki K, 'Neocolonialism, Anticommons Property and Biopiracy in the (Not-so-brave) New World Order of International Intellectual Property Protection' (1998) 6(1) *Indiana Journal of Global Legal Studies* 11–58.

Araujo BM, *The EU Deep Trade Agenda: Law and Policy* (OUP, 2016).

Banerjee R and Majumdar M, 'In the Mood to Compromise? Extended Protection of Geographical Indications under TRIPS Article 23' (2011) 6(9) *Journal of Intellectual Property Law & Practice* 657–63.

Bannerman S, *International Copyright and Access to Knowledge* (CUP, 2016).

Bartels L, 'The Trade and Development Policy of the EU' (2007) 18(4) European Journal of International Law 715–56.

Beckford G, *Persistent Poverty, Underdevelopment in Plantation Economies of the Third World* (first published OUP, 1972; Zed Books, 1983).

Belletti G, Marescotti A, and Touzard J-M, 'Geographical Indications, Public Goods, and Sustainable Development: The Roles of Actors' Strategies and Public Policies' (2017) 98 *World Development* 45–57.

Bentley B, 'The "Extraordinary Multiplicity" of Intellectual Property Laws in the British Colonies in the Nineteenth Century' (2011) 12(1) *Theoretical Enquiries in Law* 161–200.

Bhagwati J, *Free Trade Today* (Princeton University Press, 2002).

Bienabe E and Marie-Vivien D, 'Institutionalizing Geographical Indications in Southern Countries: Lessons Learned from Basmati and Rooibos' (2017) 98 *World Development* 58–67.

Bonadio E, Corthésy N, Mimler M, Daley McClure D, Williams Y, and Deslandes S, 'Maximizing the Benefits of Origin Products in An Emerging Economy - the Impact of Geographical Indication Protection in Jamaica' (2023) 5 *European Intellectual Property Review* 1–16 (available at SSRN, https://papers.ssrn.com/sol3/papers.cfm?abstract_id=4368537).

Bonadio E and Poyser C, 'Protecting Jamaican Geographical Indications: The Cases of "Jamaica Jerk", "Jamaica Rum" and "Blue Mountain Coffee"' (2021) 5 *European Intellectual Property Review*.

Bonadio E, Williams Y, and Khan B, 'Protecting Geographical Indications in the English, French and Spanish-Speaking Caribbean' in A and Bonadio E (eds), *The Future of Geographical Indications: European and Global Perspectives* (Edward Elgar, 2025).

Bowen S, 'Development from Within? The Potential for Geographical Indications in the Global South' (2010) 13(2) *Journal of World Intellectual Property* 231–52.

Brauneis R and Schechter R, 'Geographic Trademarks and the Protection of Competitor Communication' (2006) 96 *Trade Mark Review* 782–849.

Brownell M, 'Coffee Trademark Licensing for Farmers: Brewing a Farmer-Owned Brand' (2009) 14 *Drake Journal of Agricultural Law* 291–327.

Byiers B and de Roquefeuil Q, *Monitoring the EU-CARFIORUM EPA: Where are We and What are the Next Steps?* (ECDPM, 2012).

——, 'Monitoring Regional Integration in Practice: Reflections from the EU-CARIFORUM Economic Partnership Agreement' in de Lombaerde P and Saucedo Acosta EJ (eds),

Indicator-Based Monitoring of Regional Economic Integration: Fourth World Report on Regional Integration (Springer, 2017).

Cadogan M, 'A TWAIL Constructivist Critique of the IP and Development Divide in the Age of Innovation – has the Protection of Place-based Goods Changed the Narrative for the Caribbean?' in Suzy Frankel (ed), *The Object and Purpose of IP* (Edward Elgar, 2019).

Calboli I, 'Expanding the Protection of Geographical Indications of Origin Under TRIPS: "Old" Debate or "New" Opportunity?' (2006) 10 *Marquette Intellectual Property Law Review 181* (Marquette Law School Legal Studies Paper No 06-19).

Chandola H, 'Basmati Rice: Geographical Indication or Mis-Indication' (2006) 9(2) *Journal of World Intellectual Property* 166–88.

Chimni BS, 'Third World Approaches to International Law: A Manifesto' (2006) 8 *International Community Law Review* 3–27.

—— 'Capitalism, Imperialism, and International Law in the Twenty-First Century' (2012) 14(1) *Oregon Review of International Law* 17–45.

Commission, 'Global Europe: Competing in the World, A Contribution to the EU's Growth and Jobs Strategy' (2006) COM.

—— 'Trade, Growth and Intellectual Property - Strategy for the Protection and Enforcement of Intellectual Property Rights in Third Countries' (2014) COM.

—— *EU Aid for Trade Progress Report 2020: Review of Progress on the Implementation of the Updated EU Aid for Trade Strategy of 2017* (Publications Office, 2020).

—— *Ex-Post Evaluation of the Economic Partnership Agreement (EPA) between the European Union and CARIFORUM* (Publications Office, 2021).

—— 'Report from the Commission to the European Parliament, the Council, the European Economic and Social Committee and the Committee of the Regions on Implementation and Enforcement of EU Trade Agreements' (2021) COM.

—— 'Study on Control and Enforcement Rules for Geographical Indication (GI) Protection for Non-agricultural Products in the EU' (2021) COM.

Commission, Directorate-General for Trade, Plaisier N, Shafique T, Fuenfzig M, Luff D, and Snoeijenbos S, *Ex-post Evaluation of the EPA between the EU and its Member States and the CARIFORUM Member States: Final Report* (Publications Office, 2021).

Commission, Directorate-General for Trade, Silva SP, Singh R, Thompson K-A, and Hare P, *Monitoring the Implementation and Results of the Cariforum-EU EPA: Final Report* (Publications Office, 2015).

Contardi M, 'No Proprietary Protection for Individual Non-geographical Components of Protected Geographical Denominations, says AG Hogan' (2019) 14 *Journal of Intellectual Property Law and Practice* 838–40.

Coombe RJ and Malik SA, 'Rethinking the Work of Geographical Indications in Asia: Addressing Hidden Geographies of Gendered Labor' in Calboli I and Wee Loon N-L (eds), *Geographical Indications at the Crossroads of Trade, Development, and Culture: Focus on Asia-Pacific* (CUP, 2017).

Coombe RJ and Malik SA, 'Transforming the Work of Geographical Indications to Decolonize Racialized Labor and Support Agroecology' (2018) 8(3) *UC Irvine Law Review* 363–412

Cortés Martin JM, 'International protection of Geographical Indications: the WTO Multilateral Register Negotiations' in Gangjee D, *Research Handbook on Intellectual Property and Geographical Indications* (Edward Elgar, 2016) 183–201.

Corthésy N, 'Trade Marks, Country Names and Misappropriation of National Identity' (2017) 12(4) *Journal of Intellectual Property Law and Practice* 297–306.

—— 'Brand New IP: "Country Name Designation" – from France with Love' in Gervais D (ed), *The Future of Intellectual Property* (Edward Elgar, 2021)

——'Country Name Designation and International IP Protection of National Competitive Identities' (2021) 16(4-5) *Journal of Intellectual Property Law and Practice* 357–67

Covarrubia P, 'The EU and Colombia/Peru Free Trade Agreement on GIs: Adjusting Colombian and Peruvian National Laws?' (2021) 16(4-5) *Journal of Intellectual Property Law and Practice* 330–38.

Cunningham A, 'Consultancy to Prepare Technical Position Paper on CARIFORUM's Priorities for the Second Five-year Review of the CARIFORUM-EU EPA' (Final Report, 13 December 2020).

Delputte S and Williams Y, 'Equal Partnership Between Unequal Regions? Assessing Deliberative Parliamentary Debate in ACP-EU Relations' (2016) 1(4) *Third World Thematics: A Third World Quarterly Journal* 490–507.

—— 'Equal Partnership between Unequal Regions? Assessing Deliberative Parliamentary Debate in ACP–EU Relations' in Langan M and Price S (eds), *Sustainable Development in Africa–EU Relations* (Routledge, 2018).

—— 'Parliamentary Deliberation in Inter-regional Relations: Insights from the ACP-EU JPA' in Raube K, Müftüler-Baç M, and Wouters J (eds), *Parliamentary Cooperation and Diplomacy in EU External Relations* (Edward Elgar, 2019).

Dias Blue A, *The Complete Book of Spirits: A Guide to Their History, Production, and Enjoyment* (HarperCollins, 2004).

Diaz-Marta VZ and Kyrylenko A, 'The Ever-growing Scope of Geographical Indications' Evocation: from Gorgonzola to Morbier' (2021) 16(4-5) *Journal of Intellectual Property Law and Practice* 442–49.

Dinwoodie GB, 'Developing Defenses in Trademark Law' (2009) 13(5) *Lewis and Clark Law Review* 99–153.

Døhlie Saltnes J and Steingass S, 'Fit for Creating Partnerships of Equals with the Global South? Tensions in the EU's Development Policy Post-2020' (2021) 7(4) *Global Affairs* 523–40.

Drahos P, 'Developing Countries and International Intellectual Property Standard-Setting' (2005) 5(5) *The Journal of World Intellectual Property* 765–89.

Eeckhout P, *External Relations of the European Union: Legal and Constitutional Foundations* (OUP, 2004).

Eslava L, *Local Space, Global Life: The Everyday Operation of International Law and Development* (CUP, 2015).

Eslava L and Pahuja S, 'The State and International Law: A Reading from the Global South' (2020) 11 *Humanity: An International Journal of Human Rights, Humanitarianism and Development* 118–38.

Esquivel A, 'Will Coffee be the New Wine? The EU–Central American Association Agreement and the European Shaping of GIs in Costa Rica' (2021) 16(4-5) *Journal of Intellectual Property Law and Practice* 310–15.

Fanon F, *The Wretched of the Earth* (first published SARL, 1961; Grove Press, 2004).

Fidler D, 'Revolt Against or From Within the West?: TWAIL, the Developing World, and the Future Direction of International Law' (2003) 2 *Chinese Journal of International Law* 29–76.

Field C, 'Negotiating for the United States' in Watal J and Taubman A (eds), *The Making of the TRIPS Agreement: Personal insights from the Uruguay Round negotiations* (WTO, 2015) 129–58.

Ford L, 'EU Trade Governance and Policy: A Critical Perspective' (2013) 9(4) *Journal of Contemporary European Research* 578–96.

Gammage C, 'Overcoming the Development Deficit of Article XXIV: Promoting Equality through North-South RTAs' (2016) 9(1) Law and Development Review 69–93.

—— *North-South Regional Trade Agreements as Legal Regimes: A Critical Assessment of the EU–SADC Economic Partnership Agreement* (Edward Elgar, 2017).

Gammage C and Novitz T, 'The Concept of Sustainability and its Application in International Trade, Investment and Finance' in Gammage C and Novitz T (eds), *Sustainable Trade, Investment and Finance* (Edward Elgar, 2019) 1–29.

Gangjee D, 'Melton Mowbray and the GI Pie in the Sky: Exploring Cartographies of Protection' (2006) 3 *Intellectual Property Quarterly* 291–306.

—— 'Demerara Sugar: A Bitter Pill to Swallow?' (2011) 24 *Intellectual Property Journal* 1–13.

—— *Relocating the Law on Geographical Indications* (CUP, 2012).

—— 'Spanish Champagne: An Unfair Competition Approach to GI Protection' in Cooper Dreyfuss R and Ginsburg JC (eds), *Intellectual Property at the Edge: The Contested Contours of IP* (CUP, 2014) 105–29.

—— 'Genericide: The Death of a Geographical Indication?' in Gangjee D (ed), *Research Handbook on Intellectual Property and Geographical Indications* (Edward Elgar, 2016) 508–48.
—— *Research Handbook on Intellectual Property and Geographical Indications* (Edward Elgar, 2016).
Gathii JT, 'International Law and Eurocentricity' (1998) 9(1) *European Journal of International Law* 184–211.
—— *African Regional Trade Agreements as Legal Regimes* (CUP, 2011).
—— 'TWAIL: A Brief History of its Origins, its Decentralised Network, and a Tentative Biography' (2011) 3(1) *Trade, Law and Development* 26–64
—— 'Rejoinder: Twailing International Law' (2019) 98(6) *Michigan Law Review* 2066–71.
—— 'Africa and the Radical Origins of the Right to Development' (2020) 1 *TWAIL Review* 28–50.
Goffe M and Williams Y, 'The Relevance of Intellectual Property and Traditional Knowledge Frameworks for the Protection of Rastafari as Religious and Indigenous Rights-Holders' in Bonadio E, Khan B, and Luchi N, *Religion and Intellectual Property* (forthcoming, 2026).
Goffe M, Williams Y, and Malcolm-Buchanan D, 'A Reparatory Justice Approach to Land Reform for Climate Resilience Post-Hurricane Melissa' UWI Policy Brief no 10, 11 December 2025.
Green L, *Rock/Water/Life: Ecology and Humanities for a Decolonial South Africa* (Duke University Press, 2020).
Guerrieri F, 'The Farm to Fork strategy as an External Driver for Change: Possible Impacts on Nested GI Rule Systems' (2021) 16(4-5) *Journal of Intellectual Property Law & Practice* 331-40.
Gunzel O, 'Ashes to Ashes for Cheese Featuring the "Morbier" Visual Appearance?' (2021) 16(4-5) *Journal of Intellectual Property Law & Practice* 293–94.
Haight Farley C, 'Looking Beyond the Known Story: How the Prehistory of Protection of Geographical Indications in the Americas Provides an Alternate Approach' in Calboli I and Wee Loon N-L (eds), *Geographical Indications at the Crossroads of Trade, Development and Culture* (CUP, 2017) 212–34.
Handler M, 'Rethinking GI extension' in Gangjee D (ed), *Research Handbook on Intellectual Property and Geographical Indications* (Edward Elgar, 2016) 146–82.
Haskell J, 'TRAIL-ing TWAIL: Arguments and Blind Spots in Third World Approaches to International Law' (2014) 27(2) *Canadian Journal of Law and Jurisprudence* 400–01.
Heath C, 'How Would Geographical Indications from Asia Fare in Europe?' in Calboli I and Wee Loon N-L (eds), *Geographical Indications at the Crossroads of Trade, Development and Culture* (CUP, 2017) 186–211.
—— 'The Budweiser Cases: Geographical Indications v Trade Marks' in Gangjee D (ed), *Research Handbook on Intellectual Property and Geographical Indications* (Edward Elgar, 2016) 396–439.
Henry C, Williams B, and Benjamin A, 'Moving forward with EPA implementation in the Caribbean: The Example of Antigua and Barbuda' (2011) 10(1) *Trade Negotiations Insights* 8.
Heron T, 'Asymmetric Bargaining and Development Trade-offs in the CARIFORUM-European Union Economic Partnership Agreement' (2010) 18(3) *Review of International Political Economy* 328–57.
Hopewell K, 'Multilateral Trade Governance as Social Field: Global Civil Society and the WTO' (2015) 22(6) *Review of International Political Economy* 1128–58.
Howlett M and Cashore B, 'Public Policy: Definitions and Approaches' in Gilberto Capano G and Howlett M (eds), *A Modern Guide to Public Policy* (Edward Elgar, 2020).
Hughes J, 'Coffee and Chocolate – Can We Help Developing Country Farmers through Geographical Indications?' (2009) *Intellectual Property Institute* 1-152.
Hughes J, Beresford L, Kur A, Plevan K, and Scafidi S, 'That's a Fine Chablis You're Not Drinking: The Proper Place for Geographical Indications in Trademark Law' (2007) 17(4) *Fordham Intellectual Property, Media and Entertainment Law Journal* 933–78.
Kanwar V, 'Not a Place, but a Project: Bandung, TWAIL, and the Aesthetics of Thirdness' in Eslava L, Fakhri M and Nesiah V (eds), *Bandung, Global History, and International Law: Critical Pasts and Pending Futures* (CUP, 2017).
Keukeleire S and Delreux T, *The Foreign Policy of the European Union* (Routledge, 2014).

Kourouma A, *Les Soleils des Indépendances* (Éditions du Seuil, 1968).
Krishna S, *Globalization and Postcolonialism: Hegemony and Resistance in the Twenty-first Century* (Rowman & Littlefield, 2009).
Langan M and Price S, 'The EU and "Pro-Poor" Contributions to Sustainable Development in the Post-2015 Consensus' (2016) 1(4) *Third World Thematics: A Third World Quarterly Journal* 431–36.
Lodge J, 'A Trade Partnership for Sustainable Development' in Zampetti A and Lodge J (eds), *The CARIFORUM-EU Economic Partnership Agreement: A Practitioners' Analysis* (Kluwer Law International BV, 2011)
Lorde A, *Sister Outsider: Essays and Speeches* (Crossing Press, 2007).
Madhav K, 'The TWAIL Discourse: The Emergence of a New Phase' (2007) 9(3) *International Community Law Review* 291–304.
Mancini MC, Guareschi M, Bellassen V, and Arfini F, 'Geographical Indications and Public Good Relationships: Evidence and Policy Implications' (2022) 21(2) *EuroChoices* 66–71.
Manners I, 'Normative Power Europe: A Contradiction in Terms?' (2002) 40(2) *Journal of Common Market Studies* 235–58.
Marie-Vivien D, 'From Plant Variety Definition to Geographical Indication Protection: A Search for the Link Between Basmati Rice and India/Pakistan' (2008) 11(4) *Journal of World Intellectual Property* 321–44.
—— 'Protection of Geographical Indications in ASEAN countries: Convergences and challenges to awakening sleeping Geographical Indications' (2020) 23(3-4) *Journal of World Intellectual Property* 328–49.
Martens D, Orbie J, Van den Putte L, and Williams Y, 'Civil Society Meetings in EU Trade Agreements: Recommendations and Lessons for EPAs' (2016) 93 *ECDPM: The Centre for Africa–Europe Relations* 1–10.
Matthews P, 'Increasing Revenue in Developing Nations through Intellectual Property Rights: Why a Diversified Approach to Intellectual Property Protection with a Focus on Geographical Indications is the Best Method' (2010) 7 *Buffalo Intellectual Property Law Journal* 201–17.
Meunier S and Nicolaïdis K, 'The European Union as a Conflicted Trade Power' (2006) 13(6) Journal of European Public Policy 906–25.
Montero P, 'Towards a Core Unitary Legal Regime for Geographical Indications in the European Union Digital Market' (2021) 16(4-5) *Journal of Intellectual Property Law & Practice* 427–34.
Mulik C and Crespi JM, 'Geographical Indications and the Trade Related Property Rights Agreement: A Case Study of Basmati Rice Exports' (American Agricultural Economics Association Annual Meeting, Denver, 1–4 August, 2004) (New Name, 2008: 'Agricultural and Applied Economics Association') 1–26.
Murray-Evans P, *Power in North–South Trade Negotiations: Making the European Union's Economic Partnership Agreements* (Routledge, 2019).
Mutua M, 'What is TWAIL?' (2000) 94 *American Society of International Law* 31–38.
—— 'The Transformation of Africa: A critique of rights discourse' in Isa FG and de Feyter K (eds), *Human Rights and Diversity: International Human Rights Law in a Global Context* (UDP, 2009) 898
Natarajan U, Reynolds J, Bhatia A, and Xavier S, 'Introduction: TWAIL: On Praxis and the Intellectual' (2016) 37(11) *Third World Quarterly* 1946–56.
Ng CW, Adebola T, and Brown AEL, 'Place-Branding Experiences – Perspectives From Three Case Studies' in Ng CW, Adebola T, and Brown AEL (eds), *Place-Branding Experiences: Perspectives from Intellectual Property Owners, Users and Lawyers* (Edward Elgar, 2024).
Nkrumah K, *Neo-Colonialism, The Last Stage of Imperialism* (International Publishers Co, 1965)
Novitz T and Pieraccini M, 'Agenda 2030 and the Sustainable Development Goals: "Responsive, Inclusive, Participatory and Representative Decision-Making"?' in Pieraccini M and Novitz T (eds), *Legal Perspectives on Sustainability* (Bristol University Press, 2020) 39–66.

Okediji R, 'The International Relations of Intellectual Property: Narratives of Developing Country Participation in the Global Intellectual Property System' (2003) 7 *Singapore Journal of International and Comparative Law* 315–85.
Okyere M and Denoncourt J, 'Protecting Ghana's Intellectual Property Rights in Kente Textiles: The Case for Geographical Indications' (2021) 16(4-5) *Journal of Intellectual Property Law & Practice* 415–26.
O'Kicki M, 'Lessons Learned from Ethiopia's Trademarking and Licensing Initiative: Is the European Union's Position on Geographical Indications Really Beneficial for Developing Nations' (2008) 6 *Loyola University of Chicago International Law Review* 311–37.
Omachi M, 'A Tale of Two Approaches: Analysis of Responses to EU's FTA Initiatives on Geographical Indications (GIs)' (2019) 18(1) *Chicago-Kent Journal of Intellectual Property* 153–206.
Orbie J, 'The Graduation of EU Development Studies: Towards a Post-colonial Turn?' (2021) 7(4) *Global Affairs* 597–613.
Orbie J, Martens D, Oehri M, and Van den Putte L, 'Promoting Sustainable Development or Legitimising Free Trade? Civil Society Mechanisms in EU Trade Agreements' (2016) 1(4) *Third World Thematics: A Third World Quarterly Journal* 526–46.
Orbie J, Martens D, and Van den Putte L, 'Civil Society Meetings in European Union Trade Agreements: Features, Purposes, and Evaluation' (2016) 3 *Centre for the Law of EU External Relations* 1–48.
Ortino F, 'Investment Treaties, Sustainable Development and Reasonableness Review: A Case Against Strict Proportionality Balancing' (2017) 30(1) *Leiden Journal of International* Law 71–91.
Otto D, 'Subalternity and International Law: The Problems of Global Community and the Incommensurability of Difference' (1996) 5(3) *Socio-Legal Studies* 337–64.
Parliament, Directorate-General for External Policies of the Union, Josep Coll, *Criteria for Differentiation and Methods for Phasing out EU's Development Cooperation in light of the Commission's Proposal for a Development Cooperation Instrument (DCI) for 2014–2020* (Publications Office, 2012).
Parmar P, 'TWAIL: An Epistemological Inquiry' (2008) 10(4) *International Community Law Review* 363–70.
Phillips V, 'Indigenous Peoples and the Role of the Nation State' (2007) 101 *American Society of International Law* 319–23.
Pieraccini M and Novitz T, 'Introduction' in Pieraccini M and Novitz T (eds), *Legal Perspectives on Sustainability* (Bristol University Press, 2020) 1.
Peter Carl M, 'Evaluating the TRIPS negotiations: a plea for a substantial review of the Agreement' in Watal J and Taubman A (eds), *The Making of the TRIPS Agreement: Personal insights from the Uruguay Round negotiations* (WTO, 2015) 99–122.
Peukert A, 'The Colonial Legacy of the International Copyright System' in Diawara M and Röschenthaler U (eds), *Staging the Immaterial. Rights, Style and Performance in Sub-Saharan Africa* (Sean Kingston, forthcoming).
Rahmatian A, 'Neo-Colonial Aspects of Intellectual Property Protection' (2009) 12(1) *Journal of World Intellectual Property* 40–74.
Reinbothe J, 'Negotiation for the European Communities and their member states' in Watal J and Taubman A (eds), *The Making of the TRIPS Agreement: Personal insights from the Uruguay Round negotiations* (WTO, 2015) 187–208.
Richardson B, *Sugar: Refined Power in a Global Regime* (Palgrave Macmillan, 2009).
Risang Ayu Palar M, Ramli AM, Epi Sukarsa D, Citra Dewi I, and Septiono S, 'Geographical Indication Protection for Non-agricultural Products in Indonesia' (2021) 16(4-5) *Journal of Intellectual Property Law & Practice* 405–14.
Rodney W, *How Europe Underdeveloped Africa* (first published Bogle-L'Ouverture Publications, 1962; Pambazuka Press, 2012).
Schiavetti D, 'Genericness in US Certification Marks: the "GRUYERE" Case' (2021) 16 (4-5) *Journal of Intellectual Property Law & Practice* 298–300.
Shiva V, *Biopiracy: The Plunder of Nature and Knowledge* (North Atlantic Books, 2016).

Sunner L, 'How the European Union is Expanding the Protection Levels Afforded to Geographical Indications as part of its Global Trade Policy' (2021) 16(4-5) *Journal of Intellectual Property Law & Practice* 341–47.

Sylvander B, Isla A, and Wallet F, 'Under What Conditions Geographical Indications Protection Schemes Can Be Considered as Public Goods for Sustainable Development?' in Torre A and Traversac J-B (eds), *Territorial Governance: Local Development, Rural Areas and Agrofood Systems* (Physica-Verlag, 2011), 185-202.

Taubman A, 'Thinking Locally, Acting Globally: How Trade Negotiations Over Geographical Indications Improvise "Fair Trade" Rules' in Gangjee D, *Research Handbook on Intellectual Property and Geographical Indications* (Edward Elgar, 2016) 202–42.

—— *A Practical Guide to Working with TRIPS* (OUP, 2011).

Teuber R, 'Geographical Indications of Origin as a Tool of Product Differentiation: The Case of Coffee' (2010) 22 (3-4) *Journal of International Food & Agribusiness Marketing* 1–28.

Tran Wasescha T-L, 'Negotiating for Switzerland' in Watal J and Taubman J (eds), *The Making of the TRIPS Agreement: Personal insights from the Uruguay Round negotiations* (WTO, 2015) 159–86.

Upreti P, 'The Battle for Geographical Indication Protection of Basmati Rice: A View from Nepal' (2023) 54 *International Review of Intellectual Property and Competition Law* 710–31.

Wells HP, 'A Leap of Faith: TWAIL Meets Caribbean Queer Rights Jurisprudence—Intersections with International Human Rights Law' (2020) 43(1) *Dalhousie Law Journal* 397-433.

Williams E, *From Columbus to Castro: The History of the Caribbean* (Vintage, 1984).

—— *Capitalism and Slavery* (UNCP, 1994).

Williams Y, 'Shifting Between Hegemony and Dominance? A Neo-Gramscian Analysis of the EU as a Structural Foreign Policy Actor: The Singular Case of the Cariforum-EU Economic Partnership Agreement' (2015) 1 *Bruges Regional Integration and Global Governance Papers* 1–36.

—— 'The EU as a Foreign Policy Actor: Shifting Between Hegemony and Dominance' (2015) 3(1) Caribbean Journal of International Relations and Diplomacy 7–33.

—— 'Geographical Indications and Cannabis' in Natalie Corthésy, Enrico Bonadio, and Yentyl Williams (eds), *Intellectual Property and Cannabis* (Edward Elgar, 2025).

Williams Y, Gray A, and Eugene C, 'Groundings and Rastafari: Re-territorializing Caribbean Indigenous Knowledges' in Nhakid C, Nhakid-Chatoor M, Fernandez Santana A, and Wilson-Scott S (eds), *Affirming Methodologies: Research and Education in the Caribbean* (Routledge, 2022) 157–72.

Williams Y, Khan B, and Bonadio E, 'Geographical Indication Laws in the Caribbean: Towards Post-Colonial Justice for former Plantation Economy Crops? The Case of Rum' (2025) *European Intellectual Property Review* 1.

Yilmaztekin HK, and Yalcın BE, 'Turkish Law on Infringement of Geographical Indications and its Degree of Alignment with the EU Law' (2021) 16(4-5) *Journal of Intellectual Property Law & Practice* 376–73.

Yu P, 'TRIPS and its Discontents' (2006) 10(2) *Marquette Intellectual Property Review* 369–410.

Zappalaglio A and Mikheeva E, 'The New Russian Law of Geographical Indications: A Critical Assessment' (2011) 16(4-5) *Journal of Intellectual Property Law & Practice* 368–75.

ONLINE SOURCES

Acosta C, 'Marca Pais de Ron Dominicano in Riesgo' *Listindario* (Santo Domingo, 14 June 2017), https://listindiario.com/economia/2017/06/14/470069/marca-pais-del-ron-dominicano-en-riesgo.

ACP Secretariat, 'The Protection of Geographical Indications (GI): Generating Empirical Evidence at Country and Product Level to Support African ACP Country Engagement in the Doha Round Negotiations' (*ACP*, 2011), http://acp.int/fr/content/protection-geographical-indications-gi-generating-empirical-evidence-country-and-product-lev.

Barbados Loop, 'Big 3 in Barbados Rum Apply for GI - Geographical Indication' *Barbados Loop* (Bridgetown, 21 July 2022), https://barbados.loopnews.com/content/big-3-barbados-rum-apply-gi.
Bishop V, 'J'Ouvert Rum Angers Trinis' *Trinidad Express* (Port of Spain, 21 June 2021), https://trinidadexpress.com/news/local/j-ouvert-rum-angers-trinis/article_8a4092ac-d227-11eb-9254-936fbfb2e932.html.
BBC, 'Actor Michael B Jordan to Rename J'Ouvert rum after Nicki Minaj criticism' (*BBC*, 23 June 2021), https://bbc.co.uk/news/entertainment-arts-57581240.
—— 'Jamie Oliver's 'jerk rice' Accused of Cultural Appropriation' (*BBC,* 21 August 2018), https://bbc.co.uk/news/newsbeat-45246009.
Bedessee Brands, 'Bedessee Brands', https://bedesseebrands.com/.
Bird K, Diamant T, Grant U, Higgins K, Quiztow R, Turner L, and Vandemoortele M, 'Ethiopia Trademarking and Licensing Initiative: Supporting a Better Deal for Coffee Producers through Aid for Trade' (*ODI*, 2009), https://cdn.odi.org/media/documents/5946.pdf.
Bodenhausen G, *Guide to the Application of the Paris Convention for the Protection of Industrial Property* (WIPO, 1968) 25, https://wipo.int/edocs/pubdocs/en/intproperty/611/wipo_pub_611.pdf.
Brink T, 'Perspectives on Geographical Indications: Prospects for the Development of the International Legal Framework' (*WIPO*, 26–28 June 2007), https://wipo.int/edocs/mdocs/geoind/en/wipo_geo_bei_07/wipo_geo_bei_07_ibid_81778.pdf.
Brixton Distillery, 'Brixton Distillery', https://brixtondistillery.com/ and outlawrum.co.uk.
Bruce-Gardyne T, 'Flavoured Rum: Surfing the Wave' (*The Spirits Business*, 14 September 2022), https://thespiritsbusiness.com/2022/09/flavoured-rum-surfing-the-wave/.
Brundtland Commission, 'Report of the World Commission on Environment and Development: Our Common Future' (*UN*), https://sustainabledevelopment.un.org/content/documents/5987our-common-future.pdf.
Bufete Messina and Lugo IP, 'Geographical Indications: Dominican Republic View' (*IPCA*, November 2017), https://ipca.website/wp-content/uploads/2019/09/GIDominicanRepublicBufeteMessinaLugoIP.pdf.
Burrell I, 'Rum Colonisation has to Stop' (*Harpers*, 2022), https://harpers.co.uk/news/fullstory.php/aid/30060/Soapbox:_Rum_colonisation_has_to_stop.html.
Campari Group, 'J Wray and Nephew Limited', https://camparigroup.com/en/news/2019-12-31/j-wray-nephew-limited.
Caribbean Export Development Agency, 'Caribbean Export Report – Unlocking the Profit Potential of the Caribbean Highlights Growing Trend for Caribbean Rums across Europe' (*Caribbean Export,* 12 November 2020), https://carib-export.com/news/caribbean-export-report-unlocking-the-profit-potential-of-the-caribbean-highlights-growing-trend-for-caribbean-rums-across-europe/.
Caribbean Policy Research Institute (CAPRI), 'The Impact of the EPA on Caribbean Economies' (*CAPRI Caribbean,* 2009), https://www.capricaribbean.org/documents/impact-epa-caribbean-economies.
Caribbean Public Health Association, 'COVID-19 Response' (*CARPHA*, 2020), https://carpha.org/More/Media/Articles/ArticleID/366/CARPHA-COVID-19-Response#prettyPhoto.
Caribbean Regional Negotiating Machinery, 'The Cariforum-EC Economic Partnership Agreement (EPA) Special and Differential Treatment Provisions in the EPA' (*CARICOM*), https://caricom.org/documents/9679-special_and_differential_treatment_provisions.pdf.
Caribbean Review, Trademark Battle over Demerara Gold' (*Caribbean Review*, September 2010), https://caribbeanreview.org/2010/09/trademark-battle-over-%E2%80%98demerara-gold%E2%80%99/.
CARICOM, 'Building Geographical Indications for the Caribbean's Origin Linked Products' (*CARICOM*, 2015), https://caricom.org/building-geographical-indications-for-the-caribbeans-origin-linked-products/.
—— 'Crisis Related to Dominicans of Haitian Descent and Haitian Migrants in the Dominican Republic' (*CARICOM,* 13 October 2015), https://caricom.org/crisis-related-to-dominicans-of-haitian-descent-and-haitian-migrants-in-the-dominican-republic/.

—— 'ICT Ministers Approve CARICOM Secretariat Led Action Plans to Fast Track Digital Transformation' (*CARICOM*, 11 February 2022), https://caricom.org/ict-ministers-approve-caricom-secretariat-led-action-plans-to-fast-track-digital-transformation/.

CARICOM Today, 'Intellectual Property in Focus' *CARICOM Today* (Georgetown, 2020), https://today.caricom.org/2020/01/31/intellectual-property-in-focus/.

—— 'The Caribbean Trade with Europe Moving into a New Era' *CARICOM Today* (Georgetown, 25 June 2020), https://today.caricom.org/2020/06/25/the-caribbeans-trade-with-europe-moving-into-a-new-era/.

CARIPI, 'CarIPI' (*International IP Cooperation)*, https://internationalipcooperation.eu/en/caripi.

Channel 5 Belize, 'A Management System to Monitor & Evaluate Impact of EPA' *Channel 5 Belize* (Belmopan, 27 February 2020), https://edition.channel5belize.com/archives/199108.

CIEL, 'Intellectual Property in European Union Economic Partnership Agreements with the African, Caribbean and Pacific Countries: What way Forward after the Cariforum EPA and the interim EPAs?' (*CIEL*, 2008), https://ciel.org/Publications/Oxfam_TechnicalBrief_5May08.pdf.

Commission, 'WTO Talks: EU Steps up Bid for Better Protection of Regional Quality Products' (*Europa*, 28 August 2003), https://ec.europa.eu/commission/presscorner/detail/en/IP_03_1178.

—— 'Technical File for Scotch Whisky' (*Europa*, 6 September 2013), https://ec.europa.eu/geographical-indications-register/eambrosia-public-api/api/v1/attachments/45004.

——, 'Summary of Treaty' (*EC EUROPA*, 20 March 2017), https://ec.europa.eu/world/agreements/prepareCreateTreatiesWorkspace/treatiesGeneralData.do?step=0&redirect=true&treatyId=7407#:~:text=The%20CARIFORUM%20is%20a%20regional,Nevis%2C%20Surinam%2C%20and%20Trinidad%20and.

—— 'Agri-Food Trade Statistical Factsheet' (*Europa*, 13 March 2020) 296, https://ec.europa.eu/info/sites/info/files/food-farming-fisheries/farming/documents/agrifood-china_en.pdf.

—— 'Andean Community' (*Europa*), https://ec.europa.eu/trade/policy/countries-and-regions/regions/andean-community/index_en.htm.

—— 'Commission Strengthens Geographical Indications to Preserve High Quality and Reinforce Protection' (*Europa*, 31 March 2022), https://ec.europa.eu/commission/presscorner/detail/en/IP_22_2185.

—— 'Intellectual Property: Commission Boosts Protection of European Craft and Industrial Products in the EU and Beyond' (*Europa*, 13 April 2022), https://ec.europa.eu/commission/presscorner/detail/en/IP_22_2406.

—— 'Internal Market, Industry, Entrepreneurship and SMEs' (*Europa*), https://ec.europa.eu/growth/smes_en.

—— 'The EU-CARIFORUM Economic Partnership Agreement' (*Europa*), https://trade.ec.europa.eu/access-to-markets/en/content/eu-CARIFORUM-economic-partnership-agreement.

Council of the EU, 'Economic Partnership Agreement between the CARIFORUM States, of the one part, and the European Community and its Member States, of the other part' (*Consillium*), https://consilium.europa.eu/en/documents-publications/treaties-agreements/agreement/?id=2008034.

Difford's Guide, 'Goslings Since 1806', https://www.diffordsguide.com/producer/1122/gosling-brothers/story.

Economic Commission for Latin America and the Caribbean (ECLAC), 'Study on the vulnerability and resilience of Caribbean Small Island Developing States (SIDS)' (*CEPAL*, 7 December 2011), https://cepal.org/sites/default/files/publication/files/38568/LCCARL354_en.pdf.

Eslava L, 'TWAIL Coordinates' (*Critical Legal Thinking*, 2 April 2019), https://criticallegalthinking.com/2019/04/02/twail-coordinates/.

EUIPO, 'Dan Sukker Råsocker Strö Rørsukker Demerarasukker Ruokokidesokeri', https://euipo.europa.eu/eSearch/#details/trademarks/002557965.

——, 'Demerara', https://euipo.europa.eu/eSearch/#details/trademarks/007577661.

——, 'Demerara Gold', https://euipo.europa.eu/eSearch/#details/trademarks/006068779.

European Centre for Development Policy Management, 'Dominican Republic – CARICOM: Unfinished Business' (*ECDPM*, 2013), https://ecdpm.org/work/political-economy-of-regional-integration-volume-2-issue-7-october-2013/dominican-republic-caricom-unfinished-business.

European Economic and Social Committee, 'Joint Statement from the Fifth Meeting of the CARIFORUM-EU Consultative Committee' (9 December 2019), https://eesc.europa.eu/en/documents/joint-declaration/joint-statement-fifth-meeting-cariforum-eu-consultative-committee.

European Parliament, 'DCAR: The Delegation to the CARIFORUM-EU Parliamentary Committee' (*Europa*), https://.europarl.europa.eu/delegations/en/dcar/about/introduction.

—— 'Third Meeting of the CARIFORUM-EU Parliamentary Committee' (*Europa*, 1 November 2017), https://.europarl.europa.eu/cmsdata/162842/1153920EN.pdf.

Ewin-Chow D, 'Five Ways That COVID-19 Has Changed What Food Insecurity Looks Like In The Caribbean' (*Forbes*, 31 March 2020), https://forbes.com/sites/daphneewingchow/2020/03/31/five-ways-that-covid-19-has-changed-what-food-insecurity-looks-like-in-the-caribbe-an/?sh=34d69519143e.

Federacion de Cafeteros, 'Coffees from Antioquia, Cauca, C/marca and N. de Santander win 6th competition "Colombia, Land of Diversity"' (*Federacion de Cafeteros*, 15 April 2021), https://federaciondecafeteros.org/wp/listado-noticias/coffees-from-antioquia-cauca-c-marca-and-n-de-santander-win-6th-competition-colombia-land-of-diversity/?lang=en.

Goslings Rum, 'The Story', https://www.goslingsrum.com/the-story.

Gucht K de, 'A Partnership of Equals' (*EuroParl*, 4 December 2010) 4, https://europarl.europa.eu/intcoop/acp/60_20/pdf/speech_de_gucht_en.pdf.

GUYSUCO, 'Guyana Sugar Corporation Inc', https://guysuco.gy/index.php?lang=en.

Hamrick D and Kaina Fernandez-Stark K, 'Barbados in the Rum Global Value Chain' (*Duke Global Value Chain Centre*, August 2017), https://gvcc.duke.edu/wp-content/uploads/2018.01.11_The-Rum-Global-Value-Chain_PUBLIC-1.pdf.

Humphrey E, 'CARIFORUM EPA Negotiations: Initial Reflections on the Outcome' (*Europa*, 13 February 2008) 3, https://trade.ec.europa.eu/doclib/docs/2008/april/tradoc_138606.pdf.

Imani Development, 'Interview with Dr Nicholas Charalambides on M&E in Trade Agreements', https://imanidevelopment.com/interview-with-dr-nicholas-charalambides-on-me-in-trade-agreements/.

International Labour Organization (ILO), 'Guyana Launches Study of the Socio-Economic Impact of the Closure of GUYSUCO Sugar Estates on Workers' (17 June 2021), http://ilo.org/caribbean/newsroom/WCMS_803904/lang--en/index.htm.

International Law Association, 'Sustainable Development and the Green Economy in International Trade Law', https://www.ila-hq.org/en_GB/committees/sustainable-development-and-the-green-economy-in-international-trade-law.

International Trade, 'Technical Summary of Final Negotiated Outcomes: Canada-European Union Comprehensive Economic And Trade Agreement' (2013), http://international.gc.ca/trade-agreements-accords-commerciaux/assets/pdfs/ceta-aecg/ceta- technicalsummary.pdf.

International Trade Administration, 'Harmonized System (HS) Codes', https://trade.gov/harmonized-system-hs-codes#:~:text=The%20Harmonized%20System%20is%20a,taxes%20and%20for%20gathering%20statistics.

International Trade Centre, The Coffee Guide, 4th edn (Intracen, 1 October 2021) 13–20, https://intracen.org/resources/publications/the-coffee-guide-fourth-edition.

IP Kitten, 'Trade mark Ruling Muzzles Free and Honest Speech says Court of Appeal' (2010), http://ipkitten.blogspot.com/2010/05/trade-mark-ruling-muzzles-free-and.html.

Jack E, 'Demerara Rum: History of the Versailles Still' (*Rum Auctioneer*, 5 November 2019), https://rumauctioneer.com/news/history-of-the-versailles-still.

Jessop D, 'Has the EU-CARIFORUM EPA worked?' *Dominican Today* (Roseau, 5 February 2021), https://dominicantoday.com/dr/opinion/2021/02/05/has-the-eu-cariforum-epa-worked/.

JIPO, 'GIs and the Cannabis' (Zoom conference, 30 March 2022).

Kaiteur News, 'Guyana among three Caribbean countries producing more than 50% of its own food' *Kaiteur News* (Georgetown, 21 June 2022), https://kaieteurnewsonline.com/2022/06/21/guyana-among-three-caribbean-countries-producing-more-than-50-of-its-own-food/.

Kidd H, 'Appleton Estate' (*Jamaican Products*, 10 June 2018), https://jamaicanproducts.com.au/2018/06/10/appleton-estate/.

Kieley M, 'How important is a GI for Barbados Rum?' (*The Spirits Business*, 26 June 2020), https://thespiritsbusiness.com/2020/06/producers-clash-over-a-gi-for-barbados-rum/.

Koch S, 'From Poverty Reduction to Mutual Interests? The Debate in Differentiation in EU Development Policy' (*DIE-GDI*, 2013), https://die-gdi.de/en/briefing-paper/article/from-poverty-reduction-to-mutual-interests-the-debate-on-differentiation-in-eu-development-policy/.

Kyrylenko A, 'Russia Adopts Law that Shakes Cognac and Champagne Importers' (*IP Kitten*, 3 July 2021), https://ipkitten.blogspot.com/2021/07/russia-adopts-law-that-shakes-cognac.html.

Lein B, Krätke F, van Seters J, Keijzer N, and Montoute A, 'Differentiation in ACP-EU Cooperation: Implications of the EU's Agenda for Change for the 11th EDF and Beyond' (*ECDPM*, 2 October 2012), https://ecdpm.org/wp-content/uploads/2013/10/DP-134-ACP-EU-Cooperation-Implications-EU-Agenda-Change-11-EDF-2012.pdf.

Loop News, 'CARIFORUM Ministers Express Concerns at EPA Evaluation' *Loop News* (Kingston, 12 November 2021), https://caribbean.loopnews.com/index.php/content/cariforum-ministers-express-concerns-epa-evaluation.

Maharaj D, 'Building Caribbean Food Security via Technology – A Caribbean Export Perspective' (*CARICOM Today*, 10 April 2021), https://today.caricom.org/2021/10/04/building-caribbean-food-security-via-technology-a-caribbean-export-perspective/.

Martens P, 'Can Traditional Knowledge Owners and Producers in Developing Countries Use GIs for Protection and Economic Development Gain' (2012) SIEL 3rd Biennial Global Conference, available at SSRN, https://ssrn.com/abstract=2083680.

Mazzeo J, 'Will Barbados rum get its own GI?' (*Wine Mag*, 25 October 2022), https://winemag.com/2022/10/25/barbados-rum-get-own-gi/.

Medley H, 'Rum Fight gets New Referee' *The Gleaner* (Kingston, 20 September 2019), https://jamaica-gleaner.com/article/business/20190920/rum-fight-gets-new-referee.

Mejía F, 'Ron Dominicano Busca Denominación de Origen' (*Forbes*, 9 May 2022), https://forbes.do/editors-picks/2022-05-09/ron-dominicano-busca-denominacion-de-origen-2.

MICM, 'Joint Communiqué: Third Meeting of the Joint CARIFORUM-EU Council' (16 July 2015), https://micm.gob.do/images/pdf/direcciones/comercio-exterior/Joint-Communique-Tercera-Reunion-del-Consejo-Conjunto-EPA---CARIFORUM.pdf.

Miller J, 'How Does Water Quality Affect Rum Production' (*Inuakena*), https://inuakena.com/misc/how-does-water-quality-affect-rum-production/.

Ministry of Agriculture, 'Guysuco', https://agriculture.gov.gy/guysuco/.

Morgan E, 'CARICOM: GDP as an Indicator of the Status of National Economies – a False Impression' *CARICOM Today* (Georgetown, 21 December 2021), https://today.caricom.org/2021/12/15/caricom-gdp-as-an-indicator-of-the-status-of-national-economies-a-false-impression/#:~:text=On%20a%20regional%20level%2C%20the,income%20is%20US%244%2C%20348.

Mount Gay Rum, 'The Stages of Rum Making', https://mountgayrum.com/rum-making/.

Newton TC, 'Intellectual Property and Cocktails: What Everyone Should Know About Protecting Their Cocktail Creations' (*Tales of the Cocktail*, 30 August 2017), https://talesofthecocktail.org/behind-bar/intellectual-property-and-cocktails-what-everyone-should-know-about-protecting-their-cocktail-creations/.

Nicholls A, 'EU–CARIFORUM EPA Monitoring Report finds five-fold increase in EU FDI to CARIFORUM' (*Caribbean Trade Law*, 29 January 2021), https://caribbeantradelaw.com/2021/01/29/eu-cariforum-epa-monitoring-report-finds-five-fold-increase-in-eu-fdi-to-cariforum/.

Organization of African, Caribbean and Pacific States, 'About Us' (*OACPS*), https://www.oacps.org/.

Origin/WIRSPA, 'International Online Forum on Spirits GIs: Trends & Opportunities of Cooperation' (Zoom conference, 19 October 2022).

Our Today, 'CARIFORUM Slams "Glaring Weaknesses" in European Commission Evaluation of EPA' *Our Today* (Kingston, 13 November 2021), https://our.today/cariforum-slams-glaring-weaknesses-in-european-commission-evaluation-of-epa/.

Parlament, 'Minutes of the Fourth Meeting of the Joint CARIFORUM-EU Council' (*Parlament*, 17 November 2017), https://parlament.gv.at/PAKT/EU/XXVI/EU/04/11/EU_41137/imfname_10852841.pdf.
Pietrek M, 'Barbados Rum Cheat Sheet' (*CocktailWonk*, 4 December 2018), https://cocktailwonk.com/2018/12/barbados-rum-cheat-sheet.html.
Rail E, '9 Reasons the Dark 'n Stormy® Will Stand the Test of Time' (*VinePair*, 23 June 2020), https://vinepair.com/articles/9-reasons-the-dark-n-stormy-will-stand-the-test-of-time/.
Ramírez A, 'USMCA and its Effects on the Exportation of Tequila' (*Casa Sauza*, 17 December 2021), https://casasauza.com/en/tequila-process/usmca-effects-on-exportation-tequila#:~:text=The%20USMCA%20protects%20GI%2C%20which,the%20tequila%20industry%20as%20well.
Rampersad K, 'Intellectual Property Issues Strike at the Heart of the Steelpan' *Trinidad and Tobago Guardian* (Port of Spain, 29 July 2011), https://guardian.co.tt/article-6.2.447523.a608c18300.
Rum Authority, 'The Molasses vs Sugar Cane Juice Issue', http://therumauthority.com/rum-101/the-molasses-vs-sugarcane-juice-issue/.
SICE, Ministry of Foreign Trade and International Cooperation (MOFTIC) Digest, 'Geographical Indications in the Context of Guyana' (*SICE*, 2003), http://ctrc.sice.oas.org/TRC/Articles/Guyana/Moftic4.pdf.
—— 'National Development Strategy (Guyana) – Chapters 9–20' (*SICE*), http://ctrc.sice.oas.org/TRC/Articles/Guyana/NDS_Ch9_20.pdf.
South Centre, 'EPA Negotiations: State of Play and Strategic Considerations for the Way Forward' (February 2008) 10, http://southcentre.org/publications/AnalyticalNotes/Other/2008Feb_State_of_Play_and_Way_Forward.pdf.
Starbroek News, 'Bedessee Can Use Demerara Gold Trademark in North America – GuySuCo' *Starbroek News* (Georgetown, 4 March 2015), https://stabroeknews.com/2015/03/04/news/guyana/bedessee-can-use-demerara-gold-trademark-in-north-america-guysuco/.
Statista, 'Main traded goods between the European Union and the Caribbean Forum in 2018 *(in billion euros)*', https://statista.com/statistics/1101582/eu-cariforum-trade-by-product/.
Steele K, 'Basmati Rice: The New Authenticity Rules Aiming to Remove Sub-standard Varieties from the Market' (*The Conversation*, 29 December 2022), https://theconversation.com/basmati-rice-the-new-authenticity-rules-aiming-to-remove-sub-standard-varieties2-from-the-market-196818.
Ten to One Rum, 'Ten to One', https://tentoonerum.com/.
The Tribune, 'One from Ten Equals 0' *The Tribune* (Nassau, 6 May 2019), http://tribune242.com/news/2019/may/06/one-10-equals-0/.
Trademark Elite, 'DEMERARA RUM OVD GEORGE MORTON LIMITED DUNDEE', https://trademarkelite.com/uk/trademark/trademark-detail/UK00000763011/DEMERARA-RUM-OVD-GEORGE-MORTON-LIMITED-DUNDEE.
Trademarks, 'Trade Mark application no UK00001081589', https://trademarks.ipo.gov.uk/ipo-tmcase/page/Results/1/UK00001081589.
UK FCDO, UK–CARIFORUM EPA (Zoom conference, 13 June 2023).
United Nations, 'About Small Island Developing States', https://www.un.org/ohrlls/content/about-small-island-developing-states#:~:text=Small%20Island%20Developing%20States%20(SIDS,social%2C%20economic%20and%20environmental%20vulnerabilities.
—— 'Sustainable Development Goals: 17 Goals to Transform our World', https://www.un.org/en/exhibits/page/sdgs-17-goals-transform-world#:~:text=GOAL%201%3A%20No%20Poverty%20GOAL,10%3A%20Reduced%20Inequalities%20GOAL%2011.
—— 'United Nations Gifts', https://www.un.org/ungifts/steel-pans.
—— 'Potential of Traditional Medicine Should be Fostered, Economic and Social Council President Tells Panel on Attaining Millennium Development Goals in Public Health (2009), https://ibid.un.org/press/en/2009/ecosoc6385.doc.htm.
United Nations Conference for Trade and Development (UNCTAD), 'Guyana, A National Trade Strategy' (2020), https://unctad.org/system/files/official-document/ditctncd2020d3_en.pdf.

United States Patent and Trademark Office, Response to Office Action, Serial Number 78589307, Application No 78589307 (*USPTO,* 17 January 2007), http://tmportal.uspto.gov/extemal/portal/tow?SRCH=&isSubmitted=true&details=&SELECT=U S+Serial+No&TEXT=78589307#.

—— 'Shirkina Sun-dried Sidamo' (*USPTO*), http://uspto.gov/main/trademarks.htm.

West Indies Rum and Spirits Association, 'Unlocking the Potential of Authentic Caribbean Rums, Rum Market Report' (*WIRSPA*), https://wirspa.com/wp-content/uploads/ACR%20Publications/Rum-Market-Report.pdf.

Williams Y, 'The Caribbean-EU EPA – Lessons for African-EU EPAs' (*YouTube*, 10 January 2017), https://youtube.com/watch?v=VN9Xl2InTcQ.

—— 'ACP YPN at the 4th CARIFORUM EU Consultative Committee, St Lucia' (*ACP YPN*, 12 April 2018), http://acpypn.com/2018/12/04/acp-ypn-at-4th-cariforum-eu-consultative-committee-st-lucia/.

—— 'Post-Cotonou and Innovation? Lessons Learned from Intellectual Property provisions on Geographical Indications in the EU-ACP Economic Partnership Agreements' (*Afronomicslaw*, 31 May 2019), https://afronomicslaw.org/2019/05/31/post-cotonou-and-innovation-lessons-learned-from-intellectual-property-ip-provisions-on-geographical-indications-gi-in-the-eu-acp-economic-partnership-agreements-epas.

—— '"Doing and knowing" IEL through the lens of Caribbean Rastafari philosophy (IEL Collective Symposium II)' (*University of Bristol Law School Blog, Legal Research*, 26 March 2020), https://legalresearch.blogs.bris.ac.uk/tag/barry-chevannes/.

Williams Z, 'Here's the Main Issue Behind the Jamie Oliver Jerk Rice Row – and it's not cultural appropriation' *The Guardian* (London, 22 August 2018), https://theguardian.com/commentisfree/2018/aug/22/heres-the-main-issue-behind-the-jamie-oliver-jerk-rice-row-and-its-not-cultural-appropriation.

Willsher K and Roth A, 'Shampanskoye, French Champagne Industry in a Fizz over Russian Law' *The Guardian* (London, 5 July 2021), https://theguardian.com/world/2021/jul/05/shampanskoye-french-champagne-industry-in-a-fizz-over-russian-law.

WIRSPA–CarIPI, 'International Online Forum on Spirits GIs: Trends and Opportunities of Cooperation' (*OriGIn*, 19 October 2022), https://origin-gi.com/wp-content/uploads/2022/10/Lendor_DO_Ron_Dominicano.pdf.

World Bank, 'Agriculture, forestry, and fishing, value added (% of GDP) – Ethiopia', https://data.worldbank.org/indicator/NV.AGR.TOTL.ZS?locations=ET.

—— 'GDP (current US$) – Russian Federation', https://data.worldbank.org/indicator/NY.GDP.MKTP.CD?locations=RU.

—— 'GDP (current US$) – Dominican Republic' (*World Bank*, 2020), https://data.worldbank.org/indicator/NY.GDP.MKTP.CD?locations=DO.

—— 'Population, total – Barbados' (*World Bank*, 2023), https://data.worldbank.org/indicator/SP.POP.TOTL?locations=BB.

World Intellectual Property Office, 'Copyright, Monthly Review of the United International Bureaux for the Protection of Intellectual Property' (*WIPO*, 1 January 1970), https://wipo.int/edocs/pubdocs/en/copyright/120/wipo_pub_120_1970_01.pdf.

—— 'Lisbon Agreement for the Protection of Appellations of Origin and their International Registration' (*WIPO*, 1979), https://wipo.int/lisbon/en/legal_texts/lisbon_agreement.html#P15_193.

—— 'The Paris Convention for the Protection of Industrial Property (as amended on September 28, 1979)' (*WIPO*).

—— 'Appellations of Origin', https://wipo.int/ipdl/en/lisbon/lisbon-map.jsp.

—— 'Contracting Parties, Lisbon Agreement', https://wipo.int/treaties/en/registration/lisbon/.

—— 'Contracting Parties, Madrid Agreement for the Repression of False or Deceptive Indications of Source on Good', https://wipo.int/treaties/en/ip/madrid/#:~:text=According%20to%20the%20Madrid%20Agreement,importation%20must%20be%20prohibited%2C%20or.

—— 'Intellectual Property and Traditional Medical Knowledge', https://wipo.int/export/sites/ibid/tk/en/documents/pdf/background_briefs-e-n6-web.pdf.

—— 'Joint Recommendation Concerning Provisions on the Protection of Marks, and Other Industrial Property Rights in Signs, on the Internet', https://wipo.int/edocs/pubdocs/en/wipo_pub_845.pdf.
—— 'The Madrid Agreement for the Repression of False or Deceptive Indications of Source', https://wipolex.wipo.int/en/text/286776.
—— 'The Paris Convention "Contracting Parties"', https://wipo.int/treaties/en/ip/paris/.
—— 'WIPO-CARICOM Seminar on Intellectual Property', https://wipo.int/meetings/en/details.jsp?meeting_id=3717.
World Trade Organization, 'Papers circulated in the negotiations' [WTO Docs IP/C/M 29 & IP/C/W289] (*WTO*, 6 March 2001 and 29 June 2001), https://wto.org/english/tratop_e/trips_e/gi1_docs_e.htm, 25 May 2020.
—— 'Trade Policy Review – Guyana (WT/TPR/S/122)' (*WTO*, 1 October 2003), https://docsonline.wto.org/dol2fe/Pages/SS/directdoc.aspx?filename=Q:/WT/TPR/S122-0.pdf&Open=True.
—— 'Economic Partnership Agreement Between The Cariforum States And The European Union (Goods And Services) Questions And Replies' (*WTO*, 4 October 2018), https://docs.wto.org/dol2fe/Pages/FE_Search/FE_S_S009-Html.aspx?Id=248529&BoxNumber=3&DocumentPartNumber=1&Language=E&HasEnglishRecord=True&HasFrenchRecord=True&HasSpanishRecord=True&Window=L&PreviewContext=DP&FullTextHash=371857150.
—— 'Briefing Note: Small, Vulnerable Economies', https://www.wto.org/english/thewto_e/minist_e/min11_e/brief_svc_e.htm#:~:text=Small%2C%20vulnerable%20economies%20(SVEs),uncertainties%20and%20environmental%20shocks%201.
—— 'Module IV Geographical Indications', https://wto.org/english/tratop_e/trips_e/ta_docs_e/modules4_e.pdf.
—— 'Trade-Related Aspects of Intellectual Property Rights Agreement', https://wto.org/english/docs_e/legal_e/27-trips_01_e.htm.

Index

www.ingramcontent.com/pod-product-compliance
Ingram Content Group UK Ltd.
Pitfield, Milton Keynes, MK11 3LW, UK
UKHW021907150926
475560UK00003B/239

9 781509 991358